AFTER THE BLITZ

AFTER THE BLITZ

THE *LUFTWAFFE* BOMBING OF BRITAIN, 1941–1943

STEPHEN MOORE

UNIVERSITY PRESS OF KENTUCKY

Scholarly publisher for the Commonwealth,
serving Bellarmine University, Berea College, Centre College of Kentucky, Eastern Kentucky University, The Filson Historical Society, Georgetown College, Kentucky Historical Society, Kentucky State University, Morehead State University, Murray State University, Northern Kentucky University, Simmons College, Spalding University, Transylvania University, University of Kentucky, University of Louisville, University of Pikeville, and Western Kentucky University.

Editorial and Sales Offices: The University Press of Kentucky
663 South Limestone Street, Lexington, Kentucky 40508-4008
www.kentuckypress.com

Cataloging-in-Publication data available from the Library of Congress

ISBN 978-1-9859-0331-9 (hardcover)
ISBN 978-1-9859-0333-3 (paperback)
ISBN 978-1-9859-0329-6 (pdf)
ISBN 978-1-9859-0328-9 (epub)

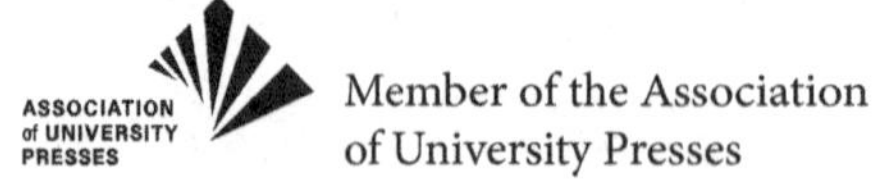

Contents

Abbreviations and Terms

AI	Aircraft Interception radar, also widely (and erroneously) referred to as Air Intercept and Airborne Interception
AOC	Air Officer Commanding (RAF)
AOC-in-C	Air Officer Commanding-In-Chief (RAF)
ARP	Air Raid Precautions
ATS	Auxiliary Territorial Service
AufklGr	*Aufklärungsgruppe*, reconnaissance *Gruppe*
C-in-C	Commander-in-Chief
CH/CHL	British early warning radar network: Chain Home for long-range detection and Chain Home Low for low-level coverage
Do	Dornier (German aircraft manufacturer)
EHS	Emergency Hospital Service
ErgGr	*Ergänzungsgruppe*, reserve training unit: *Luftwaffe* Operational Training Unit
ErprGr	*Erprobungsgruppe*, experimental (test) unit
FIU	Fighter Interception Unit
Fw	Focke-Wulf (German aircraft manufacturer)
GCI	Ground Control Interception radar
GEE	Code name for British bomber radio navigation aid
Geschwader	Composed of three *Gruppen*, with around one hundred aircraft
Gruppe	*Luftwaffe* combat group, consisting of around thirty aircraft
He	Heinkel (German aircraft manufacturer)
HE	High Explosive bombs
IC	Incendiary Containers (for thirty-six 1kg incendiary bombs)
in	inch

Ju	Junkers (German aircraft manufacturer)
KG	*Kampfgeschwader*, twin-engine bomber *Geschwader*
KGr	*Kampfgruppe*, twin-engine bomber *Gruppe*
KW	Kilowatt
LAM	Long Aerial Mine weapon
Luftflotte	*Luftwaffe* 'Air Fleet'
Luftwaffe	German Air Force
MAP	Ministry of Aircraft Production
mph	miles per hour
MU	Maintenance Unit
Mutton	Code name for LAM
OTU	Operational Training Unit
RAF	Royal Air Force
SKG	*Schnellkampfgeschwader*, single-engine fighter-bomber (night) unit
SFTS	Service Flying Training School
SLC	Searchlight Control (radar)
Tons	2,240 pounds/1,016 kilograms (Imperial [British] unit—from British sources)
Tonnes	1,000 kilograms (metric [SI] unit—from German sources)
UK	United Kingdom of Great Britain and Northern Ireland

Figures and Tables

TABLES

FIGURES

Introduction

SEPTEMBER 1941: NEWCASTLE UPON TYNE, UNITED KINGDOM

On the evening of 1 September 1941, a seventeen-year-old apprentice motor mechanic in Newcastle upon Tyne finished a double shift to begin his journey home. From the Minories garage in Jesmond, a suburb in the north of the city, he went by bus to the city centre and then east towards Walker where he lived. During this journey, around twenty-eight Junkers (Ju) 88 bombers of III / *Kampfgeschwader* (KG) 30 were approaching the city from the east, crossing the coast north of Newcastle to begin their bombing runs.[1] As the bus travelled east along New Bridge Street, it passed over the Manors railway interchange, which included a large goods station. Just after 2200, bombs started falling around the riverside areas of St Lawrence and St Peter's, amongst industrial sites and the London and North Eastern Railway line to Tynemouth.[2] This was a common occurrence: The *Luftwaffe* had sporadically bombed the city since the previous winter, normally along the Tyne to disrupt the enormous amount of shipbuilding taking place on both sides of the river. At 2220, two bombs, one 1,000kg and the other 500kg, penetrated the roof of the Manors goods station and completely wrecked the reinforced concrete structure of the building down to the ground-floor level. The building was being used as a food distribution depot, and 1,500 tons of flour, 160 tons of sugar, and 20 tons of bacon caught fire and were destroyed in the aftermath of the attack.[3] The shock wave from the exploding bombs was felt across the surrounding area, including the trolley bus the young man was sitting in on Shields Road, two kilometres from the goods station.

That young man was Derrick Moore, my father, and on our weekly Sunday visit to my grandparents, we would pass the surviving concrete basement of the

Manors goods station, which was still in use as a British Rail storage depot. He rarely talked about his war service after being called up in 1942 but occasionally admitted he had probably been in more danger during the Newcastle air raids than while in Italy. Over many car journeys to Walker, I learnt that the bombed station continued to burn for days after the attack, and he still remembered the smell of burnt meat and sugar lingering in the air. As I grew older and developed an adult interest in air power, particularly the bombing war, I become aware that the Manors raid was the heaviest *Luftwaffe* attack on Newcastle during the war, even though it took place after the Blitz had ended.[4]

Although widely known and generally remembered in Europe, the Blitz bombing campaign against the United Kingdom in 1940–1941 is not as well understood on the other side of the Atlantic. During the summer of 1940, the *Luftwaffe* (German Air Force) failed to win air superiority over the country in a campaign that has been documented as the Battle of Britain. Few historians have realised that this was also an offensive counter-air campaign to make a German invasion attempt possible if they achieved air superiority.[5] Despite prioritising daylight bombing, night attacks against industrial and port targets had taken place since the fall of France. By September, German bomber losses were unsustainable, and daylight operations declined as the night bombing campaign of the Blitz began. Although originally targeted against London, operations widened during the rest of 1940 and into 1941 with more emphasis on ports and industrial cities. Historians disagree on when the Blitz ended, but the conventional historiography maintains that this was when aircraft were redeployed to support the invasion of the Soviet Union in June 1941 after the final major raid against London on 10–11 May. The 'official' view is that the remaining forces concentrated on mine laying and nuisance bombing, which made me question whether the Manors raid was a historical anomaly.[6]

The critical position of the London attack on 10 May in the historiography has been contradicted by several claims, and despite assertions to the contrary, that raid did not signal the end of the London Blitz. Neither was it the last major attack of the Blitz but merely the last major raid on London. The formal end of the Blitz up to the start of the 'Baby Blitz' (Operation 'Steinbock'), the last German attempt at a night bombing offensive against London in 1944, can be described as somewhat of a black hole in Second World War air power historiography, and this book is an attempt to recover the evidence to document this neglected period. Preliminary research to justify the feasibility of this project highlighted the inconsistencies of this argument, confirming that attacks continued throughout the rest of 1941, including a heavy raid on London in July, and Hull continued to be attacked regularly after the end of the Blitz.[7] The Air Historical Branch opinion was that the *Luftwaffe* employed its small force in the most effective manner possible by mounting attacks of great accuracy and concentration.[8] The *Luftwaffe* continued to deploy aircraft for coastal mining and shipping attacks after the Blitz ended, but these operations peaked at the end of 1941 before a sharp decline in 1942.[9] Although bombing escalated again in April 1942 as the *Baedeker* campaign against cathedral cities began, the historiography has been distorted by accepting German propaganda that emphasised these as attacks on British culture, since the *Luftwaffe* continued to bomb targets associated with industrial or communications objectives, especially after attacks on 'cultural targets' tailed off from the middle of 1942, and many alleged *Baedeker* objectives were attacked for the same reasons. The resumption of raids on London in 1943 has marginalised the wide-ranging attacks across the United Kingdom that took place between the periods of bombing against the capital at the beginning and end of the year.

This book challenges the conventional narrative around the end of the Blitz as bombing continued into the summer, followed by a second campaign in autumn 1941. I will show that subsequent bombing in 1942 and 1943 followed the same pattern and that by allowing propaganda claims to conflate the *Baedeker* campaign, the official and subsequent historians have misrepresented the continuing operations of the *Luftwaffe*. Most studies of bombing ignore the effects attacks had on the social life, political outlook, and individual perceptions of those being targeted, and operational histories often consider themselves as distinct from these consequences, but this book will consider what the bombing campaigns against the United Kingdom were intended to achieve and their impact on the populations that were bombed.[10] Other conclusions will be retrieved from previously discounted evidence, by reexamining military and government records that in many cases have not been used by historians since the British Official Histories were written in the 1950s. Until the primary sources were declassified, historians relied on these publications without being able to verify their conclusions independently. Noble Frankland has highlighted how senior government officials tried to influence the writing of the Official Histories, to 'suit the conventions of the official mind'.[11] This study has highlighted factual errors and questionable interpretation of evidence, which historians who relied on these Histories, or secondary sources written using them, have reinforced in the historiography.

In order to place the operations that took place after May 1941 into context, a short review of developments up to that date is now necessary, noting significant events and highlighting recent research.

THE PROGRESS OF BOMBING UP TO THE MIDDLE OF 1940

The potential of the aeroplane to independently decide the outcome of war was initially proposed in the decade after heavier-than-air flight was first achieved.[12] During the Second World War, the bombing of industrial infrastructure, communications, and population centres killed a million people around the world, six hundred thousand of whom were in Europe. Millions more were displaced while strategic bombing advocates attempted to prove their theories.[13] The first air force to attempt such a strategy was the German *Luftwaffe* during the Blitz on the United Kingdom during 1940–1941. This ended when aircraft were redeployed to support the invasion of the Soviet Union in June 1941 after failing to destroy the British economy.

The First World War established both the decisive importance of air superiority and the difficulty of finding and accurately hitting targets.[14] The interwar period gave opportunities for advocates of air power to advance their theories, and the perceived efficacy of the bomber reached a new level after a speech by Stanley Baldwin in the House of Commons in 1932, when he insisted that 'the bomber would always get through'.[15] The rise of the Nazis in Germany and the formation of the *Luftwaffe* then changed the balance of air power in Europe.[16] Difficult weather conditions over the United Kingdom—some of the most unpleasant meteorological conditions of any major country, 'particularly in the winter months of frequent storms, fog and dense cloud'[17]—would hardly have assisted any attacks, as it was acknowledged that favourable bombing conditions existed over the country for only a quarter of the year.

While replenishing their losses following the Polish campaign, *Luftwaffe* planners looked ahead during the Phoney War to potential targets in case attacks on the United Kingdom were authorised. The German plans shown in table 0.1 illustrate the strategic aims of the *Luftwaffe* that contrast with the popular, incorrect impression of it as an army support arm, as only 15 percent of the *Luftwaffe* was intended for such support in 1939.[18]

TABLE 0.1
Luftwaffe Plans for Air Warfare on England

Groups of Targets	Details
1. Warships at sea and in port, in the following order of priority:	Aircraft Carriers Battlecruisers Battleships
2. Dockyards in which warships are built	(a) Tyne (b) Clyde (c) Birkenhead (d) Barrow in Furness
3. Harbour installations	(a) Liverpool (b) Manchester Ship Canal (c) Bristol Channel: Avonmouth (d) Cardiff (e) Swansea
4. Important military target	Billingham (90% of British high explosive industry, similar to German *lounaworke*)

TNA: AIR 20/7701, Air Ministry: Papers Accumulated by the Air Historical Branch, Translations from Captured Enemy Documents, Vol. II (1947), Translation VII/26, Plans for Air Warfare on England, appendix I.

After Churchill reversed British policy and authorised attacks on German targets, the *Luftwaffe* exploited the occupation of the Netherlands to reciprocate, and a directive authorising air operations over the United Kingdom was signed on 24 May 1940.[19] Small numbers of aircraft began to attack targets over southern England by both day and night, contributing to the number of attacks on towns during the war (see appendix 1). These *Störangriffe* (nuisance raids) were more accurately 'schooling flights' to familiarise crews with target areas, anti-aircraft defences, and alternative attack routes.[20]

Once the main assault on Royal Air Force (RAF) airfields during the Battle of Britain began, the command-and-control system used by Fighter Command forced a change in *Luftwaffe* tactics.[21] Surplus bombers not being utilised in daylight raids were transferred to night attacks on the industrial Midlands from 28 August 1940 onward.[22] The Germans believed that any invasion would require the destruction of civilian order and morale in London, and as the deadline for the *Luftwaffe* to achieve air superiority had already passed, forcing Fighter Command to defend London would ensure the final elimination of RAF resistance.[23]

THE BLITZ: THE ATTACKS ON LONDON

The London attack on 7 September by one thousand aircraft marks the conventional start of the Blitz in the historiography, which was characterised by 'major' attacks, where it was intended to drop more than one hundred tonnes of high explosive (HE) bombs.[24] Since the first major raid (*Grossenangriffe*) on the United Kingdom took place at Liverpool on 28–29 August, this should be considered as a more appropriate start date, as shown in table 0.2, with three successive major raids as part of the night offensive on industrial targets.[25] The omission of these raids from the Blitz chronology demonstrates the 'London-centric' narrative of the historiography, which conflates the 7 September daylight attack marking the change of German tactics in the Battle of Britain with the start of the night Blitz on the capital, despite large-scale night attacks already taking place. Over the next ten months, there were 135 major raids on the United Kingdom in three phases, of which only the first followed an uninterrupted pattern. London was bombed on seventy-six consecutive nights, apart from 3 November due to bad weather.[26] Only ten nights during this period did not qualify as major raids, when fewer than one hundred tonnes were dropped on the city (see appendix 2).[27]

The authorities had based their civil defence plans on the expectation of a daylight knockout blow, so night provisions were inadequate for when shelters would be occupied for over twelve hours, requiring facilities that had not been planned for.[28] Overy has suggested that a lack of suitable shelters led to high casualties during early bombing raids, with an average of six thousand deaths per month from September to November 1940 (see appendix 3).[29] By the end of November, civilian deaths from bombing in London exceeded those in the whole of the British army up to that date. The increasingly chaotic state of the capital meant that there was still only shelter provision for 40 percent of the population by the end of that month.[30]

AIR DEFENCE AGAINST THE BLITZ

British anti-aircraft guns were controlled using a fixed azimuth system, and the attackers quickly recognised the dangers from sound locators and

TABLE 0.2
Phases of the Blitz

Phase	Title	Duration	Attacks
1	Attacks on Liverpool and London	28–29 August to 13–14 November 1940	62 major attacks, 59 on London
2	Attacks on Industry and Ports	14–15 November 1940 to 19–20 February 1941	31 major attacks, 7 on London
3	Attacks on Ports	19–20 February to 27–28 July 1941	42 major attacks, 6 on London

Compiled from TNA: AIR 41/17; ADGB:III, i–ii and appendix 4.

searchlights by increasing operating altitude to above fifteen thousand feet. Within forty-eight hours, the gun defences of London had been doubled, and they were ordered 'to blaze away with everything they had, whether they had a target or not'.[31] The barrage was militarily ineffective but served to force the raiders to fly so high that there was no possibility of accurate targeting.[32] Britain had entered the war with an aerial command-and-control system integrated into a nationwide radar network.[33] The characteristics of British radar stations limited precision, as the radar stations faced seawards, and detection ceased as soon as raiders crossed the coast, which made the network unsuitable for night defence.[34] At the time that the Blitz started, night defence rested on six squadrons of underpowered Blenheims equipped with experimental and unreliable radar.[35] In addition, two squadrons of Defiant turret fighters relegated from the daylight battle due to their vulnerability were also available, but these lacked radar, and crews had uneven night flying experience.[36] The technical complexities of night air defence greatly exceeded those of daylight operations, as a fighter with a two-man crew and heavy armament for momentary nocturnal interceptions was essential. A completely new type of ground-based radar was required to guide the fighter to within detection range, where Aircraft Interception (AI) radar would enable the pilot to make visual contact and move into a firing position.[37]

The ability of radio pulses to detect approaching aircraft was first demonstrated, in Britain, in 1935.[38] In this context it is hardly surprising that prototype AI radar was not ready until the summer of 1939.[39] This had limited range, but an erroneous claim that the minimum range could be reduced to an acceptable figure severely disrupted the development programme.[40] The air officer commanding-in-chief (AOC-in-C) of Fighter Command, Air Chief Marshal Sir Hugh Dowding, urged the Air Ministry to equip twenty-one Blenheim fighters with AI sets so that training and development of operational tactics could begin, effectively turning the research team into a small-scale manufacturing unit.[41]

By December 1939, the first two Marks of AI had been declared operationally useless; the only positive development from testing these systems was that it became clear that highly accurate Ground Control Interception (GCI) radar would be required to guide fighters into AI range and that the intercepting aircraft needed to have a 25 percent excess of speed over the intended target.[42] The RAF had recognised the ineffectiveness of the night defences, and the creation of the Night Interception Committee in early 1940 resulted in the formation of the Fighter Interception Unit (FIU) to test all new equipment, but the more powerful AI Mark III still suffered from an unsatisfactory minimum range of one thousand feet, which was unsuitable for visual contact.[43] The prototype of the first really effective set, AI Mark IV, only began testing in July, coinciding with the availability of the first Bristol Beaufighters, tracking targets from nineteen thousand down to four hundred feet.[44] The unit was unwisely located at Tangmere in the middle of 11 Group, so all of its aircraft were either destroyed or damaged due to enemy action during the Battle of Britain, meaning that operational evaluation could not start until 4 September, and AI Mark IV–equipped Beaufighters only began to enter service in October 1940.[45] During the 17 October meeting that led to his sacking, Dowding resisted the suggestion to use single-engine visually intercepting ('Cat's Eye') fighters at night on the grounds that they would be useless, objecting to 'orders which I believe to be dangerous and unsound'.[46] The desperation of Fighter Command to achieve anything can be demonstrated by the use of Hampden bomber aircraft as improvised night fighters at the end of 1940. Air Marshal Sholto Douglas issued the order for such patrols to be initiated within twenty-four hours of assuming command of the fighter defences on 26 November.[47] As the Hampdens were too slow to catch German bombers, this tactic was abandoned on 14 December in favour of increased use of single-engine fighters at night.[48] At this time, orders were issued for AI fighters to close to within one hundred yards before opening fire 'from underneath' the target, while a review of tests for night fighter squadrons showed that of 169 pilots, there were 19 with 'below average' night vision, meaning that 11 percent of personnel were not capable of fighting at night.[49]

THE BLITZ MOVES AWAY FROM LONDON

Although early *Luftwaffe* attacks were aided by blind bombing systems, by February 1941, the neutralisation of German navigation aids meant that only 20 percent of bombs were falling in the target area.[50] As British aircraft operated near radio beams, German crews were instructed to leave the beam 'in illuminated areas' to 'mitigate the effect of night fighters'.[51] The second phase of the Blitz commenced with the major attack of Coventry on 14–15 November. Because of the successful jamming of *Knickebein*, *X-Gerät* was used by a pathfinder force to mark the target with incendiaries to allow the rest of the bomber force to follow up the attack. Although it superficially looked like an indiscriminate raid on a city centre, Coventry actually had a large concentration of factories in the city, and many important targets were damaged.[52] The *Luftwaffe* attacked London twice in November 1940 and would return another five times during these 'Attacks on Industry and Ports'.[53] Three nights of heavy bombing against Birmingham then followed before a sequence of raids at the end of November on ports, interspersed between two other attacks on London. Further raids on industrial towns and ports ensued in December, with the *Luftwaffe* beginning to concentrate bombing on a single target and repeating the practice at brief intervals to impede recovery.[54]

Massive nighttime raids on industrial targets in major British cities assumed the character of indiscriminate bombing, since accuracy was impossible due to technical limitations.[55] An early RAF survey described German attacks as flawed due to the assumption they were designed to terrorise the population and were uneconomical. It soon became clear, however, that the pattern was to attack ports, food supplies, and the aircraft industry, with the ability to achieve a reasonable concentration of hits on urban areas where there were multiple targets.[56] Special studies were made of the bombing of Hull and Birmingham to understand how fire combined with high explosives to affect different housing areas and population density, and from late 1940, the government made sure that lessons learnt from early bombing were communicated to the authorities responsible for civil defence.[57] German objectives for 1941 reflected war-essential targets, uniting the blockade strategy with the campaign against British aircraft production.[58] Although no major attacks took place from the middle of January until early March, and during two weeks in March–April 1941, many smaller attacks continued, and the number where more than ten fatalities were caused was still significant.[59] Nearly one thousand people were killed during these two 'hiatuses' without major attacks, despite claims of the *Luftwaffe* being operationally 'burnt out' by end of 1940.[60] The lack of effective British defences resulted in a striking reduction in German bomber losses but did nothing to prevent a high accident rate.[61]

Since the start of the Blitz, a system of night decoy sites had been established across the country to simulate burning buildings and divert attacking bombers away from the intended target. By January 1941, forty-two towns and cities outside of London were covered by the decoy system, but the performance of these 'Starfish' sites, specifically intended to protect civilian targets, was inconsistent.[62] Many 'Starfish' attacks were light, and their performance was uneven; the networks around Liverpool and Birmingham were too far out from the cities to be effective. Although it is claimed that 5 percent of German bombing effort was wasted against these sites, most of this was during the Blitz itself, and the proportion diverted during the period after the Blitz and covered by this study was negligible.[63]

The *Luftwaffe* had shown a marked reluctance to venture farther north than Yorkshire in force at night throughout 1940, and the first major raids did not occur there until Glasgow was attacked in March 1941. Further sporadic attacks followed on Hull, Tyneside, and Belfast, but given the importance assigned to the Clyde, Humber, and Tyne in German target selection, it appears surprising that only ten of the fifty-one major attacks in 1941 were directed against those locations.[64] From the start of the Blitz, temporary self-evacuation ('trekking') from bombed areas had strained transport links and welfare facilities, although many of those who trekked out of cities each night to avoid further attacks would still return to work in devastated areas by day.[65] If welfare provisions after attacks, both immediate (rescue, medical, and mortuary) and longer term (shelters, rest centres, emergency repairs, and rehousing) were efficient and timely, morale after heavy raids remained notably robust.

THE ESCALATION OF RAIDS FROM APRIL 1941

Casualties remained high in the spring of 1941 as bombing attacks spread out into areas less well prepared and lacking the resources now being provided for in London (see appendix 2). The *Luftwaffe* returned in March to bomb London in the first major raid of the third phase of the Blitz. During April, there were two further raids against London, which were the heaviest of the entire Blitz, before western and southern ports claimed the attention of the *Luftwaffe* for the rest of the month, including an attempt to obliterate Plymouth completely. Merseyside was then attacked for seven consecutive nights, with half of the docks put out of action, 1,400 killed, and over 70,000 made homeless during 'May Week'. The consequences to the city and the country could have been far worse if the *Luftwaffe* had concentrated their total effort on Merseyside and not diluted it with attacks on other targets at the same time. Hull was the recipient of the major raid on 8–9 May, having received the secondary (but still major) attack the previous night. This resulted in 450 deaths in the city over the two nights, with considerable damage to the docks and 10 percent of the population made homeless, before the *Luftwaffe* switched back to London for the raid that has been considered the climax of the Blitz.[66] As the 10–11 May attack on London marked the end of concentrated, often continuous, periods of bombing, it has been considered by many as the end point of the Blitz, but chapter 1 will present evidence to dispute this, show the continuation of attacks into the 'late Blitz period', and provide an alternative end date.

1

The End of the Blitz and the Continuation of Raids During 1941

10 MAY 1941: LONDON: THE CLIMAX OF THE BLITZ

The termination of attacks on London creates uncertainty for a precise date of the end of the Blitz. To establish a baseline for a comparison with subsequent attacks requires an analysis of the 10 May London raid. By May 1941, the Blitz had been in progress for eight months, and although earlier raids on London (16 and 19 April) were heavier, the attack on 10 May has assumed a critical position in the historiography of the Blitz. Whether the various claims for this attack are justified requires careful consideration that can only be achieved by considering the events of that night in detail.

Between 7 September and 13 November 1940, London sustained fifty-seven major raids, apart from the night of 3 November.[1] Throughout this sequence of seventy-six attacks (not all them were major raids), bomb damage that wrecked train lines and blocked roads meant the simple act of travelling to work could take hours longer than usual.[2] The various pipes and cables that supplied utility services running underneath the streets were inevitably damaged, leading to further hardship.[3] Places of work would regularly suffer damage overnight or be demolished by bombs.[4] As the Blitz continued, despite concentrating the majority of bombing operations on other objectives, the political significance of the capital meant that the *Luftwaffe* returned to attack London at irregular intervals. These raids disrupted the clearance and repair work that had become a part of daily life, and they prolonged the disorder from bombing. A surprise discovery after heavy bombing had been that the psychological effects of air raids were much less severe than expected. Waves of 'war neurosis' did not materialise and the preparations made to deal with such cases were found to be redundant.[5] There was, however, a surge in stress-related medical complaints.[6] As the most bombed city in the United Kingdom, London would have exhibited signs of such disorders first.[7] Although the phenomenon of the 'Blitz Spirit' as a myth has been downplayed by some revisionist historians, none has denied that it existed, although the reality was obviously more complex than the legend, with Calder conceding that 'myth does not deny things, its function is to talk about them'.[8] There is plenty of evidence to demonstrate that the population did work together to endure atrocious conditions, even if stories of uniform cheerfulness and defiance can be dismissed as false.[9]

Six waves of aircraft were despatched to London on 10–11 May. There were 340 German bombers operating over the city in a very heavy attack until 0200, when it began to ease off, with the last enemy aircraft reported as having 'left the country at 0500 hours'.[10] A total of 571 sorties were flown by the *Luftwaffe*, and as a 'maximum effort' raid, some crews ended up flying two or even three times that night.[11] The all clear was not initiated until 0524, by which time 718 tonnes HE/2,392 Incendiary Containers (IC), each holding thirty-six 1kg bombs had been dropped on London.[12] The *Luftwaffe* remained consistent with its targeting doctrine and attacked the docks, causing fires on both sides of the Thames from Romford in the east to Hammersmith in the west. As on 29 December 1940, the river was at low ebb, and water was in short supply.[13] The fire services were severely tested, with 2,154 separate conflagrations being reported across the city.[14] The damage and destruction caused to important and historic buildings, including the Deanery of Westminster Abbey, the War Office, Law Courts, the Mansion House, and the British Museum, were extensive.[15] Fourteen hospitals were involved in treating casualties, and Civil Defence installations, fire stations, and rest centres were damaged.[16] The British Museum fire consumed a quarter-million books, and £100,000 of gin was destroyed in the City Road. On a functional level, one-third of the streets in Greater London were blocked; 155,000 homes were without gas, water, or electricity; and every main railway station apart from one was blocked and closed.[17]

For twenty-four hours, only Marylebone station could function; in forty-eight hours, King's Cross, Euston, Paddington, and Liverpool Street were again operational, but Victoria and Waterloo did not reopen for a week. Thirty miles of underground track were destroyed, with many stations effectively closed.[18] The clearance of the roads progressed slowly, hampered by 162 unexploded bombs across the city.[19] Analyses of the cumulative effect of multiple air raids on the civilian population cannot just consider death and injury. The effect on morale from the denial of the basic needs of living was significant enough, but around 2.25 million people had also been made homeless due to air raids between September 1940 and May 1941. Almost two-thirds of those were in London, meaning that one person in six within the Greater London area was without a home.[20] The fires across London were so extensive that pumps were in use for eleven days. The 'exhausted' Civil Defence forces and a 'badly shaken' population waited for the final blow that would finish off the capital.[21] At an emergency meeting on 11 May, Civil Defence chiefs reported that 'two more nights of this and London will be at a standstill'.[22] Then once again, the *Luftwaffe* changed targets when the morale of the population was at its lowest point.[23]

The literature on 10 May 1941 emphasises several contradictory claims. Despite assertions by Calder, Gibbon, and Townsend, this raid did not signal the end of the London Blitz.[24] Neither was it the last major attack of the Blitz—as claimed by Gardiner, Gilbert, Levine, Richards, Webb and Duncan, and Whiting—but merely the last major attack on London.[25] The 10th of May has also been described by Price, Webb and Duncan, and Townsend as the heaviest raid of the Blitz, but the 718 tonnes HE/2,392 IC dropped that night was exceeded on both 16 April (remembered by Londoners as 'The Wednesday' [890 tonnes HE/4,200 IC]) and 19 April (similarly recalled as 'The Saturday' [1,026 tonnes HE/4,522 IC]), with more incendiaries also being dropped on 19 March (3,397 IC).[26] A similar claim by Calder for 10 May as being the worst raid of the Blitz is worthy of further consideration.[27] More fires were started on 16 April (2,250), causing extensive damage to public buildings, railways, and underground and road services.[28] A contemporary report considered that, in general, the 10 May attack was not as severe as that of 16 April.[29] The deciding factor in determining which was 'worse' has to consider the fatality figures. The 16 April raid had claimed 1,179 lives and caused 2,233 serious injuries, while the consequences of 19 April exceeded any previous attack: 1,208 dead and 1,061 seriously injured. As the 10 May attack resulted in 1,436 deaths and 1,792 serious injuries, it must be considered the worst raid of the Blitz.[30]

Perhaps the main reason why the 10 May raid stood out subsequently is that it highlighted London and the emergency services as harassed, desperate, and exhausted.[31] The Civil Defence personnel, wardens, rescue, first aid, and fire services together with the rest of the struggling population had experienced seventy-two attacks since the previous September.[32] A contemporaneous report conceded that 'morale was strained and here and there weakened', normally after repeated raids on the same target.[33] One more raid could have taken this beyond recovery, although whether this would have prompted a general collapse of morale or a more temporary effect cannot be known. Both Plymouth and Southampton had earlier seen a serious but temporary failure of civilian morale after a breakdown in local authority organisation caused a delay in repairs to utilities and housing.[34] Another reason why this raid stands out in the literature may have more to do with the significance that it had on London itself rather than on the Blitz across the country as a whole, providing an example of history being influenced by events in the national capital city, due to a 'London-centric' historiography. After three devastating raids in just over a month, it is feasible that the morale of the population of London was at its most vulnerable, and post-traumatic stress disorder then imprinted the final attack on people's memories.[35] As a collective memory, this, then, became part of the developing historiography of the Blitz.

Although raiding continued on 11 May, the *Luftwaffe* did not return to London on that night, with widespread bombing by 250 aircraft across the country. The Royal Observer Corps identified this night as the finish of 'the big night bombing offensive that had begun in September 1940', demonstrating the ambiguity of interpreting when the Blitz actually ended.[36] Many of these attacks were against Royal Air Force (RAF) airfields, resembling the 'Intruder' operations employed by both sides since the end of 1940 but with much larger numbers of aircraft than the average of six aircraft per night normally used.[37] Although the 'Late Blitz Period' marked the end of concentrated, often continuous bombing, longer lulls had occurred earlier in the Blitz campaign, with no attacks for nine weeks between January and April 1941. The unusually poor weather prompted these later lulls as much as the availability of aircraft.

CONTINUATION OF ATTACKS THROUGHOUT MAY

The extension of *Luftwaffe* raids throughout the rest of 1941 was encapsulated in the Air Historical Branch (AHB) narrative that documents the night battle until the end of that year. This listed thirty-three attacks between the

TABLE 1.1

Summary of Raids Between 12 May and 31 December 1941 Where More Than Thirty Aircraft Were Involved

Area	**Town**	**No. of Raids During Period**	**Total No. of Raids per Area**
Inland Towns	Birmingham	May: 16–17*; June: 4–5*, 11–12; July: 4–5, 8–9; August: 12–13 (6)	9 (2 major*)
	Manchester	June: 1–2; October: 12–13 (2)	
	London	July: 27–28 (1)	
Ports and Industrial Centres	Tyneside	May: 15–16; September: 1/2, 30–1; October: 2–3, 21–22; December: 8–9, 29–30 (7)	24 (2 major*)
	Hull	June: 28–29; July: 10–11, 14–15, 17–18*; August: 17–18; October: 12–13 (6)	
	Southampton	June: 21–22*, 25–26; July: 7–8; September: 20–21 (4)	
	Birkenhead	June: 24–25; October: 22–23 (2)	
	Liverpool	October: 20–21; November: 1–2 (2)	
	Sunderland	September: 11–12; November: 7–8 (2)	
	Chatham	June: 13–14 (1)	

Adapted from TNA: AIR 41/17; ADGB:III, 121.

middle of May to the end of December 1941, which straddled the 'Late Blitz Period' and continued Phase 3 of the Blitz attacks on ports. The narrative identified several major raids after 10 May and pointed out that significant *Luftwaffe* activity persisted over the country for several months. Although most civilian deaths took place before 12 May 1941, the AHB estimated in 1949 the number of deaths between that date and the end of the year as 1,585.[38] The point at which the Blitz ended and the autumn campaign against ports began is unclear, reflecting the uncertainty of a definitive end date in the historiography. By extrapolating data from other parts of the AHB narrative, it is possible to identify the dates of the listed attacks and provide a framework for analysis, as shown in table 1.1.

The widespread enemy activity against RAF stations during the night of 11–12 May was across the east and south of the country, with no operations on the west coast.[39] The War Cabinet stated that thirty-nine stations reported attacks, but many were so insignificant that they were not recorded in the Group Operations Record Books.[40] Of those documented, within the Fighter Command 11 Group area (including London), bombs were dropped on the airfields at Tangmere, Ford and Martlesham, although little damage was caused.[41] Further south and south-west, in the 10 Group area, Exeter, Middle Wallop, and Warmwell were attacked.[42] The most extensive activity took place in the Midlands, where within the 12 Group area, three separate attacks were launched against Leconfield, which caused a large number of fires and a certain amount of damage to buildings, although the airfield remained operational.[43] In addition, the stations at Matlask, Duxford, Linton, Watton, Driffield, and Scampton were also attacked, although without appreciable damage being caused. Further north, in the 13 Group area, the *Luftwaffe* operated along the north-east coast, between Blyth and Hartlepool. Again, airfields were singled out for attention, with both Acklington and Usworth being attacked, but little damage was reported.[44] Some unrecorded strikes were documented in the daily reports of damage on key points, which also included attacks that are not mentioned in the Fighter Command records.[45] These wide-ranging operations initially appear to have been random, but closer examination reveals a pattern.

During the Battle of Britain, only 60 percent of *Luftwaffe* attacks were directed against operational fighter stations, but just five of the twenty-eight stations attacked on 11–12 May were nonoperational.[46] As Usworth continued to operate the same type of aircraft (Hurricanes) in a training role, its change in status would have been difficult to discern. Additionally, the other two training airfields were also using operational aircraft in the training role. One-fifth of the attacks were against night fighter bases, just at the time when those aircraft were beginning to cause significant losses to German bombers. The aim of offensive 'Intruder' operations was to disrupt flying activity on and around enemy airfields, especially against bomber bases. Only at Wellesbourne did significant destruction occur, with one aircraft being wrecked and three damaged.[47] Both sides used such tactics, although, as previously stated, this night was unusual for the large number of *Luftwaffe* aircraft operating in this role. If a fraction of those aircraft had been used for airfield suppression, then the majority could have been better deployed against one of the cities attacked earlier in that month, when infrastructure and morale were still in a fragile state. As the *Luftwaffe* consistently switched targets throughout the Blitz, the diluting effects of such bombing meant this scenario was unlikely to occur.

The British authorities recognised the attempt to concentrate attacks against night fighter bases, which continued at a lower level on the following night.[48] The pattern of abandoning attacks just at the point when another may have been disastrous had been identified from the beginning of the month. More long-range bombers operated against the country in the first ten days of May than during any similar period, but the limitations of *Luftwaffe* strength were being revealed. The Air Ministry commented that 'it would be too early to predict how far the enemy's experiences of the past week are likely to deter him from night-bombing in force, but he seems already to be examining the advantages of dispersed raids, to our benefit'.[49]

Throughout the Blitz, the municipal fire brigades had struggled to avoid being overwhelmed by heavy attacks, endorsing the pre-war establishment of the Auxiliary Fire Service to supplement the regular provision.[50] Mutual aid between neighbouring fire services was intended to prevent escalation, but often one brigade's hoses would not fit another's hydrants.[51] Lack of standardisation was one of the major reasons for the creation of a National Fire Service, which was announced in the House of Commons on 13 May 1941.[52]

Sporadic *Luftwaffe* activity continued on all but one of the subsequent nights until 15–16 May, when the first of the significant *Luftwaffe* attacks on the AHB list took place. That raid, which was nominally against Newcastle, presents significant challenges to historical research. The Bomb Census did not begin to operate in Region 1 until 7 July 1941, so the attack predates those records.[53] The 13 Group Operations Record Book notes three incursions within the Group boundaries over this particular night.[54] No damage from these attacks was reported to the War Cabinet as militarily significant.[55] Bombs were dropped on a gasworks at Middlesbrough and on the Walker shipyards on Tyneside, where yard facilities sustained minor damage and the tracks for the pier travelling crane were affected by blast damage.[56] Damage was also caused to a gasometer four hundred yards from the shipyard, with reports of attacking aircraft machine-gunning the area.[57] Although sizeable numbers of aircraft were operating that night—more than on any night since 11–12 May—as no serious damage or casualties were inflicted, this attack was correctly considered as insignificant.

There could be no doubt about the significance of the raid against Birmingham on the following night of 16–17 May, which involved 140 aircraft, even if their exact target was less clear.[58] Aircraft were plotted approaching mainly from the east coast, with some over the south and west, which suggested to Fighter Command that many of the aircraft were lost. A recent study proposes that the usual *Luftwaffe* reference point—the London, Midland, and Scottish Railway line to the east of the city—was not visible due to late moonrise and cloud cover.[59] Few German operational records for 1941 still exist, but those for KG4 covering this raid have survived. The one *Gruppe* of KG4 based in the west was assigned to bomb Birmingham, together with KG28 and KG30. Given average serviceability, these units would produce an attacking force of around 150 aircraft.[60] The first wave consisted of incendiary bombs, the majority of which missed Birmingham and ended up falling to the east, on Nuneaton.[61] The fires at Birmingham were quickly brought under control and potential beacons were extinguished, but in Nuneaton, local services were overwhelmed by the large number of fires.[62] Early damage to the telephone system disrupted the coordination of Civil Defence services, so the second wave of attackers was already over the town before fires were under control.[63] Both of the later waves targeted the centre of the fires with heavy bombs or mines, which fell on the residential and shopping areas of the town.[64]

RAF records note that it was a very dark night, and this contributed to a lack of interceptions, especially to the west of Birmingham.[65] Further east, Defiants of 151 Squadron damaged a Dornier Do 17 over Birmingham and a Heinkel He 111 south of Derby. An Aircraft Interception (AI) Beaufighter of 25 Squadron intercepted a He 111 and shot it down near the Lincolnshire coast.[66] The most serious difficulty faced in Nuneaton was caused by the breakdown in communications during the early stages of the raid.[67] The road system was badly affected, with many routes being totally blocked and main rail links obstructed in two places.[68] Further disruption was caused locally in Nuneaton, with one train derailed and another line cut by a bomb crater. Both hospitals were damaged early in the attack, compromising medical services, and casualties included a very high percentage of killed to wounded (eighty-one killed to eighty-nine seriously wounded).[69] Out of fourteen thousand houses, it was estimated that at least six thousand sustained damage, with 8 percent wrecked or subsequently requiring demolition, due to the very heavy types of bombs and mines used in the attack.[70] Rescue and first aid services began to arrive from 0320, and additional resources were provided by RAF medical teams.[71] Five factories in the town were slightly damaged, and two had to cease production due to loss of electrical supply, with part of the Daimler Company works being destroyed by fire.[72] Several factories were also hit in the Birmingham area, but all damage was negligible and production unaffected.[73]

While German documents record that 160 tonnes HE/58 IC were dropped on Birmingham that night, British sources are more sceptical.[74] Initial estimates were of 150 bombs being dropped on Nuneaton.[75] These were quickly reduced to six on Birmingham and forty-eight on Nuneaton, because on such a small target, many bombs missed the town altogether and fell in open country.[76] As no damage was caused by these weapons, the counting of them was variable. The Civil Defence regional report proposed that Nuneaton had been mistaken for Rugby, as the position of both towns in relation to the railway lines and Watling Street was very similar. The locations of the first-wave incendiaries, together with German communiqués mentioning Birmingham, do not support this theory and point to Birmingham as being the primary target.[77] The failure to extinguish the fires in Nuneaton meant that the subsequent waves bombed the wrong target, which is reflected by the 38 people killed in Birmingham itself compared to 113 deaths across the region.[78]

This attack has been identified as the end of the Blitz by Air Marshal Douglas, the RAF commander of Fighter Command during the 1941 campaign.[79] The Official History lists eighty-eight 'notable' attacks on the country from 14 November 1940, with 16 May 1941 as the end date, describing the attacks over the rest of 1941 as 'very slight' in comparison to the main offensive.[80] In contrast, contemporary accounts blamed poor weather over the second half of May for limiting *Luftwaffe* operations against the country. Bomber forces were still considered strong, and intensive attacks would occur over short periods and then use less favourable weather for replenishment of units to prepare for further operations.[81] Despite this, an element of the historiography stretching from the war itself up to the present day, notably Harrisson and Liddell Hart, still erroneously identifies 16 May as the end of the Blitz.[82]

Poor weather continued for the rest of the month, and only minor attacks against Merseyside on the last two nights of May were considered worth mentioning to the War Cabinet.[83] The intermittent nature of enemy activity over the country towards the end of the month has encouraged other scholars, such as Mason, Lukacs, Wood, Dupuy, and Süss to identify this as the end of the Blitz, normally in general terms such as 'until' or 'at the end of' May.[84] This end date does not fit the available evidence, as much longer lulls in bombing

TABLE 1.2

Luftwaffe Operations Towards the End of the Blitz

Month in 1941	April	May	June
Grossenangriffe	21	17	6
Major Coastal Targets	18 (90%)	15 (88%)	3 (50%)
Distribution of Coastal Attacks	2E, 12S, 4W	2E, 1S, 12W	2S, 1W
Störangriffe	412	440	221
Nuisance Coastal Targets	—	277 (63%)	100 (45%)
Distribution of Coastal Attacks	—	122E, 105S, 53W	52E, 34S, 14W
Unclassified	137	142	103
Mines Laid	433	363	647
Kampfgeschwader Available	44	44	14

Compiled from BA-MA: RL 2-IV/33, Angriffe auf England, H6132, H6139, and H6145.
Figures in parentheses are percentages of totals.

had occurred earlier in the Blitz. Operations during the second half of the month were severely limited due to poor flying weather, which also restricted RAF bombing raids during the same period.[85] In contrast, Terraine mentions the Blitz only in passing, Overy vaguely assigns the end to the spring of 1941, while only Buckley acknowledges the *Luftwaffe* 'maintaining the air war' on 'a reduced scale'.[86] Official records also show that between 17 and 28 May 1941, no enemy aircraft were destroyed at night over the United Kingdom.[87]

The *Luftwaffe* considered the Battle of Britain and the Blitz as a single campaign that lasted until the beginning of the offensive against the Soviet Union.[88] The opinion of Adolph Galland was that from April 1941, the last raids against the United Kingdom were used as a cover for the impending attack in the East.[89] Both Galland and Kesselring agree that the Blitz peaked in April 1941.[90] The end of the Blitz has often been linked in the historiography to the redeployment of German units for the offensive in the East. Although these movements started at the beginning of June 1941, an examination of contemporary records in table 1.2 indicates that forces in the West had already peaked in April, when German forces were redeployed to support the Balkans campaign, reducing the number of bomber units in the West by 30 percent.[91]

TABLE 1.3

Comparison of *Kampfgeschwader* Effort (Operations per KG) During the First Half of 1941

Month	*Kampfgeschwader*	*Grossenangriffe*	*Störangriffe*	Mines Laid
January	49	0.31	2.1	2.9
February	49	0.12	3.1	7.6
March	49	0.39	4.8	8.4
April	44	0.48	9.4	9.8
May	44	0.39	10.0	8.3
June	14	0.43	15.8	46.2

Calculated from BA-MA: RL 2-IV/33, Angriffe auf England, H6111–H6145.

Despite this, there was no appreciable reduction in the scale and concentration of attacks against the United Kingdom.[92] One explanation for this is that units had been brought up to strength during the lulls in attacks earlier in 1941, and in some cases, replacement units were equipped with new types of aircraft.[93] Units began to withdraw into Germany to prepare for 'Barbarossa' from the beginning of June, while operations continued against British cities.[94] In this context, the opinion of O'Brien that acknowledges the rest of 1941 was not free of attack but describes this period as 'a breathing space' cannot be substantiated.[95] A greater concern was that German bomber production could not keep up with losses, and the *Luftwaffe* would enter the Russian campaign with two hundred fewer bombers than at the start of operations against the West a year earlier. Despite the reduction in aircraft available, table 1.3 shows that the relative effort of units increased as 1941 progressed.[96]

REVIEW OF NIGHT DEFENCE UP TO THE END OF MAY 1941

Table 1.4 confirms that meaningful results for night fighter defence up to the end of May 1941 only became possible after the teething troubles of Ground Control Interception (GCI) and the Beaufighter/AI Mark IV combination had been overcome. Although an AI Beaufighter destroyed an enemy aircraft as early as 19 November 1940, significant quantities only occurred after ground assistance was available.[97] The first GCI station became operational

TABLE 1.4
Result of Fighter Combats During the Night Battle

Year	Month	Enemy Sorties	Destroyed (Total)	Destroyed (Single-Engine)	% Destroyed (Single-Engine)
1940	September	6,135	4		
	October	5,845	3		
	November	5,495	2		
	December	3,585	4		
1941	January	1,965	3	1	33
	February	1,225	4	1	25
	March	3,510	22	1	5
	April	4,835	49	9	18
	May	4,055	96	29	30

Compiled from AIR 41/17; ADGB:III, 116–17.

on 1 January 1941, and a total of eight were active by May 1941, having been responsible for the destruction of sixty-one enemy aircraft in that period.[98]

Although the number of AI-equipped squadrons just started to increase in May 1941, the statistics conceal the qualitative improvement of the defences (see appendix 4).[99] While only one extra squadron had been added to the order of battle compared to September 1940, all bar one (which was in the process of replacing its Blenheims) were operating Beaufighters or Havocs equipped with AI Mark IV.

Although Fighter Command had won the day battle the previous year, what is not generally realised is that the RAF expected the day offensive to resume in the spring of 1941 as a second round of a far more intense Battle of Britain, and aircraft production targets reflected this.[100] The protracted development of AI radar and the late introduction of the Beaufighter meant the *Luftwaffe* was practically unopposed during the winter of 1940. Poor serviceability prevented Beaufighters being unavailable for operations on consecutive nights, exacerbating the shortage of aircraft.[101] By December, Douglas was protesting to Air Chief Marshal Sir Charles Portal, the chief of the air staff, about the allocation of Beaufighters to Coastal Command instead of night air defence.[102] Portal, however, had to consider the overall responsibilities of the air force and to fulfill the growing commitments to army support in North Africa, so he declined to accelerate the reequipment of his squadrons.[103]

Despite the enthusiasm of the air officer commanding-in-chief (AOC-in-C) for the use of single-engine, visually intercepting 'Cat's Eye' fighters in the night battle, the results were probably not worth the effort expended. On 12 May 1941, Douglas was quoted as saying, 'AI with GCI was the most profitable means of night interception', which mirrored the statement that had cost Dowding his job six months earlier.[104]

The disappointing initial performance of AI prompted Fighter Command to consider less conventional means of air defence.[105] The long approach by the night fighter after AI 'contact' into firing position below the target, to enable a 'visual' identification against the night sky, was perceived as being slow and inefficient when compared to day fighter tactics.[106] This meant that a great deal of time and resources were wasted on schemes that Gunston has charitably described as 'clutching at any straw'.[107] The Long Aerial Mine (LAM), code-named 'Mutton', consisted of two thousand feet of piano wire with a small bomb at the top and parachutes at both ends. These were to be dropped from aircraft in front of the attacking bombers, where the wire would strike a wing, detach the top parachute, and pull the bomb down to explode on the aircraft.[108] Trials using obsolete Harrow transport aircraft were discouraging and prevented AI-equipped aircraft from using the first (and at the time only) GCI station for extended periods.[109] Instead of abandoning the experiment at this stage, the squadron was reequipped with much faster Havocs, not only continuing to dilute the effectiveness of ground control but also diverting aircraft and trained crews away from night interception duties.[110] This method of defence was intended to take advantage of concentrated streams of enemy bombers travelling to a target using a radio beam and was supported by Professor Frederick Lindemann (later Lord Cherwell), who, crucially, was Churchill's scientific advisor. Lindemann did not advocate radar, as he had not been involved in developing it, while his ideas about using aerial mines went back to 1936.[111] The influence for scientific advice that Lindemann had gained with Churchill ensured that trials with LAMs continued long after their ineffectiveness was evident.[112] The proposal to use free balloon barrages was even more perplexing; they were again equipped with wires attached to small bombs, which tied up resources for months awaiting the ideal conditions to launch them. The intention was to deploy such barrages, code-named 'Albino', on nights when conditions were unsuitable for night fighter operations.[113] Despite claims to the contrary, there is no evidence that either of these schemes destroyed a single enemy aircraft.[114] Deployment of such methods was limited to over the sea, where the wind direction would prevent the parachute- or balloon-borne bombs from being deposited overland to negate the risk of civilian casualties. This did not mean that Fighter Command learnt from these experiments: An extended waste of much greater resources would take place throughout 1942.

RE-EVALUATION OF *LUFTWAFFE* POLICY DURING ATTACKS IN JUNE

Significant raiding resumed on the first night of June, with a substantial attack of ninety-three tonnes HE/228 IC on the centre of Manchester.[115] Although described as a 'concentrated' raid by the War Cabinet, a review of the evidence does not support this assertion.[116] Aircraft converged on Manchester from the east and south, but bombing took place over a wide area of Lancashire and Cheshire.[117] Business premises in the centre of Manchester sustained considerable damage, but there was spillage of bombing into the surrounding area; in addition to the forty-eight deaths in Manchester, another forty-four persons were killed in Salford.[118] Amongst the buildings hit in Manchester was the central police headquarters, but despite extensive damage, the underground Civil Defence control room continued to operate.[119] Production at three important factories was affected and damage caused at commercial premises in the dock area, with a number of roads blocked by craters.[120] The main railway line out of the city to the north was blocked, and local train services were also disrupted after Manchester Victoria station was closed due to debris blocking lines and platforms.[121] The visibility that night was described as poor, and while patrols were flown by five squadrons from 9 Group, there was only a single combat by a Defiant of 96 Squadron, which claimed a Ju 88 as damaged.[122] Despite aircraft travelling east across the country, there is no record of any interceptions being attempted while the bombers were in the 12 Group area.[123]

The previous attack on Manchester during December 1940 had identified serious deficiencies in the Civil Defence organisation. A report made following the 1–2 June raid stated that many lessons had been learnt following the December attack. The coordination and cooperation of all branches of Civil Defence during the June raid showed significant improvement.[124] It was noted that modern steel framed or reinforced concrete construction was far more resilient to bombing than older brick buildings.[125] Given the scale of attack (up to eighty aircraft), the extended availability of *Luftwaffe* units in the west, and the widespread damage caused, it is clear that the Manchester raid was not a separate operation but instead a continuation of the Blitz.[126] The only reason the Manchester attack does not qualify as a major raid was that the weight of bombs dropped failed to reach the one hundred tonnes level. As the month progressed, the number of aircraft operating still exceeded one hundred on some nights, resulting in what O'Brien has described as 'sharp' attacks.[127]

Although more aircraft (ninety-five) operated over the country during the next AHB list attack on 4–5 June, the intended target was less than clear.[128] The Air Ministry Commentary and War Cabinet for that night do not even acknowledge that anything significant occurred.[129] German records classify this as a major raid on Birmingham, with 108 tonnes HE/167 IC recorded as being dropped, with far less effective results than the ostensibly smaller attack on Manchester three nights before.[130] Aircraft operated over a wide area of the Midlands, lacking a discernible concentration, with bombs also being dropped at various points in the Medway area without casualties or any serious damage.[131] The KG4 records state that twenty-two of their aircraft attacked Birmingham, with KG28 and KG30 assigned to the same target, all aircraft using markers dropped by *Kampfgruppe* (KGr) 100 and III/KG26. Only nine aircraft of 1/KG4 claimed to have bombed Birmingham, and similar levels of inaccuracy must have been obtained by the other attacking units.[132] The bombs in the Midlands were dropped on the urban centres of Birmingham, Wolverhampton, and Coventry and extensively across Shropshire and Worcestershire, almost exclusively on residential property and factories escaped with negligible damage that had no effect on production. Casualties were light in the cities, with three people killed in Birmingham and two in Coventry.[133] The most deaths occurred in the small towns of Darlaston, Atherstone, and Tettenhall, where a total of thirty-six people died.[134] Patrols were flown from three airfields in the 9 Group area, but no combats were achieved, with visibility described as 'moderate at best'.[135] More success was achieved over 12 Group, with Beaufighters of 25 Squadron shooting down two He 111s near the east coast.[136]

The scattered nature of the bombing makes it impossible to consider this a major raid, but the number of aircraft involved and results of the attacks mean it must be regarded as significant. Although the bad weather deprived the *Luftwaffe* of the best nights of the full moon period, this was considered the only reason for German inaction.[137] The percentage of the bomber force transferred to the East was not thought to have appreciably reduced the scale of attack that could be expected when good weather returned.[138] The wider implications of heavy bombing attacks were discussed during the War Cabinet meeting held the day after this attack. Heavy raids during April and May had prompted sizeable unregulated evacuations from coastal areas, and many people who were not homeless were using rest centres after heavy attacks. At issue was whether the policy of providing for the homeless should be extended and official arrangements made for those who left the target areas nightly to sleep in safer areas. The War Cabinet considered that while sufficient rest centres needed to be provided for all persons whether homeless or not after heavy raids, no other arrangements should be made for those who were not homeless, as to do otherwise would be bad for morale.[139]

Sporadic enemy activity continued despite the unfavourable weather, but the *Luftwaffe* did not operate in strength again over the United Kingdom until the night of 11–12 June.[140] Although identified on the AHB list as a raid on Birmingham, in reality these attacks were so widely scattered that it was difficult to pinpoint the intended target.[141] Aircraft converged on the Midlands from both the south and east, in the general area above Birmingham. The KG4 records show that eleven aircraft of 1/KG4 and seventeen of 3/KG4 attacked Birmingham, with KG28 and KG30 assigned to the same target, all aircraft using markers dropped by KGr100 and III/KG26.[142] Not all aircraft attacked their assigned target; for the eleven aircraft of 1/KG4, only one actually bombed Birmingham, while six chose coastal targets.[143] Bombs were reported at Birmingham, Coventry, Shrewsbury, and Derby, before aircraft left to the south-east.[144] There was also widespread activity across the east of the country, incidents being reported from East Anglia, Lincolnshire, and Yorkshire.[145] Parachute mines were dropped at Bristol, a gasworks seriously damaged at Dover, and a barracks hit at Portsmouth.[146] The casualty distribution reflected the scattered nature of the attacks; at Bristol, fifteen people were killed, another fifteen died at Dover, and the highest death toll of the night was twenty-five at Kings Lynn.[147] Six people also died in a factory at Walsall, and four were killed in the Portsmouth barracks.[148] The inland attacks were carried out on a very small scale, which is supported by the available German records, so this night cannot be considered as a significant raid against Birmingham or the Midlands as a whole.[149] Patrols were flown from three airfields in the 9 Group area, but no contacts were achieved.[150]

Although aircraft were active over the 12 and 13 Group areas, once again there is no record of any interceptions being attempted.[151] The lack of a sizeable concentration or of major damage at the other locations disqualifies the entire night and again demonstrates the weakness of the AHB list that bases the significance of attacks solely on the numbers of aircraft operating.

For the rest of the week, there was only slight bombing, except for 13–14 June, when there was a minor concentration over the Medway, some activity over Portsmouth, and other scattered bombing around the south and east coasts as far north as Lincolnshire.[152] The AHB list identifies this night as an attack on Chatham, but there is little evidence to support this claim. Only 3 of the 230 bombs dropped on Chatham Metropolitan Borough over the whole of the pre–Bomb Census were classified, indicating that they failed to cause any damage, while only 19 bombs fell in the whole of Portsmouth County Borough over 13–14 June.[153] In spite of this, nineteen aircraft of 1/KG4 were assigned to this operation, as well as sixteen aircraft of 3/KG4, while KG28 and KG30 also took part.[154] Thirteen aircraft of 1/KG4 claimed to have attacked Chatham, dropping 26 bombs, which exceeds the total number on the entire area for that night, emphasising the dispersed nature of this raid, and there were no reports of major casualties.[155] The absence of military damage makes this raid insignificant, nor can claims in the Official History that this attack was 'notable' be substantiated.[156] The 11 Group fighters, in contrast, had a productive night, with the Havocs of 85 Squadron shooting down a He 111 and claiming another as probably destroyed. The Beaufighters of 219 Squadron also shot down two German bombers, one of which was identified as a Ju 88.[157]

Few bombs were dropped across the United Kingdom on subsequent nights, with Home Security being 'mystified at developments'.[158] As the improved weather continued, the *Luftwaffe* made its next serious attempt on a coastal target at Southampton on 21–22 June, which German records identify as a major raid, with 136 tonnes HE/143 IC being dropped, but as Fighter Command plotted only forty aircraft over Southampton and Portsmouth on that night, the German claim is difficult to substantiate.[159] Ramsey identifies this raid as the end of the Blitz, but Home Security described German propaganda claims that 2,000 tonnes of high explosive had been dropped during this raid as 'preposterous'.[160] Bombs did cause a leak in a dry dock and considerable damage to house property.[161] In addition, Southampton central station was severely damaged by parachute mines, and the main lines were blocked by debris, normal service not resuming until 23 June.[162] In spite of this, casualties were remarkably light, with twelve civilians being killed along with eight military personnel, which was partly due to large numbers of bombs missing the city and falling in adjacent rural areas, which contributed to the total number of bombs dropped without causing damage.[163] Several of these bombs and numerous incendiaries fell on open ground, causing major fires that may have encouraged optimistic *Luftwaffe* post-raid reports.[164] As only superficial damage was caused to important military targets, including the main Southampton power station, it is again impossible to consider this a major attack.[165] In terms of bombs dropped, this must still be regarded as a significant raid, and the results of the attacks would have been considerably improved if the six parachute mines that missed the city had caused damage and another six that landed in Southampton had actually exploded.[166] The fighters of 11 Group continued to improve their expertise by shooting down two of the attacking bombers.[167]

Since the attack at Birmingham on 11–12 June, the *Luftwaffe* had confined itself to coastal targets. German radio beams for blind bombing were not used operationally after the 11–12 June attack throughout the rest of 1941, the lack of radio navigation aids hindering the concentration of forces over inland targets, although KGr100, the principal target marking unit, was known to be still present in France at Chartres until early July.[168] The British expected the Germans to use their remaining bombers for concentrated attacks of great accuracy, directed by radio bombing aids to maintain pressure on the defending forces.[169] In reality, attacks were increasingly directed towards coastal ports, and since the necessary resources for blind bombing were still available during June, the selection of these targets was probably for other operational reasons. Home Security remained unimpressed, commenting that 'it is now plain that the enemy is unlikely to attack this country in force until his bombers are released from the German Eastern Front. He will however, probably continue small scale raids (probably with big bombs) for propaganda purposes. It is impossible to guess how long this lull may last, but it is certain that Civil Defence must prepare for the renewal of very heavy attacks when it is over'.[170]

The month would be seen out with three further propaganda raids on coastal targets. On 24–25 June, bombs were dropped on both sides of the estuary at Merseyside.[171] At Wallasey, a warehouse was damaged, and bombs fell on the docks and roads, but the only significant damage was to the entrance of the Mersey tunnel at Birkenhead.[172] On the following night, land mines were dropped at several locations in Hampshire, with the only significant damage at Hedge End near Southampton, where twelve people were killed.[173] Finally, on 28–29 June, Hull was bombed, causing damage to the docks and houses in the eastern end of the town, with only one death, albeit that of the deputy chief constable of police.[174] All three of these raids appear on the AHB list and again illustrate that basing the significance of attacks solely on the numbers of aircraft operating is not convincing, although the *Luftwaffe* lost a further four bombers during these operations.[175] Further evidence of this is the source that identifies the raid on 30 June–1 July against South Wales as the heaviest attack of the week, which is not mentioned within the AHB narrative.[176]

Despite the unusually poor weather, the *Luftwaffe* succeeded in continuing the Blitz and maintaining pressure on British defenders throughout June 1941, although with sometimes indifferent results. Target selection suggested that the Germans were returning to a strategy where inland industrial towns were attacked as well as the ports bombed since February 1941. Throughout the month, however, the long-range bomber strength in the West continued to decline as units were transferred to the East, which the defenders were fully aware of in contemporary Intelligence reports. As twenty radio beam stations had been established in France by the summer of 1941, there was considerable relief that the bombers capable of using them had been transferred to the Eastern Front.[177] By the end of June, only 240 such aircraft remained to face the United Kingdom, compared to the peak strength of 1,450 twin-engine bombers at the end of March.[178] The effectiveness of the remaining force was increased by the assignment of new-model aircraft to the Western Front, while the 'older models would be used against the Soviet Union'.[179] It remained to be seen how the *Luftwaffe* would manage a credible continuation of the air war with only eight *Gruppen* available compared to a previous maximum of forty-four.[180]

The British public was hard pressed for accurate information on the progress of German air raids during the Blitz, as both local and national newspapers were vague in the extreme and caused disgruntlement amongst a wide range of the population when it was perfectly clear when a city had been attacked. The censorship of news about air raids was beginning to cause problems, with authorities outside of London complaining about inadequate and misleading reporting. In some cities, there was criticism of the government and demands that populations should have their suffering adequately documented as a matter of local pride.[181] The problems caused by the censorship of news about air raids brought about a change of policy in June 1941, when Brendan Bracken took over at the Ministry of Information. Bracken had previously worked as a journalist and was not convinced that the earlier reporting restrictions were appropriate in winning the population's trust and that a 'people's war' required a different approach to explain why controls were necessary.[182] He believed that high morale could only be achieved through an open information policy, which acknowledged the hazards of war to the population, including the threat of air raids. To do otherwise would risk the loss of faith by the public.[183]

JULY 1941: CHANGING TACTICS AS THE BLITZ ENDS

Enemy activity at the beginning of July did not at the time seem to indicate the future direction of *Luftwaffe* strategy, and although many enemy aircraft had been transferred from North-West Europe, the British were unclear whether the Blitz was over. If the Soviet campaign ended quickly, an invasion attempt on Britain by the Germans could still have been possible before the end of the year, but slower progress in the East might mean a return at short notice to 'heavy blockade-bombing'.[184] The Air Ministry Commentary believed that the Germans had only two options: invasion or continued blockade.[185] Bombing operations over the United Kingdom continued to support the British view that the Blitz was not yet over.

On the night of 4–5 July, eighty bombers operated over the country, with dispersed attacks taking place over the Midlands, the east coast, and the south-west of the country.[186] *Luftwaffe* records claim that ninety-four aircraft were despatched, of which fifty-two reached their targets.[187] As with previous operations, aircraft approached the area from different directions, preventing a coordinated attack that led to scattered and ineffective bombing.[188] Some damage to residential property was caused in Birmingham, and in Coventry, an ordnance factory was hit where five people were killed and fifteen seriously injured.[189] The 'Fighter Night' tactic had been introduced earlier in the Blitz, where Cat's Eye aircraft operated in force over a major target, while anti-aircraft fire was restricted, but this tactic was implemented over Birmingham without achieving any contacts. Patrols by AI fighters under GCI direction were more successful, with aircraft from 12 Group shooting down two attacking bombers.[190] Despite the AHB list identifying this raid as an attack on Birmingham, the most serious damage of the night was actually at Plymouth, where railway lines were severed between Devonport and the dockyard.[191] Twenty-two people died in this attack, more than in all the other locations combined.[192] Had all aircraft concentrated on one objective, it might be possible to consider the attacks on this night as significant, but the results of the bombing do not justify that.

German bombing concentration improved three nights later, when fifty-five aircraft dropped ninety-two tonnes of HE/248 IC on Hampshire in general and Southampton in particular.[193] The large number of incendiaries used caused seventy-five fires, five of which were serious, although all had been extinguished by 0430 the following morning.[194] Three important roads were temporarily closed, the main railway line was blocked by debris at the central station and damage caused to the marshalling yard. The gasworks was hit and two gasholders put out of action, completely interrupting supply to the city.[195] While 383 houses were wrecked, no damage was caused to the docks.[196] In contrast to the supposedly heavier 'major' raid on 21–22 June, thirty-five people were killed in the 7–8 July attack, demonstrating what the previous attack could have achieved with better concentration of bombing.[197] The Air Ministry Commentary considered that even though it was only moderate in force, the operation against Southampton was the most serious to take place since the raid at Manchester on 1–2 June, which makes it at least as significant as the earlier raid.[198] A 'Fighter Night' carried out by aircraft of both 10 and 11 Groups led to a Hurricane of 3 Squadron shooting down a Do 17, while a Beaufighter of the Fighter Interception Unit shot down a He 111.[199] As coastal targets were easier to locate without the use of (now-unavailable) radio aids, the decision to attempt another attack on Birmingham the following night is unclear.

Although identified by the AHB as a raid on Birmingham, German communiqués claimed a much wider area of attack for 8–9 July.[200] Over one hundred aircraft operated against targets as far apart as Aberdeen, Yarmouth, and Plymouth.[201] Eighty-eight aircraft were assigned to the Midlands, but only twenty-two actually reached their target, though they achieved negligible results.[202] Recent research suggests less than five aircraft bombed the Birmingham area.[203] Once again, aircraft approached the area from multiple directions, with overlapping formations leading to scattered bombing.[204] A 'Fighter Night' resulted in two claims for damaged bombers by Cat's Eye fighters, while aircraft under GCI control did not achieve any interceptions.[205] At Aberdeen, extensive damage was caused to industrial premises, and bombs dropped at Plymouth caused twelve fires and killed three people. The most serious damage of the night was at Yarmouth where the South Quay was bombed, 120 houses demolished, 1,000 damaged, and a gasholder destroyed, with three people killed.[206] This attack was considered so serious that 12 Group initiated a 'Fighter Night' over the town, and a Ju 88 was shot down.[207] In the Midlands, by contrast, houses were reported damaged near Wolverhampton and at Etherstone, and a railway wagon works was also bombed in Derby.[208] Because of this, the diversionary attacks on this night assumed greater significance to the British and caused difficulty in identifying where the Germans had intended to attack.[209] The scattered bombing was interpreted by the Air Ministry as an indication of the *Luftwaffe* losing faith in their electronic aids, with coastal towns taking an increasing proportion of attacks due to the simplified navigation required.[210]

Up to this point in the war, the coastal city of Kingston upon Hull had been the target of twenty-eight raids, including three major attacks, and Hull was bombed another four times during July.[211] As the weather was generally poor over the United Kingdom for the rest of July 1941, the selection of coastal objectives is unsurprising.[212] The advantages to *Luftwaffe* crews in locating coastal targets and minimising risks during poor flying conditions are obvious. The Air Ministry was unimpressed with the quality of the bomber crews left to continue the offensive in the West, describing them uncharitably as a 'scratch team'. The switch to coastal objectives was interpreted as providing easier targets for 'fledging pilots at a late stage of their training'.[213]

The poor weather continued into the following week, with mist and fog giving way to thunder and heavy rain.[214] Coastal areas experienced minor bombing from aircraft that were primarily concerned with shipping targets.[215] The attacks on Hull had been small in June and early July, but 'the tempo stepped up' on 10–11 July.[216] This was the heaviest raid of the week across the country, which lasted for over two hours from 0115.[217] Seventy-eight aircraft were used, and a good concentration was achieved, with sixty-two aircraft over the target.[218] Radar detected aircraft mine laying off Flamborough Head and East Anglia, but poor visibility prevented fighter operations until 0200. Consequently, combats were limited to a He 111, which was damaged by a Defiant of 255 Squadron north of Hull.[219] Seventy-eight fires were caused, two of which were serious, and over fifty HE bombs were dropped. Twenty-one people were killed, 8 of them when a first aid post was hit, and 1,439 were made homeless. Although communications and transport were the principal targets, there was considerable damage to house property and some industry. Gas and water mains were damaged and electrical supplies disrupted, but all had been restored by the following morning.[220] Fifty-six houses were wrecked, 88 required demolition, and 1,136 were damaged.[221] Bombs were also dropped on Yarmouth and Gorleston, damaging hundreds of houses.[222]

Although there was a minor attack on Yarmouth on the night of 13–14 July, the weather continued to discourage major enemy activity.[223] The following day, the prime minister reviewed the Civil Defence services in the capital and then addressed a luncheon given by the London County Council. His speech revealed the discomfort that the authorities experienced at the start of the Blitz and the concern that was felt when attacks were switched to provincial ports and cities in case these proved more effective than those on London.[224] The central point of the speech was to remind the audience that increased British attacks on German cities was likely to provoke retaliation in the west. A return to the heavy attacks of the previous winter was therefore considered likely, and Churchill warned that 'all engaged in our civil defence forces, whether in London or throughout the country, must prepare themselves for further heavy assaults'.[225]

The night after Churchill's speech, a significant raid took place on Hull. The *Luftwaffe* used sixty-four aircraft for this attack, of which fifty-nine reported finding the target.[226] Damage from this attack was chiefly to residential property: 105 houses were wrecked, 242 were seriously damaged, and 323 people were made homeless. A gas main was hit, causing a fire, and electricity supplies were cut off, but all utilities had been restored by the following morning.[227] Although fewer bombs were dropped than on 10–11, around thirty in total, the use of heavy bombs caused greater destruction and more casualties than would have been expected for an attack of this size.[228] Twenty-five people were killed, which was more than during the previous attack on Hull.[229] A small 'Fighter Night' was operated over Hull without any success.[230] The weather continued to be poor, with bombing confined to coastal targets of opportunity from aircraft that were primarily engaged on anti-shipping sorties.[231]

The final major raid of the Blitz took place again at Hull on the night of 17–18 July 1941. Eighty aircraft made an intensive effort, resulting in the heaviest attack on the country since the 16–17 May raid on Birmingham. Graystone considered that this attack 'in terms of fatal casualties, and probably in terms of industrial damage, was only surpassed by the May blitz'.[232] Although some of the formations involved in the attack were based in northern France, all aircraft approached Hull from the east, flying up the coast to the area around Texel in the Dutch Islands before crossing the North Sea.[233] Attacking aircraft operated below ten thousand feet, with some as low as three thousand. Another small 'Fighter Night' was operated over Hull, once again without success.[234] This attack started at 0120 and lasted for two hours, with 160 fires caused, although only 4 became serious, with 2 still out of control at 0735 the following morning. There was 'serious and extensive damage' to industrial and residential property in the centre, east, and south-west of the city.[235] Although the tonnage figures were similar for both attacks (160 tonnes against Birmingham on 16–17 May versus 174 tonnes against Hull on 17–18 July), 182 bombs were recorded as hitting Hull as opposed to only 47 during the Birmingham raid, the majority of which hit Nuneaton.[236] *Luftwaffe* records show that 114 aircraft were assigned to attack Hull, of which 108 operated over the target, demonstrating the superior concentration of bombing against coastal targets.[237] Far more incendiaries were used against Hull, however (172 IC against Hull versus 58 IC against Birmingham), but these appear to have been more scattered than against Birmingham, as far fewer serious fires developed.[238] The casualties from the earlier attack reflected the more dispersed nature of the damage, with 38 deaths in Birmingham compared to 151 over the region as a whole. Although the majority of the deaths were in Nuneaton, this figure of 113 is significantly lower than the 150 killed at Hull on 17–18 July and indicates the more intense bombing of the coastal target.[239] Given the scale of the raid, 'strong and bitter criticism' was voiced by residents at the lack of defensive measures and the ease with which German bombers operated without 12 Group fighters making a greater effort to intercept them.[240]

Although the main rail links remained intact, some goods services were disrupted and not fully restored until 21 July. Utilities were so badly affected that three-quarters of the city were still without gas on 19 July, full pressure not restored to all areas until 23 July, and telephone communications still not fully reinstated by 21 July.[241] The main industrial damage was caused by fire, with offices and warehouses being burnt out at one location, a Spillers flour mill was gutted, and part of a varnish works was destroyed.[242] The heavy casualties caused by this attack were due in part to a number of communal shelters being hit, as well as a first aid depot. Damage to residential property was extensive, with 197 houses wrecked, 286 requiring demolition, and 2,000 evacuated due to the amount of damage sustained. It was estimated that a total of 17,000 houses would require first aid repairs. Twenty-one rest centres were opened that accommodated 3,548 people in total, and provisions were made for all people who wanted to evacuate from the city.[243] Although many people had not lost their houses, they left the city, anticipating further bombing. It was calculated at the time that 10,000 people were leaving the city each night.[244] By the end of 21 July, however, the majority of these trekkers (temporary self-evacuation from bombed areas) had been able to return to their own homes.[245] Although the raids during the previous week were considered to have 'acclimatised' the population to bombing, morale was very low on 18 July and a further raid 'might have been disastrous'. The Ministry of Information asserted 'the absence of a successive raid saved us from inevitable panic', but the erratic pattern of *Luftwaffe* activity ensured that this did not occur.[246] In the space of a week, the *Luftwaffe* had sent 256 bombers to Hull, of which 229 claimed to have found the target. The German assessment was that only the 17–18 July attack 'had good success,' although the citizens of Hull might have had a different opinion.[247]

The aftermath of this attack on just one street in Hull highlights the traumatic and occasionally gruesome nature of Civil Defence work. Eight unidentified bodies were recovered from bombed-out houses as well as individual parts of bodies, such as a baby's left foot, a left arm and shoulder, a left forearm, a man's right foot, a baby's left hand, and a female scalp.[248] The low morale in the city was unsurprising, as many people would have been dealing with such stressful situations after three significant raids within seven days. When analysing the cumulative effect of multiple air raids on the civilian population, it is not just death and injury that need to be considered, and such circumstances would have been replicated across all bombed areas of the United Kingdom, although where preparations were good, such as in Hull, morale did not collapse.[249]

The experiences of the civilian population of Hull during these attacks can be illustrated by an account written by a thirteen-year-old schoolboy shortly after the attacks on the city in 1941.[250] 'The first bomb landed in the next street to us so I put my overcoat on and went to see if my Auntie was all right, as I walked into the back yard an incendiary bomb dropped right next to me so I put a sand bag over it'.[251] The all clear finally sounded at 0445, and the schoolboy then went to deliver newspapers. 'I was coming home down Bond Street when I saw the manager of Kayes salvaging tools out of his shop which was on fire and he was putting the tools in a garage yard'. The fascination of the big raid had clearly not worn off, as the schoolboy was soon out into the town again. 'As I was half down the street an unexploded bomb went off killing three people, the blast from the bomb knocked me down and broke some church windows'. The robust nature of the wartime welfare system is demonstrated by the reaction of the emergency services: 'When I got up I felt dizzy so two firemen took me to a Mobile Canteen Van where I had a cup of tea to steady my head. When I had drank my tea I thanked the firemen and went home'.

The significance of the attack on Hull means it must be considered as a possible end date for the Blitz. The number of people who registered for assistance following the 17–18 July raid was 9,478. This figure was only exceeded at Hull during the period of 7–12 May 1941, when 72,651 people registered following the two major raids on the city on 7 and 8 May.[252] The attack on Hull was the heaviest attack on the country since the 16–17 May raid on the Midlands, and the damage and casualties caused were in fact much heavier than any single raid since the 10–11 May attack on London. German communiqués emphasised the destruction caused at Hull, highlighting the 'many big explosions' observed.[253] It was one of the few occasions when Hull was identified by name in news bulletins. Graystone has suggested this was due to the precision of the bombing, leaving the Germans certain of the success of the attack and was reflected in 'spectacular claims' for the operation, some of which 'were justified'.[254]

Following the raid on Hull, there was growing dissatisfaction at the ineffectiveness of defence against night bombing. Despite speeches by government and service officials giving the impression that an effective counter to night bombing, including radiolocation (the recently announced acknowledgement of radar), had become available, the heavy bombing of cities had continued. 'It is therefore a shock to the public when they find that this is not so', commented the post-raid report from Hull, 'in spite of the authoritative source of their hope and this undoubtedly shakes confidence in the statements and advice from such quarters'.[255] The inability of the defenders to prevent bombing was in part due to the reduction in *Luftwaffe* forces after the invasion of the Soviet Union in June 1941, as German tactics changed 'to complicate the detection of approach routes' and 'fragment the response of the night-time defence', to conserve aircraft because replacements were unlikely.[256] German bombers began to take energetic evasive action, beginning with a very low approach over the sea and then frequently changing course and height overland.[257] This reduced the effectiveness of the AI Mark IV radar, as the 'floodlight' system of detection produced a large echo as a result of ground reflection. This 'ground return' corresponded to the height at which the aircraft was flying, so that below eighteen thousand feet, the maximum range of the equipment was limited to the height of the aircraft, and the *Luftwaffe* tactic of approaching at low level masked the echo of the target aircraft from an intercepting fighter.[258] The rush to introduce GCI as soon as possible meant that the 'Mobile' stations available in the middle of 1941 had several limitations. As well as manual operation of the scanning dish, unreliable height estimation, and the ability to only control one fighter at a time, the stations were unable to track aircraft below five thousand feet or before crossing the coast. This meant that the *Luftwaffe* could minimise interceptions against aircraft by attacking coastal targets or shipping. In July 1941, a Chain Home Low (CHL) station was modified to enable close control of night fighters using AI Mark IV, and it achieved successful interceptions. Fighter Command intended to use these modified stations to acquire hostile targets and then transfer the interception once the enemy aircraft was within ground radar range. Orders were issued in October 1941 for CHL stations to perform these fighter control duties, and five were available along the east coast by November. A method of radar-controlled interception over the sea was not developed in 1941, which limited opportunities for the rest of the year.[259]

The claims for the last major raid against Hull to also be regarded as the end of the Blitz are therefore strong, but a final attack must be considered to determine the end date. *Luftwaffe* operations again reverted to coastal targets of opportunity, including a minor attack on Hull on 22–23 July—when the main objective of east coast shipping was not available—and unsuccessful attacks against airfields in East Anglia on 25–26 July.[260] The weather continued to be poor until the night of 27–28 July, when London was raided in force for the first time since 10–11 May 1941.[261] Although announced as a reprisal for an RAF raid on Berlin, it was not considered heavy or concentrated, so it could be seen as insignificant.[262] Sixty aircraft operated over south-east England in the heaviest activity for ten nights.[263] Although described as being of 'light intensity', the raid lasted for two and a half hours from 0125, principally on London, with minor attacks across adjoining counties, as forty-eight *Luftwaffe* aircraft took part in operations.[264] Thirty-two fighters operated over London, with the Beaufighters of 219 Squadron shooting down two of the attackers, while those of 29 Squadron destroyed one.[265] Although sixty-nine tonnes of bombs were recorded as being dropped that night, these were scattered across the city without achieving major concentration.[266] In all, twenty-three boroughs reported bombing, and 157 HE and two parachute mines were dropped.[267] A high proportion of the bombs were light in weight, which limited major damage, although damage to residential property was heavy in the inner eastern boroughs and also to the south of the river. In Poplar, two gas mains were hit, and two water mains were also cut north of the river. The absence of incendiaries meant that only seven fires were reported, of which two were classified as medium.[268] The extended nature of London housing caused widespread casualties across the city, resulting in a total of ninety deaths, including thirty in three public shelters in Poplar.[269] Damage to railway lines caused disorder in three places, but most routes had been restored by 1800 on the following day, although services from Poplar into central London were still affected on 14 August.[270] While three factories sustained some damage, there was no serious interruption to industry.[271]

Although London was often referred to as an 'inland target', the Pool of London was one of the biggest ports in the United Kingdom, as were the docks in the East End, so that the 27–28 July attack should therefore be considered as on a port. If the AHB listing of London as inland is accepted, then this raid was the last of any consequence against 'inland' targets for the rest of 1941. The next raid of any magnitude would mark the start of the German autumn campaign against coastal targets, and as London would not be attacked again until 17–18 January 1943, this makes the attack of 27–28 July doubly significant and therefore a plausible end date for the Blitz.[272] A summary of RAF offensive 'Intruder' operations in 1941 includes a note about the 27–28 July London raid, which is the only German attack mentioned in the document, and demonstrates how it was considered at the time.[273] By August 1941, it had become clear that the Blitz had ended for the foreseeable future. In London, it seemed that continuous raids had stopped in May 1941; the later attack in July and the series of attacks across the country between May and July were considered insignificant. Recently,

Süss commented that 'in many cases' London was 'the exclusive focus and so studies often end in 1941', with the collective memory of the population already beginning to assign an earlier date based on the end of continuous raiding.[274] The actual bombing records do not support this conclusion, as attacks continued well beyond May, with much shorter lulls between bombings compared to those earlier in the Blitz.[275] As raids subsequent to 10–11 May 1941 were limited due to unseasonably poor weather, these continued attacks would probably have been much heavier in more favourable conditions. The results achieved against Nuneaton (16–17 May), Manchester (1–2 June), Southampton (7–8 July), Hull (10–11, 14–15, and 17–18 July), and London (27–28 July) demonstrate what the *Luftwaffe* could still accomplish. The bombing concentrations and damage caused when coastal targets were attacked illustrate what could be achieved in ideal circumstances, leaving no doubt that the Blitz continued well into July. Given the double significance of the 27–28 attack on London, this presents a far more logical and appropriate end date for the Blitz.

The bombing of London was discussed during the War Cabinet meeting held the day after this attack and was not considered serious. More pertinent was the discussion around whether an improvement in street lighting should be made before winter. Due to poor visibility, the blackout had previously caused serious casualties, but it was decided that action should be deferred until there was evidence that a higher standard of illumination would be accepted by the public and local authorities.[276] All leading ministries had contributed to a report on how Air Raid Precautions might be improved, which concluded there was high probability of heavy winter 'blockade bombing', and it was unlikely that the population would accept anything that might enhance target finding for German aircraft.[277] The highest-ranking Civil Defence personnel were of the opinion that ports were most at risk, with their bombing being the modern equivalent of blockade, which accurately predicted the autumn campaign about to begin.[278]

The reduction in the scale of air attacks after May had allowed the authorities to address the large number of bomb-damaged buildings across the country. By 24 July 1941, 57,721 buildings in London and 70,304 in the provinces still required repair.[279] Although a total of 1,917,091 buildings had been repaired by 24 July 1941, in many cases, only preliminary work had been carried out, and further attention was still required. Nevertheless, in less than three months, 544,585 buildings had been repaired across the

United Kingdom, and progress to complete the remaining repairs would continue throughout 1941.[280]

The critical position in the historiography for the attack on London on 10 May has been contradicted as, despite assertions to the contrary, that raid did not signal the end of the London Blitz and neither was it the last major attack of the Blitz, merely the last major attack on London. This shows history being influenced by events in the national capital city, leading to a 'London-centric' historiography. As propaganda during the Blitz was focussed on the single theme of 'London can take it', this is hardly surprising.[281] A Mass Observation report in June described Londoners already taking advantage of the 'momentary peace'.[282]

The poor weather during the second half of May limited *Luftwaffe* operations against the country, apart from the heavy attack against Nuneaton/Birmingham in the middle of the month. Although units began to withdraw into Germany to prepare for 'Barbarossa' from the beginning of June 1941, operations continued against British targets, to contribute towards the blockade of the country as a form of economic warfare.[283] Forces in the west had peaked in April 1941, before a redeployment of German forces reduced the number of bomber units in the west by 30 percent. Despite this, it has been shown there was no appreciable reduction in the scale and concentration of attacks against the United Kingdom.

Significant results for night fighter defence were only possible after the teething troubles of GCI and AI radar had been overcome. These delays and the late introduction of the Beaufighter meant the *Luftwaffe* was practically unopposed during the winter of 1940. The disappointing initial performance of AI prompted Fighter Command to consider less conventional means of air defence, some of which were so esoteric to be of no practical value. The influence of Frederick Lindemann over Churchill led to some of these schemes being pursued long after their ineffectiveness was evident.

Despite unusually poor weather, the *Luftwaffe* succeeded in continuing the Blitz and maintaining pressure on British defenders throughout June 1941, although the attacks often had indifferent results. The selection of objectives suggested a return to attacks on inland industrial towns as well as ports. Throughout the month, however, the long-range bomber strength in the west declined as units were transferred to the east. The future direction of *Luftwaffe* strategy was still not clear from enemy activity at the beginning of July, and the British were uncertain whether the Blitz was yet over.

During July, the *Luftwaffe* bombed Hull four times, including the final major raid of the Blitz, resulting in the heaviest attack on the country since the 16–17 May raid on Birmingham. Although the tonnage figures were similar for both attacks, damage and casualties were much more severe at Hull, demonstrating the superior concentration of bombing against coastal targets. Claims for the final major raid against Hull to also be considered as the end of the Blitz are therefore strong, but the attack against London on 27–28 July was the final raid of any consequence against 'inland' targets for the rest of 1941. The next raid of any magnitude would denote the start of the German autumn campaign against coastal targets, so the end of July 1941 should mark the end of the Blitz. Through considering the number of aircraft operating as a measure of significance, the AHB list has been shown to be an inaccurate summary of significant attacks during this period. As London would not be attacked again until the beginning of 1943, the attack at the end of July is doubly significant and therefore an appropriate end date for the Blitz.

From the point of view from London, it seemed that continuous raids had stopped in May 1941, and the later attack in July as well as the series of attacks across the country in between were considered insignificant. The actual record of bombing does not support this conclusion, as attacks continued well beyond May with much shorter lulls between bombings compared to the two earlier in the Blitz. As later raids were limited due to unusually poor weather for the time of year, it is probable that these continued attacks would have been much heavier in more favourable conditions. The results achieved against Nuneaton, Manchester, Southampton, Hull, and London demonstrate what the *Luftwaffe* could still accomplish, leaving no doubt that the Blitz continued well into July.

2

'East Coast Blitz'

The Autumn Campaign Against Coastal Targets

SEPTEMBER 1941: THE MOUTH OF THE TYNE RIVER, UNITED KINGDOM

The 'sentinel' towns of North and South Shields developed from the small fishing settlements at the mouth of the Tyne River and at the end of the eighteenth century were established as distinct communities, despite attempts by the Hostmen of Newcastle upon Tyne to restrict exports of coal from the towns.[1] By the twentieth century, a network of ferry crossings linked the towns, which allowed workers to travel between the shipyards, chemical plants, and engine works that lined each side of the river.[2] Both towns suffered heavy casualties during the two World Wars; a disproportionate number of men from North Shields were killed during the Great War, while 3,000 merchant seamen from South Shields died in the second conflict.[3] Although the *Luftwaffe* claimed to have carried out a 'major' raid at Newcastle on 9 April 1941, this attack has been trivialised in the historiography of the Blitz, because damage was minimal across the city with only a single fatality recorded.[4] Both the British and German authorities conflated Newcastle with Tyneside, as the majority of bombs were concentrated at the mouth of the river with attacks on North Shields, South Shields, and Jarrow. The incendiaries dropped on the timber storage yards at North Shields developed in a milelong conflagration along the riverfront, and another large fire developed in the middle of the town, gutting three major shops.[5] At South Shields, considerable damage was done to the Tyne Improvement Commission at Tyne Dock, but the other dry docks and shipyards escaped, with most damage to nearby houses.[6] Although casualties were light compared to many Blitz targets, they were not negligible; 33 people died in North Shields, and 47 were killed south of the river.[7] Only a month later, a stray bomb hit the Wilkinson shelter in North Shields, killing 106 people in one of the worst individual shelter bombings of the entire war. Over three days at the end of September 1941, both towns would be bombed in the two most destructive raids during the second half of the year.

On 30 September, thirty aircraft converged at the mouth of the Tyne, dropping bombs so quickly that no air raid warning could be sounded, demonstrating how vulnerable coastal towns were to such attacks.[8] There was serious disruption to the railway system on both sides of the river, with extensive damage to residential and business property adjacent to railway stations, where bombs inevitably missed their intended targets. Bombing was concentrated north of the river, reflected by the sixty-three people killed there, compared to twenty-six to the south. Two nights later, in a rare follow-up raid, forty aircraft returned to Tyneside, with the emphasis of the bombing reversed, leading to 'the most serious raid South Shields has yet experienced'.[9] Bombing caused heavy damage to the shipyards and overwhelmed emergency services, as sixty-seven people died. Over in North Shields, there was extensive damage, but only three people were killed. There was widespread interruption to rail services on both sides of the river, in some cases blocking lines that had just been restored after the previous attack.

These two attacks, during which 159 people died, represent the height of a largely unacknowledged autumn bombing campaign against British coastal targets during 1941. The nature of German overland bombing changed after the Blitz ended, and as raids continued into August, the focus of the *Luftwaffe* shifted substantially towards the coast, as documented in the Air Historical Branch (AHB) narrative. During September 1941, German attacks caused significant damage and disruption along the north-east coast as an 'East Coast Blitz' began, which has been largely ignored by the historiography.

SUMMER BUILD-UP TO THE CAMPAIGN AGAINST COASTAL TARGETS

In early August, with German operations on a relatively small scale, the Air Ministry believed that the *Luftwaffe* was struggling to maintain an air offensive.[10] The weather continued to be poor, with already moderate daylight conditions deteriorating at night into rain and fog; *Luftwaffe* records classed August 1941 as the worst month meteorologically since the beginning of the campaign against England.[11] Night attacks were insignificant until 12–13 August, when there was scattered bombing across the Midlands and east of the country.[12] Around thirty aircraft operated, approaching from both the west and east coasts before heading inland.[13] All airfields in the 9 Group area were non-operational on that night due to poor visibility, which also prevented concentrated bombing.[14] Some of the bombing was possibly influenced by an accidental fire at a brickworks providing an aiming point, with a goods train being derailed in the aftermath of the attack.[15] Residential property was damaged in the Dudley area, with five people killed, and eleven Royal Air Force (RAF) airfields were ineffectively bombed, apart from Bassingbourne, where barracks were hit and seven service personnel were killed.[16] Attacks took place across Lincolnshire and East Anglia, causing superficial damage to shops and houses over a wide area of Lowestoft.[17] This raid was identified on the AHB list as an attack on Birmingham, but the most serious damage caused was actually against RAF installations further east. Although visibility was satisfactory in the 12 Group area, no German aircraft were claimed as destroyed despite twenty-three patrols being flown.[18] As with the last *Luftwaffe* attempt against inland targets in July, bombing was scattered and ineffective, and the attacks on this night cannot be considered significant. *Luftwaffe* records confirm that the attacks were only moderate, with only seventeen of the fifty-three aircraft despatched reaching their targets.[19]

For the week of 13–20 August, German operations at night were confined to shipping reconnaissance. Flying conditions were generally unfavourable by both day and night; the RAF agreed with the *Luftwaffe* about the weather, with one report describing it as 'treacherous'.[20] When Hull was attacked on 17–18 August, it indicated a new phase of *Luftwaffe* activity. Residential and shopping areas were bombed in the east of the city, thirty-one houses were wrecked, twenty-seven required demolition, and seventy were seriously damaged.[21] Twenty people were killed, and fifteen were seriously injured, with some utilities being affected, although these were restored by the following evening.[22] The increase in the use of anti-personnel bombs by the *Luftwaffe*—and their general lack of effectiveness—was noted during this attack. Although intended to deny access to areas they were dropped on and to disrupt movement, they were considered only of nuisance value.[23] Other aircraft operated along the east coast from Northumberland to East Anglia, where bombing was isolated and light. The apparent indifference of Fighter Command's attitude to the attack on Hull is revealed by the 12 Group Operations Record Book, which states that 'little damage was done, most of the bombs falling on areas already damaged', a declaration that would not have impressed residents of Hull being bombed out of houses damaged in previous attacks.[24] A fundamental contradiction was that although intended for the air defence of the United Kingdom, under Air Marshal Douglas, Fighter Command had become obsessed with aggressive action. The Operations Record Books of the time reflect this, with far more emphasis being given to fighter sweeps over France than intercepting night bombers.[25] Fighter Command was suffering from an expansion of operations beyond its original function, which in modern terminology would be regarded as 'mission creep', with night air defence considered less important than offensive sweeps.[26] Although forty-two aircraft of 12 Group operated on 18 August, no enemy aircraft were sighted.[27] As Douglas considered he 'would rather shoot down fifty of the enemy bombers after they have reached their objective than shoot down only ten before they have done so', this attitude is perhaps not surprising, but the reaction of the people in Hull, had they known of this policy after previously expressing dissatisfaction at the ineffectiveness of the defences after the 17–18 July 1941 attack, can only be imagined.[28] The ineffectiveness of fighter protection was also concerning the War Cabinet, which discussed the issue on 18 August 1941. Minister of Home Security Herbert Morrison noted the increase in raiding during previous days and asked for increased fighter protection for coastal areas during the autumn and winter.[29] On the following night, the *Luftwaffe* returned to the north-east coast, with a concentration around Teesside. At West Hartlepool, nineteen people were killed, while four died at Norton-on-Tees. Although these attacks were neither heavy nor significant, they together killed more people than the ostensibly heavier raid on Hull the previous night and contributed to the casualties as the 'East Coast Blitz' began.[30]

A winter bombing campaign was already anticipated, and the management of heavy attacks was discussed in War Cabinet on 21 August. Concern was expressed that shortages were delaying the manufacture of equipment and appliances for Civil Defence, the Home Secretary commenting that 'in certain areas, particularly those which had not experienced heavy air attack, local authorities were rather slow to respond'.[31] The War Cabinet also discussed a relaxation of the blackout regulations for certain vehicles on 28 August, proposing that vehicles working for the Ministry of Supply should be allowed to carry headlamps throughout the coming winter. The prime minister suggested 'that advantage should be taken of the present period, in which we were almost entirely free from night air attack, to have adequate lighting on vehicles engaged on war work'.[32] In areas free from bombing, the daily routine of siren and shelter quickly faded from people's memory.[33]

The AHB narrative does not list any further raids from August 1941, but operational records make it clear that one further attack requires consideration. On 31 August, Hull was again attacked by the *Luftwaffe*, but the narrative has overlooked this. The 12 Group Operations Record Book admits that twenty aircraft operated over the Humber, listing the eight places bombed, including Hull, but without any emphasis on the severity of the attacks.[34] The War Cabinet also noted this attack but attributed the high casualty numbers to a direct hit on a communal shelter.[35] Shelters were intended to disperse the population in order to reduce overall casualties, but the potential for heavy casualties should a communal shelter receive a direct hit is clear.[36] The destruction of the Bank underground station shelter in London on 11 January 1941 killed 57 people, which constituted half of the fatalities in the city that night.[37] Even more extreme was the incident at North Shields on 3–4 May 1941. A single German aircraft dropped four bombs, three of which caused negligible damage, but the fourth exploded in the Wilkinson factory basement public shelter on King Street, killing 106 people.[38] Because the attack on North Shields was by a lone aircraft and the shelter hit by a single bomb, it cannot be considered 'significant', despite the loss of life.

The AHB list probably discounted the Hull attack based on the 12 Group Operations Record Book assessment of the number of aircraft involved, but the air activity chart for this night shows sixty aircraft over the north-east coast.[39] It was estimated that forty-five bombers operated overland, and the majority concentrated on Hull.[40] Another RAF report states that thirty-five aircraft attacked Hull.[41] A report by the AOC-in-C of Fighter Command acknowledges that thirty aircraft were involved.[42] There are no reports of patrols from 12 Group to intercept these aircraft, possibly due to the stealth tactics used when approaching the coast.[43] After-raid reports from Hull estimated that thirty aircraft attacked the city, and over fifty bomb hits were documented.[44] Forty-one people were killed in the raid, twenty-five of these when a communal shelter was destroyed, and six domestic shelters were also hit during the attack.[45] Industry was not seriously affected during this raid, but 83 houses were wrecked, 235 were seriously damaged, and eight hundred people were made homeless. Overall, however, casualties were reduced due to the dispersed nature of shelters in the city.[46] Houses were damaged at Bilton on the outskirts of the city where seven people were killed, while bombs were also dropped across Lincolnshire, East Anglia, and the Home Counties.[47] Sixty bombs were recorded as being dropped on Hull during the 17–18 August attack, compared to only twenty-one on 31 August, but this figure alone is misleading as much heavier bombs were used in the second attack, and the total weight dropped on 31 August was 8,450kg compared to 5,300kg on 17 August.[48] Given the widespread damage at Hull, the fact that twice as many people died than in the previous noteworthy attack on 17–18 August, and more than thirty bombers were operating, the absence of this raid from the AHB list must be based on dismissive comments in the 12 Group Operations Record Book. German records show that thirty-two aircraft reached Hull on 17 August, compared to thirty-six over the city on 31 August, and Graystone describes the 17 and 31 August attacks as being 'on a similar scale'.[49] Far less important attacks were unjustifiably documented, and the addition of 31 August to the list of significant raids is important in chronicling the autumn coastal target campaign.

A Mass Observer, who visited Hull a few days after this raid, noted that the Hull blitz 'had a fearsome reputation' as far away as Doncaster, where fires were visible and 'it looked as though all Hull was burning'.[50] The business and shopping areas had suffered heavy damage, and the population were convinced that they were the only town in the country 'to have been heavily raided since the German attack on Russia'.[51] A Civil Defence Regional Officer expressed the opinion after the war that 'the people of Hull have always been aggrieved because few outside Yorkshire recognised that their city was among the most heavily bombed in the country, and some sympathy may be felt with this attitude'.[52]

'EAST COAST BLITZ': ATTACKS ON COASTAL TARGETS DURING AUTUMN 1941

The following night, the focus of the *Luftwaffe* shifted north when Newcastle was attacked on 1–2 September, which the Germans invariably claimed to have attacked whenever they bombed the Tyneside area.[53] Although RAF

Intelligence reported that as few as twelve aircraft operated on this night, this is unlikely.[54] The number of bombs dropped indicates that around thirty aircraft were involved, and the attack has been described as 'sharp' in many accounts, but as all the bombs were dropped in little more than an hour and caused several fires, a more accurate description would be 'concentrated'.[55] *Luftwaffe* records confirm that twenty-eight aircraft operated over Tyneside, flying overland between Blyth and Seaham before converging on Newcastle.[56] The first group of bombs were dropped at 2200 east of the city centre, which caused considerable damage to residential property, blocked the riverside London and North Eastern Railway line to North Shields, and caused blast damage to a shipyard in the St Peters area, although without affecting production. Another bomb fell on a platform at Manors station but failed to explode.[57] A single aircraft attacked at Blaydon, just east of Newcastle, and dropped two bombs. Whether the aiming point was industry or railway communications is uncertain: One bomb hit an ironworks, while the other destroyed two houses and damaged eighty-eight, the debris from the wrecked houses blocking the main railway line south of the river.[58]

Further bombs dropped around the Manors railway station complex in Shieldfield caused considerable damage to property, with two direct hits on the New Bridge Street goods station, which was burnt-out, and another severing the main railway line east of Manors station, so that the east coast main line had to be diverted via Carlisle.[59] The focus of the attack then drifted north, bombs landing in Sandyford, and the London and North Eastern Railway station at Jesmond was bombed and blocked by debris.[60] As these targets were surrounded by residential property, there was 'considerable' damage in the Shieldfield and Jesmond areas, with over 100 houses being demolished and around a thousand people made homeless.[61] Fifty-seven people were killed and sixty-four seriously injured across the city, and four rest centres were required for those unable to stay in their own homes.[62] At the coast, the railway at Tynemouth was bombed, but bombs landed sixty yards north of the line, seriously damaging 33 houses and slightly damaging 196, while other bombs dropped at Wallsend blocked the same railway line. Five people were killed and eight seriously injured.[63] In addition, six RAF airfields were also bombed, none of which was serious, including the Fighter Command Sector station at Ouston west of Newcastle.[64]

Home Security concluded that 'the heavy damage and casualties, for the number of aircraft attacking Hull and Newcastle, is apparently due to the use of heavy calibre bombs and "lucky hits"'.[65] Since the end of the 'Late Blitz Period', the expansion of night air defence meant that finally an Aircraft Interception (AI) fighter squadron was based near Newcastle. The brief nature of this attack meant that opportunities for interception were limited, but patrols were scrambled, and three enemy aircraft were sighted, one of which, a Ju 88, was destroyed by a Beaufighter of 406 Squadron.[66] Aircraft returning from Newcastle flew south, and on this night, the opportunity was taken by fighters in the 12 Group area to intercept them. A Ju 88 was shot down by a Beaufighter of 604 Squadron thirty miles off the Norfolk coast, and another managed to get within visual range of a second bomber, before losing it in cloud.[67] In terms of casualties and property damage, this would be the heaviest attack on Newcastle during the war, as raids shifted to other areas of Tyneside.

The demolished goods station continued to burn and was still glowing brightly on the morning of 3 September.[68] Preparations were made to demolish the building, but this proved unnecessary, as German attacks on that night were further down the east coast, and Billingham was the only place where meaningful damage was caused.[69] By failing to return to Newcastle on a second night, the opportunity for another concentrated attack was missed by the *Luftwaffe*; the fires from the burning station would certainly have guided the attackers to their target, but operational doctrine still forbade indiscriminate bombing, and German tactics at the time instead employed a 'needle-stitch' approach to strategic bombing.[70] With railway infrastructure already heavily damaged, switching targets further south would increase disruption across east coast communities. By 3 September, however, rail traffic between Edinburgh and London was again able to travel through Newcastle, and further attacks might have considerably extended the lengthy diversion via Carlisle.[71]

For the next week, operations were widely dispersed and on a small scale, but as the operation of a single enemy aircraft within a warning zone would trigger air raid warning sirens throughout the area, leading to loss of sleep and relocation to their designated shelters, this maximised the disruption to the civilian population.[72] Although the AHB list does not identify any significant raids during this week, *Luftwaffe* records claim that thirty-six aircraft attacked Newcastle on 7–8 September, of which ten found their target.[73] British documents record that bombs were dropped in thirty-five places along the east coast, but while 13 Group Operations Record Book acknowledges that twenty-five aircraft operated within their area, most aircraft stayed over the sea, and any bombs dropped fell in open country. 'Several' patrols were despatched against these raiders, but the only interception was when a Beaufighter of 406 Squadron attacked a He 111, which was lost in cloud and then claimed as damaged.[74] Although German communiqués claimed attacks against 'military objectives on Tyne and Humber', there is no evidence that significant *Luftwaffe* activity occurred in any part of the country on that night.[75] *Luftwaffe* records indicate that the next attack, planned against Manchester on 8–9 September, was cancelled due to bad weather.[76] From 11 September, disruption tactics resumed by aircraft briefly flying overland to bomb widely scattered eastern coastal areas.[77] The AHB lists an attack on Sunderland during the night of 11–12 September, where minor damage was caused to an iron works, and although twenty-five German aircraft operated over the United Kingdom on this night, only thirteen aircraft were estimated to be between Tynemouth and Brighton.[78] Analysis of previous raids from the narrative list has shown that the number of aircraft operating is an unreliable measure of significance, and in this case, the total number of aircraft operating over the entire country appears to have justified the significance of a very minor attack against Wearside. There was no alteration in activity until 20–21 September, when a very scattered raid was made on the Southampton area.[79] This poor concentration may have been due to the raid originally being planned against Liverpool and then switched due to a bad weather forecast at a late stage.[80] An estimated sixty aircraft took part and concentrated mainly on the Solent area, with eight people killed in Gosport and one in Southampton, but only seven houses were destroyed and some utility service mains damaged.[81] An attack against Milford Haven on 23–24 September identified in *Luftwaffe* documents connected with a mining operation is absent from British records, which claimed that the small number of aircraft (thirteen aircraft despatched, ten over target) were 'deployed to good effect'.[82] Home Security records note that fifteen aircraft were overland that night, and most then headed for the Bristol Channel.[83] While minor bombing took place over south-west England and south Wales, none of this could be considered to have a 'good effect'.[84]

The next significant attack on the United Kingdom by the *Luftwaffe* took place on the night of 30 September, concentrated on Tyneside at North and South Shields, and lasted for seventy minutes.[85] Most of the damage occurred at North Shields, where fifty HE bombs were dropped, causing four medium and five small fires, the last of which was extinguished by the early morning.[86] There was extensive damage to residential and business property, with 169 houses being destroyed and 580 seriously damaged, and five rest centres opened to accommodate some 400 people who had been made homeless.[87] Despite the widespread destruction, there was no damage to war production, and although bombs fell on the docks, the only tangible damage was the sinking of two trawlers.[88] Serious damage was caused to the railway system, with a fire at the goods station and rail lines blocked at the tunnel connecting North Shields to Tynemouth, meaning trains had to terminate outside the town and people complete journeys by bus.[89] Although warden and rescue parties were considered to have worked well, there were problems with first aid and ambulance services, as half of the standby ambulances were immobilised by punctures or blast damage, requiring reinforcements from Wallsend and Whitley Bay.[90] Casualties were heavy, with 59 people killed and 64 seriously injured, which was similar to the attack at Newcastle on 1 September.[91] Further bombs fell just north of Tynemouth where another 4 people died, with 2 seriously injured.[92]

About half the number of bombs (twenty-nine HE) used on North Shields fell south of the river Tyne.[93] Only one medium fire was started, and damage was caused to the power station, temporarily cutting all electricity supplies.[94] Train lines were blocked between South Shields and High Shields stations, which interrupted traffic for nearly eight hours, and a ferry landing point was hit.[95] Property damage was less severe than North Shields but still destroyed twenty-nine houses and seriously damaged two hundred more.[96] Nineteen people were killed and 51 seriously injured, with 300 people also made homeless.[97] Widespread bombing took place in the surrounding area, but most caused little damage, apart from at Southwick in Sunderland where sixteen houses were destroyed, killing 7 people and seriously injuring another 4.[98] Although twenty-seven fighters were despatched against the attackers, the only successful interception was when a Beaufighter of 406 Squadron shot down a Ju 88 twenty miles east of Tynemouth.[99] The two raids on Tyneside at the beginning and end of that month clearly illustrate the advantages of attacking coastal targets, as concentrating aircraft was much easier and quicker to achieve than inland, greatly increasing the potential for causing damage. Of the 239 people killed and 253 seriously injured across the country in September 1941, 143 and 179, respectively, were on Tyneside.[100] These figures contradict claims by Overy that 'in September the force switched to mining operations' and 'attacks on land targets remained light and largely ineffective'.[101]

National newspapers on 1 October reported the speech given by Winston Churchill the previous day in the House of Commons acknowledging the strength of German forces, but at least one asserted that 'the enemy's only shortage is in the air. That is a very serious shortage, but for the rest he still retains the initiative'.[102] This prompted an exchange of correspondence throughout the day between Churchill and Sir Archibald Sinclair, the secretary of state for air, who highlighted the 'odd coincidence' that 'Tyneside towns were subjected to a fairly sharp attack' the previous night. He thought that 'it would be calamitous if anything I said this evening gave the impression of being at variance with your speech yesterday' and attached his proposed speech at Middlesbrough that evening.[103] Churchill was unimpressed: 'I should have thought it was sufficient to say at this moment that while the German Air Force was engaged so deeply in Russia it was doubtful whether they could maintain the same continuity of attack as last winter, but that they still had a substantial bomber force in the west and by saving up could make attacks which though not as continuous might be as bad or worse than last year'.[104]

These comments reflect the acceptance by the government that intermittent heavy attacks by the *Luftwaffe* were likely to continue, dependent on weather as well as availability of aircraft.

The only night of the following week when there was a concentrated effort against land targets was a rare return to Tyneside, taking advantage of the moonlight and late-developing fog. Much further down the coast, bombers also attacked Dover.[105] About forty aircraft operated over Tyneside for a two-hour period on 2–3 October, the emphasis of the bombing reversed compared to 30 September as most aircraft attacked south of the river, with forty-four HE bombs dropped and many fires caused.[106] The marketplace was heavily attacked, with the town hall and a public shelter receiving direct hits and damage caused to other buildings.[107] Around 250 buildings were destroyed, with 600 people made homeless, 67 people killed, and 117 seriously injured.[108] The Civil Defence and firefighting services across the town were overwhelmed; reinforcements were required from surrounding areas, and three hundred soldiers were used for working parties.[109] There was also severe damage caused to the shipbuilding and ship-repairing industries.[110] The progress of repairs was disrupted by the cutting of the gas and electricity supplies, and damage to water mains necessitated the use of water cartage to maintain supply for twenty-four hours.[111]

To the north of the river, twenty-seven bombs were dropped, some of which caused further damage to the gasworks that had been hit in the attack of 30 September.[112] Air was drawn into a tank, which formed an explosive mixture, and due to the danger from a further bomb hit, residents were evacuated from the vicinity until the afternoon of the following day.[113] Damage to residential property was extensive, twenty houses demolished and seventy-one seriously damaged, but only three fatalities were recorded despite the widespread damage.[114] The railway line blocked by the raid on 30 September was again obstructed between North Shields and Tynemouth, although service was restored by the morning of 3 October.[115] Rail services were also disrupted to the south of the river, with services between Tyne Dock and South Shields temporarily suspended due to blocked lines.[116] In the Teesside area, three houses were demolished at West Hartlepool, killing six people, while in the South Bank district of Middlesbrough, three people were killed.[117] Further rail communications were disrupted when the London and North Eastern Railway line at Middlesbrough was blocked by debris.[118] *Luftwaffe* sources for once do not attribute these attacks as against Newcastle but rather as 'heavy attacks on surface targets extended from Scotland to Newcastle to harass the local shipbuilding industry'. Around fifty aircraft were used in each of the raids, with a high percentage claiming to find the target.[119]

Twenty-eight aircraft were deployed in response to this attack, twenty-three 'Cat's Eye' fighters and five AI-equipped Beaufighters. The limitations of the original 'Mobile' Ground Control Interception (GCI) stations meant that only three AI fighters operated under ground control. One of the Beaufighters of 406 Squadron was particularly successful, destroying a He 111 at 2050 near Alnwick before shooting down a Do 217 eight miles off Tynemouth at 2120. A Cat's Eye fighter destroyed a Ju 88 twenty miles out to sea before another 406 Squadron aircraft damaged a Ju 88 off Blyth at 2200.[120] Compared to the casual reaction of 12 Group during raids on Hull, the 13 Group response to attacks on the north-east was notably superior. The availability of an AI fighter squadron (406) from the beginning of September finally provided a realistic defence for the region. The attacks on Dover consisted of fifteen aircraft in three small formations, which all dive-bombed the town. Around forty HE were dropped in these attacks, and while damage to house property was extensive, no important buildings were affected.[121] Although ten people were killed, the casualty rate was considerably lower for the equivalent number of bombs dropped at South Shields.[122]

Home Security commented that 'raids like the two on Tyneside are not heavy by comparison with the experience of last winter and spring. They are, however, a tax upon the services and population which cannot be dismissed as negligible'. They were, however, considered serious enough to be discussed by the War Cabinet.[123] The majority of casualties since the beginning of August had been on the east coast, with most centred around the two major north-east conurbations on Humberside and Tyneside identified by a Home Security analysis as a cluster of towns on the coast. As well as North and South Shields, Hebburn and Wallsend, this analysis also included Sunderland (Wearside), West Hartlepool, and Billingham (Teesside) and should more accurately be described as an attack on the north-east coast. The report argues that by concentrating on such a municipal cluster, the percentage of bombs hitting urban targets was much higher compared to a single town like Hull. For the two north-east coast attacks, it was estimated that around 80 percent of bombs fell on the towns, while against Hull, only a quarter ended up in urban areas. This argument is not convincing, however, as the two Hull raids examined (10–11 July and 17–18 August) were not the most effective *Luftwaffe* attacks during this period.[124]

Despite the continued activity on the east coast, the week after the Tyneside attacks, the prime minister reminded the War Cabinet about 'the importance of securing all possible easements while the present relative immunity from air attack continued'. An announcement had been made two weeks previously to allow improved lighting for certain vehicles. The home secretary reported that he had explained to the House the reasons why it was impractical to return to a modified pre-war system of street lighting. The discussion was summarised: 'There was no reason to suggest that the Conclusions reached on the above matters should now be reconsidered. But we must be ready to adjust our policy to meet the situation as it exists from time to time, and the position must be kept under review. All practicable steps should be taken which would make the general conditions less onerous for the people of this country during the following winter'.[125]

The decision to maintain a general blackout across the United Kingdom indicates that the War Cabinet recognised continuing attacks along the east coast could easily escalate across the rest of the country, despite assertions about 'the present relative immunity from air attack'. This debate about modifying the 'blackout' policy into a 'blackable-out' one would continue throughout the war, but opposition from local authorities in heavily attacked areas prevented any amendment of the regulations.[126]

For the next ten nights, *Luftwaffe* activity was slight at worst and negligible at best. The AHB list then identifies attacks on both Hull and Manchester during the night of 12–13 October, but according to the Air Ministry Commentary, no concentrated attack developed.[127] Seventy aircraft operated primarily above South Lancashire with the inland area around Manchester receiving particular attention, causing extensive damage to mainly residential property.[128] The only industrial damage occurred at an electrical works in Manchester, and railway services were disrupted by damage to sidings at Miles Platting and Baguley Fold.[129] Fifteen houses were demolished in the city and 3 people killed, but most bombs ended up falling further east. In the Clayton area, fifteen houses were demolished and eighteen made uninhabitable, necessitating the opening of two rest centres to accommodate 100 homeless people. The heaviest damage occurred in Oldham, where 25 people were killed and 340 made homeless, and in Denton, where seventeen houses were wrecked and 14 people killed.[130] The scattered nature of the bombing during this attack is illustrated by the other places houses were destroyed: Bolton in the west, where 11 people died, and Sheffield in the east, where another 11 were killed.[131] Bombs were also dropped further south without significant damage, with two Ju 88s being shot down by the same Beaufighter of 66 Squadron.[132] This departure from coastal bombing was only nominally centred on Manchester, but widespread attacks across the north-west caused substantial damage and casualties in the suburbs and surrounding towns, so they must be considered significant. Poor accuracy indicates that the *Luftwaffe* problem of concentration against inland targets continued from the earlier Birmingham raids, and this was the last attack on inland towns in 1941.[133] *Luftwaffe* records claim that Manchester was attacked, with fifty-eight aircraft despatched and forty-six finding their objectives, but it is clear such targets were not in the city.[134] On the east coast, bombs were dropped across Yorkshire, Lincolnshire, and East Anglia. The only appreciable destruction was in the Hull dock area, but the sinking of a lighter and damage to the railway dock were not significant and cannot justify the inclusion of Hull on the AHB list for this night.[135] Fourteen buildings were destroyed and thirteen seriously damaged, with only half of these being residential accommodation.[136]

The next two nights saw scattered light bombing with negligible results, despite German claims to the contrary. On the night of 15–16 October, forty-five aircraft were despatched to bomb the docks at Hull, but bad weather meant only thirteen found their target.[137] Bombs were dropped in fifteen places on coastal districts in Yorkshire and Norfolk, with the only damage at a Royal Navy installation in Great Yarmouth.[138] Attacks did not escalate again until three raids on consecutive nights were identified on the AHB list, commencing with an attack against Liverpool on 20–21 October when fifty-five bombers operated.[139] A gasometer was burnt-out at Bootle, and a nearby Civil Defence transport depot extensively damaged.[140] Four fires were started and twenty-two houses destroyed, with around two hundred seriously damaged.[141] Fifteen people were killed and twenty-nine seriously injured, and scattered bombing also killed eight people outside of Merseyside.[142] Eighteen fighter aircraft patrolled while this raid was in progress, with no interceptions.[143]

A far more scattered attack took place along the north-east coast cluster the following night of 21–22 October, with some activity also over Kent. Two people were killed north of the Tyne in Newcastle near the Walker Naval Yard, while on the south of the river at Hebburn, fifteen people died and nine were seriously injured.[144] Sunderland was also attacked, notably between South Hylton and New Seaham, with seven total fatalities on Wearside. Further south on Teesside, bombs were dropped on Stockton with negligible effect, but more serious damage was caused to council buildings in Redcar, with fifteen people killed in this attack, and eight seriously injured.[145] Compared to the recent north-east coast attacks, the performance of the RAF night fighters was underwhelming, as seven aircraft patrolled, but no contact with German bombers was made.[146]

The *Luftwaffe* returned to Merseyside on 22–23 October, and this time attacked Birkenhead, approaching the target from both the east and west, but the bombing was very scattered, with only six deaths.[147] In contrast, night fighter performance markedly improved. Seventeen aircraft operated, with a Beaufighter of 68 Squadron destroying one Ju 88, while another was shot down by a Defiant of 256 Squadron, although the fighters were not invulnerable, as a Beaufighter was also shot down by 'enemy action'.[148] The operations on these three consecutive nights were the only ones during that week against the United Kingdom where fatalities occurred. This prompted the three attacks to be reported to the War Cabinet the day after the final raid.[149]

It should be noted that while the emphasis of activity switched to the west towards the end of the month because of poor weather on the east coast, the heavier attacks were reserved for the shipbuilding areas on the Tyne.[150] The scattered attacks along the north-east coast caused greater casualties than over Merseyside the previous night, but both raids were still significant. The last attack of the sequence when the bombers returned to Merseyside did not cause notable damage or casualties, so the inclusion of this raid on the AHB list cannot be justified. Following the raid on Birkenhead, night activity by the *Luftwaffe* declined with no sign of an attack on a specific objective.[151] The only casualties during the rest of October occurred when a parachute mine was dropped at Altringham on 25–26 October, killing eight people and seriously injuring eighteen.[152]

By the end of October 1941, the general decline in bombing attacks across the country had prompted a review of the labour allocated to air raid shelter construction, which prompted the prime minister to comment, 'The Shelter Programme has had a pretty good run since March and although it may not be completed according to the target plan, it must be far better than last year. Having regard to the Air Raid and the Air Raid Defence situation, they must expect to have to make a definite contribution to the man-power stringency, including particularly the Army'.[153]

The lord president of the Privy Council replied that manpower was indeed one of the most serious problems for the country, and construction probably gave the largest scope for manpower economy.[154] It was now clear that only between 20 percent and 30 percent of the intended shelter programme could be completed before the end of October 1941. The comment by the lord president of manpower as a 'serious problem' demonstrated the deepening gap between available resources and what was required to continue the war. In August 1940, the Manpower Requirements Committee had calculated personnel demands up to the end of 1941. With over 1,800,000 extra recruits needed for the armed forces and Civil Defence, this predicted a potential drain of a half-million men from the munitions industry.[155] As war production also needed to expand, this could only be met by 'directing women into the munitions industries'.[156] In March 1941, Churchill had set a ceiling for the army of two million, with registration and call-up accelerated throughout the year.[157] By the middle of 1941, all men up to the current final age limit of forty-one had been registered, and those of nineteen began to be called up.[158]

Another victim of the manpower shortage was the voluntary nature of Air Raid Precautions. Legislation to combine the Auxiliary Fire Service, Police War Reserve, and a new Civil Defence Reserve into Civil Defence 'forces' was passed in April 1941, which meant people could be compelled to join them. Although this resulted in 24,400 men being drafted into the National Fire Service, shortage of personnel restricted allocations to the Civil Defence Reserve to only 260.[159] Churchill's comments on air raid shelter construction reflect his conviction that manpower needed to be conserved. At the beginning of November, he would propose that registration for military service be raised by ten years to include all men up to fifty-one, and to consider calling up young men at eighteen.[160] The continued reduction and localisation of air attacks allowed the authorities to make progress in the repair of bomb-damaged buildings in the country. By 29 October 1941, a total of 2,068,336 buildings had been repaired, meaning that 151,245 repairs had been completed in this three-month period. Since 544,585 buildings had been repaired in the previous three months, the growing manpower shortage in the country is evident.[161]

COASTAL TARGETS OF OPPORTUNITY AS ANTI-SHIPPING OPERATIONS ESCALATE

Throughout the Blitz, the *Luftwaffe* had consistently attacked coastal shipping, which comprised around 35 percent of all sorties up to the end of July. During the autumn campaign along the east coast, the Germans, recognising the importance of disrupting coastal trade, allocated 46 percent of their reduced resources against such shipping, and from September to November 1941, these aircraft sank 18 ships and damaged 43. This compares to the 55 ships sunk and 103 damaged during the seven Blitz months earlier in 1941.[162] From this point, improved British defences against attacks on coastal shipping meant that *Luftwaffe* operations had 'become nearly impossible'.[163] Sporadic activity continued around the coast, but on only two nights in November were conditions suitable for significant raids.[164] The majority of bombs dropped on the night of 1–2 November were widely scattered, with a minor concentration between Merseyside and the Deeside area of Cheshire.[165] At Birkenhead, some production was disrupted at an engineering works, a flour mill was demolished, and extensive house damage killed three people, with a rest centre opened to accommodate the homeless.[166]

Further west, at Ellesmere Port, there was considerable damage to oil installations, and a tanker was hit in the docks.[167] The route the *Luftwaffe* took over the Solent between Selsey and Bournemouth replicated that used during the previous Merseyside attack on 22–23 October, which caused heavy bomber losses along the south coast, with three being destroyed and two damaged, suggesting careless German planning. Although no industrial disruption was achieved, further bombing along the south coast killed ten people.[168] Despite the low casualty toll on Merseyside, this raid caused more industrial damage than those in October and therefore must be considered significant. A Ministry of Home Security report noted that over 80 percent of the bombs dropped were 250kg or heavier.[169] Although two squadrons flew patrols, the only interception was by a Beaufighter of 68 Squadron, which shot down one bomber, and another enemy aircraft crashed after being hit by anti-aircraft fire.[170]

For the following week enemy activity was confined to anti-shipping activities, until the night of 7–8 November when the last overland attack on the United Kingdom by multiple aircraft in that month occurred.[171] Many bombs were dropped by II/KG2 between the Tyne and Tees, with some concentration at Sunderland.[172] Damage was caused to a railway and quay in the dock area, while local rail services were suspended by an unexploded bomb next to the line.[173] A power station was also bombed, and although the water softening plant was hit, output was not affected, but residential property was extensively damaged, with seven people killed and twenty-two injured.[174] Further south, at Horden, houses were demolished and five people were killed, while bombs were also dropped to the north in Northumberland where four people were killed and seven seriously injured at Newbiggin-by-the-Sea.[175] More bombs were dropped in the river at Tynemouth and on the beach at South Shields, as well as on open ground near Billingham, Redcar, and West Hartlepool, all without causing any damage.[176] The only interception by night fighters was when a Beaufighter of 406 Squadron damaged a He 111.[177] Weather conditions on this night were clearly poor, and it was reported to the War Cabinet on 11 November that thirty-seven RAF aircraft had been lost during 7–8 November for that reason.[178] The prime minister highlighted that instructions had been given several times that attacks should not be pushed too hard during unfavourable weather. 'In battle', he said, 'heavy losses must be faced; but it was undesirable to expose our aircraft to extreme hazards in the course of routine operations'.[179] By 13 November, these comments had been translated into policy, which remained in force until the spring of 1942.[180]

The authorities had also continued to make progress in the repair of bomb-damaged buildings in the country. By the end of November 1941, a total of 2,068,336 buildings had been repaired, meaning that only 25,497 repairs had been completed in that month. The amount of refurbishment remaining was clearly no longer considered a priority, as the weekly return of repairs was discontinued at the beginning of December.[181]

German air activity remained at a low level, mostly restricted to anti-shipping operations with occasional nuisance bombing of coastal targets, causing few casualties and little significant damage during the rest of November.[182] By autumn 1941, losses of He 111s had reached the point where they had to be withdrawn from night operations.[183] Although attacks on ports such as Liverpool and Newcastle were considered desirable, the adverse weather conditions at the end of 1941 confined the *Luftwaffe* to just two opportunities.[184] Overy acknowledges the resumption of 'small raids' in December, but in reality, such attacks had continued whenever weather conditions permitted them. Attacks on 'Newcastle, Plymouth and Hull' are listed but were only significant on Tyneside.[185] The second week of December saw a brief escalation of activity along the north-east coast on two consecutive nights, of which only the second was considered significant.[186] Over forty aircraft took part in what Bomb Census Survey reports described as 'very indiscriminate bombing' on 8–9 December.[187] Over thirty tonnes of bombs were dropped clustered around the three rivers of the Tyne, Wear, and Tees, with the most casualties on the coast at Whitley Bay and Monkseaton.[188] Twenty-two people were killed, including twelve servicemen, and four seriously injured in this district.[189] Civil Defence and residential property was damaged in Newcastle, with five people being killed and eleven seriously injured in the city, and three more killed south of the river.[190] On Teesside, the London and North Eastern Railway line from Billingham to Haverton was damaged, without causing casualties, other bombs being dropped at Tynemouth, Hebburn, Felling, Sunderland, and Stockton with negligible damage and without casualties.[191] Visibility on this night was described as fair, and nine RAF aircraft operated, but the only fighter to make contact was a Beaufighter from 406 Squadron under GCI control, which damaged a He 111.[192] The low level of *Luftwaffe* activity reflected the slow but steady operational decline for bombers, as aircraft 'in commission' rates fell from

62 percent to 45 percent and fully trained aircrews from 68 percent to 45 percent between July and November.[193]

For the rest of December, *Luftwaffe* operations were 'on a very small scale' until the night of 29–30.[194] This attack was mostly in and around Newcastle, although bombs were also dropped across Durham and Yorkshire, and widespread fog present on this night would not have assisted the accuracy of the attack.[195] Most of the damage was to private property, with twenty-eight houses being destroyed and one hundred damaged, with absolutely no effect on industry connected to war work. The majority of the bombs fell within an area bordered by Sunderland, Newbiggin-by-the-Sea, Dalton, and Seaton Delaval.[196] Fourteen people were killed and twenty-six seriously injured during these attacks, and two rest centres were opened to accommodate fifty-nine people from wrecked houses.[197] Despite the poor visibility, a Beaufighter from 406 Squadron attacked a Ju 88 and shot it down over the sea.[198] This raid was significant due to the number of aircraft involved and the wide area of attack, despite the lack of industrial damage.

This examination of the AHB list reveals that it is not an accurate summary of significant attacks in 1941 following 10–11 May. The narrative analysis only used the number of aircraft operating as a measure of significance and does not consider damage caused or casualty figures.

There were considerable casualties in other attacks by smaller numbers of aircraft, but these cannot be deemed significant, and the raids to be considered are a subset of the AHB list with the addition of the 31 August attack on Hull, as shown in table 2.1.[199]

The target claims in German records, as shown in table 2.2, regardless of the actual results achieved, confirm that the autumn campaign was essentially an 'East Coast Blitz', with combined attacks on Newcastle and Hull exceeding the total of all other named objectives, with the 'sharp attacks' against Tyneside and Teesside in the early autumn of 1941 acknowledged by the Official History.[200] It is possible that many *Ausweichziele* (alternative targets) were attacked away from the east coast, but there is little evidence to support this hypothesis. The tonnage dropped on Great Yarmouth illustrates damage to a town that was never identified as a primary and only once documented as a diversionary objective.[201] Despite this, the weight of bombs used against Yarmouth was three-quarters of those dropped on the other coastal towns combined.

A list of 'principal towns which had been badly blitzed', published in December 1941, reflected the coastal nature of the German offensive, including

TABLE 2.1

Revised Summary of Raids Between 12 May and 31 December 1941 Where More Than Thirty Aircraft Were Involved

Area	Town	No. of Raids During Period	Total No. of Raids per Area
Inland Towns	Birmingham	May: 16–17*; June: 4–5* (2)	4 (2 major*) [9 (2 major*)]
	Manchester	June: 1–2; October: 12–13 (2)	
Ports and Industrial Centres	Tyneside	September: 1–2, 30–October 1; October: 2–3, 21–22; December: 8–9, 29–30 (6)	17 (2 major*) [24 (2 major*)]
	Hull	July: 10–11, 14–15, 17–18*; August: 17–18, 31–1 September (5)	
	Southampton	June: 21–22*; July: 7–8 (2)	
	Liverpool	October: 20–21; November: 1–2 (2)	
	London#	July: 27–28 (1)	
	Sunderland	November: 7–8 (1)	

#London reclassified as a port. Totals from original AHB list denoted within [ ].

TABLE 2.2

German Target Claims from July to December 1941

Target	Bombs Dropped HE	Bombs Dropped IC	Notable Raids
Newcastle	565	157	7
Hull	530	716	5
Great Yarmouth	357	68	—
Other Coastal Targets	474	440	8
Inland Towns	224	97	4
Schiffe	900	—	
Ausweichziele	825	214	
Flugplätze	159	122	

HE = high explosive bombs, in tonnes; IC = incendiary containers, each holding thirty-six 1kg bombs.

Compiled from RL 2-IV/28.

only four inland locations out of a total of twenty.[202] Although the number of significant raids on Newcastle (which were actually across the whole of Tyneside) nominally exceeded those on Hull, the conclusions of the Home Security analysis from September 1941 that the attacks against Tyneside were more accurate and caused greater damage cannot be substantiated. During 1941, 991 people were killed in Hull, while 118 died in Newcastle, and 502 fatalities occurred in significant raids across Tyneside as a whole.[203] If the numbers killed by bombing are taken over an entire year, the figures indicate that attacks on Hull were more severe than against Tyneside. The claim by Calder that since the summer of 1941—'Hull had suffered several sizeable raids after the main Blitz had ended elsewhere, [but] air attacks on Britain had been only occasional'—is, however, not supported by contemporary evidence.[204] In addition, almost 10 percent of all houses in Hull were rendered uninhabitable during 1941, and the inhabitants of another 15 percent voluntarily left undamaged homes.[205] A comparison of populations in the two areas shows the long-term damage to both cities. There was a general fall in the population across the country as military reserves were mobilised between 1939 and 1940 before attacks began, which cannot be attributed to bombing damage, which was 7 percent greater in Hull than on Tyneside.[206] The population on Tyneside did not fall further, but in Hull, there was another 9 percent decrease over the next two years, which reflects the greater damage caused on Humberside.[207] Other indications for the greater effect of bombing on Hull include a decline in attendance at religious services of all denominations and the loss of recreational facilities such as sporting clubs and youth organisations (Scouts and Guides) due to evacuation of members or damage to the premises used.[208] None of these indicators was duplicated on Tyneside.

Tyneside and Humberside were coastal targets, which minimised opportunities for the defenders to intercept the attackers. Hull was the only significant settlement in the area, on a wide estuary with the city confined to the northern bank, and Britain's third largest port.[209] German bombers routinely crossed Spurn Head from the north-east and flew along the Humber estuary before turning around to start their bombing run west of the city boundary.[210] This allowed orientation using the course of the River Hull running through the middle of the city and the bend in the Humber estuary on the eastern edge of the built-up area as references. Industry in the city was confined to a narrow strip a half-mile wide along the River Hull from the Humber estuary.[211] The targets identified by the *Luftwaffe* were either along the dock complex on the Humber or close to the River Hull. This presented a well-defined area for attacking aircraft that increased accuracy and maximised damage.[212] In contrast, the mouths of the Tyne and Wear Rivers are only ten kilometres apart, and coastline similarities between the two rivers and north of the Tyne caused target confusion. The heavy gun and balloon defences led to scattered bombing at the river mouth, frequently on the wrong river. The River Tyne runs through a steep-sided valley with various industrial areas on both sides and many similar bends, leading to inaccurate inland bombing due to mistaking a river bend and missing the intended target.[213] By 1939, the Tyneside and Wearside conurbations were close to merging, and all of these factors contributed to scattered attacks, with many bombs falling harmlessly on open ground or the rivers.

DEVELOPMENT AND RESPONSE OF THE DEFENCES TO CONTINUING NIGHT ATTACKS

Although single-engine Cat's Eye fighters achieved the most combats and destroyed more aircraft in May than in any other month of 1941, as shown in table 2.3, this did not confirm their effectiveness.

Highly concentrated raids with good visibility were the most favourable conditions for Cat's Eye fighters, which reflected combat conditions in April and May. Compared to AI fighters, Cat's Eye aircraft were unable to sight and intercept raiders if the moon was below the horizon. An AHB analysis calculated that AI fighters were seven times more likely to shoot down an enemy bomber compared to the Cat's Eye alternative.[214] Cat's Eye fighters achieved fewer than ten combats during the last five months of the year. From May 1941, the number of AI squadrons in Fighter Command Groups began to increase, with most additional squadrons formed in groups away from the south and west coasts (see appendix 4). The reduction in the overall sorties flown by AI fighters was due to many squadrons being underemployed. Relocation of those squadrons to the north-east and east coasts (where significant activity continued) did not happen, as the resumption of heavy attacks in the south-east was expected.

The defence systems can logically be divided into static and dynamic parts. Of the static defences, barrage balloons were of little use against high-level attacks, as their maximum operating altitude was only 4,500 feet.[215] By preventing low-level precision attacks on high-value targets, they forced German

TABLE 2.3

Combat Results for RAF Night Fighters in 1941

Month	Sorties		Combats	Destroyed	Enemy Sorties	Total Fighter Sorties
January	T/E	84	2 (2%)ϕ	0 (n/a)*	2,295	486 (25%)#
	S/E	402	9 (2%)ϕ	3 (33%)*		
February	T/E	147	4 (3%)ϕ	2 (50%)*	1,820	568 (46%)#
	S/E	421	9 (2%)ϕ	2 (22%)		
March	T/E	270	31 (11%)ϕ	15 (48%)*	4,125	1,005 (29%)#
	S/E	735	25 (3%)ϕ	7 (28%)*		
April	T/E	542	55 (10%)ϕ	28 (51%)*	5,125	1,384 (29%)
	S/E	842	39 (5%)ϕ	20½ (53%)*		
May	T/E	643	80 (12%)ϕ	37 (46%)*	4,625	1,988 (49%)#
	S/E	1,345	116 (9%)ϕ	59 (51%)*		
June	T/E	536	37 (7%)ϕ	20 (54%)*	1,980	1,478 (75%)#
	S/E	942	15 (2%)ϕ	7 (47%)*		
July	T/E	557	23 (4%)ϕ	20 (87%)*	1,352	895 (66%)#
	S/E	338	18 (5%)ϕ	6 (33%)*		
August	T/E	549	4 (1%)ϕ	3 (75%)*	935	1,141 (122%)#
	S/E	592	1 (0.2%)ϕ	0 (n/a)*		
September	T/E	361	10 (3%)ϕ	7 (70%)*	838	705 (84%)#
	S/E	344	3 (1%)ϕ	1 (33%)*		
October	T/E	621	36 (6%)ϕ	9 (25%)*	849	1,117 (132%)#
	S/E	496	3 (0.6%)ϕ	2 (67%)*		
November	T/E	417	15 (4%)ϕ	7 (47%)*	695	762 (110%)#
	S/E	345	0 (n/a)ϕ	0 (n/a)*		
December	T/E	440	6 (1%)ϕ	3 (50%)*	695	651 (94%)#
	S/E	211	0 (n/a)ϕ	0 (n/a)*		

ϕ % of combats per sortie.

* % destroyed per combat.

% of sorties per enemy sorties.

Adapted from TNA: AIR 41/17; ADGB:III, appendix 8.

aircraft to bomb less accurately from a higher altitude.[216] The approved total of anti-aircraft guns at the start of the war (2,232 heavy/1,200 light guns) had still not been achieved by May 1941 (1,691 heavy/940 light), and lack of accuracy meant the effectiveness of the gun barrage was confined to force *Luftwaffe* bombers higher, further reducing the accuracy of attacks.[217] Although radar control of guns was introduced in October 1940, equipment shortages meant that many batteries were still firing blindly at the end of 1941.[218] The greatest challenge facing Anti-Aircraft Command was recruitment; Lieutenant-General Sir Frederick Pile, the commanding officer of Anti-Aircraft Command, subsequently complained in his despatch that 'it very soon became evident that the quality of the conscripts allotted to the Command was inferior and that I was not receiving such a good selection of Army intake'.[219] Out of one thousand recruits in one brigade, for example, 5 percent had to be immediately discharged, 2 percent were considered mentally deficient, and 18 percent were of a medical category too low for anti-aircraft work.[220] This manpower problem reduced the number of searchlight units and led to the introduction of 'mixed' anti-aircraft batteries.[221] Regulations to enable women of the Auxiliary Territorial Service (ATS) to join anti-aircraft units were passed in April 1941, and the first mixed battery became operational by August.[222] The initial integration of these units did not impress Churchill, who commented following a visit to one of the first operational batteries that he 'learned with much surprise that the present policy of the ATS is that ATS personnel in mixed batteries should not consider themselves part of the battery, and that no "battery esprit de corps" was to be allowed'.[223] Although Pile had supported the full assimilation of women into the Royal Artillery, the ATS opposed this.[224] A pointed correspondence followed, with an exasperated Churchill ending the discussion in December 1941, insisting, 'It is up to you to make these Batteries attractive to the best elements in the ATS, and those who are now being compelled to join the ATS'. 'Also there is an idea prevalent among the ladies managing the ATS that nothing must conflict with loyalty to the ATS and that Battery esprit de corps is counter to their interest or theme. No tolerance can be shown to this'.[225] Women in mixed batteries subsequently wore the Royal Artillery and Anti-Aircraft Command badges on their uniforms, and the cohesiveness and camaraderie in mixed units were at least as impressive as in male-only combat formations.[226]

The effect of searchlight shortages was negligible since German bombers had increased altitude to avoid gunfire.[227] Searchlights were needed to illuminate attacking aircraft to assist RAF fighters, but that was impracticable at elevated altitude without greater accuracy. Radar control for searchlights (SLC) was developed during 1941, but by March 1942, only 1,082 sets had been delivered out of the required 4,000.[228] By November 1941, the ineffective deployment of searchlights (on the insistence of Air Marshal Douglas) in clusters was replaced by a new system known as the 'Fighter Box'.[229] This was the area within which a night fighter could intercept a raider using the visual indication provided by radar-controlled searchlights within the 'box'. By employing a continuous series of 'boxes', a searchlight belt was created across the country, divided into 'Indicator' and 'Killer' zones.[230] The low-level approach over the sea used by the *Luftwaffe* preventing ground radar from acquiring targets had already been understood, and coastal operations limited opportunities for interception. The modifications to Chain Home Low (CHL) stations enabling them to directly control AI fighters had been completed at ten coastal locations.[231] The factor limiting the interception of enemy aircraft was the number of fighters that could be controlled, and as the original 'Mobile' GCI installations could only control one fighter at a time, the capabilities of the forty-one stations operating at the end of 1941 in the event of heavy attacks were limited.[232]

For the dynamic defence system, a network of suitably equipped airfields for night defence had been established across the United Kingdom by September 1941, with adequate control apparatus.[233] The requirement for at least one large 'Regional Control' night fighter aerodrome for each Sector in a semicircle from Newcastle to Devonshire had been identified in the winter of 1940.[234] The provision of blind landing facilities progressed throughout 1941 to enable all-weather operations by detection of airfield homing beacons using AI, but this was still incomplete in August 1941.[235] A better meteorological service to allow night fighters to operate in bad or doubtful weather had been recognised the previous autumn and improved.[236] Sixteen Beaufighter squadrons were planned by the end of 1941 to expand the night fighter force, which was still less than the twenty that Douglas had considered necessary in December 1940, but by November, only twelve had formed in Fighter Command.[237] Ministry of Aircraft Production statistics show that 911 Beaufighters were supplied to the RAF by the end of 1941.[238] Although 270 were the IC variant without radar, the availability of so many aircraft suggests that expansion of the AI squadrons was unnecessarily slow.[239] It is therefore appropriate to review the factors affecting the availability of aircraft that prevented faster expansion of the night fighter force.

The Beaufighter prototype had only flown for the first time in July 1939, and the optimisation of aircraft, AI, and GCI into an integrated weapon system was not granted the luxury of eliminating initial production defects before active service but was performed during operations against night bomber raids over the country during the winter of 1940–1941.[240] As early as July 1940, it was noted that the 'Beaufort fighter' had serious technical defects and was behind schedule.[241] The Beaufighter was equipped with sleeve-valve engines, that had been developed just before the war, and a period of time passed before engine reliability became satisfactory.[242] Defective elevator installation and faulty attachment of carburettors occurred early in service, and an internal heating system was urgently required to protect the electrical equipment from dampness.[243] The electrical supply was poorly designed and kept cutting out, and although the aircraft had an endurance of five hours, it only carried oxygen for two hours.[244] It was inevitable that lack of experience in using AI would limit interceptions, but serious faults with the equipment itself did not help. The initial slow supply of aircraft meant that daylight training was not possible, but by November, at least one squadron was able to, which highlighted that the target aircraft position did not correlate with that on the equipment screens. After investigation, this fault was traced to poor connections in the AI equipment, with all squadrons being alerted to the problem.[245] As the first German bomber shot down by an AI-equipped Beaufighter was on 19 November, it is possible these two events were related. The maintenance and repair of complex radar equipment was hindered by a shortage of qualified personnel with many units short of radio mechanics as late as June 1941, which prompted a search for any experienced men throughout the services and government departments.[246]

By May 1941, the Beaufighter had been in service long enough for Sir Henry Tizard to arrange a meeting between the Ministry of Aircraft Production, the Air Ministry, and Fighter Command to discuss progress and agree on improvements for the aircraft and radar system. It was noted that the modified nose had greatly improved visibility, but ice formation on both sides of the windscreen caused difficulty on the approach to landing. The Beaufighter I was not considered sufficiently stable, with the Beaufighter II slightly worse. The gunsight was too bright on dark nights, and there had been failures of cannon ammunition when the casing collapsed, with jammed guns a common experience for early Beaufighter pilots.[247] Although AI was now routinely checked before operational use, the suspension of the set against the shock of rough airfields was unsatisfactory, dampness was still causing

TABLE 2.4
Introduction of RAF Fighters into Service

Aircraft	First Flight	Entered Service	Extensive Service
Hurricane	November 1935	Dec 1937 (25 months)	Dec 1938 (37 months)
Spitfire	March 1936	Aug 1938 (29 months)	Sep 1939 (42 months)
Defiant	August 1937	Dec 1939 (28 months)	May 1941 (45 months)
Whirlwind	October 1938	Sep 1940 (23 months)	Oct 1941 (36 months)
Beaufighter	July 1939	Sep 1940 (14 months)	May 1941 (22 months)

Compiled from F. K. Mason, *The British Fighter Since 1912* (London: Putnam, 1992), 254, 258–59, 268–69, 274–75, and 280–81.

problems, and aerials could break off due to ice formation. Large numbers of equipment valves were unsatisfactory and had to be rejected, and pilots stressed the need for careful selection and training of AI operators.[248] Compared to other first-generation monoplane fighters, the Beaufighter entered service much earlier and rapidly became effective in the RAF, as shown in table 2.4. Despite flying for the first time ten months after the Whirlwind, the Beaufighter entered service in the same month. The Beaufighter was in extended service, twenty-two months after first flying, before any of the previous fighters had begun operating with the RAF, so it would have been unrealistic to expect the aircraft to become established more quickly.

The RAF was clearly desperate to obtain as many Beaufighters as possible for the night battle, demonstrated by the attempts to divert aircraft from Coastal Command for AI duties by Air Marshal Douglas in December 1940. Initially there was a perception of an unnecessary time lag between delivery from the manufacturer and supply of the aircraft from the Maintenance Unit (MU) where military equipment had been installed. One report complained that on 1 November 1940, there were twenty-four Beaufighters at MUs, many already fitted with AI and other equipment and air tested, some of which had been there since 25 October.[249] This period of less than a week does not appear excessive, and records show that 84 percent of all Beaufighters passed through five MUs, singly or in combination, and that most aircraft were assigned to squadrons within thirty days.[250]

Ministry of Aircraft Production statistics show that 111 Beaufighters had been delivered to the RAF by the end of 1940.[251] The dangers of night flying meant that accidents were commonplace, with aircraft being damaged or destroyed. During the winter of 1940–1941, there was no air traffic control, airfield lighting was mediocre, and radios were poor.[252] Official sources confirm that 47 Beaufighters had been fitted with AI by November 1940.[253] On 14 December 1940, 85 Blenheims and 57 Beaufighters fitted with AI were with squadrons, suggesting that almost half of the aircraft delivered in 1940 had been destroyed or seriously damaged.[254] This trend continued as 36 Beaufighters were destroyed or badly damaged in accidents during the first three months of 1941, which was almost half of the 77 in squadron service.[255] 'At this stage of the war', a night fighter pilot recalled in the 1960s, 'the chief task confronting anybody who took off at night was to try and get himself and his aircraft back safely on the ground. The accident rate was extremely high'.[256] In May 1941, Air Marshal Douglas noted that his six squadrons had a total strength of eighty-one Mark I and five Mark II aircraft.[257]

In order to track the expansion of the night fighter force, the delivery of aircraft to and total strength of squadrons up to the end of 1941 were calculated using the Aircraft Record Cards, as shown in appendix 5, table 1. Absolute Beaufighter numbers increased very slowly during 1940 and early in 1941, due to high losses from accidents over the winter months. This meant the first-line strength only rose by twenty-nine in the first five months of 1941. Because of winter losses, it took until June 1941 before the number of Beaufighters in Fighter Command exceeded 100. After this, aircraft numbers in squadrons increased rapidly and doubled in four months. Once the weather deteriorated as winter approached, the number of aircraft fell as the accident rate increased. A shortage of Merlin XX engines affected the production of Beaufighter II aircraft late in 1941, causing Air Marshal Douglas some concern.[258] Although the number of aircraft in squadrons decreased, 121 Beaufighters were available for issue in MUs at the end of 1941.[259] Douglas had complained in December 1940 that Coastal Command diverted Beaufighters away from night fighter squadrons, so by April 1941, the achievements of the Beaufighter against the *Luftwaffe* convinced the prime minister that as many as possible should be employed for night defence.[260] Air Chief Marshal Portal shared this opinion and investigated the possibility of withdrawing aircraft from Coastal Command, subsequently discovering the amount of time required to reequip the IC version would be time consuming and not advantageous, especially with only one such squadron in Coastal Command.[261] The long-range IC version was not equipped with AI and so did not cause any diversion of aircraft from night fighter units.[262]

The efficient use of operational aircraft required an excess of fully trained aircrew, but the expansion of the night fighter force in Fighter Command during the Blitz until the end of 1941 shows the number of operational aircrew did not exceed available serviceable aircraft throughout the year.[263] Following the fall of France, the enormous demand for pilots had prompted sweeping changes within Training Command to increase output, and a series of amendments (the "First to Third Revises") reduced the course length of pilot training in Service Flying Training Schools.[264] Although compensated for by a 50 percent increase in Operational Training Unit (OTU) course length, as casualties mounted during the Battle of Britain, this course was instead reduced from four to two weeks, so it only provided conversion to the operational type being flown.[265] By September 1940, the quality of pilots provided to Fighter Command from OTUs fell to an 'unsatisfactory' level due to 'inadequate training'.[266] In order to preserve the first-line fighter force, Air Chief Marshal Dowding was forced to use a 'Stabilisation Scheme' and categorise his squadrons so that a third of them (C squadrons) were relegated to a training role, giving no opportunity for night flying instruction to be carried out, and such training did not restart until November 1940.[267] The night fighter squadrons therefore maintained their numbers using pre-war personnel and ground radar operators.[268] As these numbers were inadequate, they were supplemented by bomber pilots trained to fly at night and gunners converted into AI operators after a short training course.[269] Guy Gibson, who would later command the 'Dambusters' raid, was seconded to a night fighter squadron in November 1940, and due to his previous experience, he was operating against *Luftwaffe* bombers by late December.[270] The C squadrons steadily became more congested with pilots from OTUs, but after increasing the length of the training course to four weeks, the Stabilisation Scheme was terminated in December 1940.[271] At the same time, additional OTUs were formed to ensure that pilot supply never fell to critical levels again, including opening the first night fighter OTU in December 1940, which became the earliest opportunity to resume night training.[272]

In January 1941, it was envisaged that nine fighter OTUs (seven day and two night) would be operating by April.[273] Difficulties in operating established units and delays in forming new ones meant that pilot output remained low over winter 1940–1941.[274] In May 1941, it was clear that the existing structure could only maintain first-line strength and would not allow expansion, so an additional day and one more night OTU were opened to increase capacity.[275]

By the middle of 1941, the numbers from day fighter OTUs were deemed acceptable, with 1,324 pilots being produced in the first half of the year, and output doubled from May to June 1941, to give a monthly average that would be maintained during the second half of 1941.[276] By contrast, night OTUs only generated 152 aircrews in the first six months, which included crews for single-engine Defiants as well as twin-engine AI fighters, as shown in appendix 6.[277] This amounted to 10 percent of the day fighter training output, which used three times as many units compared to night fighters.[278] Although a second night fighter OTU was formed in April 1941, it did not start training crews until June 1941.[279] By June 1941, all seven day fighter units were producing pilots, but night fighter output was solely from No. 54 OTU, as the intake of trainees into the second (No. 60 OTU) only began in June.[280] The supply of crews to AI fighter squadrons remained a fraction of those from day OTUs, with output from the second only supplying single-engine Defiant squadrons after June, which still formed the greater proportion of the night fighter force despite their ineffectiveness, while the third only began producing crews in November 1941 and not for Beaufighter squadrons.[281] By September 1941, the Defiant squadrons no longer needed a full OTU, with that unit working below full capacity.[282] Expansion was reduced in the second half of 1941 when Fighter Command provided the aircraft and crews to form an AI squadron for the Middle East.[283] During 1941, Middle East operations escalated, and after reverses in Cyrenaica and Greece, aircraft were supplied to reinforce squadrons in Egypt and Libya.[284] Inconclusive fighting in the Western Desert then occupied British forces for the rest of the year, with the number of pilots supplied from the United Kingdom never exceeding 100 per month.[285] A far more serious drain on resources was the expanded campaign of sweeps across France from May to November 1941, which caused greater pilot losses than the whole of the Battle of Britain.[286]

Before 1941, fighter operational training had been ad hoc and unregulated. It was admitted in July 1941 by the director of Operational Training that the organisation of the first night OTU had 'been somewhat of an experiment'.[287] A day fighter syllabus was drawn up and adopted by units in March 1941, but night fighter training was only standardised in August.[288] Pilots arrived at a day fighter squadron fully trained to fly on operations, but no Beaufighters were available for training, so crews had to be converted at squadrons before their training was completed.[289] A shortage of dual-control Blenheims limited operational training, together with poor reliability of aircraft.[290] Pilots spent a month at OTUs before their radar operators joined them, flying a total of thirty hours together, including eighteen at night. Fifteen hours training was then completed on squadron with operators in Beaufighters before flying at night.[291] Since GCI interceptions were not practised at OTUs, this presumably formed an important part of squadron training.[292] Therefore the output of night fighter training units needs to be considered with caution, as these crews were far from being combat ready, one source commenting, 'It was a long time before squadrons called us "operational"', it being common for crews to spend two months at squadrons before they became operationally effective.[293]

Ever since night fighter OTUs were established, the standard of radar operators (radio observers) had been criticised.[294] In July 1941, the AI operation course was as short as three weeks, primarily because very few people had first-hand knowledge of the operational use of AI, so training was limited to theoretical use of the equipment.[295] Air Marshal Douglas commented to the Night Air Defence committee, 'Recent results prove that too low a standard of AI Operator was accepted in the past. The task demands a high standard of intelligence. Drastic weeding out of unsuitable operators has already been necessary, but limited intake has prevented this from being carried far enough. A higher standard of man is now coming in for initial training, but the training capacity is, I fear, likely to be inadequate for future needs'.[296] Therefore the issue of Beaufighters to squadrons at the end of 1941 was limited due to the lack of fully operational crews.

The other aircraft used for AI interceptions was the American-built Havoc, which also experienced shortages of aircrew throughout the year. One squadron had been equipped with Havocs in April 1941, but at the end of the year, it was still the only squadron operating in the AI role (see appendix 4). The Havoc was suitable for many different duties, and this 'multiplicity' served to delay operational implementation.[297] Another squadron was also using the aircraft in the 'Intruder' role over enemy airfields, but additional aircraft had been squandered operating the Long Aerial Mine weapon ('Mutton'). While the Intruder squadron disrupted *Luftwaffe* activity, Mutton achieved nothing except the waste of AI-trained crews and GCI resources. Despite claims to the contrary, there is no evidence that aerial mines ever destroyed a single enemy aircraft, and the weapon was declared obsolete in November 1941.[298] As the OTU supplying replacement personnel for Havocs only began producing aircrew in the same month, maintaining operational resources at the two squadrons throughout 1941 was a challenge. From July 1941, Fighter Command began to receive experimental 'Turbinlite' Havocs fitted with Helmore searchlights in place of armament. The usefulness of these aircraft can only be considered after they became operational in 1942, with the Turbinlite flights being 68 percent below personnel requirements at the end of November 1941.[299]

Once a precise form of GCI became operational in January 1941, the number of *Luftwaffe* aircraft shot down during night operations increased steadily as more Beaufighters became available. The introduction of the Beaufighter into service was faster than any other contemporary fighter, so its impact on the night battle increased in direct proportion to the number of aircraft available, but further expansion of night air defence was not limited to availability of aircraft. Although Havoc aircraft were misused, for the majority of 1941 night fighter squadrons had more aircraft than operational crews to fly them. The AHB narrative eloquently summarised the impact of deficient training.

> The situation in Fighter Command in 1940, when over one-third of the squadrons were relegated to what was, in effect, a training organisation, is a further instance of the struggle between immediate operational requirements and the long term needs of training. Had it been possible to establish an adequate OTU organisation, so that pilots from SFTSs did not have to go straight from Harts to Spitfires (an instance is recorded of a pilot arriving at a squadron having flown only a Tiger Moth) accident rates—to say nothing of operational losses—would have been lower, and there would have been a considerable reduction in operational aircraft requirements.[300]

Although this analysis applied to day fighters, the same conclusions were just as relevant to the more complex AI fighters, flying at night in adverse weather conditions.

The unseasonably poor weather of August 1941 resulted in sporadic scattered attacks, but by the end of the month, a coherent *Luftwaffe* strategy emerged, and from August, this 'East Coast Blitz' was primarily carried out against the northern half of the east coast of England. Although significant raids took place on Tyneside at the beginning and end of September, periodic activity along the east coast ensured the maximum disruption to the greatest proportion of the population. October continued in the same vein with another attack on Tyneside, before a return to light, erratic, activity.

A switch of targets towards the middle of the month seemed to indicate a return to inland towns, but the widely scattered bombing drove the *Luftwaffe* to abandon such attacks for the rest of 1941. When bombing activity escalated towards the end of the month, coastal objectives were again the target. When these attacks switched to the west because of poor weather on the east coast, the subsequent heavier attack was against shipbuilding areas on the Tyne.

During the autumn campaign, the Germans continued to allocate a large percentage of their reduced resources against coastal shipping. Attacks on ports were considered desirable, but the adverse weather conditions at the end of 1941 and heavy bomber losses confined the *Luftwaffe* to just two further opportunities each in November and December. Through considering the number of aircraft operating as a measure of significance, the AHB list has again been shown to be an unsatisfactory summary of significant attacks later in 1941. By considering target claims in German records, the autumn campaign can be shown as an 'East Coast Blitz', with combined attacks on Newcastle and Hull which minimised the risks for attacking aircraft, exceeding the total of all other named objectives.

By October, it was becoming clear that manpower was one of the most serious problems for the war effort, and the deepening gap between available resources over what was required to continue the war was apparent. As a result, the completion of the shelter construction programme was postponed, and the level of house repairs for August to October was only a third of those achieved during the period of May to July.

After July 1941, Fighter Command only achieved double figures of aircraft destroyed in one month. From May 1941, the number of AI squadrons began to increase, but as additional squadrons formed, many were based away from bombed areas, leading to many squadrons being underemployed. Effective night defence was only possible after GCI became operational in January 1941, and after this date, the number of *Luftwaffe* aircraft shot down during night operations increased steadily as more Beaufighters became available. The further expansion of night air defence stalled, but the factor that limited this was not availability of aircraft, and for the majority of 1941, night fighter squadrons had more aircraft than operational crews to fly them. The inadequate training organisation halted night flying training in 1940, which did not resume until the end of the year.

It is important, however, to acknowledge the decline in total attacks on the United Kingdom after the start of the German offensive against the Soviet Union in June 1941. Although proportionately high considering the number of aircraft involved, the overall reduction was clear after the middle of October. The polarisation of attacks towards coastal targets is evident after July 1941, with *Luftwaffe* activity over large parts of the country curtailed, while other areas continued to be bombed on a regular basis.[301] Deaths on the east and north-east coasts amounted to 696 between 13 May and 31 December 1941, which equates to 44 percent of total deaths across the country during this period.[302] Of these, 229 were killed on Tyneside between 1 September and 2 October. Such levels of casualties cannot be reconciled with the Official History stating that attacks over the rest of 1941 were 'very slight' compared to the previous offensive.[303] For people living outside of the regions affected by bombing (including government and military centres), the development of a 'London-centric' historiography is understandable, but anyone occupying areas where the *Luftwaffe* continued to mount significant attacks would have expressed a different opinion.

3

The Effect of *Baedeker* on the Resurgence of the *Luftwaffe* in 1942

APRIL 1942: BATH, SOMERSET, UNITED KINGDOM

The Romans built baths here to exploit natural hot springs and gave them the name of *Aquae Sulis* (literally, 'the waters of Sulis').[1] The subsequent settlement that developed into the city of Bath is situated on the River Avon, south-east of Bristol.[2] An abbey was established in the seventh century, and when the derelict building was restored after the Reformation, the popularity of the hot springs established Bath as a spa town and led to extensive expansion during the Georgian period, including The Circus and Royal Crescent.[3] These buildings used the creamy gold limestone that has subsequently been associated with the city as 'Bath stone'.

At the start of the Second World War, sections of the Admiralty were transferred to Bath to avoid the bombing risk of remaining in London, and during the Blitz, the city avoided the damage sustained by nearby Bristol.[4] The population surged to 83,000, from a pre-war figure of 68,801, when the city became a reception area for evacuees from areas more vulnerable to bombing raids.[5] As raids moved north and east following the end of the Blitz, it seemed that the risk of bombing had passed. The first three months of 1942 saw the *Luftwaffe* confine its efforts to mine laying and anti-shipping sorties to maintain blockade pressure on the United Kingdom while conserving aircraft by avoiding overland attacks. From April 1942, the increased effectiveness of British attacks as the area bombing campaign began led to a renewed German offensive against British cities.

The term '*Baedeker*' had become synonymous with 'guidebook' by the beginning of the twentieth century, but an unsanctioned comment by a Nazi official has led to a 'notorious association' of the guide with this series of raids since the Second World War.[6] The campaign began with two attacks against Exeter, but the first raid was so scattered that only four bombs hit the city. The two attacks on Bath over the nights of 25–26 and 26–27 April then caused the most damage and fatalities to a British city since the 10–11 May 1941 raid on London. Casualties were heavy, with 413 people killed and 357 seriously injured over the two nights of bombing.[7] The high casualty rate was attributed to direct hits on a number of hotels, 'which had no adequate shelter arrangements at all', and 'the complete absence of proper shelters' across residential areas.[8] Realising that the *Luftwaffe* was now targeting undefended towns, the authorities quickly moved mobile anti-aircraft guns to both Exeter and Bath, which were ready for action against a third night attack at Bath, but the *Luftwaffe* had moved on, as there were no more worthwhile undefended targets in the south-west.[9]

German policy was to avoid defended targets, and while widespread damage and casualties were caused during these *Baedeker* raids, their military significance remains questionable. Once the initial phase was over, the destructive effect of attacks declined as countermeasures were implemented, and the night defences caused increasing losses to German aircraft. The conflation by German propaganda of these raids into an attack on British culture has concealed any alterations in *Luftwaffe* strategy or tactics during 1942, and the previous model of significance will be used to determine whether *Baedeker* marked a significant change of tactics compared to the autumn 1941 campaign.

LUFTWAFFE ACTIVITY DURING THE FIRST QUARTER OF 1942

January 1942 started 'with enemy air activity continuing on the now customary small scale'.[10] The Royal Air Force (RAF) estimated that the *Luftwaffe* still had 200–250 bomber aircraft in the west available for attacks against the United Kingdom, and in January, 146 of these were serviceable.[11] Only 14 aircraft operated overland during the first eight days of the month, causing negligible damage.[12] The Air Historical Branch (AHB) narrative identifies only two attacks worthy of mention in January 1942, on 10–11 at Liverpool and on 15–16 against the Tyne/Tees area.[13] Other sources, however, are more dismissive of these claims. Estimates of aircraft operating overland on 10–11 January range from 14 to 24, with 'scattered and ineffective bombing' across the north-west, the north-east, the eastern counties, and over the Midlands.[14] Only at Liverpool were casualties recorded, twelve of which were fatal, and utility services were damaged, while further west at Ellesmere Port, slight damage was caused to oil pipelines.[15] The raid against the north-east coast five nights later was even more underwhelming. The War Cabinet report states that 'a number of places around Teesside were bombed', but Home Security reports only mention Morpeth, Sunderland, and Horden.[16] Since just 3 aircraft in total operated overland, that only 'insignificant damage' was caused and no casualties were reported is unsurprising.[17] Although not mentioned by the AHB narrative, much greater damage was caused on 19–20 January over East Anglia, where residential property was wrecked at both Lowestoft and Sheringham.[18] The twenty-five casualties recorded in these attacks included four fatalities and five seriously injured.[19] Such minor attacks had little significance but have been documented to illustrate the inconsistent criteria used for highlighting certain raids.

Reports of enemy activity during February 1942 range from 'little' and 'slight' to 'light'.[20] Only thirteen aircraft operated against land targets during the month, and on nineteen nights, none was overland at all.[21] The narrative does not identify any attacks against the country until those at Dover, Weymouth, and Portland in March.[22] On closer examination, these all took place on the same night, 23–24 March, in a scattered attack along the south-east and south coasts.[23] The bombs at Weymouth caused no damage, but at Portland, eighty houses were slightly damaged, and two people were injured. At Dover, however, there was 'considerable damage' to house property, with twenty-six houses wrecked and one thousand damaged in total. Water and electricity supplies were interrupted. There were fourteen fatalities and seven seriously injured.[24] By this point, *Luftflotte 3* was operating according to a directive emphasising the 'prevention of enemy landings, attacking shipping and minelaying', while the 'Intruder' operations carried out during 1941 had been drastically scaled back.[25]

April began with little change in the pattern of *Luftwaffe* activity. On the night of 2–3 April, German aircraft returned to bomb Weymouth and Dover, causing much greater damage on this occasion.[26] At Weymouth, some thousand houses were damaged, a hospital had to be evacuated, and utility services were disrupted. Civil Defence services were described as having 'been extended and to have required reinforcements'. The Dover attack demolished 12 houses and damaged over 1,300, as well as hitting the London–Dover railway.[27] Casualties at Weymouth were twenty-four people killed and thirty-nine seriously injured, while at Dover there were sixteen fatalities and eighteen serious injuries.[28] Scattered bombing along the east coast led to a far more significant attack against the Humber estuary on 13–14 April. Residential areas in both Hull and Grimsby were bombed, with most of the damage to the south of the estuary.[29] The combined casualties from these locations were seventeen killed and thirty-three seriously injured.[30] From 15 April, night overland activity showed 'a noticeable increase', and operations during the following week were 'consistently more ambitious than of late'.[31] The most serious raid of the week was on 15–16 at Middlesbrough, where public utilities were disrupted, roads were blocked, and some fires were started.[32] Thirty-nine houses were wrecked and 1,700 were damaged, with twenty-five fatalities and fifty-two seriously injured, while other minor damage occurred across Berwickshire, Durham, and Northumberland.[33] There was sporadic bombing across Hampshire on the following two nights; then on 18–19 April, the Humber estuary was attacked, and Grimsby docks were hit again. The week ended with 'isolated' attacks against Poole and 'ineffective' bombing at Weymouth/Portland.[34] Because of the reduction in overland activity by the *Luftwaffe* in November 1941, Fighter Command concluded German intentions were 'to conserve his aircraft', and up to the end of March 1942, mine laying and anti-shipping constituted 94 percent of all sorties.[35] As only eight aircraft were destroyed by RAF fighters in the first quarter of 1942, this policy of conservation appeared effective.[36] German records, however, show that anti-shipping attacks caused far higher casualties; KG2 lost thirteen crews in a five-week period during February and March.[37]

By the beginning of 1942, the focus of German effort against shipping had in any case moved to the Arctic convoys.[38] As *Luftwaffe* strategy did not change until the last week of April, it is logical to evaluate up to 22 April along with the first three months of the year, where the majority of attacks were against shipping targets, although the proportions of mine laying and land targets did begin to increase and take precedence over those on coastal shipping (see appendix 8).

THE INFLUENCE OF BRITISH BOMBING ON GERMAN TARGET POLICY

After raids against German targets began in May 1940, RAF Bomber Command had continued operations whenever weather conditions were favourable and aircraft were available. As with *Luftwaffe* attacks, RAF bombing activity was markedly reduced during the winters of 1940 and 1941.[39] Despite this, propaganda documenting British bombing between September 1939 and June 1941 confidently assured readers that 'Bomber Command will allow no pause, no breathing space. Our offensive will go on, fierce because it is relentless, deadly because it is sure'.[40] Any illusions about the effectiveness of British bombing were shattered by the publication of the Butt Report in August 1941, which concluded that only one-third of all aircraft recorded as attacking their targets had bombed within five miles of them. For the Ruhr, considered the most vital target, the proportion fell to one-tenth.[41] The realisation that Bomber Command was incapable of hitting precision targets at night with the available technology prompted a re-evaluation of British bombing strategy, described by Terraine as marking 'the end of a chapter in the history of Bomber Command'.[42]

The start of the British area bombing campaign in 1942 has become associated with the appointment of Air Marshal Arthur Harris as air officer commanding-in-chief of Bomber Command.[43] Following the Butt Report, time was spent evaluating future policy. Over the winter of 1941, the concept of concentrating aircraft over a city as a nominal target, rather than pursuing individual objectives, was developed so that most bombs dropped would still hit something instead of landing in open countryside. This became official policy when the Area Bombing Directive was issued on 14 February.[44] It was not until nine days later, on 23 February 1942, that Harris assumed command.[45]

The Boulogne-Billancourt raid on the Renault factory in the suburbs of Paris on 3 March 1942 marked the beginning of the new area bombing policy, with the largest bombing raid by the RAF up to this date: 235 aircraft concentrated over a single target and all aircraft bombing in a 110-minute period.[46] The importance of this attack was highlighted in a British publication as early as 1942 and was later reinforced by Harris in the memoirs that he published shortly after the end of the war.[47] The German reaction to the raid can be characterised by the exultant tone of the Goebbels diary entry: 'The bomb raid on Paris is the most sensational of the day. Its extent was far greater than at first imagined. It is reported to me that emotions have reached the boiling point in Paris'.[48] The critical position of the Boulogne-Billancourt raid has been subsequently strengthened in the historiography, but this has also been reassessed twice since 2012.[49] Perry has demonstrated that attempts by German and Vichy authorities to use the attack to turn public opinion against the British were unsuccessful.[50] Overy has also proposed that the German decision to resume attacks on British cities was prompted by the Boulogne-Billancourt raid instead of being attributed to the destruction of Lübeck later the same month.[51] On the same day that Goebbels made his diary entry, retaliation against British targets was discussed at a conference held by Reichsmarschall Göring. It was reported that 'the Fuehrer wanted the strongest forces possible to undertake reprisal raids on London as soon as the weather was suitable'.[52]

Although Boulogne-Billancourt was considered a successful operation, Bomber Command was unable to carry out a full-scale area attack due to operational restrictions that reflected France's status as a defeated ally rather than a belligerent enemy.[53] The RAF had finally caught up with the *Luftwaffe* in the provision of radio navigation aids during the winter of 1941, when GEE was introduced, which used a system of ground radio stations to enable an aircraft accurately fix its position, and this was a major reason for the Area Bombing Directive.[54] GEE was first used against Essen on 8–9 March, during the 'first significant British raid of the war', but results were disappointing despite 80 percent of aircraft claiming to have attacked the target.[55] Over the next month, eight other major attacks were made against Essen but without 'any substantial success achieved'.[56] GEE accuracy was 'seriously diminished in the Ruhr area', and blind bombing operations there would not be possible until other radio devices became available.[57] Visibility was limited due to the industrial smog that lingered over the built-up area between Essen and Dortmund, preventing accurate targeting.[58] Operations against other targets escalated, and Bomber Command continued its experimental tactics with an attack at Lübeck on 28–29 March, when 'the first German city went up in flames'.[59] This was a saturation attack using incendiaries centred on the *Altstadt*, 'which was largely of medieval construction so that the buildings were inflammable and the streets narrow and tortuous'.[60] Lying outside the range of GEE, Lübeck was also chosen because it could be easily identified from the air. The raid was considered 'a complete success', with most of the city centre destroyed by fire and the suburbs heavily damaged. The number of bombers used in this attack was similar to that on Boulogne-Billancourt, reflecting the operational strength of Bomber Command at this time. A thousand houses were destroyed, and four thousand were damaged, with 520 fatalities and 785 injured.[61] The German response was much more restrained than after the Boulogne-Billancourt raid. Goebbels noted, 'This Sunday has been thoroughly spoiled by an exceptionally heavy air raid by the RAF on Lübeck', the day after the raid. After speaking to the *Gauleiter* of the affected area, he reported that 'he believes that no German city has ever before been attacked so severely from the air. Conditions in parts of Lübeck are chaotic'.[62] The Lübeck attack is cited as the reason Hitler authorised the *Baedeker* raids in the historiography by Collier, Douglas, Price, Whiting, and Snelling, which was only challenged by Perry and Overy in 2012.[63] Only Rothnie notes that 'Hitler was annoyed' after Boulogne-Billancourt, but his argument for the cancellation of attacks in March due to the absence of British raids on Germany is not convincing.[64]

The day after the Lübeck attack, Frederick Lindemann (by then Lord Cherwell), discussed the possibilities of 'dehousing' civilians using area bombing.[65] Lindemann highlighted that 'the effects of raids on Birmingham, Hull and elsewhere have shown that, on the average, one ton of bombs dropped on a built-up area demolishes 20–40 dwellings and turns 100–200 people out of house and home'. From civilian experience during the Blitz, he concluded, 'Investigation seems to show that having one's house demolished is most damaging to morale. People seem to mind it more than having their friends or even relatives killed'.[66] Nothing in what Lindemann recommended was new; his summary relied on information known for some time. As Churchill held the opinions of Lindemann 'in high esteem', his paper averted 'a major crisis over the employment of Bomber Command during 1942-3'.[67]

Although Bomber Command had previously repeated attacks against the same objective, these were unsuccessful until the four raids on Rostock between 23 and 26 April. None of these raids was particularly heavy, the maximum number of aircraft operating in one night being 161, and over four nights, a relatively modest 523 aircraft were despatched to Rostock, with the results in stark contrast to the attacks on Essen, for the loss of 8 aircraft. Sixty percent of the main town area was destroyed along with 1,765 buildings, while 513 were seriously damaged. Large numbers of people 'fled' after the first raids, which significantly reduced casualties, but overall, there were still 204 fatalities and eighty-nine injured.[68] A sombre Goebbels reported, 'The British are publicising their last air raid on Rostock in the grand manner. It has been, it must be admitted, pretty disastrous', conceding 'community life there is practically at an end'.[69] Following these raids, the Germans started to use the term *Terrorangriff* (terror raid) for the first time.[70]

The German attacks, commonly described as '*Baedeker* raids', began the same night as the first operation against Rostock and have been incorrectly attributed as reprisals for those attacks since 1942.[71] As the decision to resume raids had been taken after the Boulogne-Billancourt attack, the bombing of Rostock cannot have influenced the bombing of Exeter the same night. In April 1942, the initiative in the bombing war passed from the *Luftwaffe* to RAF Bomber Command, and the Germans' proactive approach earlier in the conflict subsequently became a reactive strategy. Although Hitler insisted on reprisal 'terror attacks', *Luftwaffe* high command still advocated the selection of industrial targets. This lack of direction would dilute the effect of the weakened German bomber force in the west.

THE '*BAEDEKER*' ATTACKS

The requirement for reprisal attacks after Boulogne-Billancourt went back as far as 6 March, but it was not until late April that the first raid took place. British Intelligence had anticipated reprisals after Bomber Command began area bombing raids, and Fighter Command 'was at a high state of readiness'.[72] British Intelligence was certain that the target marking unit KG100 had returned to France by April.[73]Assistant Director for Scientific Intelligence R. V. Jones, convinced that 'a major new bombing threat to England' was imminent, gave six weeks warning for attacks in early March.[74] This was 'almost exactly' six weeks before the first raid at Exeter on 23 April, indicating that preparations for reprisal raids began in March. While noting this alert and the build-up of other units, the Joint Intelligence Committee decided that German tactics would continue on from the raids of autumn 1941 against the east coast.[75] Scientific Intelligence identified that the *Luftwaffe* were testing a supersonic frequency for their directional beams to prevent jamming and had already implemented modifications to counter this.[76] Hitler was expecting attacks on London, but *Luftwaffe* planners realised that the defences around the capital would lead to unacceptable losses of attacking bombers. The campaign was therefore directed against objectives on the periphery of the British defence system, which often lacked anti-aircraft gun defences. Given the scale of operations against the Soviet Union, few aircraft were available, and reinforcements for the west were carefully selected.[77] It was not until 14 April, over two weeks after the Lübeck attack, that a directive for a renewed offensive against British cities was issued: 'The Fuehrer has ordered that the air war against England is to be given a more aggressive stamp. Accordingly, when targets are being selected, preference is to be given to those where attacks are likely to have the greatest possible effect on civilian life. Besides raids on ports and industry, terror attacks of a retaliatory nature are to be carried out against towns other than London. Minelaying is to be scaled down in favour of these attacks'.[78]

On the same day, the British War Cabinet met to consider proposals to reduce the full-time strength of Civil Defence services to release personnel for war industry.[79] This was to address the 'serious problem' of 'the deepening gap' of manpower resources between what was available to what was required to continue the war. At the end of 1941, 400,000 personnel were employed full-time in Civil Defence, but now that 'the immediate danger was over', most were 'standing by with insufficient duties to occupy them'.[80] With Japan entering the war in December 1941, military operations expanded globally, with increased demand on a finite set of resources. Herbert Morrison, the home secretary, argued that there was 'a need to replace defensive thinking with an offensive will to victory', although he conceded that the release of a large number of full-time personnel involved 'the acceptance of a certain risk if raiding on a large scale is resumed'.[81] Since 1941, people could be 'directed' (effectively conscripted) to undertake part-time Civil Defence service, so this regulation would be used to address the shortfall in personnel numbers.[82] The full-time personnel released would be liable to recall if heavy bombing began again, and Morrison justified the scheme by citing the Air Staff forecast of a six-week warning before such air attacks could be resumed, giving an interval to train new part-time Civil Defence entrants to maintain 'services of sufficient strength'.[83] Subsequent events would reveal whether Morrison's claims were justified.

It was not until the night of 23–24 April, as Bomber Command began its raids on Rostock, that the first attack of the campaign was attempted.[84] 'This week has been one of the most lively for some time', the Air Ministry Commentary noted wryly. 'Not since last July have such raids been attempted by the enemy'.[85] Although intended as an attack against Exeter, the bombing was so scattered that the British did not detect any concentration. The number of aircraft operating was no greater than during attacks earlier in the month against Weymouth/Dover, Middlesbrough, or the Humber estuary, so there was no reason to suspect a change in strategy.[86] Rothnie has described this raid as 'a complete failure: not even the pathfinder unit KG100 found the target city'.[87] A total of 142 bombs were recorded as being dropped across the south-west, of which only 4 actually hit Exeter.[88] These caused damage to about two hundred houses as well as gas and water mains, starting ten fires, with casualties confined to five dead and two seriously injured.[89] Fighter Command despatched seventeen aircraft, and a Beaufighter of 604 Squadron destroyed a Do 217, while another of 307 Squadron probably destroyed a Ju 88.[90] The guns of Anti-Aircraft Command also achieved success, with the Exeter batteries claiming one aircraft destroyed and those at Plymouth damaging two others.[91] In one night, therefore, British defences shot down almost half the number of aircraft as in the first three months of 1942.

On the following night, a similar number of aircraft, around forty, operated overland, with a substantially more concentrated attack.[92] Twenty-five aircraft were able to bomb Exeter, where there was considerable damage to residential property and public utilities.[93] More than fifty bombs were dropped on the town, causing damage to around six thousand houses, with seventy-seven fatalities and fifty-five seriously injured. Further south along the coast, another twelve people were killed, and although damage was 'considerable', the Civil Defence Inspector General concluded that 'it was light in comparison with other towns I have visited'.[94] Despite flying ninety-two sorties, Fighter Command was unable to claim a single German aircraft.[95] 'A notable feature was the high speed of the enemy aircraft', stated the 10 Group Operations Record Book, 'several pilots reporting inability to close range'.[96] The British could not detect supersonic modulations on German directional beams, but despite normal jamming, about 50 percent of bombs dropped were on target, which puzzled Scientific Intelligence.[97] Rothnie describes the nature of the attacks as leaving the British 'mystified' by 'seemingly aimless attacks with limited German resources'.[98] At this stage, nothing in German communiqués suggested that the nature of these raids was any different to those carried out in the autumn of 1941.[99]

The two attacks on Bath over the nights of 25–26 and 26–27 April and their effects merit a detailed examination, but the accurate number of bombs dropped, and casualties sustained over the two nights were uncertain at the time, due to the Civil Defence control room records being destroyed. Post-raid assessments reconstructed the total effects of both nights, which is the approach also followed in this analysis. On the night of 25–26 April, the *Luftwaffe* attempted a double attack by adding aircraft and instructors from *Ergänzungsgruppen* to those of the frontline units.[100] Although intended as a raid on Bath, bombs were scattered across the West Country, with a sizeable minority of aircraft attacking east of Bristol.[101] Although the numbers involved were initially estimated at 90 aircraft, this was revised to 80 later in the war.[102] German sources claim 151 aircraft in two waves attacked Bath, but British records do not support this.[103] Between 50 and 60 of these actually attacked Bath, with the remainder unable to find the target; one Ju 88 of KG3 was so lost that it ended up flying across the Bristol Channel into the centre of Wales, possibly due to crew inexperience, where it was shot down by a Beaufighter of 255 Squadron.[104] While aircraft from both waves were unable to locate Bath, some did stumble upon Bristol and dropped forty-five bombs.[105] These landed predominantly in the Bedminster area, where seven hundred houses were damaged, one hundred of which made uninhabitable, with gas supplies interrupted in other districts across the city.[106] Attacks were described as 'extremely ragged' due to the strong anti-aircraft defences at Bristol.[107] As a result of these attacks, seventeen people were killed and seven seriously injured.[108] Of the other aircraft that bombed across the southwest, from Chippenham to Exeter, four people died, and ten were seriously injured.[109] The first wave, of around 45 aircraft, operated between 2150 and 0145, with the second wave of 35 aircraft, which included at least 25 from the first wave, overland from 0350 until 0605.[110] While the first wave operated over Bath, another formation that has been previously ignored in the historiography approached the United Kingdom off the east coast of Scotland. Ten aircraft approached Aberdeen from the north-west, where they dropped eight bombs on the city before heading back out to sea.[111] Tenement property and shops in Aberdeen were damaged during this attack, which killed one person and seriously injured thirteen.[112]

Due to the retrospective nature of the recording, the number of bombs dropped during the Bath attacks is disputed. Initial estimates were of around fifty bombs being dropped on each of the two nights, but since Bomb Census officers counted at least 150 bomb craters, this was clearly an underestimate.[113] The Bath Council survey shows 188 separate bombs, although this only covered the central area of the city.[114] Of the various surveys carried out, none agree on the number of bombs dropped, and 137 bombs can be discredited, were duplicated, or cannot be assigned to bombs listed on the forms.[115] Damage figures for housing were similarly disputed, with the local authority numbers being much higher than those calculated from the Bomb Census plots.[116] Unlike Bristol, Bath had no effective anti-aircraft defences, so bombing was carried out at low level (two thousand feet or less). Bombs were dropped along an east-west axis on the first night and then at right angles to this (north-south) on the second night.[117] Although twice as many bombs were dropped at Bath during the first raid, those from the second attack, which only lasted an hour and comprised thirty aircraft, were much more devastating, with around 300 people of the 413 total killed on 26–27 April.[118] In addition, 357 people were seriously injured over the two nights of bombing.[119] The bomb weights were central to contemporary explanations for the heavy casualties and extensive damage. Many 500kg craters were reported, causing a 'heavy blast effect', with the average weight of bombs used at Bath 'much heavier than that at Exeter'.[120] By analysing the composition of German bomb loads for all significant raids since May 1941, however, it is clear the percentage of heavy bombs had been increasing. Figure 3.1 shows that since the end of September 1941, the number of large (500kg or larger) bombs dropped by the *Luftwaffe* had only fallen below 50 percent on one occasion, and the percentage dropped on Exeter was higher than in either of the Bath raids.

The most pertinent factors contributing towards the heavy damage caused at Bath were documented in the numerous reports that followed the raids. The oldest part of the city was in a hollow with the surrounding buildings, consisting of three- and four-storey Georgian or Victorian terraces in 'Bath stone', built in streets rising around the town. The main damage was to residential property, from the Circus in the north towards the London, Midland, and Scottish Railway lines, through the Great Western Railway main line and Lower Bristol Road to Oldfield. Large numbers of incendiaries were also dropped during both nights, but these were mostly extinguished, apart from in some churches and the Assembly Rooms, which were destroyed by fire.[121]

Many bombs also ended up falling to the south (forty bombs) and east (thirty-nine bombs) of the city centre, so the attack was not as accurate as initially suggested.[122] With the town rising 'abruptly on all sides', blast effect was amplified and contributed to the increase in damage caused, exaggerated by the discovery of how fragile the solid-looking stone housing was. Much of the 'domestic property' consisted of stone blocks only six inches thick with thin mortar joints, while others were of rubble faced with stone, which 'provided extraordinarily little resistance to bombs'.[123] The centre of the city only survived because incendiary bomb attacks missed it completely, as firefighting was inadequate in Bath and was disrupted by 'low-level machine gunning by the enemy'.[124] Despite German claims, the only damage to the abbey was

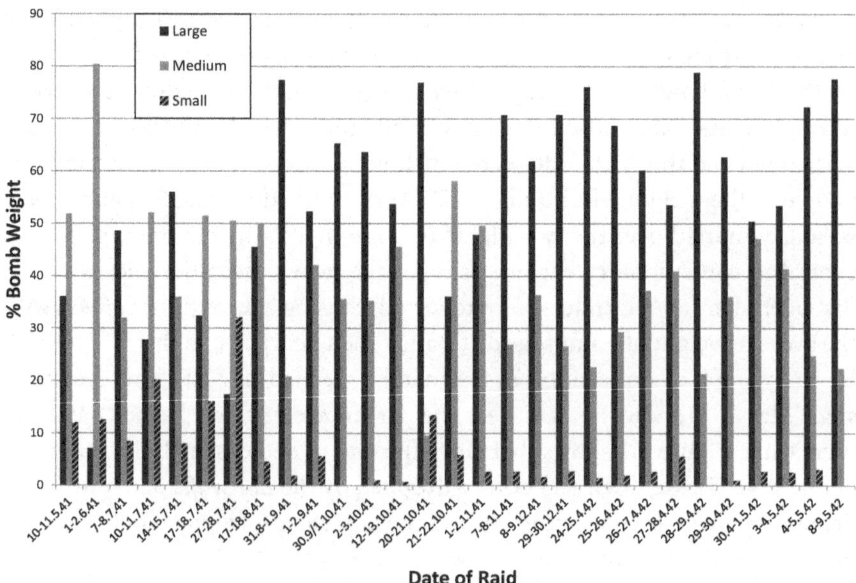

Figure 3.1: Percentage Composition of German Bomb Loads During 1941–1942 (Compiled from TNA: HO 198/57 and HO 198/247.)

from a single bomb that exploded in the recreation ground opposite, which shattered the eastern windows.[125] Although a large quantity of bombs fell on residential areas, bomb plots show that most were very close to obvious targets.[126] As the focal point of main roads and two major railway lines, damage was caused to most types of communications. Over the two nights, the central telephone exchange was evacuated, telecommunications were severely damaged, and water and gas supplies disrupted.[127] Both the Great Western Railway passenger and London, Midland, and Scottish Railway freight stations were heavily damaged, and the Great Western Railway line from Bath to London was cut, necessitating a lengthy diversion.[128] The lines westward were also blocked by a bomb that hit the Twerton tunnel, cutting the service to Bristol.[129] Although the main line to London had been restored by 28 April, lines to the west only operated freight services, with places limited in speed to 5mph as late as 30 April, and some services not restored until 10 May. There was also damage to seven factories classed as 'Key Points', and at five 'the damage was substantial'.[130]

Around these legitimate military objectives were the bombs that inevitably hit civilian targets. With only 6 percent of the 708 completely wrecked houses in Bath being council property, and fewer than 12 percent of the 1,917 seriously damaged ones, most residential damage was inflicted on the middle classes.[131] This predominantly 'private' nature of the housing at Bath caused the reappearance of 'trekking', which had not been observed since the end of the Blitz. On 26 April, most elderly and retired people 'with private means' evacuated the city, while other citizens without that opportunity or who needed to return the following day left the city for the night. The same phenomenon was also observed on 27 April, with official encouragement, leading to very long queues for buses in the evening.[132] The total number of people involved in this trekking was estimated at around 10,000.[133] The recovery of the city was protracted and involved considerable labour for a country struggling with resources. By the end of May, 8,000 houses had received 'first aid' repairs, with 2,100 men still carrying out such work, while 95 were employed to repair road damage. Utility services were almost fully restored, with only 4 percent of gas supplies remaining unconnected.[134] Overall, as Bath was a C area and possessed 'a C area mentality', the city 'stood up well to a severe test', although the 'strength of services is not anywhere adequate to deal with the scale of attack experienced, and it would be uneconomic to try and make it so'.[135] Given the economies in Civil Defence proposed by Morrison earlier that month, the government reaction to this opinion would be interesting, but no records survive.

Over Bath, Fighter Command struggled to intercept German bombers, the 10 Group Operations Record Book reporting that 'enemy aircraft appeared to be very competently handled, taking violent evasive action, consisting of weaving and usually sudden steep dives to one side. Aircraft were very fast, frustrating pilots in closing range'. On the first night, in addition to the stray aircraft shot down over Wales, Beaufighters of 307 Squadron managed to shoot down one Ju 88 and damage another, but a 'Cat's Eye' Hurricane was shot down by a different bomber.[136] A Do 217, also probably lost, was shot down off the south coast by a Beaufighter of 219 Squadron. Despite deploying sixty-seven aircraft during the 25–26 April attack, the effectiveness of the RAF response was barely adequate. On the second night, with Bath again the obvious target, a 'Fighter Night' of Hurricanes and Defiants operated over the city for two hours but only damaged two Do 217s and probably destroyed a He 111. Two 'Turbinlite' combinations and searchlight 'Fighter Boxes' were deployed without success, and Aircraft Interception (AI) Beaufighters only claimed a 'probable' as well as three damaged bombers.[137] The

10 Group aircraft were unable to oppose the tactics used by the *Luftwaffe*, which had been encountered by fighters on the east coast since the previous year. This suggests that such experience was not disseminated across Fighter Command, leading to the poor performance of 10 Group during the raids on Exeter and Bath. Due to the low-level attacks experienced at Bath, reports of German aircraft machine gunning the city are more likely to have been from British fighters shooting at them, together with spent bullets from other combats overhead falling to the ground. It had been found two years earlier in the Battle of Britain, when engaging *Luftwaffe* bombers flying at low level, that reports of Germans shooting at civilians were from the pursuing fighters.[138] Realising that the *Luftwaffe* was now targeting undefended towns, the authorities reacted with some urgency. From the pool of mobile anti-aircraft guns, twelve were moved to Exeter on 25 April, and eight to Bath on 27 April.[139] The British anticipated further attacks on such towns and therefore initiated a second phase of gun deployments, reasoning that subsequent attacks would take place across the English Channel over the south of England.[140] Anti-Aircraft Command was so short of guns that thirty-nine scheduled gun areas and 236 vulnerable points were still undefended, so the deployment of reserves was understandably sparing.[141] The next phase of the campaign then moved away from the south, which was unsurprising given the previous *Luftwaffe* policy of switching targets. The Germans believed that the Bath raids had been more devastating than the British ones at Rostock, so they returned to the tactics of autumn 1941 and switched attacks to the east coast to bomb Norwich.[142] The *Baedeker* guidebook provided information for European travellers in a standard form for every substantial town with a railway station, 'often in enough detail for the initial reconnaissance of an invading army'. Designated artistic and cultural highlights were identified with an asterisk or star.[143] On 26 April, while addressing a collection of overseas journalists after the first attack on Bath, the deputy director of the Foreign Office press department referred to *Baedeker* in this context for the first time.[144] Three days later, this was reported in the British press: 'Berlin correspondents of neutral newspapers quote German officials as saying "Now the *Luftwaffe* will go out for any building which is marked with three stars in *Baedeker*"'.[145] Goebbels was not impressed and 'took measures to prevent repetition of such folly', although he was soon taking the same position in propaganda statements.[146] As the highest rating in the guide was only two stars, this unscripted announcement was inaccurate. Although not

mentioning *Baedeker*, Hitler's speech to the *Reichstag* the following day also contained threats of 'reprisal raids'.[147]

On 27–28 April, forty-five aircraft operated over the North Sea, of which twenty-five continued overland to Norwich.[148] *Luftwaffe* resources were already strained, with the numbers supplemented by instructor crews from *Ergänzungsgruppen*.[149] The *Luftwaffe* again bombed from very low level, with HE bombs and incendiaries 'dropped indiscriminately'.[150] These caused severe damage to residential property, while the London and North Eastern Railway city station was gutted by fire. As at Bath, casualties were heavy, with 158 killed and 264 seriously injured, and by the time the raid was over, 750 people were already sheltering in rest centres.[151] The rehousing operation was complicated by 'people with big houses' being reluctant 'of taking homeless in', and many people had to return 'to their partially demolished homes'.[152] Fighter Command despatched thirty-two aircraft against the attackers, but none was shot down despite the length of time that all were overland, with four German aircraft damaged by anti-aircraft fire.[153] Over the first five nights of the renewed German offensive, Fighter Command managed to destroy only five aircraft, with two probable, from a total of 220 bombers operating, showing an alarming lack of efficacy although the low-level nature of the attacks severely shortened the range of metric AI radar sets. Before 27 April, Norwich had experienced twenty-seven air raids that had killed eighty-one people, but no guns had been available to defend the city.[154]

This renewal of attacks on the east coast prompted a further deployment of the last reserves of mobile anti-aircraft guns. The deployment of a rocket battery to York was authorised on 28 April, but due to transport difficulties, these were not in place during the raid against the city on 28–29 April.[155] Fifty aircraft flew north-west to Flamborough Head, where forty continued inland to York.[156] Aircraft arrived singly or in pairs 'at short time intervals', bombed very quickly to avoid spending time over the target, and returned to the east.[157] This raid was described by the Official History as statistically 'the most accurate of the whole *Baedeker* series'.[158] The Air Raid Precautions Inspector General was in full agreement, noting 'that only one HE bomb fell inside the city walls', with bombers following 'the line of the railway culminating at York station'.[159] Despite such accuracy, this raid was considered less severe than previous attacks, although the Guildhall (outside the city walls) was destroyed and the London and North Eastern Railway station was badly damaged.[160] Although 'statistically accurate', there was still substantial damage to residential property, generally in the vicinity of railway lines and the station, despite aircraft descending 'to below 1,000 feet when releasing bombs'. With 100 houses completely wrecked, 200 seriously damaged and about 2,500 damaged out of a total in the city of 27,000, the local authorities struggled to cope with the homeless population.[161] Twenty rest centres were opened across the city, with seventeen actually being utilised to feed and accommodate two thousand people on the night of the raid.[162] In addition to the severe damage at the passenger station, thirty-six locomotives were damaged or immobilised in the railway repair sheds, and the turntables used to move rolling stock were destroyed.[163] The efforts of the fire services meant that although the railway station was on fire, the adjoining hotel was undamaged except for broken windows, while the Guildhall burnt out without the fire spreading.[164] Casualties were lower than the three previous nights, but this attack still left seventy-nine people dead and ninety-one seriously injured.[165] Damage was also caused at Gainsborough on this night, with three people being killed, but as only one aircraft bombed the town, the damage reported appears excessive.[166] In contrast to the three previous raids, Fighter Command had a successful night against the German raiders. A 12 Group 'Fighter Night' of twenty-four Cat's Eye fighters operated over York, and a Do 217 and two He 111s were destroyed by Hurricanes of 253 Squadron.[167] Due to the longer over-the-sea approach with York thirty-five miles inland, AI fighters had more time to detect and intercept bombers. Aircraft of 68 Squadron shot down a Do 217, probably destroyed a He 111, and damaged a Ju 88. The Beaufighters of 13 Group were active, with 406 Squadron destroying a Ju 88 eighty miles east of Whitby and damaging a Do 217, with all AI combats taking place over the sea.[168] The attack on York station coincided with the arrival of the 2215 train from King's Cross, which was largely destroyed, blocking the line. On 29 April, 75 percent of passenger services operated with severe delays, while only 50 percent of freight traffic was possible, with priority given to perishables and food stuffs. By 1830, the main lines were accessible, and the backlog of services began to clear.[169]

In contrast to York, when German bombers launched their second attack in three nights against Norwich on 29–30 April, the deployed anti-aircraft guns were in position around the city, leading to 'a great wave of confidence' putting up what was described as a 'fierce' barrage during the raid.[170] The number of aircraft operating on this night increased to seventy-five, of which forty-five continued overland to attack Norwich.[171] This attack was directed at the centre of the city, causing extensive destruction to both commercial property and residential buildings.[172] The railway goods station was damaged cutting the main line to Cambridge, and utility services were disrupted especially in the centre of the city.[173] Despite the AHB narrative noting this raid was heavier and more concentrated than the first attack, casualties were actually much lighter, with 67 people killed and 86 seriously injured, giving a total of 225 killed and 350 seriously injured during the two attacks on Norwich.[174] Fourteen thousand houses were damaged over these two nights, representing 37 percent of the total number in the city, 1,400 of which were completely wrecked.[175] The 12 Group Operations Record Book neglects to document anything for this raid, but other RAF records reveal that the improvement shown by Fighter Command over York was not maintained the following night. Spitfires of 266 Squadron operated as Cat's Eye fighters, destroying one Do 217, probably destroying another and damaging a Ju 88. Only one AI fighter made an interception, a Beaufighter of 68 Squadron, but it could only damage a He 111.[176] Despite their barrage, no aircraft were brought down by the hastily installed anti-aircraft guns.

The AHB narrative then observes that 'the enemy offensive slackened' until it was 'renewed on 3/4 May' but neglects the 30 April/1 May attack at Newcastle.[177] The inconsistent documentation of German raids has been previously noted for the attack at Hull on 31 August 1941. The Official History is similarly silent, and only Snelling acknowledges the raid on Newcastle.[178] The return to an industrial target has led to this attack being discounted, but since more bombs were dropped on this night except for the first raid at Bath and the attack at York, this omission is unclear. Although the thirty-five aircraft operating was less than at York, twenty-five continued towards Tyneside, matching the number for both Exeter and the first Norwich raid.[179] In contrast to the previous six nights, no major concentration was achieved, despite KG100 operating, and bombs were scattered widely across Tyneside.[180] The authorities initially believed this was a *Baedeker* attack on Durham City, an assumption that will be considered later.[181] The presence of a balloon barrage and permanent heavy anti-aircraft batteries around Newcastle may have persuaded less experienced crews to minimise their time over the target, compromising bombing accuracy, and although several minor railways were damaged at South Shields, Beamish, Hull, and Cromer, there was little interference with traffic.[182] The urban nature of the railway system on Tyneside meant many bombs that missed railway lines hit residential districts, killing

TABLE 3.1

Comparison of RAF Claims Against *Luftwaffe* Losses, 23–30 April 1942

		Fighter Command		*Luftwaffe*		% Overclaimed		
Date	**Target**	**Dest**	**Dam**	**Missing**	**Dam**	**Dest**	**Dam**	**Total**
23–24/4/42	Exeter	2	—	—	—	40	—	40
24–25/4/42	Exeter	—	—	5	—			
25–26/4/42	Bath/ Bristol	3	1	1	2	300	50	133
26–27/4/42	Bath	3	3	1	5	300	60	100
27–28/4/42	Norwich	—	4	2	—	—	400	200
28–29/4/42	York	7	4	2	3	350	133	220
29–30/4/42	Norwich	1	3	1	—	100	300	400
30/4–1/5/42	Newcastle	7	5	4	1	175	500	260
Totals for All Eight Raids		23	20	16	11	144	181	159

Compiled from IWM: MCR 18: GAF Losses, Reels 8 and 9; and TNA: AIR 16/889, Combats and Casualties.

forty-nine people and seriously injuring thirty-six.[183] There was a notable improvement in the performance of Fighter Command, with Beaufighters of both 141 and 406 Squadrons operating over the 13 Group area. Seven contacts were made, resulting in six combats, with a Ju 88 being destroyed and four other aircraft damaged by 406 Squadron, while another aircraft was damaged by 141 Squadron.[184] The long transition across the North Sea by German bombers to the north-east of England enabled 12 Group aircraft to exploit interception opportunities on this night. The Beaufighters of 68 Squadron destroyed four Do 217s and damaged another, while the Havoc/Hurricane Turbinlite combination of 1459 Flight/253 Squadron destroyed a He 111.[185] This was not a success for the weapon system, however, as the Hurricane pilot spotted the bomber before the searchlight was switched on, and shot it down before it was illuminated.[186] With aircraft passing northwards over the 11 Group area towards the target, a Beaufighter of 29 Squadron also shot down a He 111, making it a total of six AI kills against the attack.[187]

A review of contemporary sources, shown in table 3.1, which were compiled at different times, shows that the loss numbers recorded inevitably differed. Despite these variations, the performance of Fighter Command over the first five nights of the offensive was rather indifferent, before subsequent raids suffered much greater losses. The tendency of over-claiming aircraft as destroyed had been recognised since the Battle of Britain.[188] The survival of the *Luftwaffe* Quartermaster General's returns means that RAF claims can be compared against actual German losses for this period, which documents twenty-six aircraft missing or damaged, a figure significantly lower than from British sources.[189] Apart from 24 April, RAF claims consistently exceed the number admitted to in German records.[190] As no *Luftflotte* 3 losses were recorded for 23 April, it appears the reporting of these was included in the following night's figures, which has been considered when calculating the losses for the two Exeter attacks. These calculations demonstrate that Fighter Command consistently over-claimed throughout this period, although the highest claims (for York and Newcastle) were reflected in greater numbers of aircraft lost or damaged on those nights. Throughout the air war, countless aircraft 'confirmed' as 'destroyed' survived to return to base. The apparently terminal dive of a critically damaged aircraft was frequently an evasion tactic, with serious engine fires often extinguished during such manoeuvres. On this basis, gross over-claiming was only evident for the second Norwich raid, although aircraft types not lost or damaged were claimed on several nights, such as the three Ju 88s during the first Bath raid, the three Do 217s the following night, and the four He 111s during the York attack.[191] Although aircraft identification was difficult at night, these combats took place in the middle of summer with three-quarters to full moon enhancing visibility.[192] The distinctive twin tail shape of Dornier bombers meant they could not be confused with other aircraft indicating that those combats caused no damage at all. Head-on, the Ju 88 could be mistaken for the Heinkel, but since night interception required an approach from below and behind, the characteristic wing root cut-outs of the Heinkel and the slimmer wings and tail planes of the Junkers aircraft prevented such confusion. It is therefore likely that these combats were inconclusive, and no damage was inflicted. This is not to denigrate or trivialise the efforts of the defenders, but it demonstrates the difference between combat claims and reality. What is evident is that the increased claims made at the end of this period were mirrored by increased, albeit lower, *Luftwaffe* losses, which will be considered when evaluating subsequent night defence performance.

The nights of 1 and 2 May were uneventful despite the full moon period before the *Luftwaffe* returned again to the south-west for what Collier called 'the most devastating of the raids' at Exeter.[193] This was also described by the AHB narrative as 'the last of the concentrated *Baedeker* raids'.[194] Although RAF documents state that sixty aircraft bombed the city, they are contradicted by Home Office and Civil Defence sources, which estimate around half that number.[195] Aircraft approached from the south and then flew north, dropping flares before circling the city.[196] This raid differed from the previous attacks by concentrating on the ancient centre, which consisted 'almost entirely of densely packed blocks of buildings', and 'created an area of exceptionally high fire risk'. Over fifty-three minutes, beginning with an incendiary attack followed by HE bombs, aircraft came down to one thousand feet to attack, with fifty-four tonnes of HE and incendiary bombs dropped within the city boundary.[197] As flames spread, the Southern Railway station caught fire, and the central library and telephone exchange were destroyed.[198] Studies by the Research and Experiments Department identified that the extent of fire damage depended on inflammation risk of the target area rather than the weight of attack, as at Lübeck. Home Security considered this raid as 'unusual', because 'in contrast to relatively leisurely and scattered attacks between July 1940 and June 1941, this was very concentrated in time and area', which ignores the similar tactics along the east coast of England during autumn 1941.[199] Fire services were overwhelmed, and extra resources were required from outside areas, including police reinforcements and troops to assist with road clearance and demolition.[200] As all roads east and west of Saint David's railway station were blocked, and Southern Railway and Great Western Railway lines cut by bombs or blocked by debris, there was no shortage of work for all available labour. Railway traffic was still severely affected two days later, with a 'serious reaction on passenger and freight train working'.[201] There was widespread damage to public utilities, especially to gas mains for over seven days, but electricity and water services were restored within a day. The city hospital caught fire, and Exeter Cathedral received a direct hit, which badly damaged the east end of the building.[202] Despite the theme of German propaganda, this was the first cathedral damaged (apart from glass damage at Bath) during their campaign against 'cathedral cities'. Residential property suffered severely, with 1,700 houses destroyed and 14,000 damaged out of a total of 20,000. By 21 May, nearly 8,000 houses had received 'first aid' repairs, with 2,000 repaired in the first week after the raid.[203] With 175 fatalities and 131 seriously injured, the number of deaths from this attack against Exeter was only exceeded on 26–27 April at Bath throughout the *Baedeker* period.[204]

There were accounts of high winds during this raid, which contradicted Air Ministry weather reports. The large number of buildings burning simultaneously caused 'tremendous up draughts and drew large volumes of air along adjacent streets at high speeds', a phenomenon that would be repeated across Germany to cause firestorms at Hamburg, Kassel, Darmstadt, and Dresden.[205] The number of 'trekkers' out of Exeter was initially estimated at 10,000 per night, including people bombed out during the raid, but as local officials struggled to cope with the numbers involved, some were 'virtually destitute' for several days.[206] Although 10 Group initiated a 'Fighter Night' over Exeter and operated eighteen Beaufighters against the attackers, information in the Operations Record Book is notably sparse.[207] Other RAF records indicate that four Ju 88s were destroyed by Beaufighters of 307 Squadron in the Lyme Bay area, while those of 604 Squadron attacked and probably destroyed a further two aircraft off Portland.[208]

Logically, if the *Luftwaffe* was pursuing a policy that one German source described as 'annihilation', bombers should have returned to Exeter to finish the job.[209] The Isle of Wight was instead the subject of heavy raids against what were unmistakably industrial targets across East and West Cowes, aircraft attacking from seven thousand feet down to five hundred feet, being described as doing 'more or less what they liked'.[210] The *Luftwaffe* used two separate formations, with the first group of forty aircraft attacking at 2300 and the second wave of twenty bombing at 0300.[211] After dropping flares, the sequence of incendiaries followed by HE bombs matched tactics at Exeter, but bombers attacked in small groups of up to three aircraft at intervals of two to five minutes instead of a heavy concentration. While this may have aided the attackers in identifying the principal industrial targets, which were mostly Samuel White shipyards or Saunders-Roe aircraft works, a considerable overspill of bombs into the town of Cowes caused sixty-six deaths and serious injury to seventy-four.[212] All utility services in West Cowes were interrupted, and there was widespread damage to property, with up to three hundred houses involved, leading to six hundred people being accommodated in rest centres.[213] Two Saunders-Roe seaplane works were seriously damaged, with twenty aircraft destroyed between the two sites. While aircraft hangers on the company airfield at Somerton were severely damaged, the bombing missed the factory, with bombs also damaging the railway station in Cowes, closing the Southern Railway line between there and Newport.[214] Although nine Beaufighters and four Turbinlite combinations operated during the first attack, the only damage claim was for a He 177, which was not yet operational.[215] By the time of the second attack, bad weather had spread from the west, grounding aircraft at all stations other than the Beaufighters of 604 Squadron, which destroyed a Do 217. The Solent ports at Southampton and Portsmouth were well supplied with anti-aircraft guns, which claimed four aircraft destroyed that night.[216]

The AHB narrative considers the Cowes attack 'differed from other raids in the *Baedeker* period', despite the *Luftwaffe* selecting their usual targets (communications and industry).[217] The Official History concedes that Cowes was 'apparently chosen for its factories and shipyards rather than its appeal to the tourist', but 'thereafter almost everything went wrong for the attackers', implying that this was a German decision.[218] The reason to avoid supersonic jamming until such modulations were identified has been noted, but the Assistant Director for Scientific Intelligence was uneasy at the percentage of bombs landing on target during the previous twelve days. As this was an average of 50 percent, R. V. Jones 'could not believe this was being achieved with the ordinary modulation of the X-beams, which was of course jammed'. It emerged that a modification to enable reception of supersonic modulation had not been implemented, so operators were unable to detect it. Supersonic jamming was then used, with 'dramatic results', as the average percentage of bombs on target fell to 13 percent. Jones argues that of the 447 tonnes of bombs dropped up to the Cowes raid, 80 percent (360 tonnes) would have fallen on open country if the correct countermeasures had been used, calculating that these bombs killed four hundred people and seriously injured six hundred, in addition to the serious damage caused in the cities attacked.[219]

For the next three nights, there was minimal activity by the *Luftwaffe*, although bombs were dropped in Sussex and Kent on 7–8 May without causing casualties or notable damage. The raid on the following night was nominally centred on Norwich without concentration, and bombs were scattered insignificantly across Norfolk.[220] This attack was widespread, with aircraft approaching from the north-east, again at varying heights, with most bombs falling round an Air Ministry station at Upper Stoke, just south of Norwich, without causing any damage.[221] It was estimated that fifty aircraft were operating although only thirty-five crossed the coast, with fifteen noted in the Norwich area.[222] Most bombs exploded harmlessly in rural areas, but some caused damage to several farmhouses and cottage properties, as well as two casualties, one of which was killed.[223] Very few aircraft appeared to be interested in flying over Norwich itself, probably because 'balloons were up to 6,500 feet and AA fire was in operation and searchlights exposed'.[224] After detecting supersonic modulation, British radio countermeasures were properly implemented, with jamming drastically reducing bombing accuracy.[225] Thirty aircraft were despatched against the attackers, with the 12 Group Operations Record Book noting 'one inconclusive combat', and only one aircraft was claimed as destroyed by the ground defences.[226] The records for this raid, however, indicate a rare case of British underestimation of German losses. RAF records claim that a Do 217 damaged by anti-aircraft fire crashed after hitting a barrage balloon cable.[227] The Operations Record Book assumes this was the result of an attack on the radar station at Upper Stoke, but the Home Security report for the aircraft shot down there states that machine guns were used and does not mention balloon cables or the aircraft type at all, while the 'joint' claim was from a heavy anti-aircraft gun battery, so it appears that these two claims were erroneously consolidated into one.[228] This analysis is supported by the *Luftwaffe* Quartermaster General's returns recording the loss of two Do 217E4s on that night.[229]

The AHB narrative describes Norwich 'as the last raid of the *Baedeker* period', but then contradicts this by claiming that 'isolated extensions of this type' continued later against Canterbury.[230] Conversely, Home Security identifies the Bath, Exeter, York, and Norwich attacks during this period as the 'heavier *Baedeker* raids' followed by those against Weston-Super-Mare and Canterbury.[231] Regardless of what constituted a *Baedeker* attack, both at the time and subsequently, German activity was considerably reduced for several weeks after the Norwich raid. The previous two weeks had seen significant deaths and heavy damage to nonindustrial towns and cities for relatively low German losses. The night defences were becoming increasingly effective, with 13 aircraft claimed destroyed in the three raids of May, and German records confirmed 11 as missing or total losses.[232] The severity of the attacks was magnified by the compact size of the targets, Exeter having a population of 60,000 over 4,700 acres, Bath with 70,000 over 5,100 acres, and Norwich 120,000 people within 8,000 acres. The 'substantial' effect of these raids had only been possible without effective radio countermeasures and took place before supersonic modulations were confirmed.[233] Although the effect on war production was minimal, better selection of targets (as in the case of Cowes) could have caused significant damage if attacks had continued on the same scale. By the end of this phase of attacks, it was estimated that *Luftwaffe* long-range bomber effort against the country was only 20 percent of the same period in 1941, and it was noted that this was 'some measure of the present dispersal and commitments of the German Air Force'.[234] Attacks on land targets during the last eight days of April were 130 percent greater than the whole of the year to this point and meant the *Luftwaffe* effectively abandoned mine laying operations (see appendix 8). A comparison of British and German bombing during the *Baedeker* period shows that the commitments of the *Luftwaffe* to the Eastern Front and Mediterranean had compromised its ability to sustain an offensive. While the *Luftwaffe* sent 495 aircraft against the United Kingdom during those two weeks, Bomber Command had despatched more at one target over four nights (523 against Rostock).[235] As it was less than a month since the proposals to reduce the full-time strength of Civil Defence services to release personnel for other war work, those discussions would have been contradicted by the reports reaching Herbert Morrison. While a reduction in personnel had been accepted as a risk if large-scale raiding was resumed, those attacks had been envisaged against major cities with larger infrastructure and organisation and not the smaller nonindustrial towns chosen by *Luftwaffe* planners. Civil Defence organisation for places such as Exeter and Bath 'was probably reasonable for the scale of attack they were led to expect' and was severely strained by the heavier attacks at the end of April.[236] The events of the previous two weeks prompted such areas to pay 'special attention to meet heavy air attack' for 'possible targets of "cultural"' significance. The Regional Commissioner could not see how 'we shall be able to achieve the one-third reduction which a month ago I had hoped could be carried through', due to difficulties in finding part-time Civil Defence volunteers to replace the full-time posts. 'It is clear that we cannot proceed in vulnerable places to reduce our whole-time strength until the system of direction into part-time Civil Defence is working effectively', wrote the Commissioner, a conclusion unlikely to please Morrison.[237]

EVALUATION OF *BAEDEKER* ATTACKS COMPARED TO PREVIOUS RAIDS

The success of German propaganda can be gauged by the extent that the 'notorious association' of the *Baedeker* guide appears in British documents by the end of April 1942. While all sources agree the campaign began on 23 April, the AHB and Official History cannot agree on an end date, citing 9 and

31 May, respectively.[238] Secondary sources extend this further, Rothnie until 6 June, Whiting as far as August, and Snelling that the offensive continued until 'autumn' 1942, illustrating that the whole *Baedeker* concept was fundamentally flawed.[239] The *Luftwaffe* view was that by September 'operations were confined to nuisance raids'.[240] An examination of the significant raids during 1942 does not indicate a change in *Luftwaffe* strategy or tactics, showing that *Baedeker* was a continuation of the autumn 1941 campaign with increased resources. In many cases, the attacks failed to put more than thirty aircraft over the target, which was no greater than autumn 1941, although such activity was possible over a greater number of nights. All these targets either were ports, contained major railway stations, were centres of war industries, and/or had also previously been attacked during the Blitz, with the majority on the coast or close to the sea, as even York, thirty-five miles inland, was less than fifteen minutes flying time from the coast.

If supersonic jamming had been used from 23 April, the reduction in bombing accuracy would have led to scattered ineffective bombing, as at Newcastle on 30 April. There would not have been a dramatic increase in casualties for German propaganda to take advantage of, and the 'myth of *Baedeker*' would never have occurred. A comparison of the 29 April raid on York with autumn 1941 attacks, such as at Newcastle on 1 September, illustrates that the tactics and objectives of the *Luftwaffe* remained the same. Both involved similar numbers of bombers, centred on a major railway station, causing major damage, and significantly disrupted the east coast main line, requiring lengthy diversions. Damage to residential property adjacent to railway lines was heavy in both cases, with similar casualties; the Newcastle attack killed fifty-seven people, and there were seventy-nine fatalities at York. In neither raid were the cathedral churches in the cities targeted, as at York this lay inside the city walls and the New Bridge Street goods station was east of Newcastle city centre. Where the attacks differed was in the use of incendiary bombs, with a much higher proportion used at York compared to Newcastle, but the proportion of incendiaries began to rise again during the later months of the 1941 campaign. The objectives and doctrine of the *Luftwaffe* continued to be railway communications in both cases.

Such legitimate military objectives were the goals of these attacks and not historic buildings within 'cultural centres'. The much-publicised campaign against 'cathedral cities' caused serious damage to only one (Exeter) and minor damage to another cathedral church (Bath Abbey). The attack on

Bath came about when Göring opposed Hitler's demands for attacks on London. Hitler wanted to disrupt government and military offices, but Göring pointed out that many of these had been evacuated to Bath, which was added to the target list.[241] Both Norwich and York had been previously targeted by the *Luftwaffe*, although not to the same extent during this period. There had already been seven raids on York before the April 1942 attack, which had killed two people and seriously injured six, as well as 'extensive and sundry house damage'.[242] The York raid was designed to disrupt the whole railway network in the north-east, including Hull, to interrupt convoys to the Soviet Union.[243] One commentary on the York raid questioned 'the supposed *Baedeker* policy', as 'the Minster or other ancient buildings which are mostly built of light coloured stone, such targets were clear enough and large enough to bomb without the use of flares'.[244] The redeployment of guns and balloon barrages after the first sequence of raids denied the *Luftwaffe* further easy targets, and what was perceived as another policy change was actually an adjustment to changing circumstances. Göring insisted that a greater proportion of incendiaries be used during attacks and that for attacks on industrial targets, crews 'must be instructed more definitely than before to attack the target actually ordered'.[245]

If the Germans had seriously considered attacks on 'cultural centres', they were plentiful within the *Baedeker* guide.[246] The attack against Newcastle on 30 April was initially thought to be a *Baedeker* raid on Durham City, so it is appropriate to evaluate what could have been achieved if this had occurred. The historic part of the city, the cathedral (described in *Baedeker* as 'the finest of all Norman methods of building') and castle, separated by Palace Green, is on an elevated peninsula with the river looping around them.[247] The main line railway and cathedral tower would have guided aircraft to this target only ten miles from the sea, and in an area much smaller than Bath or Exeter, a similar incendiary attack could have devastated the centre of the city. Similar targets within easy reach of the south coast included Salisbury and Winchester.

THE IMPACT OF RECURRING ATTACKS ON THE *LUFTWAFFE*

The losses sustained by the *Luftwaffe* during the *Baedeker* period differ depending on the source, but by 14 May, British Intelligence estimated that

25 percent of total sorties during the two weeks ending 9 May had been made by Reserve Training Units (*Ergänzungsgruppen*) flying obsolescent Do 17s and He 111s, and so 'sustained painful losses' to the instructor crews used would have serious consequences to the subsequent bomber training programme.[248] Nine of the aircraft lost during this period had been from the 'fourth *Gruppen*' out of a total of nineteen, meaning that *Ergänzungsgruppen* aircraft suffered a loss rate two and a half times greater than the other 75 percent of *Luftwaffe* formations.[249] Losses were serious enough for two *Gruppen* to be transferred to *Luftflotte* 3 from the Mediterranean in May 1942, in addition to those transferred to the west before the start of the April offensive, at a time when such aircraft were required for the air battle against Malta, resulting in more bombers being deployed against the United Kingdom than in the whole of the Mediterranean theatre. Although RAF Intelligence estimated that six *Ergänzungsgruppen* in the *Luftflotte* 3 area were 'operational or partly operational' on 21 May 1942, the numbers of crews capable of efficient flying must have been meaninglessly small.[250]

There was a low level of enemy activity over the next ten nights. Only two aircraft were plotted overland, although scattered daylight attacks on convoys and coastal targets continued.[251] The resumption of raids on 19 May confirmed that *Luftwaffe* tactics had not changed. Ninety aircraft operated offshore between Spurn Head and the Tees estuary, with around thirty bombers crossing the coast for a general attack north of the Humber.[252] Fifty HE were dropped on Hull itself, but around the same number also hit targets in the outlying areas, with no evidence of KG100 operating.[253] The attack was centred on the Alexandra Docks area, where twenty-six fires were started, the most serious of which in a large warehouse.[254] As usual, stray bombs hit residential property around the docks, with 236 houses being demolished, 620 seriously damaged and 1,106 slightly damaged.[255] The London and North Eastern Railway line was blocked just north of the dock area, 52 people were killed, 56 seriously injured, and 2,500 made homeless.[256] The peripheral bombs hit a worthwhile target, with an ammunition dump on an RAF station at Hedon set on fire, but bombs dropped on the Blackburn aircraft factory at Brough only caused broken windows.[257] Thirty-five 12 Group aircraft were despatched on patrols, but although there were nine contacts, there were no visual sightings.[258]

No aircraft were plotted overland for the next four nights, until a scattered raid on Poole during the night of 24 May.[259] Although seventy-eight aircraft were plotted, only thirty-two were identified as taking part in the attack.[260] How many actually crossed the coast is debatable, considering Home Security stated that 'most of the bombs that were dropped fell in the water', although one report identifies the target as Branksea Island.[261] Only 9 houses were wrecked, with the total number of houses damaged estimated at 180, with some damage to utility services.[262] Casualties were similarly low, with just nine fatalities and five seriously injured.[263] Another change in British strategy would then influence target selection for subsequent German attacks.

The policy of conservation adopted by the *Luftwaffe* was abandoned in April 1942 when attacks on centres of population were ordered by Hitler following the escalation of Bomber Command attacks. Nazi propaganda presented as reprisals on British cultural centres, popularised at the time as *Baedeker* raids, and were referred to as such in British documents by the end of April. The *Luftwaffe* continued to target communications and industry, mainly in coastal areas, but with greater destruction against undefended towns before radio countermeasures began. The heaviest month of night bombing was during April with 739 tonnes, and half of the total weight of 2,458 tonnes dropped at night was during April and May. In contrast, during the 14–15 November 1940 raid at Coventry, 450 tonnes were dropped in a single night, showing that 'the night air offensive against the United Kingdom in 1942 was of modest proportions'.[264] Once target options on the south coast were exhausted, the *Luftwaffe* was forced to return to the east coast, in a campaign that differed little from the one during the autumn of 1941. The experience gained by the defences covering the North Sea during the previous year meant that German losses increased considerably after 28 April, demonstrating British night air defence improvements. The military significance of *Baedeker* was negligible, and the 14 April Führer Directive urging 'the greatest possible effect on civilian life' within Britain that prompted the offensive has been described as achieving 'nothing at all', apart from tying down twenty-one hundred anti-aircraft guns and fifty day and sixteen night fighter squadrons and increasing 'the British population's staying power'.[265]

4

After *Baedeker*

Continuation of Luftwaffe *Operations Throughout 1942*

JULY 1942: WEST MIDLANDS, UNITED KINGDOM

Since the scattered attack at Manchester in October 1941, the *Luftwaffe* had avoided inland targets and concentrated their limited resources against coastal objectives. This policy was maintained during the *Baedeker* period—even York was only fifteen minutes flying time from the coast. Sporadic attacks on coastal targets continued throughout June, with the notable exception at Nuneaton, when twenty aircraft caused damage to railway and industrial areas. The West Midlands had not been attacked since the August 1941 raid on Birmingham, which had been a complete failure, British records noting this as the first 1942 target 'to lie well inland'.[1] Nuneaton then appeared to be the exception that proved a rule, like Manchester in 1941, with a return to coastal objectives. Fifty percent of bombing in July was concentrated into seven nights from 25–26 July, continuing raids against the north-east coast before a switch to the industrial Midlands, where three raids over four nights resulted in enemy activity at its highest since the last week of April 1942.[2] A raid on 27–28 July against Birmingham caused 'considerable' damage, followed two nights later by an attack mainly on Birmingham and Wolverhampton that was the heaviest raid on the United Kingdom since Bath on 25–26 April, although significantly fewer bombs were dropped compared to 27–28 July, and damage was slight. By the following night, the *Luftwaffe* had exhausted most of its carefully conserved assets: Only forty-five aircraft were left to attack Wolverhampton, ending the inland offensive just as quickly as it began.

The British considered the operation of two hundred bombers in the West Midlands over three nights as notable, but resources were never available for another attempt on an inland target.[3] Despite the number of aircraft operating, only forty-six tonnes of bombs were dropped on Birmingham, demonstrating that inland concentration remained difficult.[4] The distinction between the *Baedeker* period raids during April and May compared with those from June onwards is unclear in the historiography and can only be resolved using the previous model of significance. German activity peaked with attacks on Birmingham at the end of July, but losses during these raids and sorties against the Allied operation at Dieppe weakened the *Luftwaffe* so much that the 1942 campaign was effectively over. Increased German losses were due to the steady build-up of night fighter squadrons and introduction of new aircraft and weapons throughout 1942. The British had adopted a policy of trying anything for night defence during 1940, and although by 1942 it was obvious that Aircraft Interception (AI) / Ground Control Interception (GCI) was the most effective system, Fighter Command persisted with less effective measures until the end of the year.

THE 'THOUSAND BOMBER' RAIDS

Although the British 'thousand bomber' raids were exaggerated for propaganda purposes, at this stage of the war, it was a significant achievement and a genuine attempt by Bomber Command to concentrate a large force against a single target. The reasons for these raids show that such embellishment was as much for British as well as German consumption. Although the science of navigation was 'still not perfect', Bomber Command had achieved concentrated bombing on several occasions after March 1942.[5] Air Marshal Harris was aware of 'a chorus of criticism' against area bombing, so during May he planned an attack to 'stamp his authority on his new command', getting approval to send a thousand bombers against a single German city.[6] An attack by 250 aircraft had been regarded as 'strong bomber force in itself', but a single Bomber Group would contribute that number of aircraft alone.[7] Assembling the 'Operation Millennium' force required 'very nearly the absolute maximum of British bomber strength', but the entire first-line strength of Bomber Command 'still left a considerable gap between Harris's intention and reality'. This required aircraft from bomber Operational Training Units (OTUs), and 367 aircraft for this raid were operated by either instructor or trainee crews.[8] This force was twice the size of any ever sent by the *Luftwaffe* against the United Kingdom, and Harris admitted this 'was no mean task in 1942'.[9] Harris knew the risk of committing his total frontline strength and all his reserves to a single operation, and the potential consequences to the future training and expansion of Bomber Command.[10]

The initial target was Hamburg, but deteriorating weather meant that Cologne (Köln) was selected as an alternative objective.[11] All aircraft involved were in place by 26 May, which caused disruption to Bomber Command's training programme as OTU aircraft relocated to other airfields.[12] The 1,047 aircraft were concentrated over Cologne in a stream, completing the raid in ninety minutes. Damage was heavy: 3,300 buildings were destroyed and 7,908 damaged, with 59,000 people made homeless in addition to 486 fatalities and 5,000 injuries. Despite the destruction, however, the city was not 'wiped out' as Harris had intended.[13] A second attack was planned, and although the forecast was less than ideal, disruption to training could not be tolerated much longer, so 956 aircraft, including 347 from training units, were sent to Essen two nights later. Locating this city was difficult, and no concentration was achieved on the extensive Krupps armaments works.[14] Heavy clouds over Essen on this night combined with the usual industrial haze gave 'almost complete protection' to the city.[15] The despatch of 2,000 aircraft in three nights was, however, a significant demonstration of the increasing strength of British bombing.

Harris considered making thousand bomber attacks a permanent feature of the bombing offensive, estimating two to four consecutive thousand bomber raids on a city the size of Cologne 'would have the effect of virtually destroying the objective to the extent of putting it out of action for any foreseeable duration of the war'.[16] A final raid of this size was attempted in 1942, when 1,006 aircraft attacked Bremen on 25–26 June. Two-thirds of the force claimed to hit the target, but since only 572 buildings were destroyed and eighty-five people killed, this implies many bombs missed the city.[17] Losses were the heaviest of the three raids, and they also included twenty-two aircraft from OTUs (over 40 percent of the losses), all but one manned by trainee crews.[18] Bomber Command was 'back on the map' both with the public and the government, but Harris then found himself having to argue why further operations were impracticable after originally advocating them.[19]

Bomber Command had only thirty operational squadrons, plus the OTUs that supplied them. The thousand raids had attempted to overwhelm the defences by using a concentrated bomber stream, but 123 bombers did not return over the three raids.[20] Bomber Command would not despatch over a thousand aircraft to a single target again until 1944, and under very different circumstances.[21] The use of OTUs was discontinued due to bad weather, rising losses, and the evident damage that was being done to the training programme.[22] Overy describes how some of these units were 'close to mutiny' at the loss of instructors and the demands made of trainees flying obsolescent aircraft to make up the numbers for the thousand bomber raids.[23] Despite Harris's ruthless and single-minded reputation, once the thousand bomber raids threatened the sustainability of his command, they were quietly discontinued, which his *Luftwaffe* counterpart proved incapable of doing. Subsequent raids therefore concentrated on effectiveness, and the number of aircraft despatched increased naturally as Bomber Command continued to expand.

The Research and Experiments department was making 'an essential contribution to understand what bombing could achieve' by this stage of the war.[24] The study of air raids effects during the Blitz to 'throw light on the technique of enemy attack' was the beginning of the Bomb Census, initially operated in London, Birmingham, and Liverpool.[25] This was extended to obtain more detailed information for the design of countermeasures, and a 'rational understanding of the relation between weapon and effect' was developed. Enemy bombs were identified from their fragments, and the craters were formed and compared with damage plots and casualty surveys; the most important conclusion was that the effect of incendiary bombs had been greatly underestimated before the war. While British bombers carried between 15 percent and 30 percent incendiaries, diluted throughout the attacking force, the Germans used much larger numbers of aircraft, with 30 percent to 60 percent of incendiaries concentrated in the first wave 'to maximise the fire power of the force'.[26]

This practical assessment of German bombing was used by the Royal Air Force (RAF) to plan a bombing strategy, and the number of incendiaries dropped per month by Bomber Command tripled between February and July 1941, demonstrating scientific innovation 'in a functional military context'.[27] Further collaboration with the services estimated the effectiveness of the larger light-cased bombs and urged their use in area attacks.[28] The increase in scientific studies into bombing effects on structures produced a separate division (RE8), which provided 'a stream of scientific studies' on the results of air attacks on cities and introduced the critical concept of 'standardised casualty rate' to bombing analysis.[29] The RE8 division was then officially requested to supplement the intelligence activities of the Air Ministry to generate independent interpretations from the photographic surveys of bombed German cities.[30] When Morrison's plans to reduce the numbers of full-time Civil Defence personnel were implemented in 1942, it was acknowledged that 'the centre of the work' of the Research and Experiments department had swung towards offensive work, and RE8 used Bomb Census data to relate areas of damage to what could be seen on aerial photographs. After the thousand bomber raid against Cologne, a steady stream of damage reports was sent from RE8 to the Air Ministry, and such assessments were only possible from the observation of German attacks on the United Kingdom from 1940 onwards.[31]

GERMAN RESPONSE TO ESCALATION OF BRITISH ATTACKS

The German reaction to the raid on Cologne meant the renewal of *Luftwaffe* attacks on the United Kingdom was predictable.[32] Canterbury had previously escaped the raids against 'virtually every other major centre of population in Kent', but the deployment of anti-aircraft guns to the city during April indicated the British expected that immunity to end.[33] Göring had approved an attack on Canterbury as early as 16 May, but the 'sense of shock' at 'the unprecedented scale of the Cologne attack' prompted Hitler to order an immediate response, and Canterbury was chosen as 'a reprisal for the terrorist raid on Cologne' on 31 May.[34] The decline of *Luftwaffe* meant that fewer than fifty aircraft were sent on this raid, compared to the thousand despatched to Cologne by Bomber Command.[35]

Thirty aircraft approached from the north, dropping flares and incendiaries centred on the cathedral for subsequent aircraft to aim at, some diving to one thousand feet to attack, while the rest bombed from various heights.[36] Twenty-six tonnes of bombs seriously damaged an area in the centre of the city immediately south of the cathedral, using large calibre HE bombs and large numbers of incendiaries.[37] The mobile balloon barrage scheduled for Canterbury was not in place, allowing bombing from very low level.[38] Many incendiaries were dropped in containers of 120 so low that they fell as a cluster rather than spreading out, landing 'on one building causing fires which it was impossible for Fire Guards to deal with unaided'.[39] The total number of 'dwelling houses' destroyed was six hundred, with forty-five fatalities and forty-six injured.[40] Casualties were 'comparatively light' due to sufficient warning for people to take shelter, with the main attack also falling onto business districts. The cathedral was unscathed apart from blast damage to windows, although the library was hit by a bomb, with witnesses convinced 'that the evidence points to a deliberate attempt to wreck it', as large numbers of incendiaries burnt out in the cathedral precincts.[41] Since Canterbury provided the junction between the two railway lines for east and south Kent, such damage would cause widespread disruption. Although the West Station was damaged by bombs, all lines remained open as both stations lay outside the city walls away from the devastated zone, demonstrating deliberate selection of a 'cultural target' for the first time.[42] The major effect on communications was the destruction of a transport company garage, which resulted in the loss of forty-nine buses.[43] German communiqués stressed the importance of Canterbury 'as a strong garrison town and of economic importance as a grain marketing centre. This raid repays Cologne three-fold. Canterbury burning everywhere'.[44] Although 11 Group operated an increasingly rare 'Fighter Night' over the city, none of the twenty-three aircraft patrolling made any claims.[45] AI fighters were more successful, with a Beaufighter of 29 Squadron probably destroying a Do 217, while another of 219 Squadron shot down a Ju 88.[46]

Immediately after this raid, the planned balloon barrage arrived at Canterbury, but German attention had already shifted north of the Thames estuary.[47] The Official History concedes that the *Luftwaffe* 'modified the scale and direction of its attack, devoting more of its effort to places of some industrial or maritime value and less to those of purely aesthetic interest', but the attack against Ipswich on 1–2 June conformed to previous *Luftwaffe* strategy.[48] About twenty aircraft approached the Suffolk coast, and a proportion made a shallow penetration to Ipswich, with only fifteen HE bombs dropped as well as four thousand incendiaries.[49] These fell mostly on the east and south-east areas of the town, including a hit on Ipswich dock as well as four factories.[50] The incendiaries intended for the London and North Eastern Railway line ended up in an adjacent housing estate, and others dropped near a railway bridge landed on Bixley Heath, starting a gorse fire. This was then possibly confused with a flare, and five 500kg bombs were dropped on the heath shortly afterwards.[51] Twenty-one houses were wrecked, 41 seriously and

488 otherwise damaged, while five people were killed and eleven seriously injured. Due to the low-level nature of this attack, many incendiary containers failed to open until they hit the ground, reducing fire areas and limiting casualties.[52] A Havoc of 85 Squadron damaged a Ju 88 off Ipswich, and three enemy aircraft were claimed as damaged by anti-aircraft guns, with nothing claimed as destroyed.[53]

On the following night, about forty aircraft approached Kent from the Thames estuary, but whereas Bomb Census records insist 'the entire force concentrated over Canterbury where many bombs were dropped', only ten aircraft were reported over the city with six HE and 1,231 incendiaries dropped.[54] While some fires were started, all were quickly under control, with 'no damage of national importance' caused, although electricity supplies were disrupted in the Ramsgate area.[55] The balloon barrage was effective and kept the German aircraft at high level, and the raid 'was somewhat reminiscent of the abortive attack on Norwich of 8/9 May'.[56] 11 Group operated a 'Fighter Night' over Canterbury, and a Do 217 was probably destroyed by a Hurricane of 1 Squadron, while another was damaged by a Hurricane of 3 Squadron. AI fighters also operated, with a He 111 shot down by a Beaufighter of 29 Squadron and a further Do 217 destroyed by a Havoc of 85 Squadron. A Ju 88 crossing the Thames estuary on the way to Canterbury was also shot down by anti-aircraft guns.[57]

On the night of 3–4 June, 'a military objective at Poole was attacked' by 'a relatively large' force of bombers.[58] Although seventy-five aircraft were plotted, only thirty aircraft bombed the Poole area, and the numbers operating and bombing were very similar to the 24–25 May attack described in chapter 3. Flares were dropped, described as 'very brilliant', and light anti-aircraft guns expended many rounds to shoot them down. Aircraft bombed in pairs, one dropping incendiaries and the other HE, and bombing 'was in no sense, indiscriminate', Home Security insisting that 'definite targets were attacked'.[59] Thirty-four HE (fourteen tonnes) and two thousand incendiaries were dropped on the town, while another forty-seven tonnes of HE fell outside the target area, despite the use of a radio beam.[60] A RAF Reserve depot was hit, catching fire, powerhouses at a Royal Navy depot were damaged, and a 'medium fire' started at a shipyard.[61] Only three people were killed, with two seriously injured, while eighty houses were damaged, four being totally wrecked and fifty people made homeless.[62] Although 12 Group despatched twelve AI fighters and miscellaneous other aircraft against the attackers, only one Beaufighter obtained a visual but was unable to attack. In contrast, although only three German aircraft passed over 11 Group territory, a Beaufighter of 219 Squadron destroyed both a He 111 and a Ju 88 off the Isle of Wight.[63]

On 4–5 June, attention turned to the north-east coast in what German communiqués insisted were 'attacks on dock and harbour, Sunderland'. Of fifty aircraft operating, only seventeen passed overland, while the rest concentrated on mine laying.[64] In reality, this raid was against Teesside, although a ship was damaged in Sunderland harbour, and the loading of two others was delayed by an unexploded bomb. Most bombs fell in the Middlesbrough and Hartlepool areas, with no more than slight damage caused.[65] The most serious incident of the night was at Lowestoft, where a single aircraft dropped four 500kg bombs, which killed two people.[66] With attacks occurring all down the east coast, AI fighters of both 12 and 13 Group operated. Beaufighters of 141 Squadron shot down a Do 217 and damaged another off the north-east coast, while a stray Beaufighter of 25 Squadron claimed to have damaged an unidentified enemy aircraft off Whitby. Further south, another Beaufighter of 68 Squadron shot down a Ju 88 just south of Lowestoft.[67]

No aircraft were overland the following night, but on 6–7 June, fifteen aircraft attempted a half-hearted attack against Canterbury. The twenty HE bombs that were dropped only damaged some telephone cables and started a few fires, while an unexploded bomb restricted rail traffic on the Ashford and Margate lines.[68] There were no civilian casualties from this attack, and no German aircraft were intercepted or damaged by anti-aircraft guns. The Air Historical Branch (AHB) assessment of this period is ambiguous; while it considers that the Canterbury raids 'were similar to Baedeker attacks', the two attacks on Poole were interpreted as 'anti-invasion measures' and disregard the east coast operations completely.[69] Rothnie, however, considered Canterbury as 'a very inconclusive end to the *Baedeker* raids'.[70]

RESUMPTION OF GERMAN ATTACKS

The trivial scale of German effort after the third Canterbury attack demonstrates the strain previous attacks had placed on the *Luftwaffe*. The maximum number of aircraft overland at night reached ten only once, with a total of ten aircraft operating across four other nights and no aircraft overland at all on nine nights.[71] On 21–22 June, forty-five aircraft operated along the south coast, with twenty-six attacking Southampton, bombs falling on the centre and east of the city, as bombs were spread over a wide area from Surrey to Hampshire.[72] The Regional Commissioner described damage as 'scattered and not important' and was not concentrated on any particular part of the city, due to the 'particularly strong anti-aircraft defence'.[73] This 'strong' defence, however, only claimed one aircraft as damaged.[74] Despite this, thirty-four people were killed and forty-four seriously injured, with 133 houses being wrecked and 659 seriously damaged.[75] The most significant damage of the night was at Eastleigh, where a cabling works was seriously damaged and seven people were killed.[76] Both 10 and 11 Groups operated against the attackers, with a Beaufighter of 604 Squadron shooting down a He 111 off Ventnor, while another of 29 Squadron claimed to have destroyed a He 177, which was not yet operational.[77]

On 24–25 June, around forty-five aircraft operated over a wide area of East Anglia and the Midlands, counter to the usual policy of coastal targets, with about twenty concentrated at Nuneaton.[78] Incendiaries were dropped first, followed by HE about a half-hour later, with concurrent further incendiaries.[79] This tactic generally reflected the use of radio aids, but in this case, there was no 'likely target in the area covered by the IBs, which is very approximately 6 miles in extent'.[80] Nuneaton was deliberately selected as the target with a 'beacon fire' at Oldbury Hall, and the Birmingham searchlights operated throughout.[81] The 'vital and extensive' London, Midland, and Scottish Railway marshalling yard was severely damaged, with sidings disrupted and all four tracks of the main line blocked with debris, which were not cleared until the following day, and the line to Birmingham remained closed until 26 June.[82] Nineteen houses were wrecked and 244 seriously damaged, while eighteen people were killed and thirteen seriously injured.[83] The only significant industrial damage was to a factory producing components for the new Avro Lancaster bomber, so the delivery of finished aircraft 'was delayed for some weeks'.[84] Despite a long approach and deep penetration across the country, only one 9 Group Beaufighter achieved an interception, without observing any damage to the bomber.[85] Further east, AI fighters of 12 Group were more successful, with Beaufighters of 25 and 68 Squadron destroying three Do 217s, while Mosquitoes of 151 Squadron destroyed a Do 217 and two He 111s and damaged another.[86] The Official History laconically remarked that the *Luftwaffe* change in target emphasis 'clearly did nothing to improve its chances', as both Southampton and Birmingham 'were well defended targets;

and a Midland city was not as easily found as Bath or Exeter'.[87] The Air Ministry Commentary observed that Nuneaton was 'the first of the recent towns attacked to lie well inland' and speculated 'that raids may not be confined to short-range targets'.[88]

On 26–27 June, thirty aircraft from KG2, KGr106, and KG100 operated, the majority of which attacked Norwich.[89] Thirty-three HE bombs and over eight thousand incendiaries were dropped in a concentrated attack of thirty minutes, causing sixty-six fires which destroyed 150 houses and damaged 2,000.[90] The 'considerable number of incendiaries dropped' also caused 'extensive damage' to the London and North Eastern Railway goods yard and damaged 'many of the city's most prominent buildings', including the roof of the cathedral.[91] Only fourteen people were killed and eleven seriously injured, but extensive house damage meant that eleven rest centres were required for homeless residents.[92] Forty-four aircraft operated against this attack, eighteen in an increasingly rare 'Fighter Night', where a Spitfire of 610 Squadron shot down a Ju 88.[93] 151 Squadron was transitioning between aircraft, so as a Mosquito claimed one Do 217 destroyed, another crew in a Defiant damaged two Do 217s. Further south, a Beaufighter of 29 Squadron shot down a He 111 off Harwich in the 11 Group area.[94]

On the 27–28 and 28–29 June, the *Luftwaffe* attacked their most pertinent target of the whole 1942 campaign to the participating bomber crews. The coastal resort of Weston-super-Mare appeared unexceptional, being dismissed by *Baedeker* as 'a popular watering-place', apart from the Bristol Aircraft factory just to the east of the town.[95] After constructing 176 Beaufighters during 1941, the factory was now producing the improved VI night fighter version.[96] The importance of this meant a balloon barrage was present, but it only covered the aircraft factory.[97] Forty aircraft operated on each night, but only twenty bombed on the first night compared to thirty-five on the second.[98] The Regional Commissioner asserted that 'the attack was against the town, and not against the factory', but over the two nights, eighteen incendiary containers and two HE bombs landed within the works perimeter, with other HE just to the south, without damage, as all incendiaries missed buildings and aircraft.[99] On both nights, bombing began over the aircraft factory, with attacking aircraft initially descending below five hundred feet, reverting to above the balloon barrage after one struck a cable, which resulted in HE bombs falling on residential areas north of the railway lines.[100] Eleven of the fifty-six bombs dropped over the two nights were wasted by falling into the sea.[101] Many incendiary bombs on the first night fell harmlessly to the south of the town, but on the second night, these landed on the central and north sides. Many incendiary cases either failed to open after dropping or landed in the sea, so the forty fires reported after the first raid and the seventy after the second could have been significantly increased by more accurate aiming.[102] Fifty houses were wrecked and three hundred seriously damaged out of a total of five thousand, with 350 personnel transferred from Bath to carry out first aid repairs, and the balloon barrage was moved a half-mile west to protect the town. On the first night, the majority of damage was to residential areas, but it was on the main shopping centre on the following night.[103] After minor damage to railway targets on the first night, passenger and freight sides of the main line station were 'considerably disorganised by extensive damage' during the second attack, which still affected services at the end of the month.[104] Thirty-six people were killed and seventy-nine seriously injured during the first raid, while seventy-four died with 151 serious injuries on the second night.[105] Eighteen AI aircraft were operated by 10 Group on 27–28 June, with the Beaufighters of 307 Squadron shooting down one Do 217 and damaging another two, but the three 'Turbinlite' and ten 'Cat's Eye' fighters also patrolling achieved nothing. On the following night, an unsuccessful 'Fighter Night' was operated, but a Beaufighter of 307 Squadron shot down a Do 217, while another was damaged by a Mosquito of 264 Squadron.[106] Anti-aircraft fire during the first attack was restricted by low-flying aircraft, but 'a good barrage' on the second night led to one aircraft destroyed.[107] A balloon unit reported damage to an enemy aircraft, with 'pieces of wing and engine cowling found at a balloon site', but this was almost certainly a misreporting of the low-flying aircraft that hit a cable during the 27–28 attack.[108] The Air Ministry Commentary concluded that the *Luftwaffe* was conducting large numbers of reconnaissance, mine laying, and anti-shipping operations and was still 'capable of carrying out these activities and launching attacks against land targets' when 'the weather is suitable'.[109]

The prime minister's attention had been diverted from the home front, but this attitude changed towards the middle of the year. After observing uninhabited damaged houses, Churchill requested details of similar property across the country so that they could be used to house US servicemen arriving in the country. A survey subsequently showed 158,000 houses that could be made serviceable, but a shortage of labour was the stumbling block. It was intended to use such housing indirectly to meet accommodation shortages, with government departments transferring back to London from towns where the US Army required housing.[110] Compared to the number of houses waiting to be repaired in November 1941, the numbers in the provinces had increased considerably, and no progress had been made in London. The 1942 *Luftwaffe* attacks on provincial targets had caused widespread damage across the country, leaving many houses uninhabitable, and by addressing this problem over the summer, many houses could be repaired before the winter months.

The frequency of raids throughout June and July can be charitably described as patchy, although O'Brien has argued that 'these cannot be swept aside by an historian as irrelevant'.[111] Very little happened during the first twenty-four nights of the month, with significant concentration of twenty aircraft achieved only twice, both in the Tyne-Tees area.[112] Incendiary bombs were dropped across east Newcastle and Wallsend on 7–8 July, causing fires at Walkergate hospital. More incendiaries were dropped at Stockton and Middlesbrough, most hitting West Hartlepool and the ICI works at Billingham, together with HE bombs, where there was extensive damage.[113] While the hospital damage at Newcastle was to a civilian target, the buildings were located only two hundred metres east of a major railway repair works, one of the principal communication targets under *Luftwaffe* doctrine. 13 Group responded to these attacks with ten aircraft from the two available AI squadrons. Only one of the twelve contacts made resulted in combat, when a Beaufighter of 219 Squadron shot down a Do 217 off the Northumberland coast. A single aircraft was then detected heading towards the Tynemouth area two hours after the raid ended, leading to another 219 Squadron Beaufighter damaging a Do 217 off Whitby.[114]

The same number of aircraft successfully concentrated against Teesside the following night, dropping a similar tonnage of bombs. Although some bombs were dropped on Middlesbrough and Stockton, the majority fell in the Billingham area, causing further extensive damage to the ICI chemical works.[115] The 13 Group response to the attacks was more successful than the previous night, with eight aircraft between the two AI squadrons achieving five contacts, all of which resulted in combat, and Beaufighters of 406 Squadron shooting down three Do 217s and a He 111 off the north-east coast.[116]

The bombing war caused disagreements in War Cabinet at this time over the release of information to the public about the 1940–1941 Blitz.[117] The Ministry of Home Security had commissioned an information pamphlet entitled

'Front Line', as 'the story of the Civil Defence of Britain against the heavy air bombardment of 1940-41'.[118] Although publication had been approved by the Censor, objections were then raised by Sinclair, the secretary of state for air, because it would 'tell the enemy about the effects, moral and material, of every important raid on this country and about our counter-measures'.[119] Morrison argued that 'every important weakness in Civil Defence touched upon in the book and the manner of its remedy has been exhaustively discussed in the press'. He also objected to the Air Ministry's allegation that 'the book makes clear that the German attack was directed indiscriminately against civilian objectives and not selectively against economic and military ones; and that it failed'. Morrison refuted this by pointing out that 'the Germans indulged in indiscriminate attack not by *à priori* choice, but primarily because of the great difficulty of exact aiming at night', and then asked, 'Is not the RAF now engaged in a form of attack similar in many respects to the German raids of 1941?'[120] The general view of the War Cabinet (implying that not all agreed) was that the book was too detailed and should 'be rewritten in more general terms'.[121] Morrison gave no doubt of his views on publication: 'Front Line is the story of how British men and women for nine months stood alone against Hitler and won a people's battle not in any ideal or metaphorical sense, but by the defeat of the enemy's purpose in hard and bloody fact. It is needed now as a refreshment to our own spirit, a reminder to the Empire and to our American allies, and a contribution to that greater Russian knowledge of our war record which is now agreed to be desirable'.[122]

The final pamphlet undoubtedly had a propaganda value but also conveys a candid sense of the civilian struggle during the Blitz. There is no record of what amendments were made to the manuscript, but the figures recorded within it are remarkably accurate when compared to official records, as a comparison of casualties in selected towns with the official record does not reveal any censorship of figures.[123]

Following the 'damage to factories of national importance' on 8 July, enemy activity was much reduced until the resumption of attacks on 25–26 July again at Middlesbrough, the first of four significant raids over six nights.[124] Although Norman described the Middlesbrough attack as the 'heaviest air raid' on the town, this was in terms of physical damage rather than fatalities.[125] Once again, twenty aircraft were overland, with bombs being dropped on Middlesbrough, West Hartlepool, and Billingham.[126] Damage was caused to the nitric acid plant at the ICI works, reducing explosive production for over three months, and bombs in residential areas seriously damaged thirty-five houses.[127] Twelve tonnes of HE were dropped on Billingham, while five tonnes of HE and 1,500 incendiaries fell on Middlesbrough, where twenty fires were started.[128] The large numbers of bombs produced relatively low casualty numbers, with fifteen fatalities and thirty seriously injured, but sixty-five buildings were wrecked and eighty-six seriously damaged.[129] A Turbinlite combination operated without success together with seven Beaufighters, of which one from 219 Squadron shot down two Do 217s off Tynemouth.[130]

After no activity on the following night, on 27–28 July, a significantly larger *Luftwaffe* formation of sixty aircraft operated over the Birmingham area.[131] This was a 'concentrated attack' causing 'considerable damage', with seventeen Key Points affected, compared to the last major attack on the city when ten Key Points were involved.[132] This analysis is misleading, however, as on 16 May 1941, Nuneaton was the primary target rather than Birmingham (113 deaths versus 38, forty-eight HE versus six, and 2,088 incendiaries, of which the majority missed Birmingham), compared to 73 killed and 130 injured from sixty-five HE (twenty-two tonnes) and 4,500 incendiaries dropped on 27–28 July.[133] The incendiary bombs did not cause extensive fires, but property still 'suffered considerable damage'.[134] Three factories were completely gutted by fire, but the majority only experienced slight damage, which still exceeded the industrial damage caused by the 150 aircraft on 16 May 1941.[135] As usual, some aircraft missed the primary objective, with bombs dropped as far apart as Sheffield and Norwich, although most other damage was caused at Smethwick, just outside Birmingham, where 18 people were killed and 93 seriously injured.[136] Compared to the highly localised activity on the north-east coast during the earlier July attacks against Middlesbrough, on these nights the *Luftwaffe* operated across the entire country between the Humber and Thames estuaries.[137] Most Fighter Command patrols took place around Birmingham (9 Group) and across the country towards the east coast over the North Sea (12 Group), although some aircraft strayed into other Group areas. During 27–28 July, eighteen AI and three Cat's Eye fighters patrolled in 9 Group, but the only contact was by a Beaufighter of 255 Squadron, which claimed a He 111 as damaged.[138] The 12 Group fighters flew sixty-four patrols resulting in ten combats, with six aircraft claimed as destroyed and two damaged, which were all Do 217s.[139] Two of these were claimed by Mosquitoes of 151 Squadron and another by a Beaufighter of 409 Squadron, the Beaufighters of 68 Squadron claimed three more and damaged another, while the final Do 217 claim was by a Turbinlite combination of 1459 Flight.[140] In all, eleven aircraft were claimed as shot down, with eight damaged.[141]

After minimal activity during the following night, the *Luftwaffe* returned on 29–30 July with a hundred aircraft concentrated over Birmingham and Wolverhampton, with a smaller number bombing Bedford.[142] Considering the larger number of aircraft operating, significantly fewer bombs were dropped, with thirty HE and three thousand incendiaries dropped on Birmingham and twelve HE on Coventry, around 65 percent of 27–28 July.[143] Incendiaries caused 223 fires within the city of Birmingham, with another 68 across the West Midlands, compared to the 131 on 27–28 July.[144] An increased number of twenty-eight Key Points were affected, including six railways, and of the twenty-one factories attacked, three were extensively damaged, but other damage was slight.[145] Casualties were centred on Birmingham, with 95 fatalities and 289 seriously injured, while 11 were killed and 28 seriously injured at Bedford.[146] Although more German aircraft operated, patrols in 9 Group were restricted to fifteen AI fighters plus a 'Fighter Night' of six Hurricanes over Birmingham, and a single combat took place when a Beaufighter of 456 Squadron shot down a He 111.[147] Reduced patrols of forty-seven aircraft were flown by 12 Group, leading to seven combats. Mosquitoes of 151 Squadron destroyed a Do 217 and damaged another, with a further one shot down by a Beaufighter of 68 Squadron while Beaufighters of 25 and 409 Squadron both claimed Do 217s as damaged. A He 111 was probably destroyed by 409 Squadron, and a Turbinlite of 1459 Flight damaged an additional Do 217.[148] Total claims for the whole country amounted to nine aircraft shot down and nine damaged.[149]

The 29–30 July raid was the heaviest attack on the United Kingdom since Bath on 25–26 April 1942, which the AHB identified as 'the peak of the German Air Force's capabilities at this time', and subsequent night activity unsurprisingly failed to match the scale of the previous two attacks.[150] Forty-five aircraft operated, and although Birmingham was bombed again, the main concentration was against the Wolverhampton-Walsall area.[151] Incendiaries were extensively used, with very few HE dropped, causing considerable damage to both industrial and domestic property, although only eleven Key Points were affected, with eight people killed and twenty-eight seriously injured.[152] Of the seven factories attacked, only one was extensively damaged, with slight damage to the others.[153] The Air Ministry Commentary was unimpressed, describing raiding as 'ragged and much of it wasted effort', in contrast to the response of the air defences.[154] Although fewer German aircraft operated, 9 Group flew twenty-nine patrols of both AI and Cat's Eye fighters. The only combat was by a Beaufighter of 255 Squadron, which damaged a He 111, while some aircraft used the searchlight 'Fighter Box' system of control.[155] Further east, 12 Group flew patrols of twenty-five aircraft against attackers passing over Group territory, with a Do 217 shot down and another damaged, while a Ju 88 was also shot down by Beaufighters of 68 Squadron.[156] The extensive nature of *Luftwaffe* operations also presented other opportunities, with three aircraft claimed destroyed by 10 Group and three damaged by 11 Group.[157]

Although it was not obvious at the time, the *Luftwaffe* could no longer despatch large raids against the United Kingdom and would not attempt anything comparable until Operation 'Steinbock' in 1944. The Air Ministry acknowledged widespread destruction, including significant damage to vital industries, and Richards estimates thirty-eight factories were destroyed or seriously damaged with sixty-five 'notably damaged'.[158] In total, 237 houses were destroyed, 2,087 seriously and 7,306 otherwise damaged, mostly during the first two raids.[159] The *Luftwaffe* could only despatch twelve aircraft to Hull on the following night, in a return to their usual coastal policy.[160] This caused minor damage to the docks, but stray bombs hit adjacent housing, killing twenty-seven people and seriously injuring seven.[161] Ten aircraft also laid mines off the east coast, and with all enemy activity 'confined to 12 Group area', a greatly increased number of thirty-two patrols by thirty-seven aircraft were flown. Only three interceptions resulted from these patrols, which produced one combat when a Beaufighter of 68 Squadron shot down a Do 217 off Spurn Head.[162]

The German bombing offensive that began at Exeter on 23–24 April finally ended on 1–2 August when twenty aircraft operated over East Anglia, nominally centred on Norwich.[163] Only seven HE and 4,500 incendiaries were dropped on the city, which started two serious fires and caused 'substantial damage' to commercial premises, with five people being killed and twenty-seven injured.[164] Weather conditions over 12 Group were described as 'unfavourable', and no interceptions were made.[165] The ineffectiveness of the attacks on 31 July–1 August and 1–2 August only affected a total of three Key Points between both targets.[166] Throughout the rest of August, small numbers of German aircraft operated overland, with the Air Ministry

Commentary describing activity 'of little or no interest' with 'negligible' damage, until documenting a major attack at Leeds on 27–28 August.[167] As only ten aircraft were involved with two Key Points affected, this claim appears exaggerated, especially as casualties were light, with five fatalities and six seriously injured.[168]

The Official History observes, slightly harshly, that the July attacks on Birmingham 'accomplished little', and the AHB narrative finds it 'difficult to find any clear policy behind the German night operations between the close of the *Baedeker* raids and the attacks on Birmingham at the end of July', but these matched the pattern adopted since the end of the Blitz.[169] British victory claims were optimistic compared to German records, but *Luftwaffe Kampfgruppen* were still suffering unsustainable losses. By 1944, British estimates of German losses had been revised down to twenty-five aircraft over the three nights, which compares favourably to the twenty-three lost.[170] Several of the bombers supposedly 'destroyed' by British fighters did return to occupied territory before being either abandoned or destroyed during crash landings. German reports complained that experienced crews transferred from the Eastern Front were 'not equal to the demands made by night operations against Britain'.[171] The decline of the German bomber force can be illustrated by the seven aircraft lost by *Ergänzungsgruppen* over the three nights.[172] This deterioration can be further demonstrated by comparing RAF and *Luftwaffe* bomber operations during the last week of July 1942. Both sides mounted five raids during this period, but the total number of German aircraft used (237) was fewer than in the smallest British attack on Hamburg (256), with a total of 1,929 aircraft despatched by Bomber Command.[173]

A German commentary from 1944 observed that 'the task which had easily been performed previously by 600 bombers now had to be carried out by 60'.[174] British losses amounted to nearly half of total German aircraft used, with a loss rate considered unacceptably high, especially for OTU crews, but the damage to the training programme had been recognised, and this involvement was subsequently rescinded, as described earlier. The RAF training system was therefore prevented from serious damage, while the *Ergänzungsgruppen* were no longer able to provide sufficient crews to replace the heavy losses in July to continue meaningful operations against the United Kingdom.[175] The AHB narrative considers 'this sharp decline in enemy activity was a clear indication of the failing strength and effectiveness of the German night-bomber force'.[176] The German commentary notes that operations between April and August 1942 'made the greatest demands on the crews', as the bombing force dwindled and average life expectancy of an aircrew decreased to 15.2 operations against the United Kingdom. The increasing effectiveness of fighter defences forced the *Luftwaffe* to reduce the length of raids during 1942 and 'take continuous evasive action' to limit casualties.[177] Resuming raids on inland targets (Birmingham) only increased aircraft losses, and German planners acknowledged the dangers of British airspace. Some bomber units used a circuitous route to the west close to the Irish coast before crossing Wales to approach targets in the Midlands.[178] Fighter Command documents clearly show that the British were aware of changes in tactics used during bombing attacks.[179] Within four to six weeks of a new method of attack being introduced, the British defenders had found a solution.[180]

The final blow to the viability of the German bombing force came during the Allied operation against Dieppe on 19 August 1942. Although the amphibious landing was 'a dismal tactical failure', the large air operation that supported it inflicted severe damage on *Luftwaffe* aircraft attacking troops and shipping.[181] The former Operations Officer of KG2, writing in 1944, stated that the *Kampfgruppe* 'lost twenty-five percent of the aircraft which went into action' during the Dieppe operation.[182] *Luftflotte* 3 lost a total of nineteen bombers during 19 August, with eighteen damaged, of which twelve and eight respectively were from KG2, which appears to have been the most heavily engaged unit.[183] By September 1942, the average operational strength of KG2 had fallen to twenty-three crews, compared to the eighty-eight available at the beginning of the year.[184] By now the *Ergänzungsgruppen* had been stripped of instructor crews, and the three aircraft of IV/KG77 that crash-landed on 29–30 July after running out of fuel indicate that novice aircrews were now making up the numbers.[185] Lack of personnel disrupted the bomber training programme in the summer of 1942, aggravated by fuel shortages that reduced training flying hours.[186] Göring subsequently acknowledged that aircrew supply 'became difficult during the year of 1942' as the supply of replacements became 'quite broken and disrupted'.[187] The AHB condemned 'the unsound basis on which German strategical air planning was then based where political considerations may be allowed to assume an overriding importance', leading to 'a thoroughly uneconomical way of applying the night bombing effort'.[188] Only 16 percent of *Luftwaffe* sorties were overland before the start of the 1942 raids, then attacks on land targets were maintained at a minimum of 50 percent, and attacks on shipping continued at a reasonable level until the end of July, with coastal mine laying becoming insignificant throughout this period (see appendix 8). Although 'in-commission' rates for *Luftwaffe* aircraft improved at the beginning of 1942, heavy commitments in the east meant these fell after June. From this point, aircraft strength fell steadily, reducing German forces by five hundred aircraft before the end of 1942.[189] With shortages of both aircrew and aircraft, the bombing units of *Luftflotte* 3 were in no condition to continue meaningful operations, and apart from a brief spell in October 1942, nothing significant was attempted for the remainder of the year.

The prime minister continued to monitor the repair of uninhabited damaged houses, but a shortage of labour delayed progress, especially in the southern region, where available workers had been required for first-aid repairs following the *Baedeker* attacks. Despite these workforce issues, most repairs were in the provinces, with much less progress in London.[190]

THE EFFECTS OF THE MANPOWER SHORTAGE ON CIVIL AND AIR DEFENCE

The global war during 1942 prompted the British government to reconsider how the conflict could be sustained. The minister of production circulated an 'alarmist' review of 1943 production prospects in September 1942, estimating personnel requirements for service and munitions production at two million over the next twenty-one months. No specific proposals to address this were made, so the document 'was untimely and to an extent inexpert' but accurate in stating that 'we are nearing the stage of complete utilisation of our man-power'.[191] By the middle of October, although the Ministry of Labour survey was yet to be discussed, the lord president submitted recommendations for recruitment into the services up to the end of 1942.[192] It had also become clear that 'the stringency of the man-power situation was now such that it would be necessary to call men up at age 18' to fulfil service commitments for November and December.[193]

The 1942 Ministry of Labour survey was 'an important development in the technique of manpower budgeting', summarising the manpower requirements for service and supply departments against the available supply of men and women and proposing how 'the gap between supply and demand might be further narrowed'.[194] The mobilisation of manpower by the end of the third year of the war had gone further than in 1918, the fourth and final year of the First World War.[195] The requirements of 'the planned strengths and programmes up to the end of 1943 were calculated at 2.5 million men and women' by the survey. As only 1.6 million were available, this gave 'a prospective deficiency' of 900,000, so the division of manpower shortages between the three branches of the armed forces was inevitable.[196] Churchill identified the U-boat as the greatest danger, so the highest priority was given to ships and weapons for the Battle of the Atlantic.[197] The threat of air attacks being repeated on the scale of 1940–1941 was considered unlikely, and invasion was remote, so 'further reductions should therefore be made in Civil Defence and in ADGB'.[198] Churchill then proposed the intended cuts, but this 'as was to be expected, did not pass uncriticised', especially for Civil Defence.[199] By the end of 1943, Civil Defence strength was to be cut by 110,000, which Morrison as home secretary considered 'a very drastic proposal which involves risks which the Cabinet should appreciate and accept as a whole'. Most Civil Defence resources were 'found in areas which are admittedly liable to sporadic and dangerous air raids', and halving full-time strengths meant that 'extensive fires might have to be left to spread and burn themselves out, and casualties might be trapped under ruins'. Reductions in Civil Defence were from the current establishment, unlike the armed forces, which would restrict further growth. Since the beginning of 1942, both Civil Defence and police services had given up 'substantial numbers of men and women to the forces or to industry, and are invited to make still further reductions on a large scale'.[200] At the height of the Blitz, 128,000 men and 48,000 women (176,000 in total) had been in Civil Defence, but by mid-1942 this was reduced to 146,000. A total reduction of 75,100 was then suggested, compared to the 110,000 originally proposed, to be completed by the end of 1943.[201] Overall, the reductions were ratified during the War Cabinet meeting of 11 December 1942. Due to the cuts imposed on the Ministry of Aircraft Production, these 'would result in a loss of 14 heavy bomber squadrons by the end of 1943'. Cuts to Civil Defence were the amended figure of 75,000, rather than the 100,000 proposed by Churchill, which was recorded as 'a heavy reduction, responsibility for which would, of course, be accepted by the War Cabinet as a whole'. Any personnel released 'should be made available for Civil Defence duties in the event of serious emergencies', but neither the means to release them nor how serious an emergency should prompt this was specified by the War Cabinet.[202] This shortage of manpower was demonstrated by the minimal progress made on housing repairs during the second half of 1942. With new damage and previous incomplete repairs, the number of houses still requiring attention remained around 100,000 throughout the period, Churchill commenting that 'progress was too slow' after 'pressing this for months'.[203]

REDUCTION IN GERMAN ACTIVITY DURING LAST THREE MONTHS OF 1942

German night attacks had become 'increasingly costly', so day sorties increased 'largely at the expense of the night effort'.[204] The percentage of aircraft used for mine laying rose slightly in August before being abandoned for the rest of the year, while the number of aircraft making attacks overland was greatly reduced. There were fewer daylight attacks from September 1942, and from October onwards, the comment 'no overland activity' is increasingly present in British records, with 'nothing to report' by the end of December 1942.[205] A Mass Observation report in September 1942 highlighted the indifference of the British public to continued German attacks. Against a background of the wider war, 'directed employment', and rationing, civilians were only concerned about 'where to shelter and how to sleep during heavy raids'. Safety was no longer a concern, as it was noted that 'if you're hit, that's the end'. The fear of night bombing 'was mostly inspired by noise—the sirens, bombs, guns', but there was a 'feeling that the war would not last much longer'.[206] German records comment that lack of resources confined the *Luftwaffe* to day and night 'nuisance raids' from September 1942 onwards in an attempt 'to shield the squadrons from loss as far as possible', but this 'did not result in any noticeable reduction in the losses'.[207] The Air Ministry Commentary noted that *Luftwaffe* units were 'undergoing a programme of reorganisation and reequipping' with 'greatly increased training activity' by bomber *Ergänzungsgruppen*.[208] The AHB narrative describes *Luftwaffe* night activity 'on a smaller scale than any time since before the autumn of 1941' (see appendix 8). This escalated briefly with five attacks in October, with not all considered significant.[209] Only eight aircraft operated against the north-east coast on 11–12 October, bombing around 'the mouth of the Tyne', with the most serious damage at South Shields gasworks.[210] Air Ministry reports acknowledge that 'a few bombers' attacked, but 'without affecting a concentration', while another source notes bombs falling on Sunderland, Monkseaton, and Tynemouth. Although twenty people were killed and similar numbers injured, this attack was minor compared to autumn 1941.[211] The majority of bombs dropped during the subsequent attack on 16–17 October were over Teesside, with three at Sunderland. As the most serious damage from this raid was listed as 'a food store' and few casualties were caused, this attack was only significant as the one time in 1942 when an AI fighter successfully used the searchlight 'Fighter Box', shooting down a Do 217 near Sunderland.[212] The attacks on the east Midlands were even more tenuous, as on 21–22 October, *Luftwaffe* activity was again along the east coast.[213] Some damage was caused to a steelworks at Scunthorpe, but no bombs were dropped west of the Humber estuary.[214] On 24–25 October, the second east Midlands attack, the report to War Cabinet stated that bombing 'was confined to areas of the East Coast'.[215] Bombs were dropped on Humberside and in Lincolnshire, with 'a considerable number of houses' wrecked at Grantham, where thirty-two people were killed and seventeen seriously injured.[216]

While the four raids described above cannot be considered significant, the attacks on Canterbury during 31 October and 1 November 1942 demand closer attention. The first wave was a low-level attack by thirty Focke-Wulf Fw 190 fighter-bombers in the late afternoon, although another source describes this as being 'at dusk'.[217] The weather 'was not good', with 10/10 cloud at a base of five hundred feet as the attack started around 1700, so visibility would have been tenuous at best. The balloon barrage was being raised as the attack began, and 'one enemy plane fouled a balloon cable' as the others bombed at low level over residential areas of the city.[218] The second and third waves were Do 217s, and attacked at 2000 (fifteen aircraft) and 0100 (twenty aircraft) at heights between four thousand feet and ten thousand feet.[219] Accuracy was unimpressive; even for the low-level fighter-bombers, nearly a quarter of the forty bombs ended up 'in rural areas', while only two HE from the second wave landed within Canterbury Borough, due to anti-aircraft fire driving 'the raiders away from their objective'. This poor accuracy reflected the lack of experienced twin-engine bomber crews, continued by the third wave where nearly half of the thirty-six HE and a third of sixty-six incendiary bombs dropped 'fell in the adjacent rural areas'.[220] Although the railway system 'was temporarily interrupted', there was 'no damage of national importance', and most damage was to residential property, with 90 houses wrecked, 300 seriously and 1,650 otherwise damaged, killing thirty-three people and seriously injuring eighty-three.[221] The Air Ministry Commentary describes the fighter-bomber attack as 'an expensive enterprise', with nine of the attackers destroyed 'and accomplishing little in return'.[222] During the night raids, the Beaufighters of 29 Squadron shot down four Do 217s, two from each wave, with one crew responsible for three of them.[223]

A further two German bombers were claimed at night after the Canterbury raid, with only thirty-six aircraft overland during the last two months of the year.[224] The redeployment of three *Kampfgeschwader* to the Mediterranean after the Allied invasion of North Africa on 8 November disrupted operations, and although two of these units returned to France after the German occupation of *Vichy* France at the end of November, the logistical challenges of supporting the movement of nearly one hundred aircraft with ground crew, ammunition, and spare parts between two locations in quick succession should not be underestimated, and since only the most 'combat-ready' units could be considered for such transfer, the operational value of the units left facing the United Kingdom must have been moderate at best.[225]

The superior performance of the centrimetric AI Mark VII continued during this period, despite the lack of potential targets, being responsible for five of the six aircraft destroyed.[226] By the end of 1942, there had been 'a gradual dwindling' of the number of AI Mark VII sets available as they had 'been found to have a short life' as well as a lack of spare parts. The production of the replacement AI Mark VIII was not possible during 1942, and the first sets would not reach squadrons until January 1943.[227]

DEVELOPMENT OF BRITISH NIGHT DEFENCES DURING 1942

With the *Luftwaffe* conserving aircraft by concentrating on mine laying and anti-shipping operations during the winter of 1941–1942, only eight aircraft were destroyed by RAF fighters in the first quarter of 1942. At the start of the *Baedeker* phase, Fighter Command destroyed eight German bombers in the first four attacks, all against targets in 10 Group. The next set of raids were against cities along the east coast, within 12 and 13 Group areas, where fighters and Controllers already had experience of opposing enemy operations, leading to fifteen aircraft being shot down during the next four attacks on the east coast.

Before 1942, the long detection wavelength of AI sets had limited the minimum operating height and detection range due to 'ground return', as described in chapter 1. The cavity magnetron enabled the RAF to introduce

TABLE 4.1

Combat Results for RAF Night Fighters in 1942

Month	Sorties		Destroyed	Enemy Sorties	Total Fighter Sorties
January	T/E	357	4 (1.1%)*	573	551 (96%)#
	S/E	194	0 (n/a)		
February	T/E	218	2 (0.9%)*	318	367 (115%)#
	S/E	149	0 (n/a)		
March	T/E	224	2 (0.9%)*	519	392 (76%)#
	S/E	168	0 (n/a)		
April	T/E	738	17 (2.3%)*	975	1,135 (116%)#
	S/E	397	3 (0.8%)*		
May	T/E	584	14 (2.4%)*	791	771 (97%)#
	S/E	187	0 (n/a)		
June	T/E	976	21 (2.2%)*	760	1,262 (166%)#
	S/E	286	3 (1.0%)*		
July	T/E	1,348	27½ (2.0%)*	681	2,003 (294%)#
	S/E	655	5½ (0.08%)*		
August	T/E	1,462	21½ (1.5%)*	626	1,886 (301%)#
	S/E	424	0 (n/a)		
September	T/E	1,128	10 (0.9%)*	319	1,380 (433%)#
	S/E	252	0 (n/a)		
October	T/E	122	6 (4.9%)*	202	124 (62%)#
	S/E	2	0 (n/a)		
November	n/r	n/r	n/r	58	n/r
December	T/E	}647	1 (0.2%)*	124	647 (192%)#
	S/E	}	0 (n/a)		

* % destroyed per sortie.

% of sorties per enemy sorties.

n/r Not recorded.

Adapted from TNA: AIR 16/525; and AIR 16/889.

the AI Mark VII radar set that used a 10cm (centimetric) wavelength at the end of 1941.[228] Tactics to eliminate 'ground return' were also developed for aircraft equipped with AI Mark IV to perform interceptions down to three thousand feet, and improved radar operator training increased the ratio of combats achieved.[229] Although the number of sorties flown by the *Luftwaffe* during the first quarter of 1942 remained high, the lack of casualties reflected the low-risk nature of the operations. Sortie numbers peaked in April during the *Baedeker* raids and remained high until August 1942. Increased fighter sorties were flown against these raids, as shown in table 4.1, rising progressively throughout the year. Throughout 1941, the use of Cat's Eye fighters had only been effective during highly concentrated raids, and unfavourable conditions in 1942 meant few enemy aircraft were intercepted, officially described as 'moderate results', with five aircraft destroyed during six 'Fighter Nights'.[230] The superiority of the AI/GCI weapon system was finally proven, and single-engine night fighters were phased out during the first half of the year. As Defiant squadrons transitioned to twin-engine aircraft, many non-operational squadrons briefly existed, which were not active until after the *Baedeker* period ended. During the July attacks on Birmingham, however, these additional squadrons were suitably trained and experienced, and the *Luftwaffe* suffered unacceptable losses. Fighter Command finally reached the figure of twenty AI squadrons late in 1942, which Air Chief Marshal Douglas had demanded while the Blitz was still in progress. This was despite losing two squadrons for overseas service in September, replacements for which were still reforming and not operational by the end of 1942.[231] The de Havilland Mosquito was developed from 'a revolutionary concept' using wooden construction to give higher speed and a greater payload than comparable aircraft of conventional design. Although originally intended as an unarmed bomber, an AI fighter requirement was added early in the design process.[232] The first operational aircraft was delivered to 157 Squadron in January 1942, and modifications identified by this unit meant 151 Squadron only became the second operator of the new fighter in April 1942. The first operational Mosquito patrol was flown by 157 Squadron on 27 April, but there were no successful combats during the *Baedeker* attacks.[233] The superior performance of the Mosquito as an AI fighter was not significant during 1942, as by October only five fighter squadrons had received them, with not all operational (see appendix 4), and also because the aircraft used AI Mark V. This was the metric AI Mark IV equipped with a target indicator for the pilot, which was described by an experienced radar operator as a 'blunder' and 'retrograde step', since it distracted the pilot during the final stages of the interception and led to contacts being lost that could have been held with AI Mark IV.[234] By the end of 1942, 'some disquieting rumours of continued trouble with AI Mark V' had reached the Air Ministry.[235]

Single-engine night fighter squadrons continued to decrease, despite successful trials with AI Mark VI in both Defiants and Hurricanes. By the middle of the year, the Defiants had gone, and Hurricane numbers were falling as squadrons were posted overseas, leaving few single-engine fighters for night use (see appendix 4). A brief resurgence of Hurricane numbers seemed likely when twelve were fitted with AI Mark VI and delivered for operational trials in October 1942. Distributed between three squadrons, it was intended that they would be used instead of Cat's Eye fighters to operate within the searchlight box zones.

The ten Turbinlite flights (equivalent to five squadrons of Havocs) were beset by aircrew shortages over the winter of 1941–1942. The urge to validate the aerial searchlight concept was apparent in the orders issued to Fighter Groups in April 1942 during the *Baedeker* raids: 'I am particularly anxious to use the Turbinlites and these also should be put into the air early'. Douglas noted in the same order 'a curious reluctance on the part of all concerned to employ Turbinlites operationally'.[236] The expectations of Turbinlite capabilities by RAF commanders and the government, ('we should depend on dark nights upon our turbinlite flights for our defence') were clearly not shared by operational units and crews, with this misuse of resources going back to 1940.[237] The support of Frederick Lindemann had extended the use of the Long Aerial Mine (LAM) long after the shortcomings of the weapon became obvious; Lindemann was convinced it was 'self-evident that the easiest way to intercept at night is to turn night into day by the use of artificial light', persuading Churchill to coerce the RAF into trials with 'chemical searchlights' in September 1940.[238] This was to be achieved by the use of flares, released in pairs from under the wings and towed three feet behind the trailing edge, in close proximity to the fuel tanks, a fire hazard that must have impressed the trial crew almost as much as being illuminated as a perfect target for every *Luftwaffe* gunner in the sky.[239] Documentation on the outcome of this trial has not survived; either it was sufficiently encouraging, or Lindemann's relentless lobbying meant that the trial continued. By the end of October 1940, four Fairey Battles had been assigned to 29 Squadron, just as they were transitioning from Blenheims to Beaufighters, presenting an unnecessary distraction as they tried to perfect the process of AI interception.[240] The Battles were TT or target-towing aircraft, with a wind-powered winch that normally extended a target drogue, essentially a long windsock, at a respectable length behind the aircraft as a gunnery target, which at least kept these flares an acceptable distance from any fuel source.[241] The squadron Operations Record Book mentions flare trials for the first time on 26 November, when aircrew were instructed in launching flares and using the winch, but states this was not the first time such procedures had been practised. Towed flares were used to illuminate a Blenheim that night, which could not be seen if the flare was more than one hundred yards away from the target aircraft. The evaluating aircrew were underwhelmed by the trial, considering that an attacking aircraft would be dazzled by the flare before an attack could be made, and the flare made the towing aircraft an easy target. Their conclusion was that the idea of chemical searchlights 'is open to serious criticism', but Fighter Command, presumably under pressure from Lindemann (and ultimately Churchill), was 'anxious for further tests', which the squadron was to carry out 'at the first suitable opportunity'. Such opportunities appear to have been limited, with only two further tests in December and a final trial in February 1941, after which experiments were suspended.[242] By this time, an aerial searchlight powered by lightweight (in 1941 terms) batteries was under development, with a trial installation hailed as having great promise. Air Chief Marshal Portal, the chief of the air staff, had reservations about atmospheric conditions negating searchlight beams, but Lindemann persevered, also suggesting the revival of 'flare methods'.[243]

As an 'Intruder' aircraft, the Havoc was faster and more robust than the Blenheim and was comparable to early Beaufighters as an AI fighter. The only way to accommodate both the AI radar and searchlight in a Havoc was for the aircraft to be unarmed, so equipping ten flights with Turbinlite aircraft denied Fighter Command additional AI squadrons when it was a short of Beaufighters. The impact of this policy can be illustrated by the previously used Aircraft Record Cards methodology to show that the delivery of aircraft to squadrons was initially slow as LAM conversions were prioritised over those for 'Intruder' or AI versions, which did not begin to arrive until March 1941. Appendix 5, table 2 shows that the number of aircraft available increased slowly and did not reflect actual availability. Only one Havoc AI fighter squadron was operational by April 1941, and the priority given to

LAM delayed the AI fighter for two months when the Blitz was at its height.[244] Without the distraction of questionable weapon systems, aircraft and crews could have been found to equip another two squadrons towards the end of the Blitz to compensate for low Beaufighter numbers.

The fact that LAM and then Turbinlite were sponsored by Lindemann with his innate bias against AI is almost certainly the reason for this, and many Havocs remained unused during the first half of 1941.[245] The large number of civilians used for aircraft conversion and equipment supply was a major security concern, so discussion of tactics was restricted, and diagrams and other information were 'not displayed where they could be seen by anyone other than those directly concerned'.[246] Such exceptional precautions would have been more impressive if the formation of units had been as inspiring; only thirty pilots were available for Turbinlite units at the end of November 1941.[247] Turbinlite remained completely unused during the first part of 1942, in case the mass attacks 'of the order of fifty aircraft' resumed.[248] By April 1942, there were only seventy Turbinlite Havocs on strength compared to the ninety required, with no further aircraft available for conversion. The supply of Havocs, which could have significantly increased AI fighter numbers while Beaufighter availability was low, was therefore wasted without ever being used.

As the only way to fit both the AI radar and searchlight in Havocs was to remove the guns, another aircraft was required to shoot down anything illuminated by the Turbinlite searchlight. This required the use of Hurricane 'satellite' or 'parasite' fighters, and Lindemann never considered the coordination and tactics required for this. Using GCI/AI, the formation had to close to within one thousand feet, but the Havoc did not then close into visual range. The Hurricanes moved forward to intercept, and after twenty seconds, the Havoc illuminated the target. Gunston argues that a German bomber would bank as soon as it was illuminated, then 'the Hurricanes got in each other's way, and the Havoc's way; or they obstructed the beam'. This meant that 'the target got away, while a Havoc and two rather hapless Hurricanes floundered about completely lost, and with their pilots' night-adapted vision destroyed'.[249] 'Having got to a position from which the Havoc could illuminate the target, it seems almost beyond belief that anybody could imagine that it wouldn't be better to aim cannon shells rather than a searchlight'.[250] In hindsight, it is difficult to argue how taking the guns out of a fighter and replacing them with a searchlight could ever be a good idea or to see why it was ever considered in the first place. Night interception was a complex process consisting of multiple steps; the failure of any would prevent an interception. The Turbinlite system complicated and extended the process, reducing the opportunity of a successful combat. After finally being cleared for operations during the *Baedeker* attacks, early results of the tactic were hardly encouraging, with only two enemy contacts during the period. In the first contact, the Havoc succeeded in holding the enemy aircraft in its searchlight beam for over ten seconds, but for 'various reasons the satellite fighter was unable to get into a position suitable for combat'. Although the second contact on 30 April–1 May resulted in a He 111 being claimed as destroyed, the Hurricane was in visual range before the searchlight was deployed, and it attacked without the German bomber being illuminated.[251] The scepticism of Controllers and crews is evident, as only three Turbinlite sorties were flown in April 1942, with full moon conditions negating any possible advantage of searchlight illumination.[252] On 4 May, however, one Turbinlite did achieve a successful 'combat', but due to its nature, the details were heavily suppressed.[253] Near Norwich a Havoc illuminated a bomber, which was shot down by the accompanying Hurricane.[254] This success was quickly overshadowed by the realisation that the aircraft was an RAF Stirling returning from a bombing operation.[255] The crew parachuted to safety, but as they were 'stupidly brought to the same airfield as the errant Turbinlite flight; there was nearly a riot'.[256]

Douglas was clearly underwhelmed by lack of success, commenting that *Luftwaffe* tactics 'of flying fast and low whilst taking constant avoiding action are not easily dealt with by the Turbinlite' and that there was not 'any immediate likelihood of proving the worth of the Turbinlite system'.[257] Operational crews complained that 'many useful trained night fighter crews were tied up in this operation for over a year' and were sure that 'the powers-that-be certainly persisted far too long with Turbinlites'.[258] Although still urging the priority of Turbinlite over AI fighters well into September 1942, Douglas conceded that 'the results of such opportunities as have occurred have proved disappointing'.[259] In his memoirs, Douglas complained about the LAM as a 'complete waste of time', taking 'a whole year of frustrating experiments' before he was able to convince Churchill that the idea 'was worthless and he agreed to abandon it'. As for Turbinlite, however, he insisted it was 'a more promising idea' although costing 'a great deal of money and time and effort' and the 'weight of all its equipment and the obstruction in its nose slowed up the Havoc too much when it came to chasing the enemy bombers'.

He complained of 'technical difficulties which were hard to overcome', but then conceded that Turbinlite was 'surpassed in effectiveness by the straightforward radar-equipped night fighter'.[260] It should be noted that armed AI Havocs had no difficulty in chasing enemy bombers.

The operational record of Turbinlite throughout these six months was underwhelming, one bomber was damaged, the other results were inconclusive, and since all but three satellite Hurricane squadrons had been withdrawn for overseas service, Fighter Command converted the Turbinlite flights into 'composite' squadrons with six each of Turbinlite and Hurricanes.[261] In an extraordinarily defensive memorandum, Douglas complained that since becoming operational *Luftwaffe* activity had 'been on a small scale' using 'shallow penetration combined with the taking of routine evasive action', which was 'difficult to counter with Turbinlites' and that 'the system has never yet been tried against large scale raids penetrating deep over this country', which ignores the two periods of heavy raiding around the end of April and July.[262] These attacks took place in conditions of bright moonlight, which Douglas does not mention, although he separately concedes that 'during the moon period each month the light is not effective and is not required'. Referring to the large-scale attacks of 1940 where the *Luftwaffe* used radio aids for bombing on dark nights, he argues that 'at that time AI was still in a very experimental form, and the standard of training required to operate it was very low'. 'Consequently, although AI contacts were achieved', he argued, 'few were converted into visuals', completely ignoring that the Blenheims used at the time were too slow to chase the bombers they were intercepting.[263] By the time of the first searchlight installation, the five AI fighter squadrons had shot down double figures of German bombers for the third month running, demonstrating the improvements in training and experience of night interception.[264] The uncompromising support of Lindemann and his hostility towards AI radar meant there was no likelihood of the system being abandoned, effectively denying extra AI fighters to Fighter Command. Therefore, Douglas's assertion that 'had the Turbinlite scheme been fully operational in this early phase a measure of success might have been achieved' is not credible. Douglas concluded his account of Turbinlite operations (or lack of them) with a table, shown in table 4.2, demonstrating the superior performance of the AI Mark VII radar, introduced around the same time as the searchlight system.[265]

Douglas noted that the AI Mark VII results were achieved by thirty-seven aircraft distributed between four squadrons, which together claimed 25 percent of all aircraft destroyed by AI fighters while forming around 10 percent

TABLE 4.2
Combat Results for Night Defence Weapon Systems During 1942

System	Sorties	Detected	Visual	Combat	Dest	Prob	Dam
Turbinlite	355	38	11	5	1	1	2
AI Mark VII	8,082	215	95	59	28	11	14
AI Mark IV &V		—	—	—	95	24	77

TNA: AIR 41/49; ADGB, V: 62.
It is unclear where the 'extra' combat claims for Turbinlite originated.

of the AI fighter force.[266] If the 'great deal of money and time and effort' spent on the ninety Turbinlite aircraft had been used to increase the quantity of AI Mark VII radar sets, the number of aircraft shot down by Fighter Command during 1942 could have been significantly increased.[267] After explaining why the continued use of Turbinlite was 'extremely difficult to justify', Douglas then recommended that the 'squadrons should be retained for a further period' to assess 'the true worth of this weapon', although the worth (or lack of it) was already clear. He suggested that if 'such an opportunity does not occur before 1 January 1943, then I am of the opinion that the Turbinlite squadrons should be abolished', which was a significant date.[268] Douglas handed over Fighter Command to Air Marshal Trafford Leigh-Mallory at the end of November 1942 and would not have the responsibility of abandoning a scheme that he had supported for over two years.[269] Ultimately, there were very few nights when it was 'so dark that the average trained night fighter pilot' could not 'obtain a visual of his target once within firing range'. As soon as a target was illuminated, it would break out of the beam 'usually by turning one way and then, when the Havoc had set up the 'wrong' bank, by reversing the turn'.[270] German aircraft would also bank when an AI fighter opened fire, but instead of an innocuous light, damage could be inflicted before the target aircraft took evasive action. On 17 December 1942, the Turbinlite squadrons were finally abolished, due to 'the stringency of the manpower situation' and because 'the development of more effective means of night defence did not justify the continued locking up of considerable resources'. The release of these resources allowed six extra aircraft to be assigned to each of ten AI squadrons for use as 'Intruders' and permitted 'the manning of searchlight boxes by twin-engine aircraft', effectively ending the use of single-engine fighters for night interception in Fighter Command.[271]

The question remains why Douglas persisted with LAMs and Turbinlite despite the clear inadequacies of these systems. The AHB narrative describes the system 'as something of a 'white elephant', while a former pilot is more scathing, saying that it amounted to the 'flogging of dead horses'.[272] It should be noted that Douglas saw his predecessor (Dowding) get sacked for refusing to endanger pilots by using single-engine fighters at night and, because of the aggressive support of Lindemann (and his powerful ally in Churchill), decided that he should perhaps go along with such methods in order to keep his job. Once Douglas knew his time at Fighter Command was coming to an end, Turbinlite could be discontinued without risking his career.

The use of 'impractical schemes' for night defence was not limited to Turbinlite but also extended to the free balloon barrages introduced in 1941, following an initial launch over London on 27 December 1940, code-named 'Pegasus'.[273] Subsequent operations were reclassified as 'Albino', intended to defend cities against night attack 'when weather conditions such as fog make it impossible for our fighters to leave the ground', and 'Petard', against mine laying aircraft in the Thames estuary.[274] 'Albino' was 'maintained in a state of readiness' from September 1941 'on any night with favourable wind conditions' until December 1942.[275] The scale of attacks never justified a release, and over the intervening year, improvements in training and equipment of night fighter squadrons meant they could operate in much poorer weather conditions than when 'Albino' had been introduced. On 24 December, 'Albino' was abolished, despite the objections of the Admiralty, because the possibility of damage to RAF aircraft operating over Europe was considered greater than to *Luftwaffe* bombers, and the 'scheme was using too much manpower'.[276] 'Petard' was at least used operationally with two releases, although these caused more damage on the ground than to attacking aircraft. During March, several balloons fouled power lines on the Isle of Sheppey, leading to power cuts in the area. The remaining unexploded units killed three servicemen and injured three others during salvage operations, while two children died when a unit they picked up exploded.[277] After this last release of 'Petard', the system was abolished on 28 October 1942, allowing the personnel to be redeployed elsewhere in Balloon Command.[278] It should be noted that although he promoted 'Mutton', Lindemann was not a supporter of free balloon barrages and was not responsible for their continued use.

The shortage of anti-aircraft guns during 1942 meant that redeployments during the *Baedeker* period exhausted equipment reserves. The guns were hampered by a shortage of Searchlight Control (SLC) sets, with only a quarter of those required available at the beginning of the year; but of the 4,000 sets needed, by December 1942, 2,715 searchlights had been equipped.[279] Although the searchlight 'Fighter Box' system of fighter control was introduced in November 1941, *Luftwaffe* activity overland during the first three months of 1942 was slight and did not lead to any interceptions.[280] Overall the scheme 'achieved little success throughout the year', as on 80 percent of occasions, 'the system failed to give the fighter aircraft adequate indication of the locality of the target'. Only one aircraft was probably destroyed by fighters during the whole of 1942 using 'Fighter Boxes'.[281]

The interception of German aircraft by fighters continued to be controlled by the radar systems introduced in 1940 and developed in 1941. Overland *Luftwaffe* raiders were tracked, and night fighters were directed by GCI stations, but these 'Mobile' installations could only control one fighter at a time. By the middle of 1942, the first 'Fixed' GCI station was operational, although described as being 'in a somewhat experimental state', and was initially capable of handling two interceptions concurrently, doubling radar efficiency, but it was expected eventually to 'be possible to undertake four interceptions simultaneously'. Although thirty-two 'Fixed' sites were initially planned (to replace a network of forty-one 'Mobile' installations), by the end of 1942, it had been decided to complete only twenty-one of these and provide 'Intermediate' GCI stations at the other locations to replace the original 'Mobile' equipment.[282] Aircraft 'flying a steady course at a reasonable height' over the sea continued to be intercepted under Chain Home Low (CHL) control up to fifty miles from the coast.[283] Identifying aircraft following interception assumed greater importance after 1941 as RAF fighters were more likely to encounter British bombers returning from 'raiding regularly in strength' than *Luftwaffe* aircraft, and a method of avoiding mistakes such as the Stirling bomber being shot down by a Turbinlite was required.[284] During 1940, an Identification Friend or Foe (IFF) system was developed where radar waves triggered a transponder in RAF aircraft, allowing British formations to be discerned.[285] When centimetric radar was introduced, the IFF equipment was not activated by the shorter wavelength, making target verification difficult, but by October, IFF Mark III, which was triggered by centimetric radar, had been successfully developed.[286]

At the start of 1942, operational training was standardised to eliminate the 'undesirable local variation in carrying out the syllabus' across all day fighter OTUs.[287] In contrast, the night fighter training units remained inconsistent in the first half of 1942 as they were still training for different roles, only one of which provided crews for Beaufighter squadrons. As the Defiant was phased out of service during 1942, single-engine training was discontinued, but a shortage of Blenheims prevented expansion of twin-engine training, and it took until the middle of 1942 'before the aircraft supply had improved somewhat' and the night fighter OTUs could be reequipped with operational aircraft (see appendix 7). Two of the OTUs (No. 54 and No. 60) were provided with Beaufighters, with the latter unit finally brought up to full strength, while the third (No. 51 OTU) was allocated Havocs to supply crews for Turbinlite and 'Intruder' squadrons.[288] These three units were now producing more crews than the squadrons could absorb, and No. 60 OTU began to train Beaufighter crews for maritime reconnaissance until it was handed over to Coastal Command in November 1942.[289] Douglas had previously complained that those selected for radar operator training had been of 'too low a standard'. During the first half of 1942, there was 'still concern over the low standard of pupils on their arrival at the Night OTUs', so a Navigator Radio School (No. 62 OTU) was formed at the end of June. This improved the standard of training so much that advanced training on new types of AI was introduced at night fighter training units.[290]

The efficiency of day fighter OTUs continued to increase, but the more complicated training for night fighting required a higher number of units per operational squadron. The complex nature of night training can be illustrated by comparing the annual performance of the OTUs. In 1941, 90 percent of operational training output had been produced for day fighters, with the night fighter organisation only properly established towards the end of the year.[291] With No. 60 OTU not producing twin-engine crews until after March and then progressively switching to Coastal Command training for the majority of the year, to produce nearly 15 percent of total operational training output for night fighters should be considered a significant achievement.[292] Mosquito night fighters were introduced by converting squadrons established on other types onto new equipment, which slowed down the process. During 1941, the number of operational night fighter crews never exceeded the number of serviceable aircraft, and while operational crews exceeded the number of serviceable aircraft for the first four months of 1942, as shown in appendix 6, this surplus only reached a maximum number of twenty-four in March.[293] Figures fluctuated from April to August, which coincided with many squadrons reequipping and non-operational, before the numbers of operational crews increased sharply towards the end of the year, despite several squadrons being posted overseas and their replacements not operationally ready. The number of operational crews available in Turbinlite flights/squadrons and the output from the unit that supplied them would have enabled the AI squadrons to operate with 140 percent more crews than aircraft to match the day fighter squadrons and increased operational efficiency by reducing the number of sorties flown per crew and decreasing combat stress. While numbers of all pilots fell after October 1942 as squadrons were posted overseas in the build-up to the invasion of North Africa, those remaining were still sufficient to deal with any *Luftwaffe* threat in the West, described in German documents as 'an excellently organised night fighter defence system'.[294] Compared to the winter of 1940–1941, there was a much-decreased level of German activity during 1942, so there was a lower casualty rate in Fighter Command, with only forty night fighters lost, which greatly reduced the need for replacements.[295]

By 1942, the changes to training that reduced the course length at Service Flying Training Schools during the pilot supply crisis of 1940 (the "First to Third Revises") had produced unexpected and unwelcome consequences, as described in chapter 2. The reduction in advanced training had been compensated for by a 50 percent increase in operational training course length, but during 1941, 'a progressively-mounting accident rate' was evident, which increased 'sharply as pilots went onto more complex types'.[296] The accident rate increased exponentially throughout the stages of flying training, with the operational training accident rate initially much higher than for actual squadrons.[297] Although the standard of training 'was not materially different from that produced before pilot training was revised in 1940', the accident rate increased 'sharply as pilots went onto more complex types', suggesting that although they were being taught to handle the aircraft, they lacked general flying experience. By 1942, the Service Flying Training School course length had been increased from twelve to fourteen weeks as part of the flying training 'New Deal', with an extra fifteen hours of flying to increase experience before joining an OTU.[298]

The distribution by weight of night bombing for 1942 (figure 4.1) shows that most of the German effort remained close to coastal urban areas. Norwich was the urban target where the most bombs were dropped during the year (196 tonnes), but despite the popular perception of 1942 attacks on cathedral cities, the *Luftwaffe* continued to concentrate on coastal industry and ports.

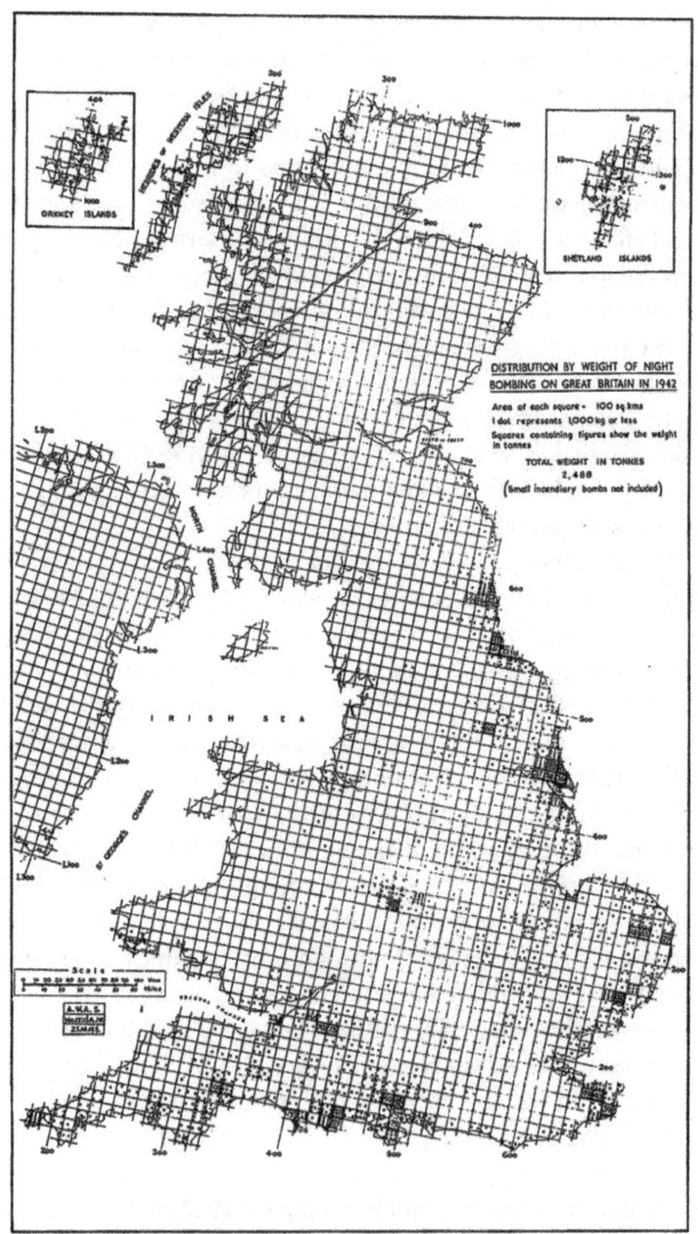

Figure 4.1: Distribution of Night Bombing on the United Kingdom in 1942 (TNA: AIR 41/49; ADGB:V, 66.)

Although the most heavily bombed cities were Norwich, Bath (143 tonnes), Canterbury (109 tonnes) and Exeter (108 tonnes), the most frequently attacked town was Great Yarmouth, which demonstrates the accumulative nature of bombing convenient coastal 'targets of opportunity'. The industrial areas along the north-east (Teesside: 152 tonnes) and east (Humberside: 187 tonnes) coasts were attacked regularly by the *Luftwaffe*, and despite the three significant attacks at the end of July, including the first time one hundred aircraft had operated over the country on a single night since June 1941, only 46 tonnes of bombs were dropped on Birmingham, demonstrating the continuing difficulties of concentration on an inland target. For the first and last three months of the year, overland German bomber activity was minimal, as the *Luftwaffe* sought to conserve resources. The middle portion of the year was characterised by attacks reacting to British bombing strategy, showing the Germans had lost the initiative in the bombing war. The AHB narrative states that apart from Birmingham and *Baedeker*, cities, ports, and coastal towns were the main night targets, but the historiography ignores that this was the basis of *Luftwaffe* strategy for most of 1941 and into 1942. The AHB believed that German successes in Russia and the Mediterranean during 1942 would have led to far heavier attacks against the United Kingdom.[299]

By 1942, the shortage of manpower in the United Kingdom meant that the expansion requirements for the armed forces and essential industries could no longer be fulfilled, leading to large-scale cuts in plans across the services and industry. Air and Civil Defence were subject to severe reductions, and it was accepted that the decrease in air raid provisions was a risk if heavy bombing resumed in the future. The slight reduction in the nominal strength of the night fighter force due to manpower shortages was compensated for by the reequipment of squadrons with newer aircraft and the elimination of unsatisfactory esoteric methods of night defence. These included the Free Balloon Barrages and Cat's Eye fighters, but the greatest waste of resources was the Turbinlite system, which continued long after its ineffectiveness was obvious, mainly for political reasons. The maturity and reliability of the AI/GCI system were undisputed, and centimetric radar proved a success, only limited by lack of equipment. The improvement in night fighting was paralleled by a steady decline in the strength and effectiveness of German attacks, despite the *Baedeker* attacks and raids on Birmingham. These 'maximum effort' attacks caused the interruption of training at *Ergänzungsgruppen* units, as losses rose to 10 percent during some raids.

5

The Night Raids of 1943

JANUARY 1943: LEWISHAM, SOUTH-EAST LONDON

The only significant attacks on the United Kingdom during the first three months of 1943 were against London. Berlin had not been bombed since November 1941, but once Bomber Command resumed attacks, German reprisals were almost inevitable.[1] A night raid on 17–18 January was followed by a daylight incursion on 20 January with fighter-bombers operating at low level. German jamming of British radar systems confused the tracking of this formation and allowed twenty-eight Fw 190s to reach the edge of London at midday.[2] At the same time, part of the balloon barrage closest to the approaching raiders had been grounded for maintenance, and orders to raise the balloons were only given as the raiders reached the inner suburbs. During this time, a 500kg bomb dropped on the Sandhurst Road School in Lewisham demolished the dining room where many children were spending their lunch hour. Forty-four people were killed in this attack—thirty-eight children, many of whom were evacuees who had returned home after an eighteen-month absence of raiding, and six teachers—but the intent of this attack is debatable.[3] Although described as 'mass murder of innocents' in press reports, the practicalities of accurate bombing at low level and high speed within a heavily defended city must be considered, and the press reports concentrated more on the dignified nature of the mass burial reflecting the wishes of the bereaved that the deaths should not be linked to the war.[4]

By 1943, the operational capability of the *Luftwaffe* was severely compromised by a lack of long-term planning, which was considerably exacerbated by the weakness of forces in the west. Raids across the rest of the country during the middle of the year were inserted between politically motivated attacks on London at the beginning and end of 1943, and the importance of these provincial raids has been previously discounted based on miscalculating the number of attacking aircraft. Some of the more significant provincial raids have been analysed to demonstrate changes in effectiveness and tactics. Although fighter-bombers had been used by day against the United Kingdom since 1940, this year saw the first high-level raids at night against inland targets, and 'Intruder' attacks on RAF airfields resumed after eighteen months. While the London raids achieved almost nothing militarily, two of them are worthy of further study, which are the bombing of the Sandhurst Road School and the accident at the Bethnal Green shelter, which provoked controversy and accusations of a cover-up.

By 1943, effective methods of night air defence were well understood, so as squadron numbers fell, equipment quality and training improvements increased combat efficiency, and reorganisation reduced personnel without impacting operations. The pilot output from day Operational Training Units (OTUs) greatly exceeded demand, leading to the closure of some units, but for night squadrons, the formation of an additional training unit became necessary to maintain satisfactory manning levels.

The social circumstances arising from evacuation and bombing damage as the war progressed increased state intervention into everyday life, and the impact of this on the civilian population also needs to be considered. The state felt it was necessary to disassociate this intervention from the social stigma of traditional Poor Relief and was further illustrated by the development of the Emergency Hospital Service (EHS) so that a comprehensive service after the war became inevitable. Post-war reconstruction was seen as an opportunity to redefine urban development, but government action limited the scale of redevelopment.

THE OPERATIONAL CAPABILITY OF THE *LUFTWAFFE* IN THE WEST

On 10 January 1943, the operational bombing capacity of *Luftflotte* 3 was at the lowest since the beginning of the war: with only 122 long-range bombers available, 67 of which were serviceable, the Air Historical Branch (AHB) described the types in service as differing 'little from those employed in 1940 and 1941'.[5] In July 1942, 201 aircraft had been available to *Luftflotte* 3, with 142 serviceable.[6] Losses of instructors and other experienced aircrew during 1942 had deprived units of replacements, while further losses and lack of new aircraft throughout 1943 compounded operational difficulties. From outnumbering the RAF 372 percent in 1940 *Luftwaffe*, bomber strength declined in the west, so by 1943, the expanded RAF Bomber Command contained 360 percent more aircraft than *Luftflotte* 3 did.[7] The British aircraft industry outperformed Germany from the start of the war; and despite doubling resources, German production only increased by 30 percent from 1941.[8] The size of the British aircraft industry meant that in the case of failure, sufficient alternative designs were available. A lack of competence in *Luftwaffe* high command (Göring) and technical development (Udet) meant the German aircraft industry lacked such resilience. This meant the Fw 190 only become operational in 1941, while the Me 210 required a complete redesign, so the obsolescent Bf 110 had to continue in production.[9] German medium bomber designs were marginally improved, but no new types reached combat units by 1943.[10] The protracted development of the He 177 as Bomber 'A', which began in 1937, illustrated all that was wrong with German aircraft development.[11] The obsession of *Generaloberst* Ernst Udet with dive-bombing made it compulsory for all *Luftwaffe* bombers, which even Göring considered unreasonable for a four-engine strategic bomber, although the decision to rescind this requirement would have been more impressive if made earlier than September 1942.[12] This legacy left the aircraft with twin-coupled (two engines driving one propeller) motors to reduce drag, with poor reliability and safety.[13] The nickname of *Luftwaffenfeuerzeug* (*Luftwaffe*'s lighter) leaves the opinion of aircrews in little doubt.[14] In addition to operational hazards, 'when the engines didn't catch fire, the wings came off. Or vice versa. Sometimes only the tail assembly disintegrated'.[15] A redesign using four individual engines was still at the prototype stage when abandoned late in the war.[16] British bomber development, however, was much more comprehensive, with the Halifax and Manchester originally designed using Rolls-Royce Vulture coupled engines, although Handley Page switched to four engines before their prototype was finalised.[17] Avro persevered with the Vulture, and the Manchester was an excellent airframe compromised by its engines, leading to high aircraft losses. Realising the problem, as the Manchester entered service in November 1940, a four-engine prototype was nearing completion. This flew as the Lancaster in January 1941 and was so clearly superior that production was quickly switched over to the new aircraft. By June 1942, within nineteen months of entering service, the Manchester had been completely superseded by the new aircraft.[18] In a similar timeframe to the He 177, the British produced five heavy bomber designs, company designers often making decisions in weeks that took their German counterparts months, of which two remained in service for the rest of the war.

There were few significant operations over the United Kingdom during 1943 other than the renewal of attacks on London, but widespread damage and casualties from sporadic raids continued along the east and south coasts. The capabilities of the *Luftwaffe* failed to live up to Hitler's ambitions for 'non-stop shuttle attacks'.[19] The AHB narrative describes the Mediterranean as 'the graveyard of the *Luftwaffe*', because heavy losses of aircrew and aircraft there led to a serious deterioration in aircrew quality.[20] While such losses were severe, 50 percent of the total *Luftwaffe*, there were other reasons for the decline. Allied successes in North Africa forced the *Luftwaffe* to deploy additional transport aircraft to support the *Afrika Korps*, closely followed by the airlift to supply the Stalingrad pocket. The movement of so many transport aircraft effectively closed all instrument and multiengine training schools.[21] By the end of January 1943. the losses in the Mediterranean and Stalingrad had destroyed a 'prohibitive' 56 percent of the transport force. As the Germans retreated in Tunisia, the only means of supply by April 1943 was from the air, and Murray argues that this 'third slaughter of German transport aircraft' impacted on the entire *Luftwaffe*, as 'all the instructor crews were shot down' during the airlift.[22] Operational losses and fuel shortages forced a reduction in training hours from 1942, which began 'a general shift against the Germans until the last half of the year [1943] when *Luftwaffe* pilots were receiving barely one-half of the training hours given to enemy pilots'.[23] RAF training hours had been increased during 1941, which reduced the accident rate, and as the war went on, the Allies extended the training period for pilots. The absence of a pilot reserve forced the *Luftwaffe* to lower standards to maintain frontline strength compared to the Allied air forces. The fighting in Italy meant 'a large air force in the Mediterranean was of no value', and during the autumn, long-range bomber units were transferred west.[24] German bomber numbers steadily increased throughout 1943, mostly by restricting offensive operations.[25] These larger forces were intended to deliver 'short, heavy and devastating' attacks, which did not begin until January 1944.[26]

The AHB narrative identifies sixty attacks at night on the United Kingdom during the first half of 1943.[27] Just eighteen attacks by more than ten long-range bombers are listed for the whole year, compared to twenty-nine in 1942, twenty of which involved more than twenty tonnes of bombs.[28] Only significant raids have therefore been analysed, unless an attack demonstrated a change in effectiveness and tactics. The only two attacks of more than fifty aircraft were both on London. Collier has described raids over the rest of the wider country during the first three months of 1943 as 'remarkably unsuccessful' and 'utter failures'.[29]

The appointment of *Oberst* Dietrich Peltz as *Angriffsfuehrer England* in March 1943 'to direct the air war against England' was prompted by criticism of the German bombing efforts against the United Kingdom during the latter half of 1942.[30] Hitler and Göring did not understand the 'technical problems of an air force' and interpreted *Luftwaffe* coastal operations 'as a sign of cowardice'.[31] Predictably, Goebbels noted that 'the Fuehrer will in no circumstances let air warfare continue in a slipshod way', and 'that the British terror will be answered by terror from our side'.[32] Peltz formed a new pathfinder unit for target marking to improve accuracy, but it was several months before I/KG66 became operational.[33] The danger from British aircraft prompted a programme of equipping bombers with tail-warning radar, while faster aircraft that could outpace night fighters were added to *Luftflotte* 3. A *Gruppe* was gradually equipped with Messerschmitt Me 410s (the redesigned Me 210), and Fw 190s of SK10 were used for night operations.[34] While the AHB opinion of *Luftwaffe* bombers was low, Price argues that these were 'revitalised', with 'a maximum speed of about 20mph greater', and 'carried additional armour protection'.[35] The Mosquito could exceed 350mph, but the performance of the earlier Beaufighters, which still equipped five squadrons (a quarter of all units), had deteriorated so much that '280 mph at 14,000 feet' was considered 'a tolerable performance for a Beaufighter I' by 1942.[36] Aircraft rarely operated at their outright top speed, unless an intercepting fighter was spotted, so the faster German bombers could therefore outrun older Beaufighters after an unsuccessful stealth approach.

THE RETURN OF THE *LUFTWAFFE* TO LONDON

The only significant attacks on the United Kingdom during the first three months of 1943 were against London. Berlin had not been bombed since November 1941, but Bomber Command resumed attacks in January, so German reprisals started on the night of 17–18 January, the first raid on London for eighteen months.[37] The two January attacks resembled those on Canterbury at the end of October 1942, with one night raid, and the other a day attack by fighter-bombers operating at low level. Unlike Canterbury, there was a two-day delay between raids, due to poor weather and aircraft redeployments to provide sufficient fighters for the day attack.[38]

Most sources agree that over one hundred aircraft took part in a two-phase attack on 17–18 January, many units flying double sorties and *Ergänzungsgruppen* supplementing the shortage of operational crews.[39] German communiqués described the first phase attacking 'WSW of the big bend in the Thames', while aircraft of the second bombed 'targets between Albert Bridge Battersea to Belmont Works'.[40] Estimates of aircraft numbers in each wave ranged between thirty-five and sixty in the first wave (twenty to thirty aircraft reaching their targets) and forty to fifty-eight in the second wave (ten to fifteen reaching target).[41] The Official History notes that as the weather was cloudy, many bombs were dropped short of target, with less than two-fifths within the London Civil Defence Region.[42] O'Brien identified around 45 tonnes of bombs dropped, although German propaganda claimed 128 tonnes and RAF Intelligence records show a total of 95 tons and 299 bombs dropped.[43] Damage was confined to the docks and districts south of the river, causing 'widespread' damage, 'not of a heavy character', with additional damage from anti-aircraft shells. Bombs were also dropped at forty-four places in Kent, twenty-two in Sussex, and four in Surrey.[44] Despite many incendiaries being dropped, most fires were negligible, as half the containers failed to open, suggesting they had been dropped too low, so the incendiaries did not deploy.[45]

Total estimates of aircraft bombing the London region were between thirty and forty-five, but the bomb tonnage gives a more realistic number of fifty-six.[46] Just under half of all bombs dropped fell outside of London, showing the inexperience of many German aircrews. This was the largest raid on London since 10–11 May 1941, and the heaviest attack on the country since Birmingham on 29–30 July 1942, but the damage that was caused most resembled that from the scattered and indecisive London raid on 27–28 July 1941. Although seventy-eight people were initially reported killed, this figure appears too high and needs to be assessed in conjunction with the casualties from the 20 January attack.[47] The approach over Kent gave Fighter Command extra time to intercept raiders, 11 Group patrols being 'increased and maintained throughout the raid'.[48] Against the first wave, Beaufighters of 29 Squadron destroyed a Ju 88 and a Do 217 and damaged two other Do 217s, while a Mosquito of 85 Squadron destroyed an additional Ju 88. The second wave saw 29 Squadron shoot down two more Ju 88s and Do 217s, with a Beaufighter of 141 Squadron damaging another Ju 88. Anti-Aircraft Command also damaged another two aircraft: a Do 217 and a Ju 88.[49]

Although not a night raid, the 20 January attack on London must be considered as part of the renewed offensive against the capital. The low-level fighter-bombers made what Price called 'their most ambitious attack since 1940', with a deep penetration to London from Kent.[50] Other *Luftwaffe* fighters 'made demonstrations off the Kent coast and over the Isle of Wight' to divert Fighter Command attention from the impending attack.[51] Twenty-eight Fw 190 fighter-bombers in two waves headed towards London at midday, while another forty fighters operated east of the Thames estuary to distract RAF fighters and escort the raiders home.[52] Complemented by an extensive jamming of British radar systems, the progress of the London raiders 'was then smoothed by a series of coincidences' that allowed 'a clear run to the target'.[53] The two formations were reported as a single raid, which led to 'confused' tracking as the aircraft crossed Kent.[54] Price estimated that this 'misconception' lasted around six minutes, which allowed the attackers to reach the edge of London.[55] Also, the part of the balloon barrage closest to the approaching raiders had been grounded to prevent interference while radar sets were calibrated.[56] The balloons were only raised as the raiders reached the inner suburbs, warning sirens sounding as the first bombs fell.[57] The AHB estimated 'not more than about twelve aircraft' reached London, the press reported six, and *Luftwaffe* records show twenty-five aircraft dropped bombs.[58] The actual number was confirmed in Bomb Census records as twenty-two bombs dropped.[59] Home Security described damage as generally 'not severe', apart from a big fire that destroyed a warehouse at the Surrey Commercial Docks.[60] Elsewhere, the President's House at the Royal Naval College, Greenwich, was 'accurately bombed', and twelve balloon sites were strafed, including four in Beckenham and Lewisham.[61]

During this raid, a 500kg bomb was dropped on the Sandhurst Road School in Lewisham, demolishing the school dining room.[62] Forty-four people were killed in this attack, with another twenty-six people killed across the southern boroughs of London.[63] Although the press reported three attackers, it is clear that only a single aircraft was involved.[64] Despite pilots usually being briefed 'to attack anything and everything liable to frighten the British public', the intent of this attack is debatable.[65] Ramsey describes how a witness saw a fighter overfly her office, 'at about eye-level' before 'bombs were heard exploding' at Sandhurst Road to the west.[66] A contemporary British map shows two important rail junctions adjacent to Manor Lane, with Hither Green station between them, and Southern Railway lines were targeted at five other points

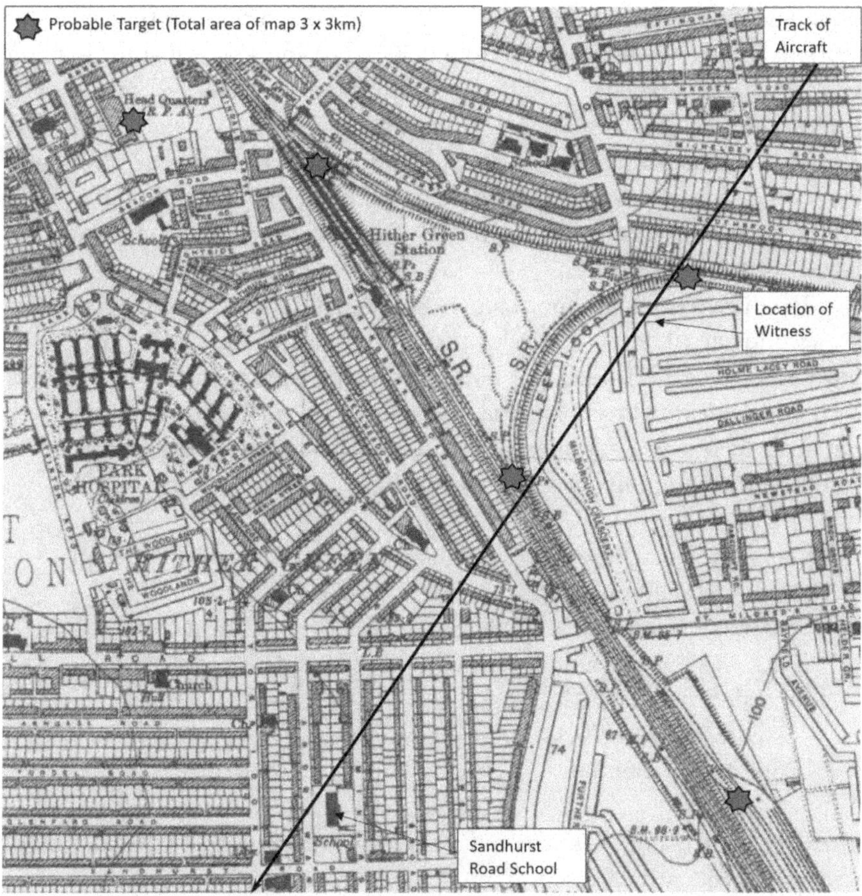

Figure 5.1: Attack on Sandhurst Road School, 20 January 1943 (Adapted from Ordnance Survey, Six-Inch, England and Wales, *London, Sheet P*, reproduced with the permission of the National Library of Scotland.)

during this midday attack.[67] In addition to communications targets, next to Hither Green junction was a Royal Field Artillery (RFA) depot.[68] Any of the railway junctions, the station, or the RFA depot were legitimate targets, but just beyond was the Sandhurst Road School, as shown in figure 5.1. Although described as 'mass murder of innocents' in press reports, the practicalities of accurate bombing at low level and high speed within a heavily defended city must be considered.[69] The *Jabo* attacks were usually coastal, and pilots had no experience of bombing inland targets. To minimise detection and escape interception, they flew at high speed (around 300mph) and so low that the horizon was lost, making navigation difficult travelling at five miles per minute. The ability of these pilots was far lower than the 'elite' ErprGr210, which still managed to bomb the wrong airfield on 15 August 1940.[70] As well as flying fast and low, carrying bombs reduced operational range, giving little time for target selection. The aircraft was flying towards the west, out of London, suggesting it had not found a target.

The distance from Manor Lane to Sandhurst Road is around a half mile, six seconds at 300mph. The pilot may have released the bomb late due to inexperience or jettisoned the bomb to escape the target area before the arrival of British fighters. It is possible the school was deliberately targeted, but other factors present make this unlikely. The unit combat report lists the results of the bombing:

> Very good grouping of hits in blocks of flats and crowds of people, violent detonations.
>
> Busy streets, obviously there was no air raid warning before the attack. High losses amongst the civilian population probable.
>
> Effect on alternative target:
>
> Direct hits in blocks of flats in the eastern part of town. Collapse of buildings observed.[71]

This 'alternative target' was almost certainly the Sandhurst Road School and was misidentified as residential accommodation. While the raid was intended to cause civilian casualties, there is no evidence that children were deliberately targeted, and the pilot may have altered course to avoid bombing the hospital next to the train depot. Thirteen Fighter Command squadrons scrambled a total of 214 fighters during this attack, but combats took place 'mainly over the Channel'.[72] Although the RAF claimed seventeen aircraft shot down, German records confirm that only nine were lost.[73] The casualties from these daylight attacks were initially reported as 70 killed, but as only a combined total of 107 killed and 158 seriously injured for the two raids is recorded officially, the preliminary figures for each day were certainly too high.[74] This attack prompted 'a thorough-going investigation into the system of raid reporting'.[75] The AHB narrative notes that 'the tardiness of the ground defences' gave rise 'to some uneasiness amongst the civil population', and comments in reports from police forces across the country ranged from 'considerable consternation' at 'the absence of balloons' to 'the reported ineffective state of the balloon barrage and the air raid warning have caused some consternation', people considering that 'the authorities have grown rather apathetic towards the dangers of daylight raids in inland areas'.[76] An enquiry concluded that a system was required to immediately notify Air Raid Warning and Balloon Control as soon as jamming began.[77]

The press reports following the Sandhurst Road School bombing concentrated more on the dignified nature of the mass burial, reflecting the wishes of the bereaved that the deaths should not be linked to the war, with the correct 'vengeance' to ensure 'that never again should this curse of war fall on the world'.[78] The use of common graves had been promoted earlier in the war predominantly to avoid a public health crisis.[79] By June 1942, the Ministry of Health was advising that 'private burials add to labour "difficulties"', but the unpopularity of mass burials stemmed from a previous association with 'pauper graves', a legacy of the Poor Law and the Workhouse.[80] Funerals were 'nationalised' to save resources, and local authorities emphasised those provided free of charge for bombing victims were in no way connected to those required under public health legislation. 'Civic dignitaries' would attend, with 'proper reverence and respect', to symbolically remove the social stigma of local authority burials.[81] Although most of the Sandhurst Road victims were buried in a mass grave, less than three months later, the relatives of the Bethnal Green accident fatalities received grants for private funerals.[82]

As mentioned earlier, many of the children killed at Sandhurst Road were evacuees who had returned home after an eighteen-month absence of raiding. Evacuation had highlighted the medical problems of working-class children, and Süss describes how younger doctors were 'blunt in their criticisms' of the health of children arriving at evacuation destinations, with many suffering 'infectious and skin diseases'.[83] Calder argues that social circumstances led to the poor health of evacuated children, and prompted by 'official fears of epidemics', seven million children were vaccinated against diphtheria free of charge between 1940–1945, leading to a 'startling decline in the number of deaths' from the disease, improving the health of British children during the war.[84] The heavy bombing during the winter of 1940–1941 hit working-class areas hardest and made thousands homeless. Limited payments were available for emergency accommodation, but these were not sufficient after heavy attacks.[85] Poor Law provision was only intended as emergency aid, Süss stating it was intended that survivors would be accommodated by the wider community so that 'the neighbourhood itself would solve some of the basic problems created by the air war'.[86] The government considered that compensation for the homeless was something that would have to wait until after the war, when 'the estimated cost reached frightening proportions'. The continuation of bombing led to reimbursement of costs to replace furnishings and clothing. The War Damage Act 1941 then entitled all affected by bombing to make a claim for free compensation irrespective of income and social status.[87] Costs of accommodation for the homeless were the responsibility of the Ministry of Health, which treated them as tenants paying 'an appropriate rate'.[88] The social stigma of paupers being forced into the Workhouse had only ended less than a generation earlier, so all payments were stressed as not being traditional Poor Relief.[89]

The next attack on London was on 3–4 March, when 'the *Luftwaffe* plumbed new depths of inefficiency' according to the Official History, because, out of one hundred tons of HE, 'only twelve tons hit the mark'.[90] This was 'another reprisal for a British raid on Berlin two nights before', described by the AHB as 'even less successful than the attack of 17/18 January'. The *Luftwaffe* claimed that 117 aircraft took part, in three waves, suggesting multiple sorties were made by crews to compensate for a shortage of aircraft.[91] RAF Intelligence estimated that 65 aircraft operated, dropping eighty tonnes of bombs for a total of 433 individual bombs.[92] The Air Ministry Commentary only identified two phases to this attack, 10 of the first wave of 35 aircraft reaching London, while 'few' of the second wave of 30 got as far as the southern suburbs.[93] Widespread 'raiding was not of a heavy nature', with four railway targets attacked, 'but the effect on essential traffic was slight', and many aircraft failed to reach London at all: 55 bombs falling within Essex, 27 in Kent, and 25 across the south-east.[94] Casualties from bombing were relatively small, but this raid was 'indirectly responsible for a massive loss of life', when 173 people were crushed to death at the Bethnal Green shelter after a woman tripped on the entrance stairs and others, falling quickly, blocked the passageway.[95] This was the largest single British civilian fatal incident during the Second World War, although enemy action also caused large losses of life in shelters, such as the bombing of the Wilkinson shelter in May 1941 at North Shields. No bombs were dropped on Bethnal Green borough during this raid, and the causes of this accident have been sensationalised or ignored within the historiography, as since April 1943, when the inquiry report was classified, there have been claims that the Bethnal Green accident was suppressed.[96] Journalists have reiterated accusations of 'cover up and rumour', claiming that details 'remain unclear', that the accident 'was kept secret for years', and there was 'panic' as 'the Tube station descended into pandemonium'.[97] The publication of a book that portrays Bethnal Green Council as a hapless victim has sustained these misinterpretations, claiming they 'repeatedly tried . . . to make safe the access to the shelter', despite 'complacency and neglect' by the government.[98] Fountain contends the 'report was suppressed and glossed over' because 'local officials' had 'wanted to insert a crush barrier at the mouth of the shelter', and he maintains that 'Bethnal Green was the victim of collusion by servants of the crown' who ignored a 'sensible and well-founded recommendation to make safe the entrance to the staircase'.[99]

Press accounts first appeared on 5 March, thirty-six hours after the incident, accurately reporting that the fall of a woman had blocked a poorly lit stairwell, with 'no sign of panic before the accident'. The lack of a handrail down the centre of the stairs was highlighted and that 'the heavy barrage' caused 'a rush of people to the shelter'. The only pertinent fact withheld was the actual location, this being described as 'a London tube shelter'.[100] Elsewhere in the press, it was already being asked 'whether or not it would be wise to fit the entrances of all large shelters with crush barriers', and the incident was concurrently reported widely across the country.[101] The initial meeting at Bethnal Green Town Hall on 4 March mentioned 'panic' at the entrance stairs for the first time. Seven buses had stopped at the entrance just as the alert sounded, causing 'congestion' to a population made 'nervy' by RAF raids on Berlin and an unfamiliar anti-aircraft barrage. A Civil Defence report contains a drawing showing the location of casualties on the staircase, confirming all fatalities were confined to the bottom thirteen of the first flight of stairs. Unlike the Tube stations in central London, Bethnal Green was not part of the active transport network. Although the structure below ground was in place, the start of the war prevented further work, so it had not been fitted out for use.[102] On 8 March, the *Daily Herald* reported corrugated iron 'umbrellas' over the entrances at Piccadilly Circus tube station, so 'better lighting can be given to the steps leading down to the main hall of the station'.[103] At Bethnal Green, a 'rush-breaker' had already been installed to 'compel people to enter slowly from each side' before entering the staircase.[104] All of this information was passed by the Censor, with only the exact location of the accident still being withheld from the public. On 12 March,

Home Security began to examine the entrances of large public shelters in their regions, without informing local authorities.[105] Originally people were expected to be able to take shelter within seven minutes, but during the Blitz, many people spent all the 'blackout time' underground, so 'the width of the entrances became of less moment'. By 1943, in 'the absence of continuous raiding', people only used shelters during the alert period, so that 'adequate means of control' at entrances was again important, and Home Security suggested that entrances could be closed by pulling gates across 'a stout central pillar' 'in case of any trouble'.[106]

The press was excluded from the public inquiry, and the secretary appointed by Home Security to assist Laurence Dunne, the selected magistrate, prepared a briefing that documented 'the absence of a crush barrier to give a "straight run in"' for the first time.[107] The inquiry ended on 17 March, Dunne concluding that a crowd surge following the discharge of anti-aircraft rockets pushed people down the stairs, leading to the fall and subsequent crush. The only reference to 'panic' was during the aftermath when the crowd 'outside the shelter were out of hand and frantic with nervousness, confusion and worry'.[108] Dunne noted the reduction in manpower available to the police since 1941, as a permanent post at the entrance was no longer possible. Manpower shortages had also 'very adversely affected' Civil Defence 'both in its quality and quantity' to an extent 'that efficiency is seriously affected'.[109] The large population of Bethnal Green meant that people had 'a marked preference for this type of shelter' and regarded it 'as a desirable haven' when it 'might prove to be a heavy raid'. Large numbers of children had recently returned to the area, which parents wanted to get underground quickly, but their presence 'retarded the speed of intake into the shelter, and the speed at which people could reach it'. The single entrance to the shelter was 'very exceptional in relation to its size', with the other two sealed off. Dunne considered that the dim lighting had 'increased the chance of a fall on the stairs' but believed the absence of a crush barrier 'as the main structural defect at the time of the accident', and that the 'main and proximate cause was a sudden rush for the entrance by 350-400 people'.[110]

The Dunne report put Herbert Morrison in a difficult position, having previously committed to publishing the findings. In a memorandum to the War Cabinet, he explained such conclusions could prompt 'the enemy to make further raids on London', where 'there are many tube shelters with restricted means of entrance, in the hope of creating a disproportionate disturbance'. Although not documented, the references to manpower shortages were also significant 'security considerations'.[111] The War Cabinet considered that dissatisfaction following the inquiry being held in private meant that if conclusions were not published, 'it would be generally assumed that there was something to hide'.

A claim for negligence against Bethnal Green Council that had been issued in March 1943 eventually reached the High Court in July 1944. This found for the plaintiff and against Bethnal Green, which identified the location of the accident for the first time. The 'negligence relied on being that the defendants failed to provide a safe and proper entry to the shelter: that the staircase was dangerous in that the steps were uneven and worn: that there was no handrail in the middle of the stairway: that the light was insufficient'. The crush was caused 'by some one, or more than one, tripping or slipping on the unsafe steps, which took place before the firing of guns, nor was there anything in the nature of rushing and surging'. As there was no one on duty at the entrance, 'those entering did not know that an accident had taken place and continued to hurry forward'. 'The defendants had been in occupation of the shelter for 2½ years and nothing had been done to the unfinished steps. After the accident changes were made to the steps and the lighting, and central handrails were put in'.[112]

Fountain insists that if Bethnal Green Council 'had been set free from the steel claw of the official secrets act' they could have argued that they 'had been assiduous in trying to make safe the access to the shelter'.[113] This comment refers to parts of the Dunne report acknowledging Bethnal Green Council had attempted to improve the shelter entrance back in August 1941.[114] A review of all surviving documentation, however, does not show the actions of the council quite so favourably. The council proposed improvements to the entrance costing £88.8.9d at the same time they were attempting to obtain funds of £110.18.10d for a library in the shelter.[115] By September 1941, the shelter building programme had been drastically reduced, and Bethnal Green probably damaged the credibility of their proposals by prioritising a library. With responsibility for the shelter split between three public organisations, agreement on any improvements was bound to be difficult, especially since the London Passenger Transport Board were concerned about liability for injuries at Bethnal Green and had requested 'a letter from the London Civil Defence Headquarters absolving the Board from any responsibility arising through the use of these tunnels as shelters'.[116] Although a roof was added to shield the stairs, and the entrance and gates were strengthened with timber, these 'improvements' were solutions to the wrong problems, not to regulate the flow of people into the shelter but to reinforce the entrance so that it would not collapse when closed off once the shelter was full.[117] The work carried out after the accident demonstrates how circumstances had changed since Winter 1940–1941, with a brick surface shelter incorporating a temporary corrugated baffle, together with improved lighting, escalators made operational, handrail improvements, and rendering risers and treads of steps with concrete.[118]

Despite the High Court judgement and witnesses at the Dunne Inquiry rejecting panic as a cause, the Official History still describes the accident as 'a grim reminder of the conditions which could ensure if people lost self-control in an air raid', and events in London during late 2017 suggest that people under threat are still suspected of panic.[119] After reports of shots being fired in the Tube station, police reported that 'passengers fled in to Oxford Circus and Regent Street causing "significant panic"'.[120] Psychologists have demonstrated that despite what 'was widely described as "panic"'. there is 'evidence to suggest people fleeing an alert are entirely reasonable'. Describing such actions as 'panic' implies 'that they are acting irrationally, excessively, and even selfishly', but this 'concerns the apparently emotional and uncontrolled actions of a few members of the public', and 'the exception all too easily becomes the rule'. Research into the 7 July 2005 London bombings and other emergencies show that 'words such as "panic" started to be used even though the actions of many other people suggested a very different picture', and while people on Oxford Street were 'running, and many looked scared and upset', their behaviour was 'largely proportionate' and were 'often helping those who are slowest'. Research has shown that where crowds have a shared group identity, they are more likely to help others and are 'less likely to push and shove at potential bottlenecks, such as the bottom of escalators, and they generally got out more quickly'.[121]

Reports of crowds being 'out of hand' at Bethnal Green were after the accident, when people in the crowd may have been looking for relatives. From the width of the steps, it can be calculated that once the stairs were blocked, it would have taken less than seven seconds for the entrance to be completely full, so the whole accident would have been over in ten seconds, which agrees with witness reports. Although a crush barrier would not have prevented the initial fall, it could have mitigated the casualty figures. The operation of the shelter had changed since the 1940–1941 Blitz, as the different tactics used by the *Luftwaffe* in January 1943 gave very little time for people to take cover. The Dunne Inquiry makes it clear that the potential risks were never properly considered. A modern risk assessment requires answers to the questions: What can go wrong? What is the likelihood that it will go wrong? What are the consequences?[122] At no stage were the relevant questions asked about Bethnal Green, the council being convinced the risk was a collapse of the entrance if a crowd tried to get into the shelter when it was full. The crush barrier that was noted as being under construction on 8 March was never considered by either the council or London Civil Defence, and there is no evidence of the council 'having conscientiously striven to make the staircase safer'; the request for library facilities weakened their argument, although a lack of consensus between the three responsible authorities did not help.[123] Spending on civil defence decreased starting with cutbacks to the shelter building programme in 1941. By 1943, proposals to withdraw 225,000 men from the building industry meant that intended repairs on 60 percent of remaining bomb-damaged houses were being reconsidered.[124] Crowd control and shelter organisation declined in a country fighting a war that was running out of money and manpower. It is unclear how much the unfinished shelter steps at Bethnal Green had deteriorated since the shelter had opened in October 1940, but they were considered bad enough to be rendered straight after the accident.

Outside of Bethnal Green, many casualties were caused by large numbers of SD-2 anti-personnel bombs, reflected by the low overall bomb tonnage. A delayed-action, hypersensitive fuse was used for the first time, which led to three fatalities as Bomb Disposal Units removed these devices.[125] Fighter Command despatched fifty-four Aircraft Interception (AI) fighters against the attackers, but a 'belt of 10/10ths cloud at 2/3000 ft' hampered operations. A Do 217 and a Ju 88 were shot down by Beaufighters of 29 Squadron, and two other aircraft destroyed by anti-aircraft guns.[126]

Night raids by *Schnellkampfgeschwader*10 began in April 1943, the Fw 190 day fighter-bomber units being amalgamated into SKG10 that month without any additional training. Climbing to 20,000ft before crossing the coast, they were directed by radio before bombing at height and high speed, with minimal accuracy. Although radio direction made these raids susceptible to attacks by AI fighters, the 'high speed and violent evasive action' of the Fw 190 made interception challenging.[127] The *Luftwaffe* was unaware of the disarray the daylight *Jabo* raids were causing and, 'to the incredulity of many of their experienced pilots', decided to switch SKG10 exclusively to night attacks.[128] From the start of the raids on 16–17 April, many of the attacking aircraft failed to find a target as large as the city of London, achieving 'remarkably little success' in what Price has described as a 'fiasco'.[129] With 'navigation so hopelessly at fault' that only two bombs were dropped within the London area, four Fw 190s landed in error at or near West Malling airfield in Kent.[130] As daylight *Jabo* operations were discontinued once night attacks began, the RAF mistakenly attributed this to limited resources, an example of both sides drawing the wrong conclusions about the use of fighter-bombers.[131] By June 1943, both day and night fighter-bomber operations had ceased, as the German surrender in North Africa meant the aircraft were required as reinforcements to the Mediterranean. The *Luftwaffe* had believed night operations would reduce operational losses, but advances in AI radar and superior British aircraft led to high German losses, a *Staffel Kapitan* of SKG10 commenting that the 'type of aircraft was neither designated for this type of mission nor was it suitable for this task'.[132]

THE SWITCH BACK TO COASTAL OPERATIONS

Although German long-range bomber activity decreased during April, the effectiveness of *Luftwaffe* attacks improved. 'Massed air attacks, chiefly against targets close to the coast' were now intended, but only with 'a good likelihood of success', allowing the time between operations to improve 'the efficiency of aircrews' by additional training 'especially in navigation and bombing'.[133] *Luftflotte* 3 records note that operations were dictated by weather that 'showed a typical April character' that only improved from 'the middle of the month'.[134] The first, at Chelmsford on 14–15 April, is not acknowledged by some sources, although the number of aircraft involved and tonnage dropped confirm that it should.[135] Although Ramsey suggests that ninety-one sorties were flown against the target, contemporary records document these as between twenty and thirty aircraft.[136] German communiqués admit to sixteen Ju 88s carrying out the attack, but claims of seventy-seven tons of bombs appear unlikely.[137] As thirty-five tonnes of bombs were dropped, with only nine tonnes falling within the borough, the British records appear to be accurate.[138] Despite 'considerable' property damage, there were no fatalities and only eight people seriously injured, with slight damage at a ball bearing works and a radio equipment factory.[139] Four aircraft were claimed as destroyed, but since four of the five shot down were Do 217s, clearly more aircraft were operating than declared.[140] Two nights later, the first of the raids by night using Fw 190s as fighter-bombers was attempted, described by the AHB as 'a fiasco'.[141]

Different 'unusual tactics paid much better a few nights later', when thirty aircraft deployed to Norway and made a low-level dusk attack against Aberdeen on 21–22 April.[142] Contemporary British sources underestimated the numbers of bombing aircraft, ranging from 'a few' by Home Security to twenty by the 14 Group Operations Record Book, but since fifty-one tonnes of bombs were dropped, this appears unduly pessimistic.[143] Aircraft attacked the residential district in the north-west of the city, half bombing from below 500 feet. Nine bombs fell around the London and North Eastern Railway station, blocking both passenger and goods lines, requiring two hundred men to restore services the following day.[144] Other significant damage was done to the Gordon Barracks, where twenty-seven servicemen were killed.[145] Despite the Bomb Census insisting that 'the town was not affected seriously by the raid', ninety-one people were killed and ninety-four seriously injured. Building damage was also extensive, with 171 houses wrecked, 736 seriously damaged, and 5,798 slightly damaged.[146] Although aircraft from Peterhead attempted to intercept, these 'Cat's Eye' fighters unsurprisingly failed, the nearest AI fighters being based at Ayr, 150 miles away.[147] A post-war account by a *Luftwaffe Bordfunker* (radio operator) who flew on this raid confirms that aircraft of KG2 flew to Norway, and because of the extreme range only 2,000kg of bombs were carried by each of the thirty aircraft despatched.[148]

Despite 'a lavish use of flares' during raids in May, the Official History notes 'only a small improvement' in accuracy, but there was 'heavier enemy activity' from the middle of the month.[149] Chelmsford was bombed on 13–14 May, although estimates by Ramsey of eighty-five aircraft and the use of Fw 190 fighter-bombers cannot be substantiated.[150] Conversely, the sixteen aircraft documented as operating are mathematically incompatible with the seventy-four tonnes of bombs dropped.[151] A low-level approach was again used, and the 'strong evasive action' employed by the *Luftwaffe* made aircraft less likely to be detected by British Chain Home (CH) and Chain Home Low (CHL) radars.[152] With the ground radar network only able to track and control one interception at a time, for many raids in 1943 the numbers of attacking aircraft were undoubtedly underestimated, and extrapolation from bomb tonnage provides a more realistic estimate of around thirty aircraft. 11 Group estimated thirty aircraft operating, although Bomb Census records describe this number as 'friendly and enemy mixed' and that fifteen attacked Chelmsford, with twenty-one tonnes of bombs recorded.[153] The main telephone exchange and a bus station were seriously damaged, with twenty-six buses destroyed, which were significant losses due to the lack of private motor transport during the war.[154] Unlike in April, 'serious damage occurred' at the Marconi radio factory, which stopped production for weeks.[155] The overspill of bombs into residential areas killed forty-four people and seriously injured forty-five.[156] Bombing was scattered, as only seventeen out of the seventy-four tons dropped fell within the Chelmsford area. Around thirty tons were spread across Suffolk, with only the three bombs dropped at Ipswich considered to be a 'definite attack', other bombs causing 'little damage'.[157] The only documented success for AI fighters was a Do 217 shot down by a Mosquito of 157 Squadron.[158] Another Do 217 was shot down by anti-aircraft guns, while a Ju 88 made a forced landing near Bury St Edmonds.[159]

Two nights later, the *Luftwaffe* attempted a double attack on the east coast, the first using low-level fighter-bombers at night. Bombing by fighters had been developed by *Erprobungsgruppe* 210 during the Battle of Britain, the accuracy of their attacks described by Mason as 'extraordinary', and the success of single-engine *Jabos* influenced future tactics on both sides.[160] Despite forty aircraft operating, only fifteen were reported overland, with fourteen bombs dropped simultaneously between Felixstowe and Southwold, some thirty miles apart, and the only significance of this raid was the tactics used.[161] As the attacking aircraft were 'at zero feet', no advance interceptions were possible, only a chance combat by two Spitfires of 317 Squadron damaged two Fw 190s, with anti-aircraft guns claiming one shot down.[162]

On the same night the *Luftwaffe* carried out the first of two raids in eight days at Sunderland, a town described by the AHB narrative that 'the Germans had persistently attempted to destroy for the past eighteen months'.[163] Although the Air Ministry Commentary states this attack on 16 May was carried out by ten aircraft, the tonnage dropped and damage caused make this questionable.[164] It is unlikely that forty-three tons of bombs were carried by so few aircraft, especially to a target across the North Sea, where bomb-load was reduced to increase range. The RAF investigation team reported that because 'of the amount of HE bombs dropped in the area, this figure appears to be too low'.[165] The Ministry of Home Security described this as 'a small scale attack' but mentions that 'a relatively large number of HE and IB caused considerable damage'.[166] These started thirty-nine fires, including two major ones, with two hundred houses wrecked, and blocked the main line at Sunderland station.[167] Seven industrial plants were damaged, but 'nothing, however, of a major character', while further down the coast, property was damaged at Seaham.[168] An Anti-Aircraft officer estimated that eighteen plus aircraft attacked, while determination from bomb tonnage gives the number at twenty-five.[169] Casualties were heavy, with sixty-eight people killed and seventy-four seriously injured in Sunderland, and thirty-three and forty-one correspondingly at Seaham.[170] Three Do 217s were claimed as destroyed, one by a Beaufighter of 604 Squadron and two by the Tyne anti-aircraft guns. Eleven AI fighters reported six visuals, of which two were identified as a Lancaster and Messerschmitt Bf 110 respectively, suggesting inconsistent aircraft recognition.[171]

On 16–17 May, Bomber Command carried out the attacks widely remembered as the 'Dambusters raid'.[172] With British propaganda exploiting the value of the operation, it was unsurprising there was a reprisal raid on Cardiff the following night, crews being urged 'to do their utmost' to reach the target.[173] Although the Air Ministry Commentary estimated ten and Bomb Census records forty aircraft, the RAF Intelligence figure of twenty-five aircraft dropping forty-six bombs appears most realistic, the attackers approaching from the south over Devon and the Bristol Channel.[174] This was the first time I/KG66 operated in the pathfinder role, which would continue until early July.[175] Aircraft flew very low until well over the coast before climbing to begin bombing, concentrating on dock and railway installations.[176] The Great Western Railway network was interrupted at five points, and only one platform remained operational at the central station.[177] Diversions for the expected trains presented 'no operational difficulty', and lines were cleared by morning.[178] While Cardiff was attacked, bombs were also dropped in thirty-five other places, including London, without major damage occurring.[179] Forty-three people were killed and fifty seriously injured at Cardiff; in London, these were eleven and sixteen respectively.[180] The 'low height made fighter action difficult', and only a single Ju 88 was shot down by a Mosquito of 151 Squadron, although anti-aircraft guns destroyed or damaged another three aircraft.[181]

The next attack on Sunderland was on 23–24 May, with estimates as low as nine aircraft, but with most bombing at low level, this is again wrong; as calculated from the ninety-two bombs on the Bomb Census, the tonnage indicates the number as twenty-one.[182] There was 'widespread damage' across the docks, industrial and residential property, which 'although extensive . . . was not serious'.[183] Eighty-three people were killed and 109 seriously injured, but while Home Security insisted 'the morale of the people was reported as excellent', another report highlighted the absence of personnel from work 'was responsible for reduced output on the day following the raid'.[184] The Bomb Census noted that 'Sunderland has no balloon barrage and the public appear to be disgruntled at the lack of defence'.[185] Ten other places along the coast were also attacked, with significant damage only at South Shields where 26 people were killed and 32 seriously injured.[186] Thirteen AI fighters operated, five contacts resulting in two combats where a Do 217 was shot down and a Ju 88 damaged by Beaufighters of 409 Squadron, while anti-aircraft guns shot down a Ju 88.[187]

The *Luftwaffe* would not achieve this level of operations again for the rest of 1943. Over ten nights, 141 aircraft were despatched and 208 tons of bombs dropped, the most serious damage being at Sunderland, where 'two moderately heavy nights attacks' killed 153 people and seriously injured 191, causing 56 percent of all fatalities in the town for the entire war.[188] The Official History was not convinced by the reintroduction of pathfinders, noting 'only a small improvement' in bombing performance.[189] On 23–24 May, Bomber Command despatched 826 aircraft to Dortmund, losing 38, which was more than bombed Sunderland on the same night, with the 15 aircraft lost by the *Luftwaffe* during this period representing an unsustainable 11 percent of the force.[190]

During 1942 RAF night fighters consistently overclaimed the number of German aircraft destroyed, but by the late July attacks the number claimed versus losses were much more realistic (see table 3.1). As table 5.1 shows, for the five attacks over ten days in May 1943, *Luftwaffe* losses exceeded the number claimed by the British, although aircraft recognition was still challenging.[191] Collier observed that improved British defences meant that 'German bomber crews led a precarious existence', the average life of a crew 'somewhere between thirteen and eighteen sorties', and were not considered experienced until a third of operations were completed.[192] Post-war, a *Luftwaffe Bordfunker* recalled that aircrew were awarded Iron Cross First-Class after 12 sorties, compared to 120 on the Eastern Front, as after each attack 'our lines were thinned by fifty percent', and 'many of my comrades never got their crosses'.[193]

TABLE 5.1
Comparison of RAF Claims Against *Luftwaffe* Losses, 14–24 May 1943

		Fighter Command		*Luftwaffe*		% Claims vs. Losses	
Date	**Target**	**Dest**	**Dam**	**Missing#**	**Dam**	**Dest**	**Total**
13–14/5/43	Chelmsford	2	—	4	—	50	50
15–16/5/43	Felixstowe	1	2	2	—	50	150
	Sunderland	3	—	1	1	300	150
17–18/5/43	Cardiff	3	1	5	—	60	80
23–24/5/43	Sunderland	2	1	3	—	67	100

Includes aircraft destroyed in crash landings.
Compiled from IWM: MCR 18: GAF Losses, Reel 17; and TNA: AIR 16/889.

Coastal attacks continued in June, with Plymouth on the south coast raided first on 12–13, by forty aircraft, although this Intelligence estimate is generous for the thirty tons dropped.[194] Damage was widespread across the city and in the dockyard, and there was severe damage adjacent to the main-line railway.[195] The Chief Constable described bombing as 'indiscriminate in character but some effort was apparently made to dislocate railway traffic', one hundred houses being wrecked and six hundred seriously damaged, killing fourteen people and seriously injuring thirty-six, but all rail services had been restored by 14 June.[196] The Beaufighters of 125 Squadron claimed two Do 217s destroyed and one damaged; and also two Ju 88s destroyed and one probable, the Plymouth anti-aircraft guns shooting down another aircraft.[197] The other attacks of note in June took place on either side of the Humber ten days apart using completely different tactics. On 13–14 June, twenty-five aircraft attacked Grimsby and Cleethorpes with a large number of incendiary and anti-personnel bombs.[198] Only eight tons were dropped, including twenty-one HE bombs, with 'considerable' fire damage at Grimsby docks and to residential properties of Cleethorpes, while operation of both the docks depot and the London and North Eastern Railway line between Grimsby and Cleethorpes was suspended due to unexploded anti-personnel bombs.[199] The AHB estimated six tons of 2kg SD-2 bombs were dropped, known as 'butterfly bombs' due to the stabilising wings used for landing, which caused them to explode if subsequently disturbed.[200] Although rarely deployed, these weapons 'had given the British defences a good deal of concern', prompting warnings to be circulated throughout Civil Defence and the national press.[201] The AHB thought the use of delayed action SD-2s was to interfere with post-raid firefighting, but since none was dropped near incendiary fires, either this was not planned or aiming was inaccurate.[202] Out of sixty-one fatalities, fifty-seven were due to SD-2 bombs, while eighty people were seriously injured from all causes, and 'the bombs continued to be a nuisance and a menace for a week'.[203] Fire damage at Cleethorpes killed fourteen people and seriously injured eight, but none of these was attributed to anti-personnel weapons.[204] Bomb Census records document that rumours were circulating in Hull 'on the morning following the Grimsby raid' about the Germans dropping anti-personnel bombs shaped like 'fountain pens, compacts, cigarette lighters, soap and scent bottles', coloured pink.[205] Fighter Command did not intercept any of the raiders, with only one aircraft damaged by the Humber anti-aircraft guns.[206]

New *Luftwaffe* tactics began on the night of 17–18 June, a German communiqué announcing 'the first operation by 12 Me 410s on Portsmouth'.[207] Home Security noted 'some damage to houses; civilian casualties were three fatal and four serious', while a naval shore establishment suffered 75 casualties, with no damage of military importance.[208] Despite German propaganda, RAF Intelligence showed only ten aircraft overland that night, with two in the Portsmouth area.[209] Hull was then attacked on 23–24 June by fifteen aircraft dropping fifteen tons of incendiary and HE bombs.[210] *Luftflotte* 3 records indicate that for 'the whole of June the weather was designated as unfavourable', so this raid was mounted due to 'favourable short-term weather conditions with stronger forces', which were significantly smaller than those used against Plymouth on 12–13 and Grimsby/Cleethorpes on 13–14 June.[211] Damage was confined to shopping and residential areas, with no disruption to railway communications.[212] Fifty-five houses were wrecked and 49 seriously damaged, with 25 people killed and 13 seriously injured.[213] Although seventeen AI fighters were deployed, there were no engagements by Fighter Command aircraft.[214] The fatalities from this raid took the deaths from bombing in Hull above 1,100, which would eventually reach 1,156.[215] Graystone describes the pattern of the bombing on Hull during the War as differing 'markedly from that of other heavily bombed cities', due to bombing 'when for much of the country the danger seemed past'.[216] This situation applied all along the east coast, from Lowestoft in the south up to Tyneside. By considering all of the urban areas along the Tyne and Wear rivers, the pattern of activity is very similar to that of Humberside, over an equivalent bombing area, with a total of 1,100 people killed in the Tyneside/Wearside area, the majority after May 1941, and gives a comparable total to Humberside, demonstrating that the effect of these attacks have been underestimated, although 2,827 houses were destroyed, significantly less than the 4,415 at Humberside.[217]

In July, only two attacks of consequence took place again on either side of the Humber estuary, around twenty-five aircraft operating on consecutive nights using conventional tactics, with dock areas and railway communications targeted in both raids.[218] *Luftflotte 3* noted that 'unfavourable weather conditions' limited 'fighting ability', so 'heavy attacks were only possible on three nights'.[219] Both Grimsby and Cleethorpes were attacked on 12–13 July, thirty-four of thirty-seven aircraft despatched reaching the target, with 'considerable damage' to the town, which missed the dock area.[220] The London and North Eastern Railway line at Grimsby was interrupted in several places, but all services had been restored by the following day.[221] There were 280 houses wrecked at Grimsby and 31 at Cleethorpes, with 250 and 150, respectively, seriously damaged.[222] Casualties were significant, with forty-five killed and ninety-eight serious injuries at Grimsby; at Cleethorpes these were nineteen and five respectively.[223] Fifteen AI fighters operated, and a Mosquito of 410 Squadron shot down a Do 217.[224] Although no aircraft were shot down north of the Humber, the Bomb Census reported 'considerable anti-aircraft fire' during this attack, with a 'deep sense of satisfaction at the intensity and promptness' of the response compared to the June raids, when 'the enemy were in action before the defences'.[225] On the following night British records document 'a small number of enemy aircraft' attacking Hull causing 'widespread' damage in central areas, dropping a 'relatively large number of HE'.[226] *Luftflotte* 3 records show fifty-two aircraft despatched, with forty-four reaching the target, which suggests further underestimation of bomber numbers.[227] Minor damage occurred in the dock area and the London and North Eastern Railway line was blocked, the Bomb Census describing bombing as 'noticeable for the degree of accuracy in aiming at railway objectives'.[228] Despite this 'accuracy', 52 houses were wrecked and 493 seriously damaged, twenty-five people killed and thirty seriously injured.[229] In the 12 Group area, thirteen AI aircraft operated without any interceptions, but further north, 13 Group Beaufighters of 604 Squadron destroyed one Do 217 and damaged a second.[230] *Luftflotte* 3 records show another fifty-one aircraft were despatched to Hull on 25–26 July, of which forty-seven reached the target, although the attack was 'severely hampered by the weather conditions', with 'poor visibility'.[231] The Air Ministry noted that twelve aircraft attacked along the north-east coast, with various places in Yorkshire reporting bombing, 'but there was no serious damage'.[232]

The AHB narrative observed that 'the character of night bombing changed from one of occasional raids by heavy bombers to sporadic attacks by high speed bombers', using Me 410s and Fw 190s against 'southern and south-eastern coastal towns rather than in the north-east'.[233] Any evaluation of *Luftwaffe* raids in the second half of 1943 must consider the Bomber Command attacks on Hamburg during the last week of July, which during the second attack 'a combination of freak weather conditions', low humidity, high ambient temperature, and no rain for several weeks allowed individual fires to combine and draw in oxygen to heat the air to one thousand degrees Celsius, a cycle that created a 'storm'.[234] Described incorrectly as 'a new and unexpected development in warfare', this firestorm killed around 40,000 people in one night.[235] In contrast, a total of 49,731 people had been killed by bombing in the United Kingdom up to this point.[236] The low British losses during this raid were attributed to the use of aluminium foil strips (known as 'Window'), causing German radar to be 'swamped by false echoes'.[237] Goebbels described Hamburg as 'a catastrophe the extent of which simply staggers the imagination', which the *Luftwaffe* did not have the capacity to emulate.[238]

Before 'Intruder' attacks dominated, there were two raids against south coast naval ports. On 11–12 August, two targets were attacked simultaneously, but while Operational Research describes fighter-bombers attacking Bournemouth and twin-engine bombers Plymouth, the 10 Group Operations Record Book reports 'a mixed force' at both locations.[239] Fifteen aircraft attacked Bournemouth, but only eight HE bombs were dropped, with two stray aircraft bombing Poole, and twenty-five attacked Plymouth predominantly with incendiaries.[240] None of the fires was considered serious, and railway targets escaped significant disruption.[241] A post-raid investigation highlighted that several containers were dropped at too low a level or were incorrectly fused; many failed to open and so incendiaries did not deploy, reducing the fire damage, as with the London raid in January 1943.[242] Seventy-five houses were wrecked and 1,200 seriously damaged at Plymouth; 13 were wrecked and 27 seriously damaged at Bournemouth.[243] Forty-three people were killed and seventy-nine seriously injured at Plymouth; and twelve were killed and twelve seriously injured at Bournemouth.[244] Eleven AI fighters operated, but the only combat was a Beaufighter of 125 Squadron shooting down a Ju 88 at the beginning of the raid.[245]

On 15–16 August, the Air Ministry Commentary estimated twenty-four aircraft bombed the east side of Portsmouth, dropping 'a relatively small number of HE', causing 'considerable blast damage' in the dock area and 'numerous incendiaries', although Price assigns ninety-one aircraft to this attack.[246] House damage was heavy, with 550 wrecked or seriously damaged, while thirty-three people were killed and thirty-six seriously injured.[247] Bombs were also dropped across Hampshire and Sussex, killing five people and seriously injuring four.[248] Night fighters had much more success in this attack, with the Mosquitoes of 256 Squadron destroying two Do 217s and a probable, with another two damaged while also destroying a Me 410. The numerous anti-aircraft guns of the Portsmouth naval base were similarly active, destroying two Do 217s and a Ju 88.[249]

'Intruder' attacks against airfields in eastern England began on 12–13 August with low-level attacks by single aircraft, usually Me 410s, although Ju 88s and Fw 190s were sometimes used.[250] There had been no 'Intruder' operations against British airfields since 1941, and the *Luftwaffe* saw such raids as 'cheap and difficult to counter'.[251] From August to October between 12 percent and 20 percent of all aircraft flying overland by night attacked airfields and RAF stations, a total of eighty attacks. The SD-2 anti-personnel bomb was used extensively, with 2,484 individual SD-2s (4.97 tonnes) dropped in twenty-eight attacks, but of the fifty-eight attacks in September and October, only ten airfields were temporarily unserviceable.[252] As Bomber Command began the 'Battle of Berlin' in October, Hitler ordered the discontinuation of German 'Intruder' operations.[253] The airfield attacks had caused 'some anxiety' to the British, who were 'amazed' when they were stopped so that raids on London could resume.[254] Fighter Command considered the threat to bomber airfields serious enough to reinforce 12 Group squadrons with additional AI Mosquitoes to counter German efforts.[255]

THE RESUMPTION OF RAIDS ON LONDON

Subsequent fast bomber operations relied on the Me 410, which was used extensively for 'Intruder' attacks between August and October of 1943 until raids on London resumed. The first attack on 7–8 October saw the long-anticipated first use of *Düppel* (the German designation for 'Window'), which disrupted British defences.[256] German aircraft followed similar courses to returning British bombers, attempting to use *Düppel* to disguise their final run over the coast towards targets. Interference varied; long wave-length CH was able to continue reporting, while CHL and Ground Control Interception (GCI) reported 'considerable' areas of the display 'blanked out', making it 'impossible to identify aircraft echoes amongst the spurious echoes'. Centimetric radar systems were far less disrupted, being able to 'distinguish between true and spurious echoes', so an AI fighter could retain a previous contact 'while passing through the affected area'.[257] The *Luftwaffe* did 'not appear to have much faith' in the potential of such jamming, many aircraft continuing to take 'violent evasive action', while Fighter Command took measures to mitigate the subsequent effect of *Düppel* on their radar systems.[258] The Air Ministry Commentary estimated around sixty aircraft took part in a three-wave attack, with one hundred HE bombs dropped, 'many of them harmlessly', of which only twenty-four fell within the London area.[259] Railway services were temporarily disrupted around Hampstead north of the Thames and Esher to the south, where there was also extensive house damage.[260] Incidents were described as 'trivial', and even a hit on the largest margarine plant in the country at Purfleet was considered 'insignificant' due to large reserve stocks.[261] Most bombs exploded harmlessly, but the built-up nature of London meant thirty-seven people were killed and ninety-nine seriously injured during these attacks.[262] Fighter Command operated twenty-three AI fighters under ground radar control, with eight others patrolling searchlight boxes against these attacks.[263] The Mosquitoes of 85 Squadron shot down two Me 410s, one of which was shared with anti-aircraft guns, and damaged another two, while the anti-aircraft guns damaged an additional three aircraft.[264] All aircraft were intercepted by fighters fitted with centimetric AI, including a Beaufighter of 68 Squadron which 'chased about ten dummy contacts' caused by *Düppel* before obtaining 'a genuine contact' and shooting down a Do 217.[265]

A mixture of Me 410s and Fw 190s (for the first time since June 1943) operated against London on 17–18 October, attacking railway targets, killing eighteen people, and seriously injuring forty-one.[266] Attacks continued for the next five nights, prompting a German propaganda broadcast to claim: 'At this moment Londoners are anxiously wondering are they coming tonight?

For eight nights running the *Luftwaffe* has been attacking London. This regular and almost mathematical activity of the German Air Force is causing real uneasiness in the English capital'. The Air Ministry Commentary was less than impressed, citing the 'regular and almost mathematical inaccuracy of the enemy's marksmanship' showing 'no signs of improvement, despite the practice which this activity must have provided'.[267] The attack on 20–21 October was the only other in this sequence of raids where significant casualties were caused, when fifteen people were killed and forty-nine seriously injured in the London area.[268] The AHB narrative is similarly dismissive of *Luftwaffe* efforts, estimating that out of 111 tonnes dropped during the month, only eight fell within the boundaries of London.[269] During November 1943 over fifteen nights, 171 German aircraft operated against London, with more than 9 aircraft used on only four occasions.[270] The Air Ministry Commentary considered 'the scale of effort slight' and that there were 'no incidents of a major character', although 131 people were still killed during the month.[271] Seventy-six of these were killed when a dancehall in Putney was hit on 7–8 November, with 114 seriously injured.[272] The only aircraft operated by the *Luftwaffe* on this night were Fw 190s, and such a 'lucky' hit reflects the random nature of attacks by this aircraft.[273] These raids by fast bombers superficially resembled Bomber Command attacks by Mosquitoes of the Light Night Striking Force which bombed various cities, especially Berlin, to 'mislead the enemy as to Main Force targets'. This analogy fails as these *Luftwaffe* attacks were the only ones being carried out against the United Kingdom; there was no 'Main Force' operating.[274] While sixty-five Me 410s operated over London during November 1943, a single Mosquito squadron despatched 149 sorties during the same month, sustaining losses of around 1 percent compared to 7 percent for German raiders.[275] The AHB narrative considered it unlikely that the *Luftwaffe* casualty rate 'was in any way affected' by the use of *Düppel*, with eleven aircraft lost during operations against London throughout November 1943.[276] The Official History argues that 'night attacks on towns and cities failed' because 'the attackers were too few, too inexperienced, too weakly led and too poorly equipped to get the better of the defences', and the British were 'amazed' that 'Intruder' operations were abandoned and resources 'wasted on scattered nuisance and reprisal raids'.[277]

Although German bombers operated against coastal targets during October and November 1943, on only two occasions did these involve more than twenty aircraft.[278] The very scattered attack at Ipswich on 3–4 November was not even reported in the War Cabinet Résumé, unlike the raid at Plymouth on 15–16.[279] In reality, neither attack was significant, with only 'temporary interference to railway services' at Plymouth, the Air Ministry Commentary describing *Luftwaffe* activity as the year ended as 'trivial'.[280] Compared to the first six months of the year, when there were no aircraft overland day or night for a minimum of five days in February and a maximum of fourteen in June, by December there were twenty-one days without overland *Luftwaffe* activity, with a minimum of ten days in October.[281]

DEVELOPMENT OF BRITISH NIGHT DEFENCES DURING 1943

The discontinuation of 'Turbinlite' confirmed the superiority of AI radar over all other forms of night air defence.[282] AI squadrons numbers peaked at twenty in October 1942, and by the start of 1943, nineteen AI squadrons remained, which fluctuated during the year as squadrons formed and were then posted overseas. Although the number of AI squadrons decreased, the quality of night defence improved as Mosquitoes replaced Beaufighters and centimetric equipment superseded metric radar (see appendix 4). Since their formation, several Fighter Command squadrons had been based in 'remote areas', where there had been 'little, or no, enemy activity for very many months'. Although squadrons had 'reached a high standard of training', their location meant there was 'no opportunity to prove themselves in operations'. Squadron deployment was established on aircraft type, which meant that Mosquito units were based on the east and south coasts due to their 'superior performance'. As centrimetric radar became more widespread, those squadrons moved to coastal areas to take advantage of the resistance of updated equipment to enemy jamming. Beaufighters reequipped with AI Mk VIII were moved from 'remote areas to forward areas' over a period of three months. A rotation of squadrons was then introduced to ensure no units were 'left in a remote location for an undue length of time'.[283] The first Mosquitoes with AI Mark VIII arrived at squadrons in March 1943, but reequipment was initially slower than for Beaufighters.[284] Although aircrew numbers 'remained at a satisfactory level', towards the end of 1942, 'no less than 144 crews', in addition to complete squadrons, were posted overseas. These personnel were replaced straight from OTUs, reducing the number of experienced crews 'to a very low level'. The improvements in operational

TABLE 5.2

Combat Results for RAF Night Fighters in 1943

Month	Sorties		Destroyed	German Sorties	Total Fighter Sorties
January	T/E	610	10 (1.6%)*	311	735 (236%)#
	S/E	125	0 (n/a)		
February	T/E	590	7 (1.2%)*	176	729 (414%)#
	S/E	139	1 (0.7%)*		
March	T/E	806	21½ (2.7%)*	415	927 (223%)#
	S/E	121	0 (n/a)		
April	T/E	567	6 (1.1%)*	260	727 (280%)#
	S/E	160	0 (n/a)		
May	T/E	757	11 (1.5%)*	395	957 (242%)#
	S/E	200	1 (0.5%)*		
June	T/E	690	9 (1.3%)*	287	767 (267%)#
	S/E	77	0 (n/a)		
July	T/E	512	11 (2.1%)*	326	600 (184%)#
	S/E	88	0 (n/a)		
August	T/E	860	16 (1.9%)*	308	947 (307%)#
	S/E	87	0 (n/a)		
September	T/E	765	11 (1.4%)*	386	809 (210%)#
	S/E	44	0 (n/a)		
October	T/E	799	13½ (1.7%)*	537	859 (160%)#
	S/E	60	0 (n/a)		
November	T/E	866	11 (1.3%)	324	915 (282%)#
	S/E	49	0 (n/a)		
December	T/E	495	4 (0.8%)*	190	535 (282%)#
	S/E	40	0 (n/a)		

* % destroyed per sortie.

% of sorties per enemy sorties.

Adapted from TNA: AIR 16/525; and AIR 16/889.

training since 1941 meant these crews were immediately operational.[285] The average number of monthly sorties flown by the *Luftwaffe* during 1943 was 326, with the number only dropping below 300 for four months. As defending fighters flew an average of 792 sorties, usually twice as many fighters operated than attacking bombers, as shown in table 5.2, so unlike previous years, more fighter sorties were always flown than aircraft attacking (see table 2.3 and table 4.1).

A comparison with combat results from 1941–1942 confirms the effectiveness of the night defences by 1943, shown in table 5.2, especially considering that the performance of Fw 190s and Me 410s at altitude exceeded that of AI Mosquitoes, restricting the number of interceptions.[286] AI Mk VIII was in service with only two squadrons in January, with MK VII used by another two, so that fourteen squadrons continued to operate metric AI Mk IV and V. The limited number of hand-built AI Mk VII radar sets operated in 1942 were gradually replaced by mass-produced AI Mk VIII, allowing the older equipment to be sent overseas, so by August, AI Mk VII was only being used for training.[287] By September, AI Mk VIII was in use by six squadrons, while the other eight continued to use AI Mk IV and V.[288] The standardised centimetric radar had clearly superior performance, with 107 aircraft destroyed, compared to 22 by metric AI fighters.[289] There was a noticeable reduction in the phenomenon of overclaiming during 1943. From German losses, the AHB estimated that 183 aircraft were lost at night over the United Kingdom, with another 32 damaged.[290] Of the 208 aircraft claimed as destroyed or probably destroyed, 88 percent were lost, demonstrating how much improved training and experience had increased the efficiency of the defence systems. Air Marshal Leigh-Mallory allowed a reduction in the size of his Command to support expeditionary operations, having insisted that in the event of a 'sustained night bombing attacks against this country', the size of the night fighter force would be restored to twenty squadrons.[291] Although the size of Fighter Command generally increased from 1941 to 1943, growth was uneven between day and night fighter units and influenced by periodic transfer of squadrons overseas (see appendix 4).

By 1943, the supply of searchlight radar sets was described as 'satisfactory', with 'more than 3,200' operational. Leigh-Mallory considered the 17–18 January raid on London as 'the first real occasion when the SLC defences have been tested', the directed searchlights contributing to the destruction of four of the six bombers shot down by night fighters. By December 1942, 2,715 sets had been delivered out of a total of 4,000 required.[292] During the first half of 1943, searchlights were withdrawn from Northern Ireland, Scotland, and parts of Wales to redeploy personnel. Searchlight and anti-aircraft gun provision was also reduced at airfields, with only 'nine important coastal night-fighter airfields' retaining 'full scale ground defences'.[293] These reductions took place before *Luftwaffe* 'Intruder' raids began in August, which could have proved costly if German attacks had been more effective. Although Leigh-Mallory insisted that these changes had 'not affected the operational efficiency of the night defence', he was concerned that the stage had been 'reached when the searchlight defences can be weakened no further'.[294] By the end of the year, however, further withdrawals meant that the searchlight belt only extended from Plymouth to Scarborough, to a depth of twenty-eight miles from the coast, although the spacing south of London had 'been thickened to 3,500 yards as opposed to 6,000 yards elsewhere'.[295] Balloon Command experienced similar reductions in the spring of 1943, eliminating twenty thousand personnel. Barrages were maintained at London, Plymouth, Falmouth, and Yeovil, and mobile units remained along the East Anglia and Kent coasts, to counteract low-level daylight attacks, the Newcastle balloon barrage being extended to cover Sunderland for 'similar reasons'.[296] All reserves of anti-aircraft guns had been exhausted during the *Baedeker* period in 1942, and reinforcement of vulnerable coastal sectors in 1943 required redeployment from other areas. Fourteen major towns received additional guns, while numerous coastal 'fringe targets' of daylight fighter-bombers were also reinforced.[297] Steady progress was made towards the approved totals for heavy (2,232) and light (1,200) anti-aircraft guns as the war progressed, with 2,635 and 4,589 respectively in service by June 1944.[298] Once 'Window' was used operationally, Fighter Command had to consider 'the best action to take should the enemy resort to this type of interference'.[299] When the *Luftwaffe* deployed their *Düppel* alternative, centimetric sets were found able to function tolerably through the interference, with radar-controlled searchlights 'often able to work through' such 'infected areas'.[300]

In 1943, full-scale trials at the first two 'Fixed' GCI stations 'to investigate the control of AI aircraft engaged on searchlight aided interception' in addition to those operating under 'normal GCI procedure' began. These trials were so successful that this system of control was extended to 'all areas of the country where searchlights are deployed'.[301] By September 1943, fifteen 'Fixed' stations were operational, the last six entering service at the end of October.[302] As the hardware improved, a shortage of controllers for GCI stations developed in Fighter Command, Leigh-Mallory complaining that many experienced controllers were being posted overseas, '[which had] proved a severe drain on my resources'. To compensate for this deficiency, training schools were established to 'ensure an adequate supply of Controllers', Leigh-Mallory envisaging 'a period during which all my stations will be badly under establishment in Controllers'.[303] By the end of 1943, these training schools had started 'to pay dividends', and he considered 'the position regarding GCI Controllers has improved'.[304] In April 1943, work started on a radar station that would still function 'in the presence' of 'Window', anticipating *Luftwaffe* use once it was deployed by Bomber Command. A chain of fifteen stations was planned, but the first two were not operational until the beginning of 1944 and therefore not available when the *Luftwaffe* began using *Düppel* in October 1943.[305]

The Dieppe operation made the RAF expect heavy casualties during the invasion of North Africa which did not materialise, so the pilot output from OTUs in 1943 'greatly exceeded the demand' (see appendix 6). This overproduction led to several day training units being closed during 1943.[306] The lowest monthly output from day units (155) was still 50 percent higher than the highest monthly output from the night OTUs (98), and the highest monthly output from day fighter operational training (389) was 400 percent more than the equivalent night total. During 1943, the efficiency of night OTUs increased by using Beaufighters for initial pilot training before operational training began. Towards the middle of the year, a new training unit was formed for 'Intruder' crews, and the elimination of Turbinlite meant the output from the two night OTUs went exclusively to night fighter squadrons.[307] Courses at day fighter units were reduced due to an excess of trained pilots, but at night units the intakes, including training of radar operators, were increased due to operational demand, and an additional Beaufighter OTU was opened. As the surplus of day fighter pilots continued to increase, three day training units were closed, and the intake at the others further reduced.[308] Courses at night training units were reduced in December 1943, despite the number of operational crews only consistently exceeding serviceable aircraft three months previously.[309] This narrow margin was never a concern, as only sixteen night fighters were lost operationally throughout the year.[310] The performance of OTUs between 1941 and 1943 in appendix 8 demonstrates the complex nature of night training.

ACCEPTANCE OF STATE INTERVENTION INTO EVERYDAY LIFE

Webster has described the expansion of medical services in the United Kingdom between the two world wars as 'a haphazard assemblage', and by the start of the Second World War, the introduction of a comprehensive health service was 'an inevitability'.[311] Although employed men could see doctors via National Insurance contributions, this excluded their families and did not include hospital care.[312] Klein describes the available health care in 1939 as 'both inadequate and irrational'.[313] The large voluntary hospitals were usually associated with a medical school attached to a civic university, while many smaller voluntary hospitals relied on generous benefactors to remain open.[314] By 1939, a system of municipal hospitals was running in parallel with voluntary institutions, but uneven coverage across the country meant provision of care was restricted.[315] In comparison with other developed European countries, 'the UK's health services were falling behind', so that medical coverage was uneven and inconsistent.[316]

The Ministry of Health planned the EHS to deal with casualties from enemy action.[317] A National Blood Transfusion service and public health laboratories were established to manage epidemic disease.[318] Although initially intended for military personnel, the possibility of a knockout blow bombing attack prompted the addition of civilian air raid casualties to the plans.[319] When war began, hospitals were cleared of patients, many seriously ill, to free up 140,000 beds, but after six years of war, the total number of civilian air raid casualties treated was 40 percent less than the number of sick people removed from hospitals in two days during September 1939.[320] Concern about ongoing civilian medical care led to adjustments of the EHS, with funded beds being transferred away from cities and new hutted hospitals being built. Free outpatient treatment was extended to civilian war casualties at hospitals at the outbreak of war, and between September 1940 and May 1941, twenty-five thousand air raid casualties were admitted to London hospitals, with forty-six thousand elsewhere in the country, so by November 1940, every 'well managed' bed could be used for sick civilians to reduce pressure on casualty accommodation. This provided government funded beds in a state-run service side-by-side with other hospital beds, and when additional beds were required, non-EHS patients were relocated at the Ministry's expense.[321]

These developments created one hospital system that was 'allocated the resources to transform the acute and casualty services', while the other 'old system was left untouched by its activities'.[322] The Ministry found that 'hospital work could not be unaffected by the general trend of social development', so health departments slowly assumed 'the role of principal advocate for the welfare of sick people'. By 1941, the government was committed to the introduction of a comprehensive hospital scheme with readily available appropriate treatment as soon as possible after the war.[323] Webster argues this was intended as 'a partnership between the public and voluntary sectors', but the Beveridge Report led to 'a radical overhaul of the health services' and the formation of the National Health Service in 1948.[324]

Casualty numbers were only ever serious during the Blitz and the later *Vergeltungswaffen* attacks, so the scale of bombing never caused a permanent breakdown in morale. The risk of 'unnatural death' from other causes remained high, as before the war, 'pain and discomfort were accepted as part of life to be endured with stoicism', while 'working class people did not expect to be comfortable' and 'patients expectations were not high. The death of children from infectious disease was the way of the world'.[325] Even at their highest in 1940–1941, deaths from bombing were never as high as individual figures for the three most deadly diseases or from other causes of 'violent death', and 'it is just possible that despite all the upheavals and destruction of air bombardment, the fear of air attack far outweighed the reality'.[326] Figure 5.2 shows that people were more likely to die from bronchitis, tuberculosis, or pneumonia, so the lack of a breakdown in morale can be understood, as bombing was never the dominant cause of unnatural death, especially from 1942 onwards, when there were twice the number of road accident deaths as from bombing.[327] Although a serious rise in deaths and the number of new cases from tuberculosis was claimed during 1940–1941, due to the clearing of infective patients from sanatoriums at the outbreak of war returning home in an infective state, this is not supported by official data.[328] While tuberculosis deaths did rise 10 percent during 1940 and 1941, there were much larger increases for other infectious diseases in the same period, with nearly three times more dying from bronchitis in 1940 and twice as many in 1941; deaths from other major infectious diseases also increased in the early war years.

This suggests that the Titmuss comments on tuberculosis cases—'How many of these were sputum positive—and consequently a danger to other people—is impossible to say'—probably indicated a small number of patients.[329] The number of deaths due to bombing exceeded other 'violent deaths', including poisoning and domestic and industrial accidents for only one year of the war (1944), partly due to the huge expansion of industry leading to increased accidents amongst inexperienced new workers, underlining the dangers of life and how unexpected death was accepted before the development of modern standards of public and industrial safety.[330]

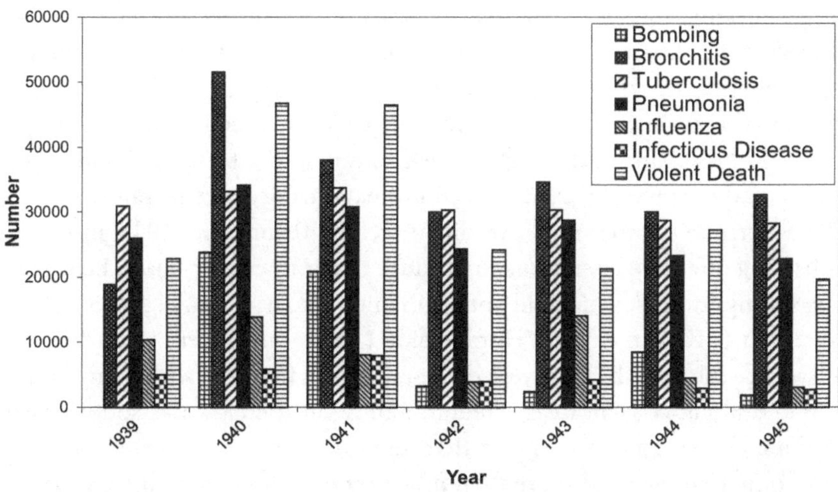

Figure 5.2: Causes of Civilian Death, 1939–1945 (Compiled from HO 191/11 and Central Statistical Office, *Statistical Digest of the War* [HMSO, 1951], 35–40.)

A further indication of the acceptance of state intervention into everyday life was the plans for post-bombing reconstruction. In January 1940, a Royal Commission recommended the extension of central government planning to correct previous failures in regional development. Planners in cities where major damage had occurred envisaged comprehensive rebuilding schemes, with Bristol, Coventry, Hull, and Southampton expecting to finance reconstruction from state funds.[331] The appointment of regional planning officers was 'fiercely opposed by the local authorities', so the government intervened to limit the scale of redevelopment.[332] The homeless population produced by the bombing of 1940–1941 created the need for quick results, so plans for high-quality projects were abandoned, although several towns contemplated a 'grand design' with the timescale extended beyond the post-war period.[333] To reduce costs during post-war austerity, many of these projects would be amended to produce brutalist high-rise 'pedantic, aggressive, uncaring' architecture.[334]

A lack of aircraft at the beginning of 1943 meant the *Luftwaffe* was unable to conduct a coherent bombing offensive against the United Kingdom. Poor decision-making meant newer aircraft were not available, German units operating updated versions of near-obsolescent designs. Heavy losses of aircraft in Russia and the Mediterranean drastically decreased aircrew replacements, the absence of an adequate reserve lowering *Luftwaffe* training standards to maintain frontline strength, which reduced quality and experience. Reprisals for raids on Berlin led to renewed attacks on London, but widespread damage and casualties continued during sporadic raids. The size of the German bomber force steadily increased throughout 1943, mostly by restricting offensive operations to produce larger forces for 'short, heavy and devastating' attacks, which did not begin until January 1944. Figure 5.3 shows Plymouth (110 tonnes) and Humberside (106 tonnes) were the urban targets where the most bombs were dropped during the year, with many bombs scattered along coastal areas, predominantly on the east and south coasts. Of the eighteen attacks by more than ten long-range bombers throughout 1943, only two involved more than fifty aircraft, both of which were against London, where many bombs fell outside the city in the wider Thames estuary (179 tonnes), showing the lack of training and experience of many German aircrews. As in 1942, the north-east and east coasts were attacked regularly by the *Luftwaffe*, raids against London predominating in the first and last three months of the year. The total weight of bombs dropped at night during the whole of 1943 was 1,778 tonnes, compared to 2,458 tonnes during 1942, 4,034 tonnes from July to December 1941 after the main effort of the Blitz had ended, and the 142,843 tonnes dropped by Bomber Command in 1943.[335]

The number of deaths from bombing declined from 3,236 in 1942 to 2,372 in 1943. The most effective attacks against the wider country were on or near the coast, with considerable damage at Aberdeen, Chelmsford, and, especially, Sunderland during April–May, with the British consistently underestimating the number of attackers due to the low-level tactics used by the *Luftwaffe*. From a peak in May, *Luftwaffe* raids gradually tailed off, although several attacks on both sides of the Humber extended the period of bombing against this area compared with those of the rest of the country. This situation applied all along the east coast, and the pattern of activity across the urban areas by the Tyne and Wear rivers was very similar to that of Humberside, over a comparable bombing area, demonstrating that the effect of these attacks has been underestimated. The *Luftwaffe* continued anti-shipping operations, but mine laying declined in the second half of the year. Operations by Fw 190s and Me 410s characterised the second part of 1943, including a return to 'Intruder' attacks against airfields that caused

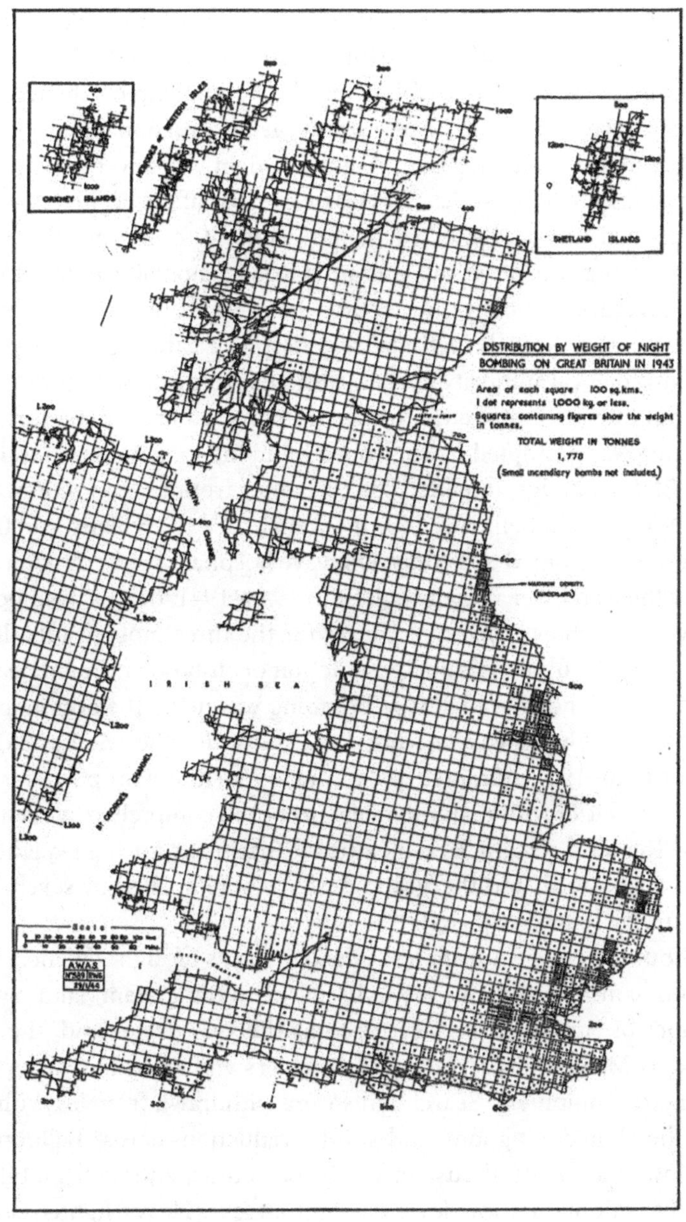

Figure 5.3: Distribution of Night Bombing on the United Kingdom in 1943 (TNA: AIR 41/49; ADGB:V, 224.)

'some anxiety' to the British, until they were stopped on Hitler's orders in October so that raids could resume on London (see appendix 7).

Accusations of a cover-up following the Bethnal Green shelter disaster have been shown to be false, since most of the information was in the public domain before the enquiry began. As the accident was never anticipated, no action was taken to address deficiencies before loss of life occurred, so claims that the council was prevented by the government to improve the entrance are unconvincing. The deaths at Sandhurst Road School illustrate the conflict between government policy and victims' families, as private mourning was subordinated and funerals 'nationalised', despite a campaign to remove the social stigma of local authority burials. Although compensation for the homeless was not intended until after the war, reimbursement for lost furnishings and clothing was prompted by continued bombing to maintain morale.

The EHS, although intended for casualties from enemy action, was by the middle of the war being used for the welfare of sick civilians, and the government was committed to a comprehensive hospital scheme as soon as possible after the war. Even at their highest in 1940–1941, deaths from bombing were never as high as individual figures for the three most deadly diseases, and despite all the upheavals and destruction of air bombardment, fear of air attack far outweighed the reality, as bombing was never the dominant cause of unnatural death, especially from 1942 onwards. The widespread heavy damage of 1940–1941 presented a planning opportunity for post-war reconstruction, and cities with major damage proposed comprehensive rebuilding schemes. The need for quick results meant that plans for high-quality projects were abandoned, and the 'grand design' contemplated by several towns did not survive to be completed.

Without interference from less effective forms of night defence, Fighter Command consolidated on the AI/GCI weapon system, and although the number of AI squadrons decreased as the year progressed, the quality improved as Mosquitoes replaced Beaufighters and AI radar was upgraded to centimetric equipment. Searchlights were withdrawn from less vulnerable parts of the United Kingdom. and similar reductions across Balloon Command allowed a twenty thousand cut in personnel, although mobile units remained to counteract low-level daylight attacks. Heavy fighter casualties that had been expected did not materialise, so the pilot output from OTUs in 1943 greatly exceeded the demand. This overproduction led to several day fighter training units being closed during 1943, but the supply of night fighter crews remained only just sufficient.

Conclusions

THE PERFORMANCE OF THE *LUFTWAFFE* DURING OVERLAND BOMBING OPERATIONS

Any assessment of German operational performance during this period needs to consider the contemporary British opinion.

> By the beginning of 1942 the German bombing offensive against Great Britain had passed its peak and the RAF bombing offensive against German cities and industry had begun to gather weight. The heaviest attacks against this country in the period under consideration were in the nature of reprisal raids. All these attempts to shake British morale proved to be failures and only reflected the decline of the German bomber arm. The enemy did not persevere with air attacks against shipping, aerial minelaying and air raids on ports which might have yielded profitable results and with the adoption of a policy of reprisals they were to a large extent abandoned by the end of 1943.[1]

This study has shown that the pattern of raids carried out from the end of May into the summer of 1941 represented 'blockade-bombing' as a continuation of the Blitz campaign. Despite unusually poor weather, the *Luftwaffe* continued operations throughout June, although the results of attacks were often indifferent. A more accurate end date for the Blitz has been determined, demonstrating that assigning this date to coincide with the transfer of aircraft to support the offensive against the Soviet Union is not valid. The Blitz did not end in May 1941 but continued until the 27–28 July raid on London. *Luftwaffe* bombing strategy suffered from inadequate application of force against a selected target; neither the intensity or duration of German attacks ever achieved a social breakdown, as the weight of bombs dropped was never sufficient to cause critical damage, or a sequence of raids against a particular city ended too soon. One more night of bombing against Liverpool at the beginning of May 1941, for example, or a follow-up attack on London after the 10–11 May raid might have led to morale collapsing. The *Luftwaffe* overestimated what the number of aircraft and the size of the payload available to them could achieve, and the failure to cause critical damage to British morale and infrastructure during the winter of 1940–1941 undermined the confidence of the German high command in the capability of strategic bombing. A successful conclusion to the Soviet campaign could have led to a German invasion attempt before the end of 1941, with slower progress expected to lead to 'heavy blockade-bombing' at short notice, so the threat of German air power continued to influence British policy despite the end of the Blitz.[2]

The concentration of attacks against coastal targets by the *Luftwaffe* after July 1941 both simplified navigational requirements and reduced the length of time aircraft spent overland. The heavy damage from this 'East Coast Blitz' was diluted by intermittent attacks on inland targets, where bombing was scattered and ineffective. Damage was caused mainly on or near the eastern and southern coasts, the concentration of bombing determining how serious damage and casualties were likely to be, especially against Tyneside and Humberside, activity only switching to the west coast when poor weather prevented operations against preferred targets. The *Luftwaffe* continued to allocate a large percentage of its reduced resources to disrupt coastal shipping trade, and such operations predominated when adverse weather only allowed four overland bombing opportunities during the last two months of the year. The list compiled by the Air Historical Branch (AHB) of significant raids from May to December 1941 has been shown as not exhaustive, because the RAF was interested in the number of aircraft operating over targets and did not consider other relevant factors such as damage caused or casualties, leading to important targets being overlooked and trivial raids being documented.

The *Baedeker* reprisal raids were presented by German propaganda as attacks on British cultural centres, but analysis of these raids has shown the *Luftwaffe* continued to target communications and industry within cities with limited military significance, despite claims to the contrary. The cultural value of Bristol was low (and it had already been heavily attacked during the

Blitz), damage to Bath and York was concentrated around railway stations, with the attack on Newcastle in the middle of the reprisal raid sequence being a return to a previous target with important industrial and communications centres. The significant raids during 1942 did not indicate a change in *Luftwaffe* strategy or tactics, demonstrating the whole concept of *Baedeker* is fundamentally flawed, as the attacks were a continuation of the autumn 1941 campaign with increased resources. All the targets either were ports, contained major railway stations, were centres of war industries, or had also previously been attacked during the Blitz, with the majority on the coast or close to the sea. The much-publicised campaign against 'cathedral cities' caused serious damage to only one (Exeter) and minor damage to another cathedral church (Bath Abbey). As raids progressed, bombing accuracy declined due to both the use of improved electronic countermeasures and losses of experienced crews that could no longer be replaced.

The change in German bombing strategy from proactive to reactive took place as Bomber Command policy altered, with political demands for reprisal raids overshadowing prudent targeting policy. The British found it 'difficult to find any clear policy behind the German night operations between the close of the *Baedeker* raids and the attacks on Birmingham at the end of July', but these still conformed to the pattern adopted since the end of the Blitz. The AHB narrative considered that apart from Birmingham and *Baedeker* cities, ports and coastal towns were the main targets for night attacks, which was the same mix of targets that had been the basis of *Luftwaffe* strategy since May 1941. The raids on the West Midlands at the end of July 1942 caused unsustainable losses to the *Luftwaffe*, and it was incapable of despatching large raids against the United Kingdom for the rest of the year. The 1942 campaign has been described as achieving 'nothing at all', except for 'increasing the British population's staying power', while these 'maximum effort' attacks disrupted training at *Ergänzungsgruppen* due to heavy losses of instructor crews.

The areas along the north-east and east coasts were again regularly attacked by the *Luftwaffe* in 1943, but aircraft shortages prevented a coherent bombing offensive against the country. The collapse of training—and lower training standards—decreased aircrew availability and reduced quality and opportunities for experience. Raids against London predominated in the first and last three months of the year as reprisals for British attacks against Berlin, and between 1941 and 1943, the areas attacked contracted and moved towards coastal areas.[3] The most effective attacks against the wider country were on or near the coast, with the British consistently underestimating the number of attackers due to the low-level tactics used by the *Luftwaffe*, as the scale of attacks on provincial targets was much higher than previously documented. The east coast attacks of 1941 and the continued raiding in 1942 have received limited coverage, as the metropolis was not bombed during these campaigns, the location of administrative centres making a 'London-centric' historiography and the populist view inevitable. Similarly, the provincial raids during 1943 received much less coverage than attacks on London, despite 90 percent of bombs falling in raids outside the capital. While heavy raiding against Humberside has been acknowledged, the pattern of activity across urban areas of Tyneside and Wearside was very similar over a comparable bombing area, demonstrating that the effect of these attacks has been underestimated. Lower numbers of bombs were dropped in successive years after 1941, with deaths due to bombing declining as bomb tonnage decreased. The AHB narrative concedes 'that the inevitable damage to house property, to public utilities, to railways and industrial premises could not be ignored, especially in its local consequences, even if its effect on the whole of the war effort was negligible'.[4]

Records show that in only three months of 1940, when both day and night raids were being mounted, and in April–May 1941, when 'maximum effort' attacks were made before the transfer of bomber units, did the *Luftwaffe* lose more than a hundred aircraft in a single month.[5] Such losses could have been mitigated if, as argued by the AHB, more attention had been paid to coastal targets, mine laying, and shipping. Overall, there were as many attacks against land targets as on shipping, with mine laying sorties nearly always at a much lower level, unless weather conditions prevented overland attacks (see appendix 7). The use of fast bombers in the second half of 1943 could have further mitigated aircraft losses, but the return to 'Intruder' attacks against airfields was abandoned for political reasons, to the amazement of the British. The overall percentage of aircraft lost by the *Luftwaffe* has been underestimated, and when daylight operations, accidents, and aircraft that failed to return are added to losses caused by the defenders, this is far higher than previously considered, which increased in consecutive years, from 4 percent of aircraft despatched in 1941 to 7 percent in 1942 and rising to 11 percent in 1943.[6] By 1943, the 'adoption of a policy of reprisals' meant German aircraft losses escalated, which, combined with the collapse of the aircrew training programme, severely disrupted *Luftwaffe* bomber operations.

THE SOCIAL IMPACT OF BOMBING ON THE BRITISH POPULATION

The consequences of bombing on the British public were influenced by government policies, and widespread preventive inoculations reduced the instance of diseases, giving an unexpected public health benefit, with free health care gradually extended to more people as the war progressed, and the health benefits to the general population led to the commitment for the introduction of a National Health Service. The risk of 'unnatural death' from other causes remained high, and at their highest in 1940–1941, deaths from bombing were never as high as the three most deadly diseases or from other causes of 'violent death', and 'it is just possible that despite all the upheavals and destruction of air bombardment, the fear of air attack far outweighed the reality'.[7] Under these circumstances, the lack of a breakdown in morale due to bombing can be understood, as it was never the dominant cause of unnatural death, especially from 1942 onwards. The number of 'violent deaths' remained significant throughout the war, underlining the extent to which other war-related factors increased the chance of unexpected death.

Towards the end of 1941, it was clear that shortage of manpower was becoming a serious problem, with a widening gap between the resources available and what was required to continue the war. Increased war production was only possible by replacing men with women and accelerating the call-up of eligible manpower, and the establishment of Civil Defence 'forces' allowed people to be compelled to serve, which undermined the previous voluntary nature of Air Raid Precautions. By 1942, these manpower shortages meant that further expansion of the armed forces and essential industries was no longer possible, so large-scale cuts were implemented. The severe reductions to Civil Defence meant it was accepted that the decrease in air raid provisions would be a risk if heavy bombing resumed in the future.

Given that the prospect of death was much more widely anticipated during the war, it is perhaps surprising that the Bethnal Green shelter accident was considered such a tragedy and the subsequent suppression of the causes such a scandal. Press reporting meant that most information was in the public domain within a few days of the incident, with only the exact location withheld, which was standard wartime policy. It was only when the Dunne Inquiry erroneously assigned the cause of the accident to 'panic' that the government was obliged to classify the conclusions to deny information to the enemy. The unsafe stairs that caused the trip and led to a crush, developing into major loss of life, were directly linked to structural defects that had been ignored since the end of the Blitz. Certain sources have insisted that the council tried to improve the entrance, and the deaths were caused because the government blocked these efforts. The ambivalent attitude of the council towards improving the shelter did not instil confidence in how it was managed, and the improvements proposed would not have prevented the accident, as the principal reason for the crush injuries was never identified. The High Court judgement in 1944 clearly identified poor lighting and the defective staircase as the accident causes, although if a crush barrier had been constructed in 1941, as some sources wrongly claim the council proposed, then the loss of life could have been mitigated or even completely eliminated, despite the reduction in police and civil defence manpower.

Following the Sandhurst Road School bombing, reports concentrated more on the dignified nature of the mass burial rather than on the actual attack, reflecting the wishes of the bereaved that the deaths should not be linked to the war. This contrasts with public opinion in 1917, when the similar deaths of children after the bombing of a school had led to demands to 'blot out a German town' after an air raid.[8] The increasing state intervention into the everyday lives of working people led to the acceptance of government involvement in local affairs. The abolition of Workhouses in 1930 meant the stigma of such institutions was still within living memory, and initial opposition to council involvement in the burial of air raid victims was prompted by the municipal interment of paupers during that period. The public was therefore wary of council assistance and the government had to stress that this was not a form of Poor Relief. The government scheme of first aid repairs and replacement of destroyed property drove councils to consider reconstruction of heavily damaged towns and led to the concept of 'centralised town planning', although most schemes did not survive post-war austerity.

THE DEVELOPMENT OF THE NIGHT DEFENCE SYSTEMS

By 1940, the RAF had integrated radar into a command-and-control system that gave Fighter Command a significant advantage during the Battle of Britain, but this technology was not precise enough for night defence. The requirement for a night interception system had been recognised, but when the Blitz started, development was not complete, meaning the *Luftwaffe* encountered little interference during operations in the winter of 1940. An analysis of Beaufighter numbers has shown that winter losses during 1940–1941 slowed down the expansion of the night fighter force such that night defence appeared ineffective. By the time the Ground Control Interception (GCI) / Aircraft Interception (AI) Mark IV / Beaufighter system achieved operational efficiency in the spring of 1941, a crisis of confidence existed in political circles about the perceived value of AI fighters. Although some of this opposition can be explained by the technological ignorance of senior officers and advisors, whose experience of air fighting was out of date and limited to single-seat biplane fighters, others, like Lindemann, who were hostile to the AI fighter concept and had access to Churchill, were able to advance their own ideas. Douglas promoted mercifully brief experiments with Hampden bombers but persisted with single-engine ('Cat's Eye') fighters long after he accepted that 'AI with GCI was the most profitable means of night interception'. The only exception within this group was Dowding, but his realistic assessment of the problems facing the expansion of night defence meant he lost his job. An array of questionable alternatives to AI proliferated during 1940–1941, including free balloon barrages that were intended for use when weather was unsuitable for aircraft to operate but were never used successfully. More serious distractions were the 'Mutton' experiments during the winter of 1940–1941 and the 'Turbinlite' aerial searchlight from March 1941, which wasted Havoc aircraft that could have equipped additional AI squadrons. The argument that 'had the Turbinlite scheme been fully operational in this early phase a measure of success might have been achieved' cannot be substantiated, as the *Luftwaffe* would have soon noted the extensive use of aerial searchlights and included night fighters in the bomber streams to attack Turbinlite aircraft once searchlights were illuminated. At the same time, Anti-Aircraft Command had not achieved the approved total of guns and searchlights, with shortage of personnel limiting the equipment that could be operated, despite the recruitment of women into mixed gun batteries.

Although Douglas insisted that twenty AI squadrons were essential for night defence, the number of operational pilots remained low during 1941, as AI-trained crews were diverted away from AI fighter squadrons to Turbinlite units, leaving night fighter squadrons with more aircraft than operational crews to fly them. An inadequate training organisation meant that while day fighter training was satisfactory by June 1941, AI fighter training was deficient throughout the year. Only twelve AI squadrons were operational by November 1941, and it took until 1942, as Defiant units began to reequip with more suitable aircraft, that numbers increased. For a short period, there were therefore many nonoperational squadrons, which unfortunately coincided with the *Baedeker* raids, where extra AI squadrons might have caused unsustainable losses to the *Luftwaffe* much earlier than the attacks on the West Midlands in July 1942. The maturity and reliability of AI/GCI were undisputed, with centrimetic radar notably superior, although lack of equipment limited impact throughout the year. The number of AI aircraft continued to grow, despite both these and day fighter units being periodically posted overseas, but the planned total of twenty squadrons was only briefly achieved in late 1942 before decreasing again. AI squadrons were always the poor relation of single-engine fighter units, in terms of both equipment (for aircraft and radar) and personnel, the provision of trained aircrew supplied from a relatively small number of Operational Training Units compared to those used for day fighters. The 'policy of over-insurance' that led to an excess of day fighter squadrons retained in the United Kingdom during 1942 has been criticised as a waste of resources, but the AHB narrative argues that 'Allied victories in Russia and North Africa could not be foretold at the beginning of the year'.[9] By the time the number of AI squadrons started to decrease, the efficiency of the night defence had improved dramatically due to technical improvements so that combat claims actually gave a realistic estimate of the number of German aircraft destroyed. With the abolition of noneffective types of night defence, Fighter Command consolidated the AI/GCI weapon system, the Mosquito replaced the Beaufighter as the standard AI fighter, and centimetric radar overtook metric systems for the first time. During 1943, manpower shortages led to the withdrawal of searchlights from much of the country, along with similar reductions in Balloon Command. The Dieppe operation in 1942 prompted the RAF to expect subsequent heavy fighter pilot casualties, but as these did not occur, the output of trained pilots in 1943 greatly exceeded the requirements, leading to several day Operational Training Units being closed, although the supply of night fighter crews remained less generous. As Bomber Command began to inflict serious damage on Germany, the same was not possible against the United Kingdom with the resources available.

This book has explored whether the military significance of bombing activity after mid-1941 has been underplayed by the existing historiography, due to the influence of the British Official Histories. Until the primary sources were declassified, historians relied on these publications without being able to verify their conclusions independently. Noble Frankland has highlighted how senior government officials tried to influence the writing of the Official Histories, and a careful review of the primary sources used for this study has highlighted factual errors and questionable interpretation of evidence within the historiography, such as what constituted a significant raid, a London-centric bias towards recording activity—which diminished the importance of bombing across the country, especially during the eighteen months when the capital was not attacked—and an underestimation of the challenges that hindered successful night interception, which historians who relied on these Histories, or secondary sources written using them, have reinforced in the historiography. In a similar way, Stephen Robinson has recently shown how Halder's German Military History Program for the US Army after the Second World War distorted military perceptions of the Eastern Front and perpetuated 'the *Wehrmacht* myths' in popular culture.[10] Until more historians revisit the primary sources used to produce other similar Official Histories, it is impossible to assess how many other false narratives are still considered to be established historical 'facts'. Despite the significant and sometime heavy damage caused by the *Luftwaffe* during this period, the results of such raids never vindicated the contentions of strategic bombing advocates as to the potential of the aeroplane to independently decide the outcome of war. As both sides of my family were living in the areas of Tyneside affected by the attacks described in this study at the time, I have reason to be personally thankful that this never happened.

Acknowledgements

Any qualification achieved via part-time study requires a measure of endurance, which is not only confined to the actual scholar. The years of work, including my MA, which led to my PhD, would not have been possible without the support of my wife, Sue, for which I continue to be eternally grateful. I also remain indebted to my sister-in-law, Jan, who continues to provide me with accommodation during my ongoing archival research visits.

This study originated from a remark made by my MA course leader, Dr Claudia Baldoli, about my independent study module. Claudia commented that the high level of post-Blitz attacks along the east coast were worthy of further study and that there might be a PhD thesis in them, with a book to follow. My thanks go to both Claudia, who had confidence in her prediction, and Dr Martin Farr for being my supervisors at Newcastle University, supporting me throughout, and providing meticulous and detailed feedback at every stage of the project. I would also like to thank Dr Felix Shultz for his help in translating some of the more esoteric *kompostia* present in *Luftwaffe* documents, Dr Matt Perry for a 'rigorous' mock viva, and Professor Richard Overy for providing access to *Luftwaffe* documents held by the Central Archive of the Ministry of the Russian Federation (TsAMO).

I am extremely grateful to Dr Brian Laslie, historian at the US Air Force Academy, for suggesting the publication of my thesis and assisting with the transition of it into a publishable book. The good advice from Brian and Natalie O'Neal of UPK helped this first-time author navigate what seemed like particularly scary situations at times, and their editorial suggestions were instrumental in turning an academic monograph into a far better book. My friend Nick Bennett volunteered to read an interim version of this document, and I am grateful for the observations that he made as a general reader, which greatly improved the quality of the final manuscript. In a similar vein, my

PhD examiners, Professor John Buckley and Dr Vicky Long, forced me to confront some of my conclusions and articulate them in a more coherent manner. I am also indebted to the anonymous readers selected by UPK for reading the drafted material and offering their comments and suggestions. I did seriously consider every single one of them, even if I subsequently chose not to change a lot of what I had written.

Professor David Edgerton challenged the validity of my calculations for the causes of civilian death during an exchange on X, the website formerly known as Twitter, which eliminated an error before publication. For this, I owe him my gratitude. I would like to acknowledge the numerous conversations with Kristen Alexander, Alan Allport, Mike Betchold, Philip Blood, Nick Hewitt, James Jefferies, Ian Kikuchi, Rob Owen, Harry Raffal, James Patton Rogers, William Sheehan, Victoria Taylor, and Matthew Willis that helped shape my ideas and improve this study, but any and all errors are solely my responsibility.

No researcher can function without the assistance of archivists, and I would like to thank the staffs of the National Archive at Kew; the Imperial War Museum; the Bath Record Office; the Hull History Centre; the Mass Observation Archive, University of Sussex; Tyne and Wear Archive Services; York City Archives; the Zuckerman Archive, University of East Anglia; and the *Bundesarchiv-Militärarchiv*, Freiburg, Germany, for their support during periods of archival research. I am especially grateful to Seb Cox, head of the Air Historical Branch (RAF) for providing access to documents held at RAF Northolt that would have otherwise been unobtainable. The role of archives and archivists continues to be undervalued in enabling new avenues of primary research, and it needs to be acknowledged that without them, a study like this would have been impossible.

Appendix 1: Most Attacked Towns in the United Kingdom

(Piloted Aircraft Only)

	Number of Attacks		Totals		
Town/City	**Day**	**Night**	**Attacks**	**Deaths**	**Houses Demolished**
London	101	253	354	29,890	82,546
Dover	76	49	125	183	945
Great Yarmouth	25	72	97	183	1,769
Folkestone	56	27	83	105	537
Hull	6	70	76	1,156	4,415
Hastings	54	21	75	154	463
Lowestoft	27	47	74	171	495
Romford	4	68	72	151	449
Portsmouth	15	57	72	855	4,736
Plymouth	13	58	71	1,107	3,754
Margate	30	40	70	53	275
Liverpool	—	68	68	2,568	5,598
Southampton	18	49	67	615	4,667
Southend	10	57	67	87	206
Portland	28	38	66	49	40
Eastbourne	39	27	66	174	475
Ramsgate	37	26	63	89	327
Gillingham	22	38	60	68	159
Bristol	5	51	56	1,238	2,909
Birkenhead	—	52	52	460	1,899
Birmingham	—	51	51	2,150	5,065

Compiled from O'Brien, *Civil Defence*, appendix VI, TNA: HO 198/243 and 245.

Appendix 2: Major Attacks on British Targets, 1940–1941

TABLE 1
August to 19/20 October 1940

Date				Bombs Dropped		Casualties	
Year	Month	Date	Target	HE	IC	Killed	Seriously Injured
1940	August	28–29	Liverpool	103	190	60	91
		29–30	Liverpool	130	313		
		30–31	Liverpool	127	225		
	September	7–8	London	649	734	1,000	1,605
		8–9	London	202	257	412	747
		9–10	London	259	315	322	629
		10–11	London	175	1,018	172	291
		11–12	London	208	328	356	377
		13–14	London	125	200	394	322
		15–16	London	367	387	230	496
		16–17	London	207	308	221	265
		17–18	London	317	651	258	331
		18–19	London	339	628	495	529
		19–20	London	312	603	178	281
		20–21	London	154	79	185	287
		21–22	London	162	329	116	264
		22–23	London	140	361	127	202
		23–24	London	310	601	217	286
		24–25	London	256	384	259	322
		25–26	London	260	441	315	362
		26–27	London	270	239	258	336

(Continued)

TABLE 1
August to 19/20 October 1940 (*Continued*)

Date				Bombs Dropped		Casualties	
Year	Month	Date	Target	HE	IC	Killed	Seriously Injured
		27–28	London	167	437	177	131
		28–29	London	325	205	252	172
		29–30	London	311	136	145	165
		30–1	London	295	105	221	206
	October	1–2	London	250	115	143	147
		2–3	London	130	300	78	53
		4–5	London	189	236	83	117
		5–6	London	242	176	60	104
		7–8	London	211	143	169	332
		8–9	London	257	264	113	307
		9–10	London	264	245	190	248
		10–11	London	269	718	200	237
		11–12	London	213	126	108	239
		12–13	London	148	24	128	433
		13–14	London	249	131	264	331
		14–15	London	304	299	240	580
		15–16	London	538	177	430	878
		16–17	London	346	187	600	427
		17–18	London	322	134	324	240
		18–19	London	172	132	150	117
		19–20	London	386	192	274	508

HE = tonnes; IC = incendiary containers, each holding thirty-six 1 kg bombs.
Compiled from TNA: AIR 41/17, appendix 4 and HO 191/11; and TWAS: T170/8.

TABLE 2

21–22 October 1940 to January 1941

Date				Bombs Dropped		Casualties	
Year	Month	Date	Target	HE	IC	Killed	Seriously Injured
1940	October	21–22	London	115	52	146	74
		25–26	London	193	193	93	202
		26–27	London	253	176	164	220
		27–28	London	127	40	115	85
		28–29	London	176	111	155	151
		29–30	London	236	109	32	22
		30–31	London	178	92	44	29
	November	1–2	London	227	130	92	151
		2–3	London	117	126	29	53
		4–5	London	184	16	48	77
		5–6	London	139	—	64	86
		6–7	London	223	4	89	182
		7–8	London	242	9	176	284
		8–9	London	133	—	79	147
		9–10	London	124	—	60	105
		10–11	London	212	7	139	229
		12–13	London	165	92	132	194
		14–15	Coventry	503	881	554	865
		15–16	London	474	1,142	142	434
		16–17	London	104	—	158	284
		17–18	Southampton	198	300	54	61
		19–20	Birmingham	403	870	450	540
		20–21	Birmingham	132	296	14	94
		22–23	Birmingham	227	457	332	493
		23–24	Southampton	150	464	89	118
		24–25	Bristol	161	333	196	139
		27–28	Plymouth	110	175	10	3
		28–29	Liverpool	356	860	278	175
		29–30	London	380	820	131	267
		30–1	Southampton	152	598	50	130
	December	1–2	Southampton	147	586	72	101
		2–3	Bristol	122	615	148	134
		8–9	London	387	3,188	250	634
		11–12	Birmingham	277	685	115	241
		12–13	Sheffield	355	457	589	488

(Continued)

TABLE 2

21–22 October 1940 to January 1941 (*Continued*)

Date				Bombs Dropped		Casualties	
Year	Month	Date	Target	HE	IC	Killed	Seriously Injured
		20–21	Liverpool	205	761	412	382
		21–22	Liverpool	280	940		
		22–23	Manchester	272	1,032	683	653
		23–24	Manchester	195	893		
		27–28	London	111	318	141	455
		29–30	London	127	618	163	509
1941	January	2–3	Cardiff	115	392	167	174
		3–4	Bristol	154	1,488	142	127
		10–11	Portsmouth	142	1,409	166 (20)θ	203
		10–11	Manchester	111	735	22	27
		11–12	London	144	598	105	385
		12–13	London	155	823	106	148
		16–17	Avonmouth	124	1,480	12	33

HE = tonnes; IC = incendiary containers, each holding thirty-six 1 kg bombs; θ = missing.

TABLE 3
February to July 1941

Date				Bombs Dropped		Casualties	
Year	Month	Date	Target	HE	IC	Killed	Seriously Injured
1941	February	NO MAJOR ATTACKS					
	March	8–9	London	130	693	212	393
		10–11	Portsmouth	193	1,291	17	25
		11–12	Birmingham	122	830	6	Not recorded
		12–13	Liverpool	303	1,782	101	98
		13–14	Glasgow	272	1,650	707	412
		14–15	Glasgow	231	782		
		15–16	London	103	397	71	121
		16–17	Bristol	165	940	255	145
		18–19	Hull	316	2,140	94	67
		19–20	London	467	3,397	751	1,170
		20–21	Plymouth	159	881	329	283
		21–22	Plymouth	187	1,003		
	April	7–8	Dumbarton	132	465	58	454
		8–9	Coventry	315	710	474 (11)θ	702
		9–10	Newcastle	152	1,396	80	59
		9–10	Birmingham	285	1,110	423	454
		10–11	Birmingham	246	1,183		
		11–12	Bristol	193	701	173	143
		15–16	Belfast	203	808	323	329
		16–17	London	890	4,200	1,179	2,233
		17–18	Portsmouth	346	1,280	14	19
		19–20	London	1,026	4,522	1,208	1,061
		21–22	Plymouth	139	1,000	590#	438#
		22–23	Plymouth	146	994		
		23–24	Plymouth	118	574		
		26–27	Liverpool	113	426	36	105
		29–30	Plymouth	210	531	#Included in 21–24 April figures	
	May	2–3	Liverpool	105	167	1,453*	1,065*
		3–4	Liverpool	363	1,387		
		4–5	Belfast	219	2,667	192	189
		5–6	Clydeside	351	1,300	487	379

(*Continued*)

TABLE 3
February to July 1941 (*Continued*)

Date				Bombs Dropped		Casualties	
Year	Month	Date	Target	HE	IC	Killed	Seriously Injured
		6–7	Clydeside	199	1,090		
		7–8	Liverpool	232	807	*Included in 2–4 May figures	
		7–8	Hull	110	268	215	153
		8–9	Nottingham	137	189	157	116
		8–9	Hull	167	540	233	144
		8–9	Birmingham	137	189	None recorded	
		10–11	London	718	2,393	1,436	1,792
		16–17	Birmingham	160	58	128 (23)θ	172
	June	4–5	Birmingham	108	167	27	20
		21–22	Southampton	136	143	12	32
	July	17–18	Hull	174	172	150	98

HE = tonnes; IC = incendiary containers, each holding thirty-six 1 kg bombs; θ = missing.

Appendix 3: Civilians Killed in the United Kingdom, 1940–1943

Date		Killed					Seriously Injured			
Year	Month	M	F	C	n/c	Total	M	F	C	Total
1940	March	1	—	—	—	1	3	2	—	5
	April	1	1	—	—	2	12	24	3	39
	May	—	—	—	—	—	3	—	—	3
	June	18	17	8	—	43	26	19	4	49
	July	199	68	32	—	299	194	114	47	355
	August	649	368	126	6	1,149	871	531	128	1,530
	September	3,023	3,013	920	12	6,968	4,543	4,164	781	9,488
	October	2,767	2,910	629	7	6,313	3,853	3,433	663	7,949
	November	2,329	2,066	604	5	5,004	3,244	2,465	538	6,247
	December	1,813	1,561	580	34	3,988	2,686	1,816	362	4,864
1941	January	801	630	216	1	1,648	1,195	663	179	2,037
	February	448	310	98	3	859	598	354	102	1,054
	March	2,222	1,683	602	106	4,613	2,743	1,876	404	5,023
	April	3,048	2,487	744	196	6,475	3,572	2,603	494	6,669
	May	2,617	2,095	791	109	5,612	2,904	1,819	416	5,139
	June	185	163	62	—	410	232	176	44	452
	July	201	194	81	3	479	225	193	73	491
	August	52	79	31	—	162	77	58	19	154
	September	109	82	48	—	239	125	97	31	253
	October	134	93	35	—	262	181	127	45	353
	November	39	37	13	—	89	78	68	17	163
	December	17	14	6	—	37	19	27	7	55
1942	January	29	67	18	—	114	25	27	7	59
	February	5	15	4	—	24	12	4	4	20
	March	18	3	—	—	21	5	8	1	13

(Continued)

Appendix 3 Table (*Continued*)

Date		Killed					Seriously Injured			
Year	**Month**	**M**	**F**	**C**	**n/c**	**Total**	**M**	**F**	**C**	**Total**
	April	382	464	129	14	989	506	446	94	1,046
	May	174	156	48	25	403	203	169	52	424
	June	122	134	39	2	297	143	183	39	365
	July	207	166	41	1	415	567	247	55	869
	August	154	183	57	8	402	215	232	63	510
	September	87	79	41	—	207	118	83	37	238
	October	80	91	55	—	226	153	170	48	371
	November	8	12	4	—	24	23	11	4	38
	December	44	52	18	—	114	57	120	20	197
1943	January	107	146	76	—	329	180	225	102	507
	February	94	138	22	1	255	133	175	37	345
	March	118	136	41	—	295	199	204	34	437
	April	63	83	26	1	173	81	95	25	201
	May	216	267	105	—	588	290	342	101	733
	June	120	66	16	1	203	137	112	33	282
	July	59	81	28	—	168	73	103	33	269
	August	39	41	29	—	109	74	72	17	163
	September	2	1	2	—	5	5	5	1	11
	October	53	48	17	—	118	119	123	41	283
	November	41	49	28	1	119	76	134	28	238
	December	3	4	4	—	10	20	20	1	41
TOTALS		22,898	20,353	6,473	536	50,260	30,798	23,939	5,233	59,970

M = male; F = female; C = child; n/c = not classified.

Adapted from TNA: HO 191/11.

Appendix 4: Composition of Fighter Command, May 1941–December 1943

	Single-Seat Fighters				Serviceable	Operational	Multi-Seat Fighter Squadrons					Serviceable	Operational
Date	Spit	Hur	Other[1]	Typh	Aircraft	Aircrew	Beau	Def	Mosq	Hav	Other[2]	Aircraft	Aircrew
02.05.41	28	36	1	—	1,039	1,185	4	7	—	1	4 (1*)	231	225
30.05.41	33	30	1	—	1,069	1,176	5	7	—	1	3 (1*)	218	264
04.07.41	42	28	1	—	1,092	1,321	9	9	—	1	4½ (1*/2½#)	245	268
08.08.41	43	30	1	—	1,240	1,272	12	9	—	1	4½ (1*/2½#)	324	286
05.09.41	44	30	1	—	1,246	1,376	12	6	—	1	4½ (1*/2½#)	299	312
03.10.41	44	28	2	—	1,251	1,447	12	6	—	1	4½ (1*/2½#)	326	333
07.11.41	54	13	2	—	1,100	1,445	12	7	—	1	4½ (1*/2½#)	314	377
02.01.42	58	12	3	1	1,133	1,501	12	7	1	1	6½ (5#)	370	413

(Continued)

Appendix 4 Table (*Continued*)

	Single-Seat Fighters				Serviceable	Operational	Multi-Seat Fighter Squadrons					Serviceable	Operational
Date	Spit	Hur	Other[1]	Typh	Aircraft	Aircrew	Beau	Def	Mosq	Hav	Other[2]	Aircraft	Aircrew
06.02.42	58	13	3	2	1,165	1,619	13	6	1	1	7 (5#)	358	418
06.03.42	59	12	3	2	1,181	1,549	14	5	1	1	7 (5#)	356	435
03.04.42	54	12	2	2	1,156	1,404	15	4	1	1	7 (5#)	393	381
01.05.42	59	12	2	3	1,130	1,343	15	3	2	1	7 (5#)	422	322
05.06.42	58	12	2	3	1,134	1,440	17	—	3	1	8 (5#)	351	372
03.07.42	59	12	2	3	1,331	1,639	18	—	4	1	7 (5#)	399	413
07.08.42	59	9	2	6	1,253	1,563	18	—	4	1	7 (5#)	398	448
04.09.42	59	9	2	6	1,196	1,525	18	—	5	—	7 (5#)	401	466
09.10.42	59	9	2	8	1,126	1,562	18	—	5	—	7 (5#)	409	492
06.11.42	47	5	2	8	995	1,208	15	—	6	—	7 (5#)	379	485
04.12.42	47	6	2	11	995	1,207	14	—	7	—	7 (5#)	367	482
08.01.43	47	5	2	14	1,011	1,195	12	—	9	—	7 (5#)	368	408
05.02.43	47	4	2	16	968	1,193	12	—	10	—	2	310	341
05.03.43	47	4	2	16	1,037	1,245	11	—	10	—	1	315	333
02.04.43	47	4	2	16	1,038	1,367	11	—	9	—	2	329	356
30.04.43	47	2	2	19	1,034	1,342	10	—	9	—	2	346	326
04.06.43	47	2	2	19	1,003	1,393	8	—	10	—	2	327	321
02.07.43	48	3	1	19	952	1,414	8	—	10	—	2	341	325
06.08.43	48	4	1	18	973	1,439	7	—	11	—	2	357	355
03.09.43	48	4	1	18	1,092	1,701	6	—	14	—	2	353	358
01.10.43	48	4	1	18	1,125	1,676	5	—	17	—	2	339	387
31.10.43	48	4	1	18	1,140	1,660	5	—	12	—	2	259	323
30.11.43	48	4	1	18	1,151	1,625	5	—	12	—	2	253	328

[1] Whirlwind and Airacobra.

[2] Blenheim, Intruder, LAM (*) and Turbinlite (#).

(Compiled from TNA: PREM 3/29/4).

Appendix 5: Replacement of Blenheim Aircraft in Fighter Command

TABLE 1

Beaufighter Squadrons in Fighter Command, 1940–1941

Date		Cumulative Deliveries	Total Initial Establishment	Beaufighter Squadrons	
				Total	**Fully Equipped**
1940	September	22	18	5	0
	October	45	29	5	0
	November	76	47	5	2
	December	96	57	5	3
1941	January	101	55	5	3
	February	123	65	5	4
	March	141	70	5	4
	April	159	79	7	5
	May	190	84	7	5
	June	228	107	9	6
	July	275	136	11	7
	August	331	177	13	10
	September	375	204	14	11
	October	410	212	15	12
	November	424	199	15	12
	December	461	189	15	12

Compiled from AHB, AM Form 78, Drawers: Battle P (Cont.) to Beaufighter T, and Beaufighter V to Beaufighter JL.

TABLE 2

Havoc Formations in Fighter Command 1940–1941

Date		Cumulative Deliveries	Total Initial Establishment	Havoc Formations	
				Total	Fully Equipped
1940	December	5	5	2	0
1941	January	8	7	2	0
	February	22	21	5	0
	March	50	42	5	2
	April	72	55	5	3
	May	87	51	5	3
	June	109	63	6	3.5
	July	140	73	10	3
	August	174	84	11	4
	September	225	97	13	5
	October	265	111	12	6
	November	295	117	13	7
	December	322	100	13	5*

* LAM squadron disbanded.

Compiled from AHB, AM Form 78, Drawer: Havoc AE to Hind K.

Appendix 6: Supply of Aircrew to Night Fighter Squadrons

Date	Aircraft Serviceable	Night Fighter Crews		Day Pilots	OTU Output	
		Total	Operational		Night#	Day
02.05.41	72* (+159)θ	64 (+185)θ	85 (+170)θ	1,185	51	229
30.05.41	72* (+146)θ	97 (+203)θ	81 (+183)θ	1,176	23	411
14.07.41	89* (+156)θ	116 (+205)θ	92 (+176)θ	1,321	27	387
08.08.41	97* (+227)θ	137 (+243)θ	91 (+195)θ	1,273	56	400
05.09.41	125* (+174)θ	181 (+252)θ	122 (+190)θ	1,376	48	475
03.10.41	147* (+179)θ	204 (+249)θ	130 (+203)θ	1,447	23	459
07.11.41	138* (+176)θ	220 (+258)θ	130 (+215)θ	1,445	27 (+13)	340
02.01.42	167* (+162)ϕ	371**	183 (+87)ϕ	1,466	22 (+21)	326
06.02.42	172* (+176)ϕ	401**	187 (+84)ϕ	1,577	34 (+20)	202
06.03.42	174* (+164)ϕ	425**	198 (+92)ϕ	1,510	41 (+25)	263
03.04.42	207* (+171)ϕ	525**	217 (+67)ϕ	1,361	55 (+22)	312
01.05.42	232* (+172)ϕ	622**	216 (+80)ϕ	1,302	36 (+23)	278
05.06.42	253* (+83)ϕ	598**	271 (+86)ϕ	1,393	41 (+12)	257
03.07.42	294* (+82)ϕ	524**	281 (+96)ϕ	1,593	28 (+19)	467
07.08.42	305* (+73)ϕ	566**	334 (+96)ϕ	1,521	23 (+21)	290
04.09.42	326* (+49)ϕ	583**	368 (+83)ϕ	1,480	42 (+22)	190
09.10.42	323* (+52)ϕ	596**	399 (+73)ϕ	1,522	18 (+16)	488
06.11.42	306* (+43)ϕ	563**	372 (+83)ϕ	1,166	27 (+19)	268

(*Continued*)

Appendix 6 Table (*Continued*)

	Aircraft	Night Fighter Crews		Day	OTU Output	
Date	**Serviceable**	**Total**	**Operational**	**Pilots**	**Night#**	**Day**
04.12.42	291* (+48)ϕ	547**	375 (+75)ϕ	1,166	18 (+30)	191
08.01.43	297*	401	309	1,195	35	193
05.02.43	287*	473	315	1,193	40	243
05.03.43	290*	470	321	1,245	36	304
02.04.43	329*	459	356	1,367	41	291
30.04.43	346*	418	326	1,342	36	258
04.06.43	327*	391	321	1,393	71	389
02.07.43	341*	390	325	1,414	50	372
06.08.43	357*	400	355	1,539	98	316
03.09.43	353*	404	358	1,701	74	348
01.10.43	339*	540	387	1,676	42	300
31.10.43	259*	401	328	1,660	77	195
30.11.43	253*	416	328	1,625	70	155

* Beaufighters and Mosquitoes (only Beaufighters before 02.01.42).
θ Number in brackets Blenheim/Havoc/Defiant.
ϕ Number in brackets Turbinlite/Defiant; ** Including Turbinlite/Defiant.
No. 60 OTU included from June to August 1942, number in brackets from No. 51 OTU (Turbinlite).
Compiled from TNA: PREM 3/29/4, AIR 16/1144, AIR 16/1145, and AIR 16/1148.

Appendix 7: German Air Activity, July 1941–December 1943

Year	Month	Total Sorties	Target Selection		
			Land#	Shipping	Mine Laying
1941	July	1,082	887 (82%)	—	195 (18%)
	August	676	370 (55%)	306 (45%)	—
	September	720	220 (31%)	405 (56%)	95 (13%)
	October	759	346 (46%)	413 (54%)	—
	November	695	198 (28%)	417 (60%)	80 (12%)
	December	695	97 (14%)	583 (84%)	15 (2%)
1942	January	368	45 (12%)	278 (76%)	45 (12%)
	February	328	13 (4%)	235 (72%)	80 (24%)
	March	504	85 (17%)	232 (46%)	187 (37%)
	1–22 April	455	128 (28%)	112 (25%)	215 (47%)
	23–30 April	537	345 (64%)	182 (34%)	10 (2%)
	April Total	992	473 (48%)	294 (30%)	225 (22%)
	May	791	395 (50%)	252 (32%)	144 (18%)
	June	757	400 (53%)	216 (29%)	141 (18%)
	July	681	383 (56%)	293 (43%)	5 (1%)
	August	626	341 (54%)	263 (42%)	22 (4%)
	September	323	105 (33%)	218 (67%)	—
	October	203	72 (35%)	131 (65%)	—
	November	63	2 (3%)	61 (97%)	—
	December	134	34 (25%)	100 (75%)	—

(*Continued*)

Appendix 7 Table (*Continued*)

Year	Month	Total Sorties	Target Selection			
			Land#		**Shipping**	**Mine Laying**
1943	January	303	150 (50%)		98 (32%)	55 (18%)
	February	183	53 (29%)		78 (43%)	52 (28%)
	March	432	251 (58%)		135 (31%)	46 (11%)
	April	259	51 (20%)	18 (7%)	115 (44%)	75 (29%)
	May	435	99 (23%)	101 (23%)	200 (46%)	35 (8%)
	June	402	122 (30%)	57 (14%)	208 (52%)	15 (4%)
	July	377	151 (40%)	—	211 (56%)	15 (4%)
	August	320	137 (43%)	38 (12%)	145 (45%)	—
	September	407	77 (19%)	37 (9%)	113 (28%)	180 (44%)
	October	535	265 (50%)	34 (6%)	116 (22%)	120 (22%)
	November	325	135 (42%)	39 (12%)	151 (46%)	—
	December	195	65 (33%)	12 (6%)	118 (61%)	—
Overall Total		14,570	6,358 (43%)		6,385 (44%)	1,827 (13%)

Overland activity split into long range and fighter-bomber from April 1943.

Compiled from TNA: AIR 40/1645.

Appendix 8: Intake and Output from Fighter Operational Training Units, 1941–1943

	1941				1942				1943			
	Day		Night		Day		Night		Day		Night	
Month	In	Out	In	Out	In	Out	In	Out	In	Out	In	Out
January	169	188	—	—	220	202	70	54	285	193	49	35
February	154	137	25	41	246	263	43	66	326	243	50	40
March	312	146	73	22	297	312	103	77	513	304	87	36
April	286	213	—	15	448	278	75	59	476	291	32	41
May	335	229	78	51	429	257	89	53	301	258	126	36
June	468	411	38	23	616	467	52	47	421	389	72	71
July	549	387	70	41	354	290	64	44	371	372	80	50
August	540	400	90	74	193	190	64	64	285	316	158	98
September	503	475	90	83	500	488	58	34	222	348	108	74
October	539	459	98	38	206	268	50	46	75	300	73	42
November	382	340	92	64	133	191	50	48	175	195	110	77
December	370	326	71	79	318	393	40	39	125	155	62	70
Jan–Jun	1,724	1,324	214	152	2,356	1,779	432	356	2,322	1,678	416	259
Jul–Dec	2,883	2,387	511	379	1,704	1,820	326	275	1,253	1,686	591	411
Total	4,607	3,711	725	531	4,060	3,599	758	631	3,575	3,364	1,007	670
%	86.4	87.5	13.6	12.5	84.3	85.1	15.7	14.9	78.0	83.4	22.0	16.6
Total Intake	5,332				4,818				4,582			
Total Output	4,242				4,230				4,034			

Compiled from AIR 16/874, AIR 16/1144, AIR 16/1145, and AIR 16/1148.

Notes

INTRODUCTION

1. T. H. O'Brien, *Civil Defence* (HMSO, 1955), 428.

2. The National Archives (subsequently TNA): HO 201/11, Ministry of Home Security, Key Points Intelligence Directorate, Daily Reports, 2–3 September 1941, 2.

3. TNA: HO 198/181, Ministry of Home Security, Research and Experiments Department, Bomb Census Papers, Raid Summaries: Region 1, Northern; May 1940–April 1942, Raid Summary TE/5/2/4/(109).

4. Tyne and Wear Archive Services (subsequently TWAS): PA.NC/5/32, Newcastle City Police, Wartime Records, Situation Reports (Regional Police Staff Officer), Air Raids 1940–43.

5. D. C. Dildy and P. F. Crickmore, *To Defeat the Few: The Luftwaffe's Campaign to Destroy Fighter Command* (Osprey, 2020), 14.

6. TNA: AIR 41/17, Air Ministry, Air Historical Branch (subsequently AHB) Narratives and Monographs, Air Defence of Great Britain (subsequently ADGB), Vol. III: Night Air Defence, June 1940–December 1941 (1949), 119.

7. B. Collier, *The Defence of the United Kingdom* (HMSO, 1957), 301; and C. Whiting, *Britain Under Fire: The Bombing of Britain's Cities, 1940–45* (Leo Cooper, 1999), 102.

8. TNA: AIR 41/17; ADGB:III, 119.

9. S. W. Roskill, *The War at Sea*, vol. I (HMSO, 1954), 497–499, and *The War at Sea*, vol. II (HMSO, 1956), 149, 161–162, 166, and 387.

10. R. Overy, "Introduction," in *Bombing, States and Peoples in Western Europe 1940–1944*, ed. C. Baldoli et al. (Continuum, 2011), 4; and R. Overy, *The Bombing War: Europe 1939–1945* (Allen Lane, 2013), xxv. Studies on the social and cultural impact of bombing began with R. M. Titmuss, *Problems of Social Policy* (HMSO, 1950). Subsequent important works include A. Calder, *The People's War: Britain 1939–1945* (Pimlico, 1992 [1969]); and N. Longmate, *How We Lived Then: A History of Everyday Life During the Second World War* (Hutchinson, 1971), although A. Calder, *The Myth of the Blitz* (Pimlico, 1992 [1991]) is of less value. More recently, J. Gardiner, *The Blitz: The British Under Attack* (HarperPress, 2010); and *Bombing, States and Peoples*, ed. Baldoli, Knapp, and Overy, have prompted further scholarship, such as C. Baldoli and A. Knapp, *Forgotten Blitzes: France and Italy Under Allied Air Attack, 1940–1945* (Continuum, 2012); M. Haapamaki, *The Coming of the Aerial War* (I. B. Tauris, 2014); B. Holman, *The Next War in the Air*

(Ashgate, 2014); D. Süss, *Death From the Skies: How the British and Germans Survived Bombing in World War II* (Oxford University Press, 2014) and J. Levine, *The Secret History of the Blitz* (Simon & Schuster, 2015).

11. N. Frankland, *History at War: The Campaigns of an Historian* (Giles de la Mare, 1998), 2.

12. T. Hippler, *Bombing the People: Giulio Douhet and the Foundations of Air-Power Strategy, 1884–1939* (Cambridge University Press, 2013), 37.

13. Overy, *Bombing War*, xxiii; and J. Keegan, *The Second World War* (Hutchinson, 1989), 576, 584, and 598.

14. W. Murray and A. R. Millett, *A War to Be Won: Fighting in the Second World War* (Belknap Press of Harvard University Press, 2000), 30–31.

15. *Parliamentary Debates (Commons)*, 270, 10 November 1932, 525–641.

16. Air Ministry, *The Rise and Fall of the German Air Force, 1933–1945* (The National Archives, 2008), 11.

17. Overy, *Bombing War*, 71 and 94.

18. W. Murray, *Strategy for Defeat: The Luftwaffe 1933–1945* (Apple, 1983), 19; and J. Buckley, *Air Power in the Age of Total War* (UCL, 1999), 127.

19. R. Overy, *Bomber Command 1939–1945* (HarperCollins, 1997), 33; and H. Boog, "The Luftwaffe and Indiscriminate Bombing up to 1942," in *The Conduct of the Air War in the Second World War: An International Comparison*, ed. H. Boog (Berg, 1992), 388.

20. Overy, *Bombing War*, 71.

21. C. Bekker, *The Luftwaffe War Diaries* (Macdonald, 1967), 169.

22. F. K. Mason, *Battle Over Britain* (McWhirter Twins, 1969), 308.

23. H. Boog, "The Luftwaffe's Assault," in *The Burning Blue*, ed. P. Addison and J. A. Crang (Pimlico, 2000), 45; and H. Umbreit and K. A. Maier, "Direct Strategy Against Britain," in *Germany and the Second World War, Vol. II, Germany's Initial Conquests in Europe*, ed. K. A. Maier et al. (Oxford University Press, 1991), 386.

24. TNA: AIR 41/17; ADGB:III, App. 4. The use of 'Blitz' to denote German attacks of British cities appeared in the press two days later, *Daily Mail*, 10 September 1940, 6.

25. Collier, *Defence of the United Kingdom*, 211.

26. Whiting, *Britain Under Fire*, 21.

27. D. Richards, *Royal Air Force 1939–1945*, Vol. I (HMSO, 1954), 205.

28. Calder, *People's War*, 179, 182, and 190.

29. Overy, *Bombing War*, 145.

30. Whiting, *Britain Under Fire*, 22.

31. Whiting, *Britain Under Fire*, 24.

32. J. Ray, *The Night Blitz, 1940–1941* (Arms and Armour, 1996), 112.

33. D. Wood and D. Dempster, *The Narrow Margin: The Battle of Britain and the Rise of Air Power 1930–40* (Arrow, 1969 [1961]), 84–87.

34. TNA: AIR 41/88, Signals, V: Fighter Control and Interception (1952), 175; and L. Deighton, *Fighter* (Jonathan Cape, 1977), 125.

35. TNA: AIR 41/17; ADGB:III, 116.

36. A. Price, *Blitz on Britain 1939–1945* (Ian Allan, 1977), 95.

37. D. Zimmerman, "British Radar Organisation and the Failure to Stop the Night-Time Blitz," *Journal of Strategic Studies* 21, no. 3 (1998): 86.

38. R. Overy, "Introduction," in *Air Power History: Turning Points from Kitty Hawk to Kosovo*, ed. S. Cox and P. Gray (Frank Cass, 2002), xiii.

39. I. White, *The History of Air Intercept Radar and the British Nightfighter 1935–1959* (Pen & Sword, 2007), 19.

40. D. Zimmerman, *Britain's Shield: Radar and the Defeat of the Luftwaffe* (Sutton, 2001), 216.

41. B. Gunston, *Night Fighters: A Development and Combat History* (Sutton, 2003 [1976]), 51.

42. Zimmerman, "British Radar Organisation," 100; and E. G. Bowen, *Radar Days* (Adam Hilger, 1987), 126.

43. White, *The History of Air Intercept Radar*, 38.

44. Zimmerman, "British Radar Organisation," 103.

45. TNA: AIR 29/27, Air Ministry: Operations Record Books, Miscellaneous Units, Fighter Interception Unit Operations Record Book (subsequently ORB); 1940–1944, 16 August 1940; and Bowen, *Radar Days*, 129.

46. V. Orange, *Dowding of Fighter Command* (Grub Street, 2008), 205. Official sources also describe these aircraft variously as 'cats-eye' and 'Catseye', but this has been standardised in the text.

47. TNA: AIR 24/507, Air Ministry: ORBs, Commands, HQ Fighter Command ORB; 1936–1940, 26 November 1940.

48. S. Richards, *The Luftwaffe Over Brum: Birmingham's Blitz From A Military Perspective* (Richards, 2015), 75.

49. TNA: AIR 24/507, HQ Fighter Command ORB, 12 December 1940.

50. Murray, *Strategy for Defeat*, 81.

51. Central Archive of the Ministry of the Russian Federation (TsAMO): f.500, *Findbuch* 12452 *Generalstab der Luftwaffe, Luftwaffe Führungsstab* papers, File 107, *'Bemerkungen zum Einsatz der Luftwaffe Nr. 14'*, 8.5.41, 13.

52. Richards, *Royal Air Force*, I:206, 210–211.

53. TNA: AIR 41/17; ADGB:III, appendix 4.

54. Richards, *Royal Air Force*, I:212.

55. Boog, "The Luftwaffe and Indiscriminate Bombing up to 1942," 390.

56. Overy, *Bombing War*, 255.

57. S. Zuckerman, *From Apes to Warlords* (Hamish Hamilton, 1978), 140–144; and Overy, *Bombing War*, 155.

58. Overy, *Bombing War*, 107.

59. TNA: HO 191/11, Ministry of Home Security, Research and Experiments Department, Unregistered Papers, Statement of Civilian Casualties and Chronological Record of Air Attacks on Great Britain and Northern Ireland, September 1939–June 1944 (1945), 6–8.

60. R. P. Hallion, "The Second World War as a Turning Point in Air Power', in *Air Power History*, ed. S. Cox and P. Gray (Frank Cass, 2002), 98.

61. Murray, *Strategy for Defeat*, 55.

62. C. Dobinson, *Fields of Deception: Britain's Bombing Decoys of World War II* (Methuen, 2000), 89.

63. Dobinson, *Fields of Deception*, 212–213 and 293–295.

64. O'Brien, *Civil Defence*, 412 and 415; and Collier, *Defence of the United Kingdom*, 506.

65. Overy, *Bombing War*, 143–144. One source describes this as 'extreme commuting', Levine, *Secret History of the Blitz*, 65.

66. O'Brien, *Civil Defence*, 417–418.

1. THE END OF THE BLITZ AND THE CONTINUATION OF RAIDS DURING 1941

1. Collier, *Defence of the United Kingdom*, 684.

2. Whiting, *Britain Under Fire*, 44; and Longmate, *How We Lived Then*, 127.

3. Calder, *People's War*, 176.

4. Longmate, *How We Lived Then*, 127.

5. E. Glover, "Notes on the Psychological Effects of War Conditions on the Civilian Population: (III) The Blitz: 1939–41," *International Journal of Psychoanalysis* XXIII (1942): 17.

6. Haapamaki, *Coming of the Aerial War*, 186.

7. Collier, *Defence of the United Kingdom*, 684.

8. Calder, *The Myth of the Blitz*, 2–3.

9. B. Purdue and J. Chapman, *The People's War? A Study Guide* (The Open University, 2004), 43.

10. TNA: AIR 25/200, Air Ministry: ORBs, Groups, No. 11 (Fighter) Group ORB: Appendices, May–August 1941, 11 Group Intelligence Bulletin No. 198, Appendix to Part II: Attack on London, Night 10–11/5/41, 1.

11. W. G. Ramsey, *The Blitz: Then and Now*, Vol. 2 (Battle of Britain Prints, 1988), 608.

12. Gardiner, *Blitz*, 344.

13. Calder, *People's War*, 214.

14. Gardiner, *Blitz*, 344.

15. TWAS: T170/8, Sunderland County Borough Council, Town Clerks Department: ARP Weekly Bulletins File No. 1, Home Security Operations Bulletin No. 45: 7–14 May 1941, 4.

16. O'Brien, *Civil Defence*, 419.

17. Calder, *People's War*, 214.

18. Gardiner, *Blitz*, 354.

19. TNA: HO 198/247, Ministry of Home Security, Research and Experiments Department, Bomb Census Papers, Summaries of Information: Number of bombs dropped on certain towns from October 1940–September 1941 and for period September 1941–March 1945 (1945), Bomb Census Summary of Information, 19th May 1941, 1.

20. J. Gardiner, *Wartime: Britain 1939–1945* (Review, 2005), 393.

21. Calder, *People's War*, 214.

22. Gardiner, *Blitz*, 358.

23. Air Ministry, *Rise and Fall of the GAF*, 96.

24. Calder, *People's War*, 214; C. F. Gibbon, *The Blitz* (Allan Wingate, 1957), 266; and P. Townsend, *Duel in the Dark* (Harrap, 1986), 209.

25. Gardiner, *Wartime*, 432; Gardiner, *Blitz*, 319; M. Gilbert, *Second World War* (Weidenfeld & Nicolson, 1989), 181; J. Levine, *Forgotten Voices of the Blitz and the Battle*

of Britain (Ebury, 2007), 460; Richards, *Royal Air Force 1939–1945*, I:217; E. Webb and J. Duncan, *Blitz Over Britain* (Spellmount, 1990), 44; and Whiting, *Britain Under Fire*, 92.

26. Price, *Blitz on Britain*, 125, Webb and Duncan, *Blitz Over Britain*, 44; and Townsend, *Duel in the Dark*, 189–190.

27. Calder, *Myth of the Blitz*, 37.

28. O'Brien, *Civil Defence*, 416.

29. TWAS: T170/8, Bulletin No. 45: 7–14 May 1941, 4.

30. Calder, *Myth of the Blitz*, 37; and Calder, *People's War*, 214.

31. Whiting, *Britain Under Fire*, 90.

32. Gardiner, *Blitz*, 358.

33. TNA: AIR 40/1654, Commentary on Gazetteer 1941–43 (1944), Short Review of Activities of the German Air Force on the Western Front Since the Outbreak of Hostilities, 4.

34. T. Harrisson, *Living Through the Blitz* (Penguin, 1990 [1979]), 164–165 and 188–189.

35. J. Lukacs, *The Last European War, September 1939–December 1941* (Routledge & Kegan Paul, 1976), 134.

36. TNA: AIR 41/11, *The Royal Observer Corps* (1946), 63.

37. TNA: AIR 41/18; ADGB, IV: The Beginning of the Fighter Offensive 1940–1941 (1947), appendix (VI) A.

38. TNA: AIR 41/17; ADGB:III, 121–122.

39. TNA: AIR 25/177, No. 9 (Fighter) Group ORB, September 1940–September 1944, 12 May 1941.

40. TNA: CAB 66/16/25, War Cabinet and Cabinet, Memoranda (WP and CP Series), Paper No. WP (41) 102, Weekly Résumé (No. 89), 8–15 May 1941, 9.

41. TNA: AIR 25/193, No. 11 (Fighter) Group ORB, May 1926–December 1941, 12 May 1941.

42. TNA: AIR 25/182, No. 10 (Fighter) Group ORB, June 1940–December 1943, 12 May 1941.

43. TNA: AIR 25/219, No. 12 (Fighter) Group ORB, April 1937–December 1941, 12 May 1941.

44. TNA: AIR 25/233, No. 13 (Fighter) Group ORB, January 1941–December 1943, 12 May 1941.

45. TNA: HO 201/9, Ministry of Home Security, Key Points Intelligence Directorate: Daily Reports, May–June 1941, 12 May 1941, 2–3.

46. TNA: AIR 41/15; ADGB, II: The Battle of Britain (1945), appendix 8 and AIR 16/874; Air Ministry: Fighter Command, Registered Files, Précis History of Fighter Operational Training Units (1944), 6.

47. TNA: HO 199/158, Ministry of Home Security, Intelligence Branch, Registered Files, Weekly Summaries of Air Raid Incidents for Weeks Ending 18 August 1940–11 January 1942, Civil Defence No. 9 Region, Summary of Air Raid Activity From 0600 Hours 11 May-0600 Hours 18 May 1941, 1.

48. TNA: AIR 16/524, Night Air Defence Committee, Minutes of Meetings and Reports, September 1940–April 1942, Progress Report by Air Officer Commanding-In-Chief on the Developments and Results Obtained in Night Interception for the Period 10 May–18–19 June 1941, 1.

49. TNA: AIR 40/1654, Commentary, 34.

50. O' Brien, *Civil Defence*, 250–251.

51. Gardiner, *Blitz*, 209.

52. Calder, *People's War*, 209.

53. TNA: HO 198/247, Bomb Census Summary, 14 July 1941, 1.

54. TNA: AIR 25/233, No. 13 Group ORB, 16 May 1941.

55. TNA: CAB 66/16/32, Paper No. WP (41) 109, Weekly Résumé (No. 90), 15–22 May 1941, 11.

56. TNA: AIR 25/233, No. 13 Group ORB, 16 May 1941.

57. TWAS: PA.NC/5/54, Occurrence Reports on Air Raids and Other Damage, 23 February 1940–17 December 1943, Air Raid Damage 16th May 1941, and AIR 25/233, No. 13 Group ORB, 16 May 1941.

58. TNA: CAB 66/16/32, Paper No. WP (41) 109, 8.

59. Richards, *Luftwaffe Over Brum*, 104.

60. Bundesarchiv-Militärarchiv (subsequently BA-MA): RL 10/38, III:1, *Kampfgeschwader* 4 (09.05.1941–18.06.1941), *Angriffe auf London, Birmingham und Chatham, Geheime Kommandosache der KG4*, 16/17.5.41, Enclosure 31 and *Gefechtsbericht der I./KG4 über Einsatz*, 16/17.5.41, Encl. 35.

61. TNA: HO 198/196, Raid Summaries: Region 9, Midland; June 1940–July 1941, Raid Summaries TL 5/2/4 (104) and (105).

62. TNA: HO 199/158, No. 9 Region, Summary of Air Raid Activity From 0600 Hours 11 May-0600 Hours 18 May 1941, 3; and HO 199/181, Nuneaton: 16–17 May 1941, Notes on Operation of Services, 3.

63. TNA: HO 198/196, Raid Summary TL 5/2/4 (105), 1; and HO 199/181, Notes on Operation of Services, 3.

64. TNA: HO 199/181, Inspector General Report, 27 May 1941, 1.

65. TNA: AIR 25/177, No. 9 Group ORB, 16 May 1941.

66. TNA: AIR 25/219, No. 12 Group ORB, 17 May 1941.

67. TNA: HO 199/181, Inspector General Report, 27 May 1941, 1.

68. TNA: HO 199/158, No. 9 Region, Summary of Air Raid Activity 11 May–18 May 1941, 2 and HO 201/9, Daily Reports, 17 May 1941, 3.

69. TNA: HO 198/196, Raid Summary TL 5/2/4 (105), 1.

70. TNA: HO 199/181, Notes on Operation of Services, 1 and Inspector General Report, 27 May 1941, 2.

71. TNA: HO 199/181, Notes on Operation of Services, 1–3.

72. TNA: HO 198/196, Raid Summary TL 5/2/4 (105), 1; HO 199/158, No. 9 Region, Summary of Air Raid Activity 11 May–18 May 1941, 2, and CAB 66/16/32, Paper No. WP (41) 109, Weekly Résumé (No. 90), 15–22 May 1941, 11.

73. TNA: HO 201/9, Daily Reports, 17 May 1941, 1–2 and 20 May 1941, 5.

74. TNA: AIR 41/17; ADGB:III, appendix 4.

75. TNA: HO 199/158, No. 9 Region, Summary of Air Raid Activity 11 May–18 May 1941, 1.

76. TNA: HO 198/196, Raid Summaries TL 5/2/4 (104) and (105).

77. TNA: HO 199/158, No. 9 Region, Summary of Air Raid Activity 11 May–18 May 1941, 3.

78. TNA: HO 191/11, Chronological Record, 10.

79. S. Douglas, *Years of Command* (Collins, 1966), 132.

80. Collier, *Defence of the United Kingdom*, 503–505 and 301.

81. TNA: AIR 40/1654, Commentary, 35.

82. Ministry of Information (subsequently MoI), *Front Line 1940–1941: The Official Story of the Civil Defence of Britain* (HMSO, 1942), 88; Harrisson, *Living Through the Blitz*, 88; B. H. Liddell Hart, *History of the Second World War* (Cassell, 1970), 108; Price, *Blitz on Britain*, 124; M. Arnold-Forster, *The World at War* (Methuen, 1983 [1974]), 303; A. Roberts, *The Storm of War: A New History of the Second World War* (Allen Lane, 2009), 102; and C. Goss, *The Luftwaffe's Blitz: The Inside Story, November 1940–May 1941* (Crécy, 2010), 188.

83. TNA: AIR 41/17; ADGB:III, appendix 9.

84. Mason, *Battle Over Britain*, 482; Lukacs, *The Last European War*, 135; D. Wood, *Attack Warning Red: The Royal Observer Corps and the Defence of Britain 1925 to 1975* (McDonald and James, 1976), 123; R. E. Dupuy and T. N. Dupuy, *The Collins Encyclopedia of Military History: From 3500 B.C. to the Present Day* (HarperCollins, 1993), 1167; and Süss, *Death From the Skies*, 3.

85. TWAS: T170/8, Bulletin No. 46: 14–21 May 1941, 4; and TNA: AIR 40/1654, Commentary, 36.

86. J. Terraine, *The Right of the Line: The Royal Air Force in the European War, 1939–1945* (Hodder and Stoughton, 1985), 262; R. J. Overy, *The Air War, 1939–1945* (Potomac, 2005), 36; Overy, *Bombing War*, 109; and Buckley, *Air Power*, 132.

87. TNA: AIR 16/663, Fighter Operational Records, September 1939–February 1942, Casualties Caused by Night Fighters During May 1941, 2.

88. Bekker, *Luftwaffe War Diaries*, 182. BA-MA: RL 2-IV/33, *Angriffe auf England: Materialsammlung*, 1940–41 (*Luftwaffe*: 8 *Abteilung*) contains information from July 1940–June 1941, indicating the German opinion on the length of the air campaign.

89. R. Holmes, *The World at War: The Landmark Oral History From Previous Unpublished Archives* (Ebury, 2007), 145.

90. A. Galland, *The First and the Last: The German Fighter Force in World War II* (Methuen, 1955), 97; and A. Kesselring, *The Memoirs of Field-Marshal Kesselring* (Greenhill, 2007 [1954]), 80.

91. TNA: AIR 40/1922, German Air Force: Order of Battle, Jan 1941–Oct 1941 (1945), Orders of Battle for 01.04.41, 10.06.41, and 01.10.41; and Air Ministry, *Rise and Fall of the GAF*, 120–122.

92. TNA: AIR 40/1654, Commentary, 37.

93. TNA: AIR 40/2444, Battle of Britain: German Account and Other Papers (1946), Translation of a German Account of the Air War Against Great Britain, 1940–1943, 6.

94. Air Ministry, *Rise and Fall of the GAF*, 162–165.

95. O'Brien, *Civil Defence*, 425.

96. Murray, *Strategy for Defeat*, 80.

97. O. Thetford, *Aircraft of the Royal Air Force* (Putnam, 1988), 147.

98. TNA: AIR 41/88, Signals, V:192, 195. A more recent source gives a lower figure of fifty aircraft, R. Jackson, *Air War at Night* (Howell, 2000), 146–147.

99. Richards, *Royal Air Force 1939–1945*, I: 214.

100. TNA: AIR 41/18; ADGB:IV, part 1, paragraph 62.

101. TNA: AIR 2/7317, Air Ministry: Registered Files (1936–1953), RAF Inspector General's reports 1940–1941, Notes on Interception of Enemy Aircraft at Night, 9 January 1941, 2.

102. TNA: AIR 16/622, Sir W. Sholto Douglas, C-in-C Fighter Command: correspondence with Sir C. F. A. Portal, Chief of Air Staff, 6 December 1940.

103. TNA: AIR 16/622, Douglas correspondence with Portal, 8 December 1940.

104. TNA: AIR 41/17; ADGB:III, 112.

105. TNA: PREM 3/22/5, Prime Minister's Office: Operational Correspondence and Papers, AIR: Night Bombing: Measures to Counteract, AI (Airborne Interception Equipment), Lindemann correspondence with Churchill, 24 October 1940, 1.

106. TNA: AIR 19/308, Air Ministry: Private Office Papers, Turbinlite Squadrons, Turbinlites, 18 October 1942, 1.

107. Gunston, *Night Fighters*, 68.

108. Richards, *Royal Air Force 1939–1945*, I:207.

109. TNA: AIR 41/17; ADGB:III, 92.

110. Gunston, *Night Fighters*, 69.

111. R. V. Jones, *Most Secret War* (Hamish Hamilton, 1978), 35.

112. W. S. Churchill, *The Second World War, Vol. II: Their Finest Hour* (Cassell, 1949), 346.

113. TNA: AIR 41/17; ADGB:III, 93.

114. TNA: PREM 3/314/4, MINES: Long Aerial Mines, Including Daily and Weekly Returns, March-November 1941, Portal correspondence with Churchill, 11 May 1941, 1.

115. TNA: AIR 40/1916, Report of Enemy Bombing 2: British Targets (1944), Table Showing German Estimate of Bombs Dropped on British Targets, November 1940–October 1941.

116. TNA: CAB 66/16/48, Paper No. WP (41) 125, Weekly Résumé (No. 92), 29 May–5 June 1941, 8.

117. TNA: AIR 25/177, No. 9 Group ORB, 1 June 1941.

118. TNA: HO 191/11, Chronological Record, 10.

119. TNA: HO 198/197, Raid Summaries: Region 10, North Western; June 1940–January 1942, Raid Summary TM 5/2/4 (126), 1.

120. TNA: CAB 66/16/48, Paper No. WP (41) 125, 10.

121. TNA: HO 201/9, Daily Reports, 3 June 1941, 2–4.

122. TNA: AIR 25/177, No. 9 Group ORB, 1 June 1941.

123. TNA: AIR 25/219, No. 12 Group ORB, 1 June 1941.

124. TNA: HO 199/194, Manchester: 22–24 December 1940 and 2 June 1941; Air Raid on Manchester 2 June 1941, 1.

125. TNA: HO 198/197, Raid Summary TM 5/2/4 (126), 2.

126. TWAS: T170/8, Bulletin No. 48: 28 May–4 June 1941, 1.

127. O'Brien, *Civil Defence*, 420.

128. TWAS: T170/8, Bulletin No. 49: 4–11 June 1941, 1.

129. TNA: AIR 40/1654, Commentary, 39 and CAB 66/16/48, Paper No. WP (41) 125, 10.

130. TNA: AIR 41/17; ADGB:III, appendix 4.

131. TNA: AIR 25/219, No. 12 Group ORB, 5 June 1941; and TWAS: T170/8, Bulletin No. 49, 1.

132. BA-MA: RL 10/38, III:1; KG4, *Geheime Kommandosache der* KG4, 4/5.5.41, Enclosure 98; and Gefechtsbericht der 1/KG4 über Einsatz, 4/5.5.41, Encl. 102.

133. TNA: HO 199/158, No. 9 Region, Summary of Air Raid Activity 1–8 June 1941, 1; and HO 201/9, Daily Reports, 6 June 1941, 1.

134. TNA: HO 191/11, Chronological Record, 10; and HO 199/158, No. 9 Region, Summary of Air Raid Activity 1–8 June 1941, 2.

135. TNA: AIR 25/177, No. 9 Group ORB, 4 June 1941; and AIR 40/1654, Commentary, 39.

136. TNA: AIR 25/219, No. 12 Group ORB, 5 June 1941.

137. TNA: AIR 40/1654, Commentary, 39.

138. TWAS: T170/8, Bulletin No. 49, 1.

139. TNA: CAB 65/18/36, War Cabinet and Cabinet, Minutes (WM and CM Series), Paper No. WM (41) 57; Conclusions of a Meeting of the War Cabinet, 5 June 1941, 67.

140. TNA: CAB 66/17/2, Paper No. WP (41) 129; Weekly Résumé (No. 93), 5–12 June 1941, 10.

141. TNA: AIR 41/17; ADGB:III, appendix 9.

142. BA-MA: RL 10/38, III:1; KG4, *Geheime Kommandosache der* KG4, 11/12.6.41, Encl. 114.

143. BA-MA: RL 10/38, III:1; KG4, *Gefechtsbericht der* 1/KG4 über Einsatz, 11/12.6.41, Encl. 118.

144. TNA: AIR 25/177, No. 9 Group ORB, 11 June 1941.

145. TNA: AIR 25/219, No. 12 Group ORB, 11 June 1941.

146. TNA: CAB 65/18/38, Paper No. WM (41) 59; War Cabinet, Conclusions, 12 June 1941, 10; and TWAS: T170/8, Bulletin No. 50: 11–18 June 1941, 1.

147. TNA: HO 191/11, Chronological Record, 10.

148. TNA: HO 198/196, Raid Summary TL 5/2/4 (107), 1; and TWAS: T170/8, Bulletin No. 50, 1.

149. TNA: CAB 66/17/2, Paper No. WP (41) 129, 7.

150. TNA: AIR 25/177, No. 9 Group ORB, 11 June 1941.

151. TNA: AIR 25/193, No. 11 Group ORB, 12 June 1941; and AIR 25/219, No. 12 Group ORB, 11 June 1941.

152. TNA: CAB 66/17/9, Paper No. WP (41) 136; Weekly Résumé (No. 94), 12–19 June 1941, 11–12.

153. TNA: HO 198/221, Statistical Records, Region 6, Pre Bomb Census Records, Portsmouth C.B.; and HO 198/227, Statistical Records, Region 12, Pre Bomb Census Records, Kent, Chatham M.B.

154. BA-MA: RL 10/38, III:1; KG4, *Geheime Kommandosache der* KG4, 13/14.6.41, Encl. 128.

155. BA-MA: RL 10/38, III:1; KG4, *Gefechtsbericht der* 1/KG4 über Einsatz, 13/14.6.41, Encl. 132; and TNA: CAB 66/17/9, Paper No. WP (41) 136, 12.

156. TNA: HO 201/9, Daily Reports, 14 and 15 June 1941; and Collier, *Defence of the United Kingdom*, 301.

157. TNA: AIR 25/193, No. 11 Group ORB, 13 June 1941.

158. TWAS: T170/8, Bulletin No. 50, 1; and W. G. Ramsey, *The Blitz: Then and Now*, Vol. 3 (Battle of Britain Prints, 1990), 41.

159. TNA: AIR 25/193, No. 11 Group ORB, 21 June 1941, AIR 41/17; ADGB:III, appendix 4; and AIR 25/193, No. 11 Group ORB, 21 June 1941.

160. Ramsey, *The Blitz*, 3:9; and TWAS: T170/8, Bulletin No. 51: 18–25 June 1941, 1.

161. TNA: CAB 66/17/19, Paper No. WP (41) 146; Weekly Résumé (No. 95), 19–26 June 1941, 10.

162. TNA: HO 201/9, Daily Reports, 22 June 1941, 3 and 23 June 1941, 2.

163. TNA: HO 191/11, Chronological Record, 10; TWAS: T170/8, Bulletin No. 51, 1; and HO 198/247, Bomb Census Summary, 23 June 1941, 2.

164. TNA: HO 198/193, Raid Summaries: Region 6, Southern; June 1940–May 1942, Raid Summary TI 5/2/4 (106), 1–2.

165. TNA: HO 201/9, Daily Reports, 22 June 1941, 2.

166. TNA: HO 198/193, Raid Summary TI 5/2/4 (104), 1.

167. TNA: AIR 25/193, No. 11 Group ORB, 21 June 1941.

168. TNA: AIR 41/13, Signals, Vol. VII: Radio Countermeasures (1950), 32; BA-MA: RL 10/38, III:1; KG4, *Geheime Kommandosache der* KG4, 4/5.6.41, Encl. 98 and 11/12.6.41, Encl. 114; and AIR 40/1922, Order of Battle 10.6.41, 3.

169. TNA: AIR 41/17; ADGB:III, 119.

170. TNA: AIR 40/1654, Commentary, 41–42.

171. TWAS: T170/8, Bulletin No. 51, 2.

172. TNA: HO 198/197, Raid Summary TM 5/2/4 (126a), 2–3; and CAB 66/17/19, Paper No. WP (41) 146, 10.

173. TWAS: T170/8, Bulletin No. 52: 25 June–2 July 1941, 1; and TNA: HO 191/11, Chronological Record, 10.

174. TNA: CAB 66/17/24, Paper No. WP (41) 151, Weekly Résumé (No. 96), 26 June–3 July 1941, 10; and TWAS: T170/8, Bulletin No. 52, 1.

175. TNA: AIR 25/193, No. 11 Group ORB, 25 June 1941; and TNA: AIR 25/219, No. 12 Group ORB, 25 June 1941.

176. TNA: CAB 66/17/24, Paper No. WP (41) 151, 10.

177. Jones, *Most Secret War*, 250.

178. TNA: AIR 40/1207, German Air Force First Line Strength During the European War 1939–1945 (1945), 1.

179. Umbreit and Maier, "Direct Strategy Against Britain," 405.

180. TNA: AIR 40/2444, Air War Against Great Britain, 9.

181. Süss, *Death From the Skies*, 65–66.

182. D. Todman, *Britain's War: Into Battle, 1937–1941* (Allen Lane, 2016), 632.

183. TNA: INF 1/679, Ministry of Information: Files of Correspondence, Home Publicity Division, Minister's Memorandum on Propaganda, Memorandum to the War Cabinet, 24 April 1942.

184. TWAS: T170/8, Bulletin No. 52, 3.

185. TNA: AIR 40/1654, Commentary, 43.

186. TWAS: T170/8, Bulletin No. 53: 2–9 July 1941, 1.

187. BA-MA: RL 2-IV/28, *Luftkrieg gegan England: Gefechtskalender Juli-Dez 1941* (*Luftwaffe*: *8 Abteilung*, *5 Okt* 1944), *Durchführung und Erfolge*, *Juli*, H6153.

188. TNA: AIR 25/177, No. 9 Group ORB, 4 July 1941.

189. TNA: HO 199/158, No. 9 Region, Summary of Air Raid Activity 29 June–6 July 1941, 1; and HO 198/196, Raid Summary TL 5/2/4 (111), 1.

190. Collier, *Defence of the United Kingdom*, 271; and TNA: AIR 25/219, No. 12 Group ORB, 5 July 1941.

191. TNA: HO 198/194, Raid Summaries: Region 7, South Western; June 1940–April 1942, Raid Summary TJ 5/2/4 (94), 1.

192. TNA: HO 191/11, Chronological Record, 10.

193. TNA: AIR 40/1916, Table Showing German Estimate of Bombs Dropped on British Targets.

194. TWAS: T170/8, Bulletin No. 53, 2.

195. TNA: HO 201/10, Daily Reports, July–August 1941, 8 July 1941, 2–3.

196. TNA: CAB 66/17/33, Paper No. WP (41) 160; Weekly Résumé (No. 97), 3–10 July 1941, 11.

197. TNA: HO 191/11, Chronological Record, 10.

198. TNA: AIR 40/1654, Commentary, 43.

199. TNA: AIR 25/193, No. 11 Group ORB, 7 July 1941.

200. TNA: AIR 40/1645, Air Ministry: Directorate of Intelligence: Intelligence Reports and Papers, Tabular Record of G.A.F. Activity Against the United Kingdom, July 1941–December 1944 (1944), July 1941–December 1943, 8 July 1941.

201. TWAS: T170/8, Bulletin No. 53, 2.

202. BA-MA: RL 2-IV/28, *Gefechtskalender, Durchführung und Erfolge, Juli*, H6153.

203. Richards, *Luftwaffe Over Brum*, 128.

204. TNA: AIR 16/606, Fighter Command Operational Research Section: Enemy Night Activity Charts, July–December 1941, 8–9 July 1941.

205. TNA: AIR 25/177, No. 9 Group ORB, 8 July 1941.

206. O' Brien, *Civil Defence*, 426; and TWAS: T170/8, Bulletin No. 53, 2.

207. TNA: AIR 25/219, No. 12 Group ORB, 9 July 1941.

208. TNA: HO 199/158, No. 9 Region, Summary of Air Raid Activity 6–13 July 1941, 1; and HO 201/10, Daily Reports, 10 July 1941, 3.

209. Collier, *Defence of the United Kingdom*, 301.

210. O'Brien, *Civil Defence*, 426.

211. TNA: HO 198/247, Bomb Census Summary, 23 June 1941, 3; and AIR 41/17; ADGB:III, appendix 5.

212. TWAS: T170/8, Bulletin No. 54: 9–16 July 1941, 1; Bulletin No. 55: 16–23 July 1941; and Bulletin No. 56: 23–30 July 1941, 1.

213. TNA: AIR 40/1654, Commentary, 44.

214. TWAS: T170/8, Bulletin No. 54, 1.

215. TNA: CAB 66/17/39, Paper No. WP (41) 166; Weekly Résumé (No. 98), 10–17 July 1941, 8.

216. T. Geraghty, *A North-East Coast Town: Ordeal and Triumph* (Hull Academic Press, 2002 [1951]), 19.

217. TWAS: T170/8, Bulletin No. 54, 1.

218. BA-MA: RL 2-IV/28, *Gefechtskalender, Durchführung und Erfolge, Juli*, H6153.

219. TNA: AIR 25/219, No. 12 Group ORB, 11 July 1941.

220. TWAS: T170/8, Bulletin No. 54, 1–2.

221. Hull History Centre (subsequently HHC): C TYA/54, Air Raid Incident Files, Raid 54, 11 July 1941, File 1, Form WDP1, 30 July 1941.

222. TWAS: T170/8, Bulletin No. 54, 1.

223. TNA: CAB 66/17/39, Paper No. WP (41) 166, 11.

224. O'Brien, *Civil Defence*, 420.

225. *Times*, 15 July 1941, 2.

226. BA-MA: RL 2-IV/28, *Gefechtskalender, Durchführung und Erfolge, Juli*, H6153.

227. HHC: C TYA/55, *Air Raid Incident Files, Raid 55, 15 July 1941, File 3, Form WDP1*, 15 July 1941; and TWAS: T170/8, Bulletin No. 54, 3.

228. TNA: HO 198/247, Bomb Census Summary, 21 July 1941, 1.

229. HHC: C TYC/6, Summary of Air Raid Casualties, Individual Air Raids, 26 June 1940–17 March 1945, Casualty Summary 15 July 1941.

230. TNA: AIR 25/219, No. 12 Group ORB, 15 July 1941.

231. TNA: AIR 40/1654, Commentary, 45.

232. P. Graystone, *The Blitz on Hull (1940–45)* (Lampada, 1991), 23.

233. TNA: CAB 66/18/2, Paper No. WP (41) 179, Weekly Résumé (No. 99), 17–24 July 1941, 11.

234. TNA: AIR 25/219, No. 12 Group ORB, 18 July 1941.

235. TWAS: T170/8, Bulletin No. 55, 1.

236. TNA: HO 198/247, Bomb Census Summary 26 May 1941, 2 and 21 July 1941, 1.

237. BA-MA: RL 2-IV/28, *Gefechtskalender, Durchführung und Erfolge, Juli*, H6153.

238. TNA: HO 198/244, Nationwide Analysis of Bombing, Comparison of Figures of Raids on Various Targets, With Those Obtained From German Sources, Hull, 17–18 July 1941.

239. TNA: HO 191/11, Chronological Record, 10.

240. TNA: HO 199/45, Hull and East Riding Information Committee, Observations on Working of Post-raid Organisations Following Air Attack 18 July 1941, Effects of Enemy Air Attack Upon Hull, 18 July 1941, 2.

241. TWAS: T170/8, Bulletin No. 55, 3.

242. TNA: HO 201/10, Daily Reports, 19 July 1941, 2.

243. TWAS: T170/8, Bulletin No. 55, 1 and 3.

244. O'Brien, *Civil Defence*, 427.

245. TNA: HO 186/606, Ministry of Home Security, ARP Registered Files, Air Raids, Exodus of People to Rural Areas From Towns Suffering Heavy Raids, Report on a Visit to Hull Following Their Heavy Raids on the Night of 17–18 July, 21 July 1941, 1–3.

246. TNA: HO 192/1284, Ministry of Home Security, Research and Experiments Department, Registered Papers; Surveys of Damage in Great Britain: Effects of Air Raids, Reports by Ministry of Information, 12–15.

247. BA-MA: RL 2-IV/28, *Gefechtskalender, Durchführung und Erfolge, Juli*, H6153.

248. HHC: C TYA/56, Air Raid Incident Files, Raid 56, 18 July 1941, File 14, Air Raid: 18 July 1941, 28 July 1941.

249. Todman, *Britain's War*, 509.

250. TNA: HO 199/453, Enemy Bombing: Investigation of Its Effects on Production, Transport and Morale, Research and Experiments Department Memo, 27 February 1942.

251. Quotations are from TNA: HO 199/453, Sydney Chapman: What Happened to me and What I did in the Air Raids. All punctuation (or lack of it) matches the original.

252. TNA: HO 192/1286, Surveys of Damage in Great Britain: Kingston-Upon-Hull, Housing and Rehousing, 18.

253. TNA: AIR 40/1645, Tabular Record, 17 July 1941.

254. Graystone, *Blitz on Hull*, 23.

255. TNA: HO 192/1254, Surveys of Damage in Great Britain: Kingston-Upon-Hull, General, Summary on the Raid 18th July 1941 in the Eastern Division, 4.

256. TsAMO: f.500, 12452, 107, *'Bemerkungen zum Einsatz der Luftwaffe Nr.* 15', 4.7.41, 2.

257. TNA: AIR 41/88, Signals, V:134.

258. TNA: AIR 10/2288, Air Ministry: Air Publications (subsequently AP) and Reports, AP1093D, Vol. I, Introductory Survey of Radar, Part II, (1947), chapter 1, paragraph 16.

259. TNA: AIR 41/88, Signals, V:204–207.

260. Ramsey, *Blitz*, 3:51.

261. TNA: AIR 40/1654, Commentary, 45.

262. TNA: CAB 66/18/7, Paper No. WP (41) 184; Weekly Résumé (No. 100), 24–31 July 1941, 8.

263. TWAS: T170/8, Bulletin No. 56, 2.

264. TNA: CAB 66/18/7, Paper No. WP (41) 184, 11; and BA-MA: RL 2-IV/28, *Gefechtskalender, Durchführung und Erfolge, Juli*, H6153.

265. TNA: AIR 25/193, No. 11 Group ORB, 27 July 1941.

266. TNA: AIR 40/1916, Table Showing German Estimate of Bombs Dropped on British Targets.

267. TNA: HO 198/247, Bomb Census Summary, 28 July 1941, 3.

268. TNA: CAB 66/18/7, Paper No. WP (41) 184, 11.

269. TWAS: T170/8, Bulletin No. 56, 2; and TNA: HO 191/11, Chronological Record, 10.

270. TNA: HO 201/10, Daily Reports, 29 July 1941, 3; and HO 199/115, Intelligence Branch Reports Nos. 1–31 on Effects of Air Raids From 1 January 1941 to 25 March 1942, Intelligence Branch Report No. 17, 4.

271. TWAS: T170/8, Bulletin No. 56, 2.

272. TNA: AIR 41/49; ADGB, Vol. V: The Struggle for Air Supremacy, January 1942–May 1945 (194?), appendix 22.

273. TNA: AIR 41/18; ADGB:IV, appendix (VI), A., 5.

274. Süss, *Death From the Skies*, 18; and J. Gardiner, "The Blitz Experience in British Society 1940–1941," in *Bombing, States and Peoples*, ed. Baldoli et al. (Continuum, 2011), 171.

275. TNA: AIR 41/17; ADGB:III, appendix 4.

276. TNA: CAB 65/19/11, Paper No. WM (41) 75, War Cabinet, Conclusions, 28 July 1941, 175.

277. TNA: HO 186/927, Air Raids, Preparations for Heavy Air Attacks, Paper No. CDC (41) 51, Civil Defence Preparations for Next Winter, 21 July 1941.

278. Süss, *Death From the Skies*, 126.

279. TNA: PREM 3/18/1, Houses Repaired by Local Authorities; AIR: German Raids, Repair etc., 1 May 1941, 22 May 1941, and 24 July 1941.

280. TNA: PREM 3/18/1, Houses Repaired by Local Authorities, Calculated from Figures on 1 May 1941 and 24 July 1941.

281. V. Chambers, "'Defend Us From All Perils and Dangers of This Night': Coping with Bombing in Britain During the Second World War," in *Bombing, States and Peoples*, ed. Baldoli et al. (Continuum, 2011), 154.

282. Mass Observation Archive (subsequently M-O): Topic Collection (subsequently TC) 23, Air Raids 1938–1945, Box 11: Air Raids in Britain, 1940–41; File 11//K: Warden Posts General Report, 13 June 1941.

283. R. Overy, *Interrogations: The Nazi Elite in Allied Hands* (Allen Lane, 2001), 342.

2. 'EAST COAST BLITZ': THE AUTUMN CAMPAIGN AGAINST COASTAL TARGETS

1. M. Barke, B. Robson, and A. Champion, *Newcastle Upon Tyne: Mapping the City* (Birlinn, 2021), 73.

2. K. Groundwater, *Maritime Heritage: Newcastle and the River Tyne* (Silver Link, 1990), 46 and 56.

3. D. Jackson, *The Northumbrians: North-East England and Its People* (Hurst, 2019), 110 and 146.

4. TWAS: PA.NC/5/32, Air Raids 1940–43.

5. TWAS: T15/1477, Tynemouth County Borough Clerks Department Records, ARP Files, 1938–1974, War Damage to Property, April–June 1941, 17 April 1941.

6. TNA: HO 199/32, Air Raid Precautions Department, Ministry of Home Security, South Shields: 9/10 April 1941; and HO 198/181, File No. TE5/2/4/(86).

7. TNA: HO 191/11, Chronological Record, 8.

8. TNA: HO 198/1, Forms BC2 and BC4, Region 1, Northern, 18–19 August 1941–4–5 June 1942, BC2 Serial No. 1/BC 2/8, North & South Shields, 30/9–1/10/41, 1; and HO 199/30, 16 August 1940–2 October 1941 Returns, County Borough of Tynemouth ARP Department, Air Raids 30 September and 2 October 1941, 15 October 1941, 1.

9. TWAS: T170/8, Bulletin No. 66: 1–8 October 1941, 1.

10. TNA: CAB 66/18/17, Paper No. WP (41) 194, Weekly Résumé (No. 102), 7–14 August 1941, 8.

11. TNA: AIR 40/1654, Commentary, 47; and BA-MA: RL 2-IV/28, *Gefechtskalender, Wetterablauf*, August, H6163.

12. Ramsey, *Blitz*, 3, 66.

13. TNA: AIR 16/606, Night Activity Charts, 12–13 August 1941.

14. TNA: AIR 25/177, No. 9 Group ORB, 12 August 1941.

15. TNA: HO 201/10, Daily Reports, 13 August 1941, 3.

16. TWAS: T170/8, Bulletin No. 58: 6–13 August 1941; TNA: AIR 25/219, No. 12 Group ORB, 13 August 1941 and AIR 40/1645, Tabular Record, 12 August 1941.

17. TWAS: T170/8, Bulletin No. 58, 2.

18. TNA: AIR 25/219, No. 12 Group ORB, 13 August 1941.

19. BA-MA: RL 2-IV/28, *Gefechtskalender, Durchführung und Erfolge*, August, H6164.

20. TNA: AIR 40/1654, Commentary, 47; and CAB 65/19/20, Paper No. WM (41) 84, War Cabinet, Conclusions, 19 August 1941, 224.

21. TWAS: T170/8, Bulletin No. 59: 13–20 August 1941, 2; and HHC: C TYA/58, Air Raid Incident Files, Raid 58, 18 August 1941, File 1, Form WDP1, 18 August 1941.

22. TWAS: T170/8, Bulletin No. 59, 2.

23. TNA: AIR 40/1654, Commentary, 48.

24. TNA: AIR 25/219, No. 12 Group ORB, 18 August 1941.

25. TNA: AIR 25/193, No. 11 Group ORB, 7 July 1941.

26. J. Hoagland, "Beware 'Mission Creep' in Somalia," *Washington Post*, 20 July 1993, A17.

27. TNA: AIR 25/219, No. 12 Group ORB, 18 August 1941.

28. TNA: AIR 41/18; ADGB:IV, part 1, paragraph 113.

29. TNA: CAB 65/19/19, Paper No. WM (41) 83, War Cabinet, Conclusions, 18 August 1941, 218.

30. TWAS: T170/8, Bulletin No. 59, 3. The *Luftwaffe* was convinced that their operations had been against Sunderland on this particular night. BA-MA: RL 2-IV/28, *Gefechtskalender, Durchführung und Erfolge*, August, H6164.

31. TNA: CAB 65/19/21, Paper No. WM (41) 85, War Cabinet, Conclusions, 21 August 1941, 231.

32. TNA: CAB 65/19/23, Paper No. WM (41) 87, War Cabinet, Conclusions, 28 August 1941, 245.

33. Overy, *Bombing War*, 186.

34. TNA: AIR 25/219, No. 12 Group ORB, 1 September 1941.

35. TNA: CAB 66/18/37, Paper No. WP (41) 214, Weekly Résumé (No. 105), 28 August–4 September 1941, 10.

36. O'Brien, *Civil Defence*, 84.

37. Gardiner, *Blitz*, 95.

38. TNA: HO 198/181, Raid Summary TE5/2/4/(93), 1.

39. TNA: AIR 16/606, Night Activity Charts, 31 August–1 September 1941. The equivalent chart for 17–18 August shows thirty-eight aircraft operating along the east coast.

40. TWAS: T170/8, Bulletin No. 61: 27 August–3 September 1941, 2.

41. TNA: AIR 40/1645, Tabular Record, 31 August 1941.

42. TNA: AIR 16/524, Progress Report by AOC-in-C on Night Interception, 1 August–10 November 1941, 1.

43. TNA: AIR 25/219, No. 12 Group ORB, 1 September 1941.

44. TNA: HO 198/182, Raid Summaries: Region 2, North Eastern; May 1940–November 1941, Raid Summary TF5/2/4/(75), 1.

45. TWAS: T170/8, Bulletin No. 61, 2.

46. HHC: C TYA/59, Air Raid Incident Files, Raid 59, 31 August 1941, File 1, Form WDP1, 31 August 1941.

47. TWAS: T170/8, Bulletin No. 61, 2.

48. TNA: HO 198/247, Bomb Census Summary, 4 and 11 September 1941, table IIA and table II.

49. BA-MA: RL 2-IV/28, *Gefechtskalender, Durchführung und Erfolge*, August, H6164 and September, H6174, and Graystone, *Blitz on Hull*, 26. This attack has also been described as 'concentrated', Ramsey, *Blitz: Then and Now*, 3, 67.

50. M-O: File Report (subsequently FR) 844, Hull, 23 August 1941, 2.

51. M-O: FR844, Hull, 3–4.

52. O'Brien, *Civil Defence*, 427.

53. TNA: AIR 16/606, Night Activity Charts, 1–2 September 1941.

54. TNA: AIR 40/1645, Tabular Record, 1 September 1941. A far more realistic estimate of twenty-eight aircraft is given by O'Brien, *Civil Defence*, 428.

55. TNA: HO 198/247, B Division Summary No. 1, 2.

56. BA-MA: RL 2-IV/28, *Gefechtskalender, Durchführung und Erfolge*, August, September, H6174; and TNA: AIR 25/233, No. 13 Group ORB, 1 September 1941.

57. TWAS: 2239/1, Newcastle upon Tyne Air Raid Precautions, Reports of Section Leaders on Property Damage and Civilian Casualties at St Peter's, Grace Street, Scarborough Road, Union Road, Albion Row and Athol Street, Newcastle, September 1941, Reports on Air Raid Damage in Byker/St Peter's area of Newcastle, 1 September 1941, 'C' Division Information Officers Report, 7 September 1941, 1; and TNA: HO 201/11, Daily Reports, 2 September 1941, 2–3 September 1941, 2.

58. TNA: HO 198/181, Raid Summaries: Region 1, Northern; May 1940–April 1942, Raid Summary TE5/2/4/(115), 1; and HO 201/11, Daily Reports, 2 September 1941, 3.

59. TNA: HO 198/1, BC4 Serial No. 1/1/8, Newcastle, 1–2 September 1941, 1; and HO 201/11, Daily Reports, 2 September 1941, 2.

60. TNA: HO 198/1, BC4 Serial No. 1/1/8, Newcastle, 1–2 September 1941, 3–4.

61. TWAS: T170/8, Bulletin No. 61, 3.

62. TWAS: PA.NC/5/54, Occurrence Reports on Air Raids, Air Raid, September 1–2, 1941 by Assistant Chief Constable, 2 September 1941; and TNA: HO 191/11, Chronological Record, 10.

63. TWAS: T15/1478, Tynemouth County Borough Clerks Department, ARP Files, 1938–1974, War Damage to Property Returns; 3 July–29 November 1941, Report Re: Air Raid on the 1st September 1941, 1; TNA: HO 201/11, Daily Reports, 2 September 1941, 2; and TWAS: 255/60, Wallsend MBC, Record of Civilian War Deaths due to War Operations, 2 September 1941.

64. TNA: CAB 66/18/37, Paper No. WP (41) 214, 11; and AIR 25/233, No. 13 Group ORB, 1 September 1941.

65. TNA: AIR 40/1654, Commentary, 49.

66. TNA: AIR 25/233, No. 13 Group ORB, 1 September 1941.

67. TNA: AIR 25/219, No. 12 Group ORB, 2 September 1941.

68. TNA: HO 201/11, Daily Reports, Weekly Report of Damage, 27 August–3 September 1941, 2.

69. TWAS: PA.NC/5/54, Occurrence Reports on Air Raids, Air Raid on City on the Night of 1st September 1941 by F. J. Crawley, Chief Constable, 2; and TNA: CAB 66/18/37, Paper No. WP (41) 214, 11.

70. Boog, "The Luftwaffe's Assault," 49.

71. TNA: HO 201/11, Daily Reports, 3 September 1941, 2.

72. TNA: CAB 66/18/41, Paper No. WP (41) 214, Weekly Résumé (No. 106), 4–11 September 1941, 8.

73. BA-MA: RL 2-IV/28, *Gefechtskalender, Durchführung und Erfolge*, September, H6174.

74. TWAS: T170/8, Bulletin No. 62: 3–10 September 1941, 2; and TNA: AIR 25/233, No. 13 Group ORB, 7 September 1941.

75. TNA: AIR 40/1645, Tabular Record, 5 September 1941.

76. BA-MA: RL 2-IV/28, *Gefechtskalender, Durchführung und Erfolge*, September, H6174.

77. TNA: CAB 66/18/46, Paper No. WP (41) 223, Weekly Résumé (No. 107), 11–18 September 1941, 8.

78. TNA: HO 201/11, Daily Reports, Weekly Report of Damage, 10–17 September 1941, 1; and TWAS: T170/8, Bulletin No. 63: 10–17 September 1941, 1.

79. TNA: CAB 66/18/49, Paper No. WP (41) 226, Weekly Résumé (No. 108), 18–25 September 1941, 11.

80. BA-MA: RL 2-IV/28, *Gefechtskalender, Durchführung und Erfolge*, September, H6174.

81. TWAS: T170/8, Bulletin No. 64: 17–24 September 1941, 1–2.

82. BA-MA: RL 2-IV/28; *Gefechtskalender, Durchführung und Erfolge*, September, H6174.

83. TWAS: T170/8, Bulletin No. 64, 2.

84. TNA: CAB 66/18/49, Paper No. WP (41) 226, 11.

85. TNA: CAB 66/19/4, Paper No. WP (41) 231, Weekly Résumé (No. 109), 25 September–2 October 1941, 12.

86. TNA: HO 198/1, BC2 Serial No. 1/BC 2/8, North & South Shields, 30/9–1/10/41, 1; and TWAS: T170/8, Bulletin No. 65: 24 September–1 October 1941, 2.

87. TWAS: T15/1490, Tynemouth County Borough Clerks Department Records, ARP Files, 1938–1974, WDP1 Returns; August 1940–March 1945, Form WDP1, 30 September 1941; and T170/8, Bulletin No. 65, 2.

88. TNA: HO 201/11, Daily Reports, 1 October 1941, 1; and TWAS: T170/8, Bulletin No. 65, 2.

89. TNA: HO 199/30, Air Raids 30 September and 2 October 1941, 15 October 1941, 1 and 8; and TWAS: T170/8, Bulletin No. 65, 2.

90. TNA: HO 199/30, Air Raids 30 September and 2 October 1941, 15 October 1941, 6–7.

91. TNA: HO 191/11, Chronological Record, 10.

92. TWAS: T170/8, Bulletin No. 65, 3; and TNA: HO 198/181, Raid Summary TE5/2/4/(117)(i), 1.

93. TNA: HO 198/181, Raid Summary TE5/2/4/(107), 2.

94. TWAS: T170/8, Bulletin No. 65, 2–3.

95. TNA: HO 198/181, Raid Summary TE5/2/4/(107), 2.

96. TWAS: T170/8, Bulletin No. 65, 3.

97. TNA: HO 191/11, Chronological Record, 10; and TWAS: T170/8, Bulletin No. 65, 3.

98. TNA: HO 198/1, BC4 Serial No. 1/2/7, Sunderland, 30/9–1/10 1941, 1.

99. TNA: AIR 25/233, No. 13 Group ORB, 30 September 1941.

100. TNA: HO 191/11, Chronological Record, 10.

101. Overy, *Bombing War*, 117.

102. *Times*, 1 October 1941, 2; and Ramsey, *Blitz*, 3, 70.

103. TNA: PREM 3/189/4, GERMAN AIR FORCE, Various, Sir Archibald Sinclair to Winston Churchill, 1 October 1941, 1–2.

104. TNA: PREM 3/189/4, Winston Churchill to Sir Archibald Sinclair, 1 October 1941, 1–2.

105. TNA: AIR 40/1654, Commentary, 51–52.

106. TNA: HO 198/1, BC2 Serial No. 1/BC2/9, North and South Shields, 2–3/10 1941, 1; and TWAS: T170/8, Bulletin No. 66: 1–8 October 1941, 1.

107. TNA: HO 198/1, BC4 Serial No. 1/2/7, South Shields, 2–3/10 1941, 7–8.

108. TWAS: T170/8, Bulletin No. 66, 2; and TNA: HO 191/11, Chronological Record, 10.

109. TWAS: T170/8, Bulletin No. 66, 2.

110. TNA: HO 201/11, Daily Reports, 3 October 1941, 1 and 4 October, 1–2.

111. TNA: HO 201/11, Daily Reports, Weekly Appreciation of Damage, 1–8 October 1941, 1.

112. TNA: HO 198/1, BC2 Serial No. 1/BC2/9, North and South Shields, 2–3/10 1941, 1.

113. TNA: HO 199/30, Air Raids 30 September and 2 October 1941, 15 October 1941, 8.

114. TWAS: T15/1490, WDP1 Returns; August 1940–March 1945, Form WDP1, 2 October 1941 and T170/8, Bulletin No. 66, 2.

115. TNA: HO 199/30, Air Raids 30 September and 2 October 1941, 15 October 1941, 9.

116. TNA: HO 201/11, Daily Reports, 3 October 1941, 2.

117. TWAS: T170/8, Bulletin No. 66, 2.

118. TNA: HO 201/11, Daily Reports, 3 October 1941, 2.

119. BA-MA: RL 2-IV/28, *Gefechtskalender, Durchführung und Erfolge, Oktober*, H6183.

120. TNA: AIR 25/233, No. 13 Group ORB, 2 October 1941.

121. TWAS: T170/8, Bulletin No. 66, 2.

122. TNA: CAB 66/19/9, Paper No. WP (41) 236, Weekly Résumé (No. 110), 2–9 October 1941, 11.

123. TWAS: T170/8, Bulletin No. 66, 4; TNA: CAB 65/19/35, Paper No. WM (41) 99, War Cabinet, Conclusions, 2 October 1941, 69; and CAB 65/19/36, Paper No. WM (41) 100, War Cabinet, Conclusions, 6 October 1941, 74.

124. TNA: HO 198/247, B Division Summary No. 5, 1–2.

125. TNA: CAB 65/19/37, Paper No. WM (41) 101, War Cabinet, Conclusions, 9 October 1941, 83.

126. O'Brien, Civil Defence, 423.

127. TNA: AIR 40/1654, Commentary, 52.

128. TWAS: T170/8, Bulletin No. 67: 8–15 October 1941, 2.

129. TNA: HO 201/11, Daily Reports, 13 October 1941, 1–2.

130. TWAS: T170/8, Bulletin No. 67, 2.

131. TNA: HO 191/11, Chronological Record, 10–11.

132. TNA: AIR 25/177, No. 9 Group ORB, 12 October 1941. Seven aircraft were operated against the raiders on this night. The 12 Group ORB stops recording operational information after September 1941, so it is not possible to ascertain the response in that Group area for this attack.

133. Price, *Blitz on Britain*, 127.

134. BA-MA: RL 2-IV/28, *Gefechtskalender, Durchführung und Erfolge, Oktober*, H6183.

135. TWAS: T170/8, Bulletin No. 67, 2.

136. HHC: C TYA/61, Air Raid Incident Files, Raid 61, 13 October 1941, File 1, Form WDP1, 13 October 1941.

137. BA-MA: RL 2-IV/28, *Gefechtskalender, Durchführung und Erfolge, Oktober*, H6183.

138. TWAS: T170/8, Bulletin No. 68: 15–22 October 1941, 1.

139. TNA: AIR 40/1654, Commentary, 53.

140. TNA: CAB 66/19/19, Paper No. WP (41) 246, Weekly Résumé (No. 112), 16–23 October 1941, 11.

141. TWAS: T170/8, Bulletin No. 68, 1.

142. TNA: HO 191/11, Chronological Record, 11; and TWAS: T170/8, Bulletin No. 68, 1.

143. TNA: AIR 25/177, No. 9 Group ORB, 20 October 1941.

144. TNA: HO 198/1, BC4 Serial No. 1/1/11, Newcastle, 21–22 October 1941, 1; and HO 191/11, Chronological Record, 11.

145. TWAS: T170/8, Bulletin No. 68, 2; and TNA: HO 191/11, Chronological Record, 11.

146. TNA: AIR 25/233, No. 13 Group ORB, 21 October 1941.

147. TNA: HO 198/64, Forms BC2 and BC4, Region 10, North Western, 12/13 October 1941–11/12 March 1943, BC2, Chester, 22/23.10.41, 1, Ellesmere Port, 22/23. 10.41, 1; and TWAS: T170/8, Bulletin No. 69: 22–29 October 1941, 1.

148. TNA: AIR 25/177, No. 9 Group ORB, 22 October 1941.

149. TNA: CAB 65/19/41, Paper No. WM (41) 105, War Cabinet, Conclusions, 23 October 1941, 108.

150. BA-MA: RL 2-IV/28, *Gefechtskalender, Durchführung und Erfolge, Oktober*, H6183.

151. TNA: AIR 40/1654, Commentary, 54.

152. TWAS: T170/8, Bulletin No. 69, 1.

153. TNA: PREM 3/27, AIR: Air Raid Shelters and Rest Centres, M977/1, Lord President of the Privy Council from the Prime Minister, 17 October 1941, 1.

154. TNA: PREM 3/27, Prime Minister from the Lord President of the Privy Council, 23 October 1941, 1.

155. Calder, *People's War*, 234.

156. Winston S. Churchill, *The Second World War, Vol. III: The Grand Alliance* (Cassell, 1950), 455.

157. Calder, *People's War*, 237.

158. H. M. D. Parker, *Manpower* (HMSO, 1950), 150.

159. O'Brien, *Civil Defence*, 550–51.

160. Churchill, *The Second World War, Vol.* III:, 454.

161. TNA: PREM 3/18/1, Houses Repaired by Local Authorities, Calculated from figures on 24 July 1941 and 29 October 1941.

162. TNA: AIR 41/17; ADGB:III, appendices 8 and 15.

163. Air Ministry, *Rise and Fall of the GAF*, 108.

164. BA-MA: RL 2-IV/28, *Gefechtskalender, Wetterablauf*, November, H6193; and *Durchführung und Erfolge*, November, H6194.

165. TNA: CAB 66/19/32, Paper No. WP (41) 259, Weekly Résumé (No. 114), 30 October–6 November 1941, 10.

166. TWAS: T170/8, Bulletin No. 70: 29 October–5 November 1941, 2.

167. TNA: HO 198/64, BC4 Serial No. M306, Ellesmere Port, 1/2.11.41, 1–2.

168. TNA: AIR 16/606, Night Activity Charts, 22–23 October and 1–2 November 1941; and TWAS: T170/8, Bulletin No. 70, 2.

169. TNA: HO 198/247, B Division Summary No. 10, Part II, 1–2 November 1941.

170. TNA: AIR 25/177, No. 9 Group ORB, 1 November 1941.

171. TNA: CAB 66/19/32, Paper No. WP (41) 270, Weekly Résumé (No. 115), 6–13 November 1941, 8.

172. TNA: AIR 25/233, No. 13 Group ORB, 8 November 1941.

173. TWAS: T170/8, Bulletin No. 71: 5–12 November 1941, 2.

174. TNA: HO 201/11, Daily Reports, 8 November 1941, 1; and HO 191/11, Chronological Record, 11.

175. TWAS: T170/8, Bulletin No. 71, 2; and HO 198/1, BC4 Serial No. 1/1/12, Newbiggin, 7/8.11.41, 2.

176. TNA: HO 198/1, BC4 Serial No. 1/2/9, South Shields, 2, West Hartlepool, 7, Billingham, 8, Serial No. 1/1/12, Tynemouth, 3, Serial No. 1/3/12, Redcar, 7, 7/8.11.41.

177. TNA: AIR 25/233, No. 13 Group ORB, 8 November 1941.

178. TNA: CAB 65/20/4, Paper No. WM (41) 111, War Cabinet, Conclusions, 11 November 1941, 141.

179. TNA: CAB 65/20/4, Paper No. WM (41) 111, 142.

180. C. Webster and N. Frankland, *The Strategic Air Offensive Against Germany* [subsequently *SAOAG*] *1939–1945*, Vol. IV (HMSO, 1961), 142.

181. TNA: PREM 3/18/1, Ministry of Health from Prime Minister's Office, 3 December 1941.

182. Ramsey, *Blitz*, 3:79.

183. Murray, *Strategy for Defeat*, 110.

184. TNA: AIR 20/7701, A Survey of German Air Operations, 1939–1944, German Air Historical Branch (8th Abteilung), 21 September 1944, 7.

185. Overy, *Bombing War*, 117.

186. TNA: CAB 66/20/22, Paper No. WP (41) 270, Weekly Résumé (No. 119), 4–11 December 1941, 10 and 13.

187. TNA: HO 198/1, BC2 Serial No. 1/BC2/27, Newcastle, 8–9-12-41, 1.

188. TNA: HO 198/247, B Division Summary No. 14, Part II, 8–9 December 1941.

189. TNA: HO 191/11, Chronological Record, 11; and TWAS: T170/8, Bulletin No. 75: 3–10 December 1941, 1.

190. TWAS: PA.NC/5/54, Occurrence Reports on Air Raids, Air Raid, 2209 hrs 8.12.41-0400 9.12.41 by Assistant Chief Constable, 10 December 1941; TNA: HO 198/1, BC4 Serial No. 1/2/10, South Shields, 8–9-12-41, 1; and TWAS: T170/8, Bulletin No. 75, 2.

191. TNA: HO 198/1, BC4 Serial No. 1/2/10, Billingham, 8–9-12-41, 10, Serial No. 1/1/16, Tynemouth, 3, Serial No. 1/2/10, Felling, 2, Sunderland, 5, Hebburn, 7, Stockton, 13, 8–9-12-41.

192. TNA: AIR 25/233, No. 13 Group ORB, 9 December 1941.

193. Murray, *Strategy for Defeat*, 94–97.

194. TNA: CAB 66/20/34, Paper No. WP (42) 3, Weekly Résumé (No. 122), 25 December 1941–1 January 1942, 9.

195. Ramsey, *Blitz*, 3, 82.

196. TWAS: T170/8, Bulletin No. 78: 24–31 December 1941, 2.

197. TNA: HO 191/11, Chronological Record, 11; and TWAS: PA.NC/5/54, Occurrence Reports on Air Raids, Air Raid, 29 December 1941 by Assistant Chief Constable, 30 December 1941, 1.

198. TNA: AIR 25/233, No. 13 Group ORB, 30 December 1941.

199. TNA: AIR 41/17; ADGB:III, 121–122 and appendix 9.

200. O'Brien, *Civil Defence*, 428.

201. On 15/16 October. BA-MA: RL 2-IV/28, *Gefechtskalender, Durchführung und Erfolge, Oktober*, H6183.

202. TNA: HO 199/396, Region No. 5 and Birmingham: Comparative Estimate of Bomb Damage, HS1/172/1, Blitzed Towns, 4.12.41.

203. TNA: HO 191/11, Chronological Record, 8–11; and TWAS: PA.NC/5/32, Air Raids 1940–43.

204. Calder, *Myth of the Blitz*, 39.

205. TNA: HO 192/1286, Kingston upon Hull, Housing and Re-housing, 26.

206. By December 1940, a million men had joined the British armed forces, Todman, *Britain's War*, 263.

207. Compiled from TNA: HO 198/245, Civilian War Deaths in Administrative Areas of England and Wales: Yearly Totals.

208. TNA: HO 192/1254, RE/B38/27/1, 1–2 and 19–22.

209. Süss, *Death From the Skies*, 233.

210. TNA: HO 192/132, Air Raid Damage, Region 2, North Eastern, Hull, 19–20 May 1942, Serial No. H.381, 1.

211. TNA: HO 192/1268, Surveys of Damage in Great Britain: Kingston-upon-Hull, Weights of Bombs Dropped and Casualties, Industry in Hull.

212. Graystone, *Blitz on Hull*, 8.

213. Groundwater, *Maritime Heritage*, 7.

214. TNA: AIR 41/17; ADGB:III, 112.

215. TNA: AIR 41/1, Balloon Defences 1914–1945, I, 192.

216. TNA: AIR 41/1, Balloon Defences, I, 263.

217. TNA: AIR 41/17; ADGB:III, 117–118.

218. M. M. Postan et al., *Design and Development of Weapons* (HMSO, 1974), 383–384.

219. F. Pile, "The Anti-Aircraft Defence of the United Kingdom from 28 July 1939–15 April 1945," *London Gazette*, no. 38149 (16 December 1947), 5974.

220. TNA: AIR 41/17; ADGB:III, 112.

221. Pile, "Anti-Aircraft Defence of the United Kingdom," 5981.

222. G. J. DeGroot, "Whose Finger on the Trigger? Mixed Anti-Aircraft Batteries and the Female Combat Taboo," *War in History* 4, no. 4 (1997): 436.

223. TNA: PREM 3/48, ANTI-AIRCRAFT DEFENCES, M1000/1, Secretary of State for War from the Prime Minister, 18 October 1941, 1.

224. DeGroot, "Whose Finger on the Trigger?," 436.

225. TNA: PREM 3/48, M1092/1, Secretary of State for War from the Prime Minister, 9 December 1941, 1.

226. DeGroot, "Whose Finger on the Trigger?," 436–438.

227. TNA: AIR 41/17; ADGB:III, 112.

228. TNA: AIR 16/525, Night Air Defence Committee, Minutes of Meetings and Reports, November 1941–August 1943, Progress Report by Air Officer Commanding-In-Chief on the Developments and Results Obtained in Night Interception for the Period 10 November 1941–31 March 1941, 12.

229. Pile, "Anti-Aircraft Defence of the United Kingdom," 5974; and W. S. Douglas, "Air Operations by Fighter Command from 25 November 1940–31 December 1941," *London Gazette*, no. 38404 (16 September 1948): 5018.

230. TNA: AIR 41/17; ADGB:III, 113.

231. TNA: AIR 16/525, AOC-in-C Progress Report, 10 November 1941–31 March 1942, 2.

232. TNA: AIR 41/88, Signals, V, 202.

233. TNA: AIR 41/17; ADGB:III, appendix 11.

234. TNA: AIR 24/531, HQ Fighter Command ORB, Appendices: Air Staff Branch, December 1940, Night Interception Report by Air Officer Commanding-In-Chief, 14 December 1940, 3.

235. TNA: PREM 3/22/3, AIR: Night Bombing—Measures to Counteract, Night Interception—Various, M808/1, Secretary of State for Air from the Prime Minister, 20 August 1941, 1; and L. Brandon, *Night Flyer* (Goodall, 1992 [1961]), 32.

236. TNA: PREM 3/22/2, AIR: Night Bombing—Measures to Counteract, Night Interception—Memoranda by A. M. Dowding, Night Interception, 3 November 1940, 2.

237. TNA: AIR 41/18; ADGB:IV, part 1, paragraph 71; and AIR 16/524, AOC-in-C Progress Report, 1 August–10 November 1941, 10.

238. AHB (RAF): Ministry of Aircraft Production Statistical Review 1939–1945 (1946), United Kingdom New Aircraft Deliveries by Type, 6.

239. AHB: Aircraft Record Cards (AM Form 78), Drawer: Battle P (Cont.)-Beaufighter T.

240. V. Bingham, *Bristol Beaufighter* (Airlife, 1994), 74.

241. TNA: PREM 3/22/2, Comparative Advantages of Summer and Winter Fighting, 15 July 1940, 3.

242. G. White, *Allied Aircraft Piston Engines of World War II* (Warrendale, PA: Society of Automotive Engineers, 1995), 134–138.

243. TNA: PREM 3/22/2, Night Interception, 30 September 1940, 1 and 3.

244. TNA: AIR 2/7317, Report no. 100, appendix A.

245. TNA: PREM 3/22/2, Night Interception, 17 November 1940, 2.

246. TNA: AIR 16/524, AOC-in-C Progress Report, 10 May–18/19 June 1941, 6. Radio mechanic was a specific RAF trade. PREM 3/22/1, AIR: Night Bombing—Measures to Counteract, Night Air Defence Meetings, Night Air Defence Meeting, 25 June 1941, 1.

247. TNA: AIR 20/4316, Sir Henry Tizard, Night Defence and Interception: Reports and Analyses, Report of Conference on Technical Aids to Night Fighting, 8 May 1941, 13–14; and G. Gibson, *Enemy Coast Ahead* (London: Goodall, 1986 [1946]), 131, 146–147.

248. TNA: AIR 20/4316, Report of Conference on Technical Aids to Night Fighting, 8 May 1941, 4.

249. TNA: PREM 3/22/2, Night Interception, 3 November 1940, 2.

250. AHB: AM Form 78, Drawers: Battle P (Cont.)-Beaufighter T and Beaufighter V-Beaufighter JL.

251. AHB: MAP Statistical Review, UK New Aircraft Deliveries by Type, 6.

252. Brandon, *Night Flyer*, 45.

253. TNA: AIR 41/88, Signals, V:129.

254. TNA: PREM 3/22/5, Report for Week Ending 14 December 1940, 1.

255. G. Warner, *The Bristol Blenheim: A Complete History* (Crécy, 2002), 299.

256. Brandon, *Night Flyer*, 48.

257. Bingham, *Bristol Beaufighter*, 75.

258. TNA: AIR 16/524, AOC-in-C Progress Report, 1 August–10 November 1941, 10 and AHB: Aircraft Deliveries Against Contract By Manufacturer, Vol. I: A-G, Bristol: Filton: T Serial Beaufighters: Contract No: B.30264/39, 1.

259. AHB: AM Form 78, Drawers: Battle P (Cont.)-Beaufighter T and Beaufighter V-Beaufighter JL.

260. Bingham, *Bristol Beaufighter*, 75.

261. TNA: PREM 3/22/3, Prime Minister from the Chief of the Air Staff, 30 April 1941, 1–2.

262. AHB: AM Form 78, Drawers: Battle P (Cont.)-Beaufighter T and Beaufighter V-Beaufighter JL.

263. TNA: PREM 3/29/4, Monthly Strength Returns, Fighter Command, 07.09.40 to 02.05.41.

264. TNA: AIR 41/4, Flying Training—Aircrew Training, 1934–1942 (1945), 309–313.

265. TNA: AIR 41/71, Flying Training during World War II: Volume 2 Part 3; Operational Training, 824.

266. TNA: AIR 41/4, Flying Training, 499.

267. Richards, *RAF*, I:192 and TNA: AIR 41/4, Flying Training, 503.

268. TNA: AIR 41/88, Signals, V:129.

269. TNA: AIR 41/71, Operational Training, 837.

270. Gibson, *Enemy Coast Ahead*, 118 and 124.

271. TNA: AIR 41/4, Flying Training, 501–502.

272. TNA: AIR 41/17; ADGB:III, 90.

273. TNA: AIR 41/71, Operational Training, 827–828.

274. TNA: AIR 41/4, Flying Training, 504.

275. TNA: AIR 41/71, Operational Training, 829–830.

276. TNA: AIR 16/1144, Record and History of Operational Training Units under Nos. 81 and 9 Groups and No. 12 Group: 1 July–31 December 1941, Vol. II, Input and Output of Pupils in 1941, 488–493.

277. The intake of courses was in the ratio of 4 singles to 21 twins, TNA: AIR 16/874, History of Fighter OTUs, 5. If the ratio for the output remained the same, this produced 24 single and 128 twin-engine crews.

278. TNA: AIR 16/1143, Record and History of Operational Training Units under Nos. 81 and 9 Groups and No. 12 Group: 1910–30 June 1941, Vol. I, 1941 Summary of Events, 105–106.

279. TNA: AIR 16/491, Training at Operational Training Units 1940–1942, AOC Fighter Command from AOC No. 81 Group, 25 July 1941, 2.

280. TNA: AIR 16/1144, Input and Output of Pupils in 1941, 488–493.

281. TNA: AIR 41/71, Operational Training, 830.

282. TNA: AIR 16/491, Minutes of a Meeting held at the Air Ministry on 29 September 1941 to Discuss the Lengthening of the OTU Course During the Winter Months and to Discuss Means of Expanding TE Night Fighter Capacity, 2.

283. TNA: AIR 16/524, AOC-in-C Progress Report, 1 August–10 November 1941, 10.

284. Richards, *RAF*, I:305.

285. TNA: AIR 16/491, Minutes of a Meeting held at the Air Ministry on 29 September 1941, 1.

286. Richards, *RAF*, I:387.

287. TNA: AIR 16/491, AOC Fighter Command from AOC No. 81 Group, 29 July 1941, 1.

288. TNA: AIR 41/4, Flying Training, 506–507.

289. TNA: AIR 41/71, Operational Training, 830.

290. TNA: AIR 16/491, Minutes of a Meeting Held at Headquarters Fighter Command on 5 August 1941 to Decide on the Establishment of Aircraft in Twin Night Fighter OTUs, 1.

291. TNA: AIR 16/1147, Record and History of Operational Training Units under Nos. 81 and 9 Groups and No. 12 Group: 15 April–31 October 1943, Vol V, A Comparison of the Training at a Night OTU: November 1941 and September 1943, 1695–1697.

292. TNA: AIR 16/491, AC E. S. Goodwin from AM W. S. Douglas, 17 March 1942, 2.

293. TNA: AIR 16/1147, Comparison of the Training at a Night OTU, 1697 and Howard-Williams, *Night Intruder*, 27 and 38.

294. The RAF re-categorised the radar operator role three times; for consistency, 'radar operator' will be used.

295. Brandon, *Night Flyer*, 18 and 24.

296. TNA: AIR 16/524, Progress Report by AOC-in-C on Night Interception, 10 May–18/19 June 1941, 6.

297. TNA: PREM 3/314/4, Prime Minister from Lord Beaverbrook, 14 March 1941, 1.

298. TNA: AIR 16/524, AOC-in-C Progress Report, 1 August–10 November 1941, 6.

299. TNA: AIR 19/308, Air Member for Personnel from Air Member for Training, 27 November 1941, 1.

300. TNA: AIR 41/71, Operational Training, 828.

301. TNA: AIR 41/17; ADGB, Vol. III, appendixes 2, 6, and 9; and Collier, *Defence of the United Kingdom*, appendix XXX.

302. Calculated from TNA: HO 191/11, Chronological Record, 9-11 and AIR 41/17; ADGB:III, 121.

303. Collier, *Defence of the United Kingdom*, 301. Other significant sources that fail to acknowledge any German activity over the UK in 1941 after the end of the Blitz include Air Ministry, *Rise and Fall of the GAF*; Bekker, *Luftwaffe War Diaries*; and Richards, *RAF*, Vol. I.

3. THE EFFECT OF *BAEDEKER* ON THE RESURGENCE OF THE *LUFTWAFFE* IN 1942

1. A. L. Rowse, *Heritage of Britain* (Putnam, 1977), 15.

2. *Universal Knowledge A to Z: A New Encyclopaedia of General Knowledge* (Odhams, 1938), 112.

3. M. Leapman, *Travel Guide to Britain* (Reader's Digest, 1999), 244–247.

4. M. Wainwright, *The Bath Blitz* (DK, 1992 [1975]), 74.

5. C. L. Dunn, *The Emergency Medical Services*, Vol. II (HMSO, 1953), 467.

6. D. M. Bruce, "Baedeker: The Perceived Inventor of the Formal Guidebook: A Bible for Travellers in the 19th Century," in *Giants of Tourism*, ed. R. W. Butler and R. A. Russell (CAB International, 2010), 102.

7. TNA: HO 191/11, Chronological Record, 11.

8. HO 199/138, Bath: Survey of Damage from 25–27 April 1942, 1.

9. N. Rothnie, *The Baedeker Blitz: Hitler's Attack on Britain's Historic Cities* (Ian Allan, 1992), 20.

10. Ramsey, *Blitz: Then and Now*, 3:94.

11. TNA: AIR 41/49; ADGB:V, 41–42.

12. TNA: AIR 40/1654, Commentary, 68.

13. TNA: AIR 41/49; ADGB:V, 42.

14. TNA: AIR 40/1654, Commentary, 68; AIR 40/1645, Tabular Record, 10 January 1942; and CAB 66/21/2, Paper No. WP (42) 22, Weekly Résumé (No. 124), 8–15 January 1942, 11.

15. TWAS: T170/8, Bulletin No. 80: 7–14 January 1942, 2; and TNA: CAB 66/21/2, Paper No. WP (42) 22, 11.

16. TNA: CAB 66/21/4, Paper No. WP (42) 24, Weekly Résumé (No. 125), 15–22 January 1942, 11; and TWAS: T170/8, Bulletin No. 81: 14 to 21 January 1942, 2.

17. TNA: AIR 40/1654, Commentary, 69; and AIR 40/1645, Tabular Record, 15 January 1942.

18. TNA: CAB 66/21/4, Paper No. WP (42) 24, 11.

19. TWAS: T170/8, Bulletin No. 81, 2.

20. TNA: AIR 40/1654, Commentary, 69–71.

21. TNA: AIR 40/1645, Tabular Record, February 1942.

22. TNA: AIR 41/49; ADGB:V, 42.

23. TNA: CAB 66/23/16, Paper No. WP (42) 136, Weekly Résumé (No. 134), 19–26 March 1942, 11.

24. TWAS: T170/8, Bulletin No. 90: 18 to 25 March 1942, 2.

25. TNA: CAB 106/1206, War Cabinet and Cabinet Office: Archivist and Librarian Files: (AL Series), Correspondence of Mr Basil Collier with the Air Ministry, Air Historical Branch, Conference between Goering, Milch, Jeschonnak, Bodenschatz, and Teske on 21 March 1942, 1.

26. TNA: CAB 66/23/16, Paper No. WP (42) 154, Weekly Résumé (No. 136), 2–9 April 1942, 9.

27. TWAS: T170/8, Bulletin No. 92: 1 to 8 April 1942, 2.

28. TNA: HO 191/11, Chronological Record, 11.

29. TNA: CAB 66/23/16, Paper No. WP (42) 154, 9; and CAB 66/23/16, Paper No. WP (42) 164, Weekly Résumé (No. 137), 9–16 April 1942, 9.

30. TWAS: T170/8, Bulletin No. 93: 8 to 15 April 1942, 2.

31. TWAS: T170/8, Bulletin No. 94: 15 to 22 April 1942, 1.

32. TNA: CAB 66/23/16, Paper No. WP (42) 164, 9.

33. TWAS: T170/8, Bulletin No. 94, 2; and TNA: AIR 40/1654, Commentary, 74.

34. TNA: CAB 66/24/6, Paper No. WP (42) 176, Weekly Résumé (No. 138), 16–23 April 1942, 10.

35. TNA: AIR 16/525, AOC-in-C Progress Report, 10 November 1941–31 March 1942, 2.

36. TNA: AIR 41/49; ADGB:V, 43.

37. TNA: AIR 40/2444, *Air War Against Great Britain*, 10.

38. H. Boog, "The Situation of the Luftwaffe from 1942 to the Beginning of 1943," in *Germany and the Second World War, Vol. VI, The Global War*, ed. H. Boog et al. (Oxford University Press, 1991), 622.

39. The number of aircraft despatched in December 1940 (1,385) was less than half of the September total (3,141). In December 1941, roughly half the number (1,411) of aircraft were used in raids compared to those in September (2,621). Webster and Frankland, *SAOAG*, IV, 431.

40. Air Ministry, *Bomber Command* (HMSO, 1941), 128.

41. Webster and Frankland, *SAOAG*, I:178.

42. Terraine, *Right of the Line*, 293.

43. T. D. Biddle, "Bombing by the Square Yard: Sir Arthur Harris at War, 1942–1945," *International History Review* 21, no. 3 (1999): 632.

44. M. Hastings, *Bomber Command* (Michael Joseph, 1979), 132–133 and Webster and Frankland, *SAOAG*, IV, 143–145.

45. R. Jackson, *Before the Storm: The Story of Bomber Command 1939–42* (Cassell, 2001), 179.

46. M. Middlebrook and C. Everitt, *The Bomber Command War Diaries, An Operational Reference Book: 1939–1945* (Penguin, 1990 [1985]), 245.

47. Air Ministry, *Bomber Command Continues* (HMSO, 1942), 43; and A. Harris, *Bomber Offensive* (Collins, 1947), 104.

48. J. Goebbels, *The Goebbels Diaries* (Hamish Hamilton, 1948), 71.

49. D. Richards and H. St. G. Saunders, *Royal Air Force 1939–1945*, Vol. II (HMSO, 1954), 122; Webster and Frankland, *SAOAG*, I:339; Jackson, *Before the Storm*, 187; and Hastings, *Bomber Command*, 147.

50. M. Perry, "Bombing Billancourt: Labour Agency and the Limitations of the Public Opinion Model of Wartime France," *Labour History Review* 77, no. 1 (2012): 73.

51. Overy, *Bombing War*, 118.

52. TNA: AIR 20/7703, Translations from Captured Enemy Documents, Vol. IV (1947), Translation VII/79, Reports of Conferences Held by Riechsmarschall Göring on 6 March and 16 May 1942, Conference Held on 6 March 1942, 1.

53. S. Kitson, "Criminals or Liberators? French Public Opinion and the Allied Bombing of France, 1940–1945," in *Bombing, States and Peoples*, ed. Baldoli et al., (Continuum, 2011), 285.

54. Terraine, *Right of the Line*, 473; TNA: AIR 10/2288, AP1093D, Vol. I, Part II, chapter 4, paragraphs 2-3; and R. Irons, *The Relentless Offensive* (Pen & Sword, 2009), 218.

55. M. Farr, "The Labour Party and Strategic Bombing in the Second World War," *Labour History Review* 77, no. 1 (2012): 144; Terraine, *Right of the Line*, 475.

56. Webster and Frankland, *SAOAG*, I:389.

57. A. Harris, *Despatch on War Operations* (Frank Cass, 1995), 10.

58. R. Blank, "The Battle of the Ruhr 1943: Aerial Warfare Against an Industrial Region," *Labour History Review* 77, no. 1 (2012): 40.

59. Harris, *Bomber Offensive*, 105.

60. Webster and Frankland, *SAOAG*, I:391.

61. Jackson, *Before the Storm*, 189.

62. Goebbels, *Goebbels Diaries*, 108.

63. Collier, *Defence of the United Kingdom*, 305; Douglas, *Years of Command*, 162; Price, *Blitz on Britain 1939–1945*, 132; C. Whiting, *Three Star Blitz: The Baedeker Raids and the Start of Total War* (Leo Cooper, 1987), 3; and S. Snelling, *Norwich: A Shattered City* (Halsgrove, 2012), 15.

64. Rothnie, *Baedeker Blitz*, 9.

65. Hastings, *Bomber Command*, 127.

66. Webster and Frankland, *SAOAG*, I, 331–332.

67. Jackson, *Before the Storm*, 186.

68. Middlebrook and Everitt, *Bomber Command War Diaries*, 259–261.

69. Goebbels, *Goebbels Diaries*, 135, 142.

70. Jackson, *Before the Storm*, 189.

71. TNA: AIR 40/1654, Commentary, 75.

72. TNA: AIR 41/49; ADGB:V, 47.

73. Air Ministry, *Rise and Fall of the GAF*, 195; TNA: AIR 40/1526, German Air Force: Order of Battle, March 1942–October 1944 (1945), Order of Battle for 21/05/42, 4, places 7/KG100 at Chartres.

74. Jones, *Most Secret War*, 251.

75. Rothnie, *Baedeker Blitz*, 11.

76. Jones, *Most Secret War*, 251–252.

77. Air Ministry, *Rise and Fall of the GAF*, 195.

78. Price, *Blitz on Britain 1939–1945*, 132.

79. TNA: CAB 65/26/9, Paper No. WM (42) 48, War Cabinet, Conclusions, 14 April 1942, 213.

80. Parker, *Manpower*, 195.

81. TNA: CAB 66/23/33, Paper No. WP (42) 153, Release of Whole-Time Civil Defence Personnel for War Industry, 10 April 1942, 3.

82. TNA: CAB 65/26/9, Paper No. WM (42) 48, 213.

83. TNA: CAB 66/23/33, Paper No. WP (42) 153, 1 and 3. The reductions consisted of one-sixth of the National Fire Service in England and Wales, one-third of the Civil Defence services, and seven thousand policemen.

84. Defined by the AHB narrative as 23 April–9 May 1942, TNA: AIR 41/49; ADGB:V, 46. This period coincided with the maximum available moonlight for the month, AIR 16/607, Description of Enemy Activity, April–May 1942.

85. TNA: AIR 40/1654, Commentary, 75.

86. TNA: AIR 40/1645, Tabular Record, April 1942.

87. Rothnie, *Baedeker Blitz*, 18.

88. TNA: HO 198/247, B Division Summary No. 34, 1.

89. TNA: HO 191/183, Report of Air Attacks on Exeter, April–May 1942, Consolidated Report on the Effects of Air Attacks on the City of Exeter, 2; and TWAS: T170/8, Bulletin No. 95: 22–29 April 1942, 4. Records show that bombs destroyed nineteen houses and seriously damaged twenty-seven more, HO 198/57, Forms BC2 and BC4, Region 7,

South Western, 8–9 July 1941–15–16 June 1942, BC4, Exeter City and County, 23–24 April 1942, 1.

90. TNA: AIR 25/182, No. 10 Group ORB, 24 April 1942.

91. TNA: AIR 16/889, Casualty Returns, March 1942–September 1943, Return of Enemy Aircraft Casualties due to Anti-Aircraft Fire, 22–29 April 1942.

92. TNA: AIR 16/607, Fighter Command Operational Research Section: Enemy Night Activity Charts, 23–24–24–25 April 1942.

93. TNA: HO 191/183, Consolidated Report, 2; and CAB 66/24/13, Paper No. WP (42) 183, Weekly Résumé (No. 139), 23–30 April 1942, 9.

94. TWAS: T170/8, Bulletin No. 95, 4; TNA: HO 191/11, Chronological Record, 11 and HO 192/868, Exeter: Bomb Damage to Various Properties, Hostile Air Attack, 23–24 April 1942, 29 April 1042, 1.

95. Rothnie, *Baedeker Blitz*, 19.

96. TNA: AIR 25/182, No. 10 Group ORB, 24 April 1942.

97. Jones, *Most Secret War*, 252. The RAF Y-Service was able to confirm KG100 were operating by identifying the call sign of the target-marking aircraft, TNA: AIR 40/1645, Tabular Record, April 1942.

98. Rothnie, *Baedeker Blitz*, 19.

99. TNA: AIR 40/1645, Tabular Record, April 1942.

100. Price, *Blitz on Britain 1939–1945*, 134.

101. Rothnie, *Baedeker Blitz*, 19.

102. TNA: AIR 16/607, Night Activity Charts, 25–26 April 1942 and AIR 40/1645, Tabular Record, April 1942.

103. AIR 40/2444, Air War Against Great Britain, 11.

104. TNA: HO 192/862, Preliminary Report on the Raids on Bath, 1; HO 198/57, Report on the IB Attack on Bath, 6 May 1942, 2; Rothnie, *Baedeker Blitz*, 19; and AIR 25/177, No. 9 Group ORB, 25 April 1942.

105. TNA: HO 198/247, B Division Summary No. 35, 25–26 April–1–2 May 1942, 3.

106. TWAS: T170/8, Bulletin No. 95, 5.

107. TNA: HO 199/138, Report on the South Western Region for the Period 1 April–9 May, 1.

108. TNA: HO 191/11, Chronological Record, 11.

109. TWAS: T170/8, Bulletin No. 95, 5.

110. TNA: HO 192/862, Situation at Bath After Raids 25–26–26–27 April 1942, 1.

111. TNA: AIR 16/607, Night Activity Charts, 25–26 April 1942.

112. TWAS: T170/8, Bulletin No. 95, 5.

113. TNA: HO 199/138, Dictated Report on Visit of Inspection to Bath on Tuesday and Wednesday, 28–29 April 1942, 1.

114. Bath Record Office (subsequently BRO): 0146, Maps Showing Bomb Damage to Properties in Bath. Of these, twenty-seven failed to explode.

115. Calculated from TNA: HO 198/57, BC4, Bath City, Somerset, 25–26–26–27 April 1941.

116. TNA: HO 192/1651, Air Raid Assessment Reports, Bath: General, 4 June 1942.

117. TNA: HO 192/862, Preliminary Report on the Raids on Bath, 1.

118. TNA: HO 199/138, Report on the South Western Region, 1.

119. TNA: HO 191/11, Chronological Record, 11.

120. As reported in TNA: HO 192/862, Situation at Bath After Raids, 1; Observations on General Effects of Blast, 1; HO 199/138, Dictated Report, Bath, 1; and Report on the South Western Region, 1.

121. TNA: HO 192/862, Preliminary Report, 1; Situation at Bath After Raids, 1; and HO 199/138, Dictated Report on Visit of Inspection to Bath, 1.

122. Calculated from TNA: HO 198/57, BC4, Bath, Somerset, 25–26–26–27 April 1942.

123. TNA: HO 192/862, Observations on General Effects of Blast, 1; and HO 199/138, Bath, 1.

124. TNA: HO 199/138, Dictated Report, 1–4; and Bath, 1–5.

125. TNA: HO 198/57, BC4, Bath, Somerset, 25–26 April 1942, 1.

126. BRO: 0146, Annotated Somerset Sheets XIV.1 and 5 Showing Bomb Damage to Properties in Bath.

127. TWAS: T170/8, Bulletin No. 95, 5.

128. TNA: HO 201/12, Daily Reports, January–June 1942, 26 April 1942, 5; and Railway Situation Report, 27 April 1942.

129. TWAS: T170/8, Bulletin No. 95, 5.

130. TNA: HO 201/12, Railway Situation Report, 28 and 30 April 1942, Daily Reports, 10 May 1942 and Weekly Appreciation of Damage, 22 to 29 April 1942, 2.

131. Calculated from TNA: HO 192/862, Summary of Air Raid Damage, Bath City, 9 June 1942; and BRO: War Damage List of Houses, Specifications and Plans: No. 1, Air Raid Damage to Council Houses, 8 July 1942.

132. TNA: HO 192/862, Preliminary Report, 4.

133. TNA: HO 199/138, Bath, 4.

134. TNA: HO 199/421, Region No. 7: May 1942–January 1943, Report on the South Western Region for the Period 10–31 May 1942, 1. On 9 May, 2,500 men had been used for first aid repairs, BRO: BC/2/1/66/2, Minutes of Bath City Council, 1631–1974, Civil Defence Committee, 19 June 1942, 2.

135. TNA: HO 199/138, Bath, 5.

136. TNA: AIR 25/182, No. 10 Group ORB, 25 April 1942.

137. TNA: AIR 16/889, Combats and Casualties, 25–27 April 1942; and AIR 25/182, No. 10 Group ORB, 26 April 1942.

138. A. Price, *The Hardest Day* (Arms and Armour, 1988), 104.

139. TNA: PREM 3/48, Memorandum for the Prime Minister on Emergency Deployment of A.A. Defences to Counter Enemy Attacks on Undefended Towns, 28 April 1942, 2.

140. TNA: PREM 3/48, Memorandum on Emergency Deployment of A.A. Defences, 2.

141. Whiting, *Three Star Blitz*, 52.

142. Goebbels, *Goebbels Diaries*, 139.

143. Bruce, "Baedeker," 93–98.

144. Snelling, *Shattered City*, 16.

145. *Times*, 29 April 1943, 4.

146. Snelling, *Shattered City*, 16.

147. Goebbels, *Goebbels Diaries*, 142.

148. TNA: AIR 16/607, Night Activity Charts, 27–28 April 1942.

149. Rothnie, *Baedeker Blitz*, 20.

150. TNA: AIR 25/220, No. 12 (Fighter) Group ORB, 1942–1943, 28 April 1942.

151. Snelling, *Shattered City*, 89 and TWAS: T170/8, Bulletin No. 95, 6.

152. M-O: FR 1285, Reports on Two Baedeker Raids, 30 May 1942, 4.

153. TNA: AIR 25/220, No. 12 Group ORB, 28 April 1942; and AIR 16/607, Night Activity Charts, 27/28 April 1942.

154. Whiting, *Three Star Blitz*, 65.

155. TNA: PREM 3/48, Memorandum on Emergency Deployment of A.A. Defences, 2.

156. Damage as listed in TWAS: T170/8, Bulletin No. 95, 7. TNA: AIR 16/607, Night Activity Charts, 28–29 April 1942.

157. TNA: HO 192/129, Air Raid Damage, Region No. 2, North Eastern, York, BC4, York City, 28–29 April 1942, 1.

158. Collier, *Defence of the United Kingdom*, 306.

159. TNA: HO 199/322, Comments and Recommendations by Inspector General and Other; Inspectors Following Country-Wide Visits, York, 1.

160. TNA: CAB 66/24/13, Paper No. WP (42) 183, 10.

161. TNA: HO 192/129, RE/B12/1/1, 1 and First Appreciation of the Air Raid on York, 4–5.

162. York City Archive (subsequently YCA): 89.38a.2, Civil Defence, Miscellaneous Correspondence Following Raid, 30 April–17 July 1942, Report on the Air Raid on the City During the Early Hours of 29 April 1942, 8.

163. TNA: HO 192/129, First Appreciation, 4–5.

164. TNA: HO 199/322, York, 1.

165. TNA: HO 191/11, Chronological Record, 11.

166. TNA: AIR 16/607, Night Activity Charts, 28–29 April 1942.

167. TNA: AIR 25/220, No. 12 Group ORB, 29 April 1942.

168. TNA: AIR 16/889, Combats and Casualties, 29 April 1942; and AIR 25/233, No. 13 Group ORB, 29 April 1942.

169. TNA: HO 201/12, Railway Situation Report, 29–30 April, 1 May 1942.

170. M-O: FR 1285, Two Baedeker Raids, 6; and Snelling, *Shattered City*, 85.

171. TNA: AIR 40/1645, Tabular Record, 29 April 1942.

172. TNA: CAB 66/24/13, Paper No. WP (42) 183, 9.

173. TWAS: T170/8, Bulletin No. 96: 29 April–6 May 1942, 3.

174. TNA: AIR 41/49; ADGB:V, 49; and Snelling, *Shattered City*, 89.

175. TNA: HO 198/202, Raid Summaries, Special Reports: Damage in Region 4 and 5, RE/B14/1/1, 1.

176. TNA: AIR 16/889, Combats and Casualties, 29 April 1942.

177. TNA: AIR 41/49; ADGB:V, 51.

178. Snelling, *Shattered City*, 87.

179. TNA: AIR 16/607, Night Activity Charts, 30 April–1 May 1942.

180. TWAS: T170/8, Bulletin No. 96, 3; and TNA: AIR 40/1645, Tabular Record, 30 April 1942.

181. TNA: HO 199/412, Region No. 1, May 1942–January 1943, Regional Commissioner's Monthly Report, May 1942, 1.

182. TNA: HO 201/12, Damage Summary, 1–2; and Railway Situation Report, 1 May 1942.

183. TNA: HO 191/11, Chronological Record, 11.

184. TNA: AIR 25/233, No. 13 Group ORB, 1 May 1942.

185. TNA: AIR 25/220, No. 12 Group ORB and AIR 16/889, Combats and Casualties, 1 May 1942.

186. Price, *Blitz on Britain 1939–1945*, 134–135.

187. TNA: AIR 16/889, Combats and Casualties, 30 April 1942.

188. TNA: AIR 41/16; ADGB:II, appendix 36.

189. Imperial War Museum (subsequently IWM): German Miscellaneous MCR 18: GAF Losses, Reels 8–9.

190. The Do 217E2 U5+MN shot down in Devon on 23 April is not present in MCR 18, indicating inaccuracies in both German and British records; Ramsey, *Blitz*, 3, 108.

191. Interpretation of the German records has led to errors in some sources. A Do 217 of Stab/KG2 was incorrectly assigned to the second Norwich raid but was actually damaged off Norwich during the York attack. The other losses from the York raid (also reported as 29 April) are completely undocumented; Snelling, *Shattered City*, 87.

192. TNA: AIR 16/607, Description of Enemy Activity, 16–30 April 1942.

193. TNA: AIR 40/1654, Commentary, 77; and Collier, *Defence of the United Kingdom*, 306.

194. TNA: AIR 41/49; ADGB:V, 51.

195. TNA: AIR 16/607, Night Activity Charts, 3–4 May 1942; and AIR 40/1654, Commentary, 77; quote the higher figure. TNA: HO 191/183, Consolidated Report, 3; and HO 198/57, BC4, Exeter City and County, Somerset, 3–4 May 1942, 1; use the lower number of aircraft.

196. TNA: HO 192/868, Final Report on City of Exeter Air Raid, 3–4 May 1942, 1.

197. TNA: HO 191/183, Consolidated Report, April–May 1942, 2–3.

198. TWAS: T170/8, Bulletin No. 96, 4.

199. TNA: HO 191/183, Consolidated Report, 2–4. The centres of both Lübeck and Exeter provided an ideal environment for incendiary attacks.

200. TWAS: T170/8, Bulletin No. 96, 4.

201. TNA: HO 198/57, Early Morning Appreciation of the Attack in Exeter, 3–4 May; and HO 201/12, Damage Summary, 4 May 1942, 2; and Railway Situation Report, 4–5 May 1942.

202. TWAS: T170/8, Bulletin No. 96, 4.

203. TNA: HO 191/183, Consolidated Report, 25.

204. TNA: HO 191/11, Chronological Record, 11.

205. TNA: HO 191/183, Consolidated Report, 5.

206. TNA: HO 199/139, Exeter, 23 to 25 April and 3–4 May 1942, Exeter, 2.

207. TNA: AIR 25/182, No. 10 Group ORB, 3 May 1942.

208. TNA: AIR 16/889, Combats and Casualties, 4 May 1942.

209. TNA: AIR 40/2444, Air War Against Great Britain, 11.

210. TNA: HO 198/53, Forms BC2 and BC4, Region 6, Southern, 19–20 February 1941–16–17 June 1942, BC3 Forms, Cowes, Isle of Wight, Hampshire, 4–5 May 1942; and BC2, Cowes UDC, 4–5 May 1942, 1.

211. TNA: AIR 16/607, Night Activity Charts, 4–5 May 1942.

212. TNA: HO 198/53, BC2, Cowes UDC, 4–5 May 1942, 1, BC3 Forms, Cowes, Isle of Wight, Hampshire, 4–5 May 1942; and TNA: HO 191/11, Chronological Record, 11.

213. TWAS: T170/8, Bulletin No. 96, 4.

214. TNA: HO 198/193 Raid Summary TI 5/2/4 (123), 2; HO 201/12, Damage Summary, 1 and Railway Situation Report, 5 May 1942.

215. The He 177 would not begin operational evaluation until July 1942 and did not enter service until the end of 1942; D. Mondey, *Axis Aircraft of World War II* (Chancellor, 1996 [1984]), 95. The existence of the aircraft had been noted by the British in September 1941; TNA: PREM 3/189/4, ACM Freeman to Winston Churchill, 13 September 1941, 1.

216. TNA: AIR 16/889, Combats and Casualties, 4 and 5 May; Enemy Aircraft Casualties due to Anti-Aircraft Fire, 4 May 1942; and AIR 25/182, No. 10 Group ORB, 4 May 1942.

217. TNA: AIR 41/49; ADGB:V, 52.

218. Collier, *Defence of the United Kingdom*, 307.

219. Jones, *Most Secret War*, 252–253.

220. TNA: CAB 66/24/33, Paper No. WP (42) 203, Weekly Résumé (No. 141), 7–14 May 1942, 8.

221. TNA: HO 198/10, Forms BC2 and BC4, Region 4, Eastern, 8–9 July 1941–12 June 1942, Raid 8/9.5.42, Preliminary Report and RDS Station (67/713208). The 'Air Ministry Station' was the Stoke Holy Cross Chain Home (CH) radar, but German intelligence would have been unaware this equipment was unsuitable for night operations; Ramsey, *Blitz*, 3, 127.

222. TNA: AIR 16/607, Night Activity Charts, 8–9 May 1942.

223. TNA: HO 199/415, Region No. 4, May 1942–January 1943, Regional Commissioner's Monthly Report, May 1942, 1; and TWAS: T170/8, Bulletin No. 97: 6–13 May 1942, 3.

224. TNA: HO 198/10, Raid 8/9.5.42, Preliminary Report. A mobile barrage of balloons had been deployed to Norwich on 1 May, which prevented accurate low-level bombing: AIR 41/49; ADGB:V, 52.

225. TNA: AIR 41/46, No. 80 Wing RAF Historical Report 1940–1945, appendices 4 and 5.

226. TNA: AIR 25/220, No. 12 Group ORB, 9 May 1942.

227. TNA: AIR 16/607, Night Activity Charts, 8–9 May 1942 and AIR 16/889, Enemy Aircraft Casualties due to Anti-Aircraft Fire, 9 May 1942.

228. TNA: HO 198/10, Raid 8/9.5.42, Balloons and RDS Station (67/713208). There was also a possible contribution from a night fighter, as another report states 'one contact made, but had to break off as E/A was approaching Balloon Barrage'; Night Fighters, Coltishall Aerodrome.

229. IWM: MCR 18: GAF Losses, Reel 9.

230. TNA: AIR 41/49; ADGB:V, 52.

231. TNA: HO 191/203, History of the Research and Experiments Department, Ministry of Home Security 1939–1945, 9.

232. IWM: MCR 18: GAF Losses, Reel 9.

233. TWAS: T170/8, Bulletin No. 95, 1.

234. TNA: CAB 66/24/33, Paper No. WP (42) 203, 6.

235. Calculated from Middlebrook and Everitt, *Bomber Command War Diaries*, 245–261; and TNA: AIR 40/1645, Tabular Record.

236. TNA: HO 199/139, Exeter, 23–25 April and 3/4 May 1942, Exeter, 2.

237. TNA: HO 199/420, Region No. 6, May 1942–February 1943, Regional Commissioner's Monthly Report, May 1942, 1.

238. Collier, *Defence of the United Kingdom*, 308.

239. Rothnie, *Baedeker Blitz*, 20; Whiting, *Three Star Blitz*, 134; and Snelling, *Shattered City*, 157.

240. TNA: AIR 40/2444, Air War Against Great Britain, 11.

241. TNA: AIR 20/8693, Hermann Goering: Interrogation at the Nuremberg Trial, 13. Such opposition must be put in the context of a post-war interrogation, although large parts of the Admiralty had been evacuated to Bath.

242. YCA: 89.32, Reports on Air Raids: York: 28 October 1940, 2.

243. Whiting, *Three Star Blitz*, 90.

244. TNA: HO 192/129, First Appreciation, 3. This page of the report has been crossed through with blue pencil, suggesting that such comments were disregarded at a higher level.

245. TNA: AIR 20/7703, Translation VII/79, Conference Held on 16 May 1942, 6.

246. The final guide published before the war contains plans of Bath, Canterbury, Exeter, Norwich, and York, which were attacked. There are also plans of eleven other cathedrals that were never targeted by the *Luftwaffe*; K. Baedeker, *Great Britain: Handbook for Travellers* (Old House, 2013 [1937]), 29, 53, 73, 105, 108, 120, 136, 181, 217, 225, 264, 265, 320, 348, 401, and 444.

247. Baedeker, *Great Britain*, xxxi.

248. TNA: CAB 66/24/33, Paper No. WP (42) 203, 6. These were calculated from wireless intercepts, as the call sign for *Luftwaffe* aircraft was also the unit designation, allowing easy identification; TNA: AIR 40/2666, RAF Wireless Intelligence Service, Periodical Summaries, Summary No. 23, March–April 1942, 2; and AIR 40/2444, Air War Against Great Britain, 11.

249. Calculated from IWM: MCR 18: *GAF Losses*, Reels 8–9. The unfamiliarity of crews with operations over the United Kingdom probably increased losses, TNA: AIR 41/49; ADGB:V, 53.

250. TNA: AIR 40/1526, German Air Force, Order of Battle for 21.05.42.

251. TNA: AIR 40/1645, Tabular Record, May 1942.

252. TNA: AIR 16/607, Night Activity Charts, 19–20 May 1942.

253. TWAS: T170/8, Bulletin No. 98: 13–20 May 1942, 1; and TNA: AIR 40/1645, Tabular Record, May 1942.

254. TNA: HO 192/132, Hull, 19–20 May 1942, Home Security Intelligence Summary No. 1980, 1.

255. HHC: C TYA/66, Air Raid Incident Files, Raid 66, 19 May 1942, File 9, Form WDP1, 19 May 1942.

256. TWAS: T170/8, Bulletin No. 98, 3; and TNA: HO 191/11, Chronological Record, 11.

257. TNA: HO 201/12, Damage Summary, 1, 20 May 1942.

258. TNA: AIR 25/220, No. 12 Group ORB, 20 May 1942. One Ground Control Interception (GCI) station directed two fighters towards German bombers, but in both cases, the targets were at the limit of radar range, and contact was lost before fighters could intercept, AIR 16/865, GCI Station, Seaton Snook: Interception Reports, Summary of Interception Operations, 19 to 20 May 1942.

259. TNA: AIR 40/1645, Tabular Record, May 1942.

260. TNA: AIR 16/607, Night Activity Charts, 24–25 May 1942 and HO 192/811, Air Raid Damage, Region 6, Southern, Poole and Bournemouth, RE/B16/2/1, 1.

261. TNA: HO 192/811, Appreciation and Report of Attack on Poole Borough 24–24 May 1942, 1.

262. TWAS: T170/8, Bulletin No. 99: 20–27 May 1942, 2.

263. TNA: HO 191/11, Chronological Record, 11.

264. TNA: AIR 41/49; ADGB:V, 65.

265. Boog, "The Situation of the Luftwaffe from 1942 to the Beginning of 1943," 622. Overy uses a similar argument to demonstrate the resources tied up by Bomber Command at the beginning of 1944, but these greatly increased figures include fifty-five thousand anti-aircraft guns and 70 percent of all fighters (780 twin engine and 870 single engine), R. Overy, *Why the Allies Won* (Pimlico, 2006), 158–160; and Air Ministry, *Rise and Fall of the GAF*, 274.

4. AFTER *BAEDEKER*: CONTINUATION OF *LUFTWAFFE* OPERATIONS THROUGHOUT 1942

1. TNA: AIR 40/1654, Commentary, 83.

2. TNA: AIR 16/607, ORS 6/1/3, 21 August 1942.

3. TNA: AIR 40/1654, Commentary, 88.

4. TNA: AIR 41/49; ADGB:V, 66.

5. Webster and Frankland, *SAOAG*, I, 402. This comment is worthy of consideration because the author served as a navigator in Bomber Command.

6. Overy, *Bombing War*, 292.

7. Harris, *Despatch*, xv.

8. Terraine, *Right of the Line*, 484.

9. Harris, *Despatch*, 13.

10. Harris, *Bomber Offensive*, 109.

11. Overy, *Bombing War*, 292.

12. Jackson, *Before the Storm*, 190–191.

13. Overy, *Bombing War*, 293.

14. Richards and Saunders, *Royal Air Force 1939–1945*, II, 137.

15. Terraine, *Right of the Line*, 489.

16. Webster and Frankland, *SAOAG*, I, 412.

17. Overy, *Bombing War*, 293.

18. Richards and Saunders, *Royal Air Force 1939–1945*, II, 137.

19. Terraine, *Right of the Line*, 490.

20. Overy, *Bombing War*, 293.

21. Webster and Frankland, *SAOAG*, I, 416.

22. Richards and Saunders, *Royal Air Force 1939–1945*, II, 138.

23. Overy, *Bombing War*, 293.

24. Overy, *Bombing War*, 256.

25. TNA: HO 191/203, History of the Research and Experiments Department, Ministry of Home Security 1939–1945, A. R. Astbury, 71–72.

26. R. Overy, "Bomber Command and the Lessons of the Blitz 1940–1941," *Royal Air Force Historical Society Journal* 55 (2013): 9.

27. Buckley, *Air Power*, 144.

28. TNA: HO 191/203, History of the Research and Experiments Department, 2.

29. Overy, "Bomber Command and the Lessons of the Blitz," 9.

30. Zuckerman, *From Apes to Warlords*, 146.

31. Zuckerman Archive (subsequently SZ): OEMU/50/2/9, Effects of Raids 1942–1945, RE8 Assessment of the 1000 Bomber Raid on Cologne, and OEMU/50/2/16, RE8 Report on Dusseldorf Raids, August and September 1942.

32. O'Brien, *Civil Defence*, 431.

33. Whiting, *Three Star Blitz*, 126.

34. TNA: AIR 20/7703, Translation VII/79, Conference Held on 16 May 1942, 7; and Webb and Duncan, *Blitz Over Britain*, 173.

35. TNA: AIR 16/607, Night Activity Charts, 31 May–1 June 1942, estimates the number at forty-five, while AIR 40/1645, Tabular Record, 31 May 1942, favours fifty aircraft. Some secondary sources grossly overestimate the numbers involved, such as seventy-seven, Rothnie, *Baedeker Blitz*, 113; eighty, O'Brien, *Civil Defence*, 431; or eighty to ninety, Collier, *Defence of the United Kingdom*, 307.

36. TNA: HO 198/65, Forms BC2 and BC4, Region 12, South Eastern, 26 August 1941–6–7 June 1942, BC2, Canterbury, 31 May–1 June 1942, 1; and AIR 16/607, Night Activity Charts, 31 May/1 June 1942.

37. TWAS T170/8, Bulletin No. 100: 27 May–3 June 1942, 1, TNA: HO 198/247, B Division Summary No. 39, 1; and AIR 40/1654, Commentary, 80. The erroneous belief that a greater proportion of heavy HE was being used has already been discussed.

38. TNA: AIR 41/49; ADGB:V, 54.

39. TNA: HO 199/261, Canterbury, 1; and 3 June 1942, Report of Raid on Canterbury, 1.6.42, 1.

40. TNA: CAB 66/25/17, Paper No. WP (42) 237, Weekly Résumé (No. 144), 28 May–4 June 1942, 10; and HO 191/11, Chronological Record, 11. The destroyed figure for dwelling houses appears excessively high, as a subsequent report gives the aggregate for all three raids in June at 510 destroyed and another 600 severely damaged, HO 192/1102, Canterbury, House Damage, Canterbury Raids: June 1942, 1.

41. TNA: HO 199/261, Report of Raid, 1.6.42, 3.

42. TNA: HO 201/12, Daily Reports, 2 June 1942, 2; and Railway Situation Report, 1 June 1942.

43. TWAS T170/8, Bulletin No. 100, 3.

44. TNA: AIR 41/49; ADGB:V, 55.

45. TNA: AIR 25/194, No. 11 (Fighter) Group ORB, 1942–1943, 31 May 1942.

46. TNA: AIR 16/889, Combats and Casualties, 31 May–1 June 1942.

47. O'Brien, *Civil Defence*, 431.

48. Collier, *Defence of the United Kingdom*, 308.

49. TNA: AIR 16/607, Night Activity Charts, 1–2 June 1942 estimates the number as eight. HO 198/10, Report on Ipswich Borough Raid June 1–2 1942, 2, quantifies this as approximately fifteen aircraft. HO 199/99, Ipswich: 2 June 1942, Abstract of Report Dated 17th June 1942 by ARP Controller, Ipswich County Borough on Raid of 2nd June 1942, 1; and HO 198/247, B Division Summary No. 39, 1.

50. TNA: HO 201/12, Weekly Summary of Damage, 27 May–3 June 1942, 4.

51. TNA: HO 199/99, Report on Air Raid on Tuesday 2nd June 1942, 1 and 4; and HO 198/10, Report on Ipswich Borough Raid, 1.

52. TNA: HO 199/99, Abstract of Report, 1–2.

53. TNA: AIR 16/889, Combats and Casualties, 2 June 1942; and Enemy Aircraft Casualties due to Anti-Aircraft Fire, 27 May–3 June 1942.

54. TNA: AIR 16/607, Night Activity Charts, 2–3 June 1942; HO 198/65, BC2, Canterbury, 2–3 June 1942, 1; and HO 198/247, B Division Summary No. 39, 1. A single aircraft had also dropped 720 incendiaries at Canterbury on 1–2 June, but these fell on open ground and caused no damage.

55. TWAS T170/8, Bulletin No. 100, 3.

56. Rothnie, *Baedeker Blitz*, 127.

57. TNA: AIR 25/194, No. 11 Group ORB, 1 June 1942; and AIR 16/889, Combats and Casualties, 3 June 1942 and Enemy Aircraft Casualties due to Anti-Aircraft Fire, 27 May–3 June 1942.

58. Whiting, *Britain Under Fire*, 135; and TWAS T170/8, Bulletin No. 101: 3–10 June 1942, 2.

59. TNA: HO 198/53, Report of an Attack on the Borough of Poole on 3/4/6/42, 1.

60. TNA: HO 198/247, B Division Summary No. 39, 1; and AIR 25/182, No. 10 Group ORB, 3 June 1942.

61. TNA: HO 201/12, Weekly Summary, 27 May–3 June 1942, 1.

62. TNA: HO 198/53, Report of an Attack on the Borough of Poole, 2; and CAB 66/25/17, Paper No. WP (42) 237, 10.

63. TNA: AIR 25/182, No. 10 Group ORB, 3 June 1942; AIR 25/194, No. 11 Group ORB, 3 June 1942; and AIR 16/889, Combats and Casualties, 4 June 1942.

64. TNA: AIR 40/1645, Tabular Record, 4 June 1942.

65. TNA: HO 201/12, Weekly Summary, 27 May–3 June 1942, 2.

66. TNA: HO 198/247, B Division Summary No. 39, 1; and TWAS T170/8, Bulletin No. 101, 2.

67. TNA: AIR 16/889, Combats and Casualties, 4–5 June 1942.

68. TNA: HO 198/65, BC2, Canterbury, 6–7 June 1942, 1, specifies twenty-five, but both AIR 40/1645, Tabular Record, 6 June 1942 and HO 201/12, Weekly Summary, 3, agree on fifteen. TWAS T170/8, Bulletin No. 101, 2.

69. TNA: AIR 41/49; ADGB:V, 55–56.

70. Rothnie, *Baedeker Blitz*, 128.

71. TNA: AIR 40/1645, Tabular Record, June 1942.

72. TNA: AIR 16/607, Night Activity Charts, 21–22 June 1942 and HO 192/817, Air Raid Damage, Region 6, Southern, Southampton, 21–22 June 1942, File No.RE/B 16/8/1, 1; and CAB 66/25/46, Paper No. WP (42) 266, Weekly Résumé (No. 147), 18–25 June 1942, 9.

73. TNA: HO 199/420, Regional Commissioner's Monthly Report, July 1942, 1.

74. TNA: AIR 16/889, Enemy Aircraft Casualties due to Anti-Aircraft Fire, 17–24 June 1942.

75. TNA: HO 191/11, Chronological Record, 12; and HO 199/420, Monthly Report, July 1942, 1.

76. TNA: HO 192/816, Air Raid Damage, Region 6, Southern, Southampton, 21–22 June 1942, Report on Damage Sustained by Pirelli-General Cable Works, 3; and HO 199/420, Regional Commissioner's Monthly Report, July 1942, 1.

77. TNA: AIR 25/182, No. 10 Group ORB; and AIR 25/194, No. 11 Group ORB, 21 June 1942.

78. TNA: AIR 16/607, Night Activity Charts, 24–25 June 1942. Predictably, German communiqués claimed that Birmingham had been bombed, AIR 40/1645, Tabular Record, 24 June 1942.

79. TNA: HO 198/63, Forms BC2 and BC4, Region 9, Midland, 23 May 1942–4–5 June 1943, BC2 Serial No. MR.528, Nuneaton, 24/25.6.42, 1.

80. TNA: HO 198/63, Report on Raid, Atherstone Rural Council, 1. No reports of radio beams are mentioned in any British document.

81. TNA: HO 199/182, Nuneaton, 24–25 June 1942, Air Raid on Nuneaton on 25 June 1942, Report of the Fire Guard Staff Officer, 1; and HO 192/934, Air Raid Damage, Region No. 9, Midland, Nuneaton, 24–25 June 1942, Birmingham, General Appreciation, 2.

82. TNA: HO 201/12, Weekly Appreciation of Damage, 24 June–1 July 1942, 1; and Railway Situation Report, 25.6.42.

83. TWAS T170/8, Bulletin No. 104: 24 June–1 July 1942, 2; and TNA: HO 191/11, Chronological Record, 12. For comparison, thirty-two houses were also demolished at Great Yarmouth by the bombs of a single aircraft.

84. Richards, *Luftwaffe Over Brum*, 109.

85. TNA: AIR 25/177, No. 9 Group ORB, 24 June 1942.

86. TNA: AIR 16/889, Combats and Casualties, 24 June 1942. The *Luftwaffe* lost four aircraft this night (Do 217 and three Ju 88s), with another two damaged (Do 217 and Ju 88), so none was a He 111, suggesting identification deficiencies in the RAF, IWM: MCR 18: GAF Losses, Reel 9.

87. Collier, *Defence of the United Kingdom*, 308.

88. TNA: AIR 40/1654, Commentary, 83.

89. TNA: AIR 40/1645, Tabular Record, 26 June 1942; and Snelling, *Shattered City*, 123. There is no evidence in German communiqués that Norwich was considered a reprisal raid.

90. TNA: HO 198/11, Forms BC2 and BC4, Region 4, Eastern, 24–25 June–22 December 1942, BC2, Norwich, 26/27.6.42, 2, Report on Raid Incidents, Norwich, 27 June, Norwich Raid 26/27 June and CAB 66/26/11, Paper No. WP (42) 281; Weekly Résumé (No. 148), 25 June–2 July 1942, 9.

91. TNA: HO 201/12, Weekly Appreciation of Damage, 2.

92. TNA: HO 191/11, Chronological Record, 12; and TWAS T170/8, Bulletin No. 104, 2.

93. TNA: AIR 25/220, No. 12 Group ORB, 27 June 1942.

94. TNA: AIR 16/889, Combats and Casualties, 27 June 1942.

95. Baedeker, *Great Britain*, 133.

96. AHB: Aircraft Deliveries Against Contract, Vol. I, Bristol: Weston: X Serial Beaufighters: Contract No: B.65570/40, 1.

97. TNA: HO 199/421, Region No. 7, May 1942–January 1943, Regional Commissioner's Monthly Report, June 1942, 1.

98. TNA: AIR 16/607, Night Activity Charts, 27–28 and 28–29 June 1942; AIR 40/1645, Tabular Record, 27 and 28 June 1942 and HO 198/58, Forms BC2 and BC4, Region 7, South Western, 27–28 June–December 1942, BC2, Weston-super-Mare, 27/28 and 28/29.6.42, 1.

99. TNA: HO 199/421, Regional Commissioner's Monthly Report, June 1942, 1; and HO 198/58, Raids on Weston-super-Mare, 3.

100. TNA: HO 198/58, Raids on Weston-super-Mare, 1–2; and HO 199/421, Regional Commissioner's Monthly Report, June 1942, 1.

101. TNA: HO 198/58, AWAS AL1, Weston-super-Mare, 27/28 and 28/29.6.42.

102. TNA: HO 198/58, Raids on Weston-super-Mare, 1–2; and HO 199/421, Regional Commissioner's Monthly Report, June 1942, 1.

103. HO 199/421, Regional Commissioner's Monthly Report, June 1942, 1–2; and TWAS T170/8, Bulletin No. 104, 3.

104. TNA: HO 201/12, Weekly Appreciation of Damage, 2; and Railway Situation Report, 30.6.42.

105. TNA: HO 191/11, Chronological Record, 12.

106. TNA: AIR 25/182, No. 10 Group ORB, 28–29 June 1942; and AIR 16/889, Combats and Casualties, 27–29 June 1942.

107. TNA: HO 198/58, Raids on Weston-super-Mare, 1–2; and AIR 16/889, Enemy Aircraft Casualties due to Anti-Aircraft Fire, 24 June–1 July 1942.

108. TNA: AIR 25/182, No. 10 Group ORB, 29 June 1942.

109. TNA: AIR 40/1654, Commentary, 83.

110. TNA: PREM 3/18/1, Correspondence between the Prime Minister and the Minister of Production, 25 May, 12 June, 14 June, and 25 June 1942.

111. O'Brien, *Civil Defence*, 432.

112. TNA: AIR 40/1645, Tabular Record, July 1942.

113. TNA: HO 198/2, Forms BC2 and BC4, Region 1, Northern, 6–7 July–20–21 December 1942, Appreciation Report, 7 July 1942 and HO 201/20, Weekly Reports, 31 December 1941–30 December 1942, Weekly Appreciation of Damage to Key Points, 1–8 July 1942, 1.

114. TNA: AIR 25/233, No. 13 Group ORB, 7 July 1942 and AIR 16/889, Combats and Casualties, 7 July 1942.

115. TNA: HO 198/2, Form AL1, Billingham, Middlesbrough and Stockton, 7–8 July 1942 and HO 192/76, Air Raid Damage, Region 1, Northern, Teesside, 1942, Appreciation Report, 8 July 1942; and First Report of Inspection of Fires Caused by Enemy Action on Nights of 6–7–7–8 July 1942, 2–3.

116. TNA: AIR 25/233, No. 13 Group ORB; and AIR 16/889, Combats and Casualties, 8 July 1942.

117. TNA: CAB 65/27/6, Paper No. WM (42) 90, War Cabinet, Conclusions, 9 July 1942, 131–132.

118. TNA: CAB 66/25/50, Paper No. WP (42) 270, Memorandum, 'Front Line', 27 June 1942, 1.

119. TNA: CAB 66/26/4, Paper No. WP (42) 274, Memorandum, 'Front Line', 29 June 1942.

120. TNA: CAB 66/25/50, Paper No. WP (42) 270, 2.

121. TNA: CAB 65/27/6, Paper No. WM (42) 90, 132.

122. TNA: CAB 66/25/50, Paper No. WP (42) 270, 2.

123. MoI, *Front Line 1940–1941*, 88; and TNA: HO 191/11, Chronological Record, 1–11.

124. O'Brien, *Civil Defence*, 432.

125. B. Norman, *Air Raid Diary: The Luftwaffe Attacks on Tees-side, 1940–1943* (Norman, 2010), 116. Most raids on Middlesbrough resulted in single figures of fatalities except for the twenty-seven killed on the night of 15–16 April 1942, TNA: HO 191/11, Chronological Record, 12.

126. TNA: AIR 40/1645, Tabular Record; and HO 198/2, Form BC2, Billingham, Middlesbrough and West Hartlepool, 25–26 July 1942.

127. TNA: HO 201/20, Weekly Appreciation of Damage, 22–29 July 1942, 2; and TWAS T170/8, Bulletin No. 108: 22–29 July 1942, 4.

128. TNA: HO 198/247, B Division Summary No. 39, 1.

129. TNA: HO 191/11, Chronological Record, 12; and HO 198/2, Additional Information, 27 July 1942.

130. TNA: AIR 25/233, No. 13 Group ORB, 26 July 1942. German records do not, however, report the loss of any Do 217s on this night, IWM: MCR 18: GAF Losses, Reel 10.

131. TNA: AIR 40/1645, Tabular Record, 27 July 1942.

132. TNA: HO 201/20, Weekly Appreciation of Damage, 22–29 July 1942, 1.

133. TNA: HO 198/247, B Division Summary No. 44, 1; and HO 191/11, Chronological Record, 12.

134. TNA: HO 201/20, Weekly Appreciation of Damage, 22–29 July 1942, 2.

135. TNA: HO 192/937, Air Raid Damage, Region 9, Midland, Birmingham, 1942, List of OUT Factories Damaged by July Raids on Birmingham, 14 December 1942, 1–2.

136. TWAS T170/8, Bulletin No. 108, 5; and TNA: HO 191/11, Chronological Record, 12.

137. TNA: AIR 16/607, Night Activity Charts, July 1942.

138. TNA: AIR 25/177, No. 9 Group ORB, 27 July 1942.

139. TNA: AIR 25/220, No. 12 Group ORB, 28 July 1942.

140. TNA: AIR 16/889, Combats and Casualties, 27–28 July 1942. German records identify only one Do 217 shot down on this night, plus another damaged, IWM: MCR 18: GAF Losses, Reel 10.

141. TNA: AIR 16/607, Night Activity Charts, 27–28 July 1942.

142. TNA: AIR 40/1645, Tabular Record, 29 July 1942; and AIR 16/607, Description of Enemy Activity, 29–30 July 1942.

143. TNA: HO 198/247, B Division Summary No. 44, 1.

144. TWAS T170/8, Bulletin No. 108, 4; and Bulletin No. 109: 29 July–5 August 1942, 2.

145. TNA: HO 201/20, Weekly Appreciation of Damage, 29 July–6 August 1942, 2; and HO 192/937, List of OUT Factories Damaged by July Raids on Birmingham, 14 December 1942, 2–4.

146. TNA: HO 191/11, Chronological Record, 12.

147. TNA: AIR 25/177, No. 9 Group ORB, 29 July 1942.

148. TNA: AIR 25/220, No. 12 Group ORB, 30 July 1942. Admitted German losses included three Do 217s shot down plus another damaged, IWM: MCR 18: GAF Losses, Reel 10.

149. TNA: AIR 16/607, Night Activity Charts, 29–30 July 1942.

150. TNA: AIR 41/49; ADGB:V, 60.

151. TNA: CAB 66/27/23, Paper No. WP (42) 348, Weekly Résumé (No. 153), 30 July–6 August 1942, 6–8.

152. TNA: HO 201/20, Weekly Appreciation of Damage, 29 July–6 August 1942, 4; and HO 192/937, Attacks on Birmingham, Coventry and No. 9 Region, 4.

153. TNA: HO 192/937, List of OUT Factories Damaged in July Raids in Midland Region, 14 December 1942.

154. TNA: AIR 40/1654, Commentary, 87.

155. TNA: AIR 25/177, No. 9 Group ORB, 30 July 1942.

156. TNA: AIR 25/220, No. 12 Group ORB, 31 July 1942.

157. TNA: AIR 16/889, Combats and Casualties, 30–31 July 1942.

158. TNA: AIR 40/1654, Commentary, 88; and Richards, *Luftwaffe Over Brum*, 110–114.

159. TNA: HO 192/937, Air Raid Damage to Dwelling-Houses During the Month of July 1942, 19 December 1942.

160. TNA: AIR 40/1645, Tabular Record, 31 July 1942.

161. TNA: CAB 66/27/23, Paper No. WP (42) 348, 9; and HO 191/11, Chronological Record, 12.

162. TNA: AIR 25/220, No. 12 Group ORB, 1 August 1942.

163. TNA: AIR 40/1645, Tabular Record, 1 August 1942.

164. TNA: HO 198/247, B Division Summary No. 45, 1; and Snelling, *Shattered City*, 153.

165. TNA: AIR 25/220, No. 12 Group ORB, 2 August 1942.

166. TNA: HO 201/20, Weekly Appreciation of Damage, 29 July–6 August 1942, 5.

167. TNA: AIR 40/1654, Commentary, 88–89, 102.

168. TNA: AIR 40/1645, Tabular Record, 27 August 1942; and TWAS T170/8, Bulletin No. 113: 26 August–2 September 1942, 2.

169. Collier, *Defence of the United Kingdom*, 309; and TNA: AIR 41/49; ADGB:V, 55.

170. TNA: AIR 40/1653, Locations of Enemy Activity Over United Kingdom: Gazetteer and Maps 1941–1945 (1945), G.A.F. Losses in Attacks on Targets in UK (From July 1941); and IWM: MCR 18: GAF Losses, Reel 10.

171. TNA: CAB 106/1206, Mössel—16 August 1942, 1.

172. IWM: MCR 18: GAF Losses, Reel 10.

173. Calculated from Middlebrook and Everitt, *Bomber Command War Diaries*, 245–261; and TNA: AIR 40/1645, Tabular Record.

174. TNA: AIR 40/2444, Air War Against Great Britain, 14.

175. Air Ministry, *Rise and Fall of the GAF*, 196.

176. TNA: AIR 41/49; ADGB:V, 61.

177. TNA: AIR 40/2444, Air War Against Great Britain, 11.

178. Richards, *Luftwaffe Over Brum*, 114.

179. TNA: AIR 16/525, Addendum to Progress Report by AOC-in-C, Fighter Command to Cover the Period 16–30 June 1942, 1.

180. TNA: AIR 40/2444, Air War Against Great Britain, 14.

181. Murray, *Strategy for Defeat*, 135.

182. TNA: AIR 40/2444, Air War Against Great Britain, 11.

183. IWM: MCR 18: GAF Losses, Reel 10.

184. TNA: AIR 40/2444, Air War Against Great Britain, 11.

185. IWM: MCR 18: GAF Losses, Reel 10.

186. TNA: AIR 41/49; ADGB:V, 61.

187. TNA: AIR 20/8693, Goering: Interrogation at Nuremberg, 10; and Air Ministry, *Rise and Fall of the GAF*, 205.

188. TNA: AIR 41/49; ADGB:V, 55.

189. Murray, *Strategy for Defeat*, 138.

190. TNA: PREM 3/18/1, Correspondence between the Prime Minister and the Minister of Production, 22 August 1942.

191. Parker, *Manpower*, 172; and TNA: CAB 66/16/32, Paper No. WP (42) 424, The 1943 Production Programme, 23 September 1942, 1.

192. Parker, *Manpower*, 174.

193. TNA: CAB 65/28/12, Paper No. WM (42) 142, War Cabinet, Conclusions, 19 October 1942, 100.

194. Parker, *Manpower*, 175–176.

195. TNA: CAB 66/31/14, Paper No. WP (42) 534, Man-Power Survey, 21 November 1942, 9–10.

196. TNA: CAB 65/28/30, Paper No. WM (42) 160, War Cabinet, Conclusions, 26 November 1942, 178–179.

197. Parker, *Manpower*, 178.

198. TNA: CAB 66/31/36, Paper No. WP (42) 556, Man-Power, 28 November 1942, 2.

199. Parker, *Manpower*, 179.

200. TNA: CAB 66/31/39, Paper No. WP (42) 559, Civil Defence and Manpower, 30 November 1942, 1–2.

201. TNA: CAB 66/31/50, Paper No. WP (42) 570, Man-Power, 9 December 1942, 12.

202. TNA: CAB 65/28/30, Paper No. WM (42) 167, War Cabinet, Conclusions, 11 December 1942, 213–214.

203. PREM 3/18/1, Minister of Production to the Prime Minister, 22 December 1942.

204. TNA: AIR 41/49; ADGB:V, 60.

205. TNA: AIR 40/1645, Tabular Record, October–December 1942. The AHB narrative contradicts these figures by noting sixty-nine mine laying sorties in December, AIR 41/49; ADGB:V, 62.

206. M-O: FR 1423, Night Bombing and the People, 17 September 1942, 1, 4, and 9.

207. TNA: AIR 40/2444, Air War Against Great Britain, 12.

208. TNA: AIR 40/1654, Commentary, 96.

209. TNA: AIR 41/49; ADGB:V, 62.

210. TNA: CAB 66/30/1, Paper No. WP (42) 471, Weekly Résumé (No. 163), 8–15 October 1942, 6 and 10.

211. TNA: AIR 40/1654, Commentary, 95; HO 198/247, B Division Summary No. 53, 1; and HO 191/11, Chronological Record, 12.

212. TNA: CAB 66/30/7, Paper No. WP (42) 477, Weekly Résumé (No. 164), 15–22 October 1942, 11; and HO 198/247, B Division Summary No. 54, 1; and AIR 16/525, AOC-in-C Progress Report, 1 October–30 November 1942, 8.

213. TNA: CAB 66/30/7, Paper No. WP (42) 477, 10.

214. TNA: HO 198/247, B Division Summary No. 55, 1.

215. TNA: CAB 66/30/23, Paper No. WP (42) 493, Weekly Résumé (No. 165), 15–22 October 1942, 10.

216. TNA: HO 198/247, B Division Summary No. 55, 1.

217. TNA: AIR 40/1654, Commentary, 98; and CAB 66/30/7, Paper No. WP (42) 510, Weekly Résumé (No. 166), 29 October–5 November 1942, 7.

218. TNA: HO 198/66, Forms BC2 and BC4, Region 12, South Eastern, 9–10 June–30 December 1942, General Narrative of Attack by Enemy Aircraft on Canterbury 31.10.42–1.11.42, 1.

219. TNA: HO 198/66, General Narrative of Attack, 1–2; and CAB 66/30/7, Paper No. WP (42) 510, 8.

220. TNA: HO 198/66, General Narrative of Attack, 2–3; and HO 198/247, B Division Summary No. 56, 1.

221. TNA: CAB 66/30/7, Paper No. WP (42) 510, 11; and AIR 40/1654, Commentary, 98; HO 192/1102, Canterbury House Damage, 2 June 1943, 2; and AIR 40/1654, Commentary, 98–99. The latter source notes 'compared to the *Baedeker* raids these figures are small'.

222. TNA: AIR 40/1654, Commentary, 98.

223. TNA: AIR 16/889, Combats and Casualties, 31 October 1942 and AIR 25/204, No. 11 (Fighter) Group ORB: Appendices, July–December 1942, 11 Group Intelligence Bulletin No. 296, Defensive Operations by the Group. German records show only two Fw 190s lost and one damaged from the Canterbury attacks, and confirm four Do 217s lost, plus another damaged, IWM: MCR 18: GAF Losses, Reels 11–12.

224. TNA: AIR 40/1645, Tabular Record, November–December 1942.

225. TNA: AIR 16/525, AOC-in-C Progress Report, 1 October–30 November 1942, 2.

226. TNA: AIR 41/49; ADGB:V, 63.

227. TNA: AIR 16/525, AOC-in-C Progress Report, 1 July–30 September 1942, 4; and 1 October–30 November 1942, 6.

228. B. Johnson, *The Secret War* (Pen & Sword, 2004 [1978]), 94–97.

229. TNA: AIR 16/525, AOC-in-C Progress Report, 10 November 1941–31 March 1942, 5.

230. TNA: AIR 16/525, AOC-in-C Progress Report, 1 April–15 June 1942, 3.

231. TNA: AIR 16/525, AOC-in-C Progress Report, 1 October–30 November 1942, 2.

232. C. M. Sharp and M. J. F. Bowyer, *Mosquito* (Faber and Faber, 1971 [1967]), 23–32 and 38.

233. Sharp and Bowyer, *Mosquito*, 148–150 and 185.

234. Brandon, *Night Flyer*, 95.

235. TNA: AIR 19/308, Secretary of State for Air to ACAS, 9 January 1943.

236. TNA: AIR 24/509, HQ Fighter Command ORB; 1942, AOC-in-C Message No. 384, 27–28 April 1942.

237. TNA: AIR 19/308, Secretary of State for Air to Air Ministry Supply Organisation, 16 March 1942.

238. TNA: PREM 3/22/6, AIR: Night Bombing: Measures to Counteract, Chemical Searchlights, Lindemann correspondence, September 1940–February 1941.

239. TNA: PREM 3/22/6, Lindemann correspondence, September 1940–February 1941.

240. TNA: AIR 27/341, Air Ministry: Operations Record Books, Squadrons, No. 29 Squadron ORB, Summary of Events, October 1940.

241. J. J. Halley, *Royal Air Force Aircraft, L1000-N9999* (Air Britain, 1993), 52.

242. TNA: AIR 27/341, No. 29 Squadron ORB, Summary of Events, November–December 1940 and February 1941.

243. TNA: PREM 3/22/6, Correspondence between Portal and Lindemann, March 1941.

244. Townsend, *Duel in the Dark*, 184.

245. AHB: AM Form 78, Drawer: Havoc AE-Hind K.

246. TNA: AIR 16/585, Turbinlite Squadrons, Turbinlite Flights, 6 September 1941.

247. TNA: AIR 19/308, Air Member for Personnel from Air Member for Training, 27 November 1941, 1.

248. TNA: AIR 16/525, AOC-in-C Progress Report, 10 November 1941–31 March 1942, 11.

249. Gunston, *Night Fighters*, 70.

250. Howard-Williams, *Night Intruder*, 59.

251. TNA: AIR 16/525, AOC-in-C Progress Report, 1; April–15 June 1942, 5 and App. A.

252. TNA: AIR 16/607, Description of Enemy Activity, April–May 1942.

253. None of the Fighter Command HQ or Group ORBs contains any information, and the incident was never mentioned in any Night Air Defence Committee Minutes or Reports.

254. TNA: AIR 27/2004, Air Ministry: Operations Record Books, Squadrons, 534 Squadron (ex 1455 Flight) ORB, 4 May 1942.

255. TNA: AIR 27/1350, 218 Squadron ORB, 4 May 1942.

256. Howard-Williams, *Night Intruder*, 59.

257. TNA: AIR 16/525, AOC-in-C Progress Report, 1; April–15 June 1942, 5.

258. Brandon, *Night Flyer*, 53.

259. TNA: AIR 16/525, AOC-in-C Progress Report, 1 July–30 September 1942, 4.

260. Douglas, *Years of Command*, 107–108.

261. TNA: AIR 41/49; ADGB:V, 62.

262. TNA: AIR 16/525, Turbinlite Squadrons, 14 December 1942, 2; and AIR 16/607, Description of Enemy Activity, April and July 1942.

263. TNA: AIR 16/525, Turbinlite Squadrons, 14 December 1942, 2–3.

264. TNA: AIR 41/17; ADGB:III, 116.

265. TNA: AIR 16/525, Turbinlite Squadrons, 14 December 1942, 2–4.

266. TNA: AIR 19/308, *NAD (42)* 11th Meeting: Turbinlite Squadrons, 17 December 1942, 2.

267. Only 150 AI Mark VII sets were built, all by hand, Gunston, *Night Fighters*, 76.

268. TNA: AIR 16/525, Turbinlite Squadrons, 14 December 1942, 4–5.

269. Richards and Saunders, *Royal Air Force 1939–1945*, II, 368.

270. Gunston, *Night Fighters*, 70.

271. TNA: AIR 16/525, Night Air Defence: Minutes of Meeting held 17 December 1942, 2.

272. TNA: AIR 41/49; ADGB:V, 61; and Howard-Williams, *Night Intruder*, 127.

273. TNA: AIR 24/531, HQ Fighter Command ORB, Appendices, Report of Operation 'Pegasus', 31 December 1940.

274. TNA: AIR 41/1, Balloon Defences, 404–406.

275. TNA: AIR 16/525, AOC-in-C Progress Report, 10 November 1941–31 March 1942, 8.

276. TNA: AIR 41/49; ADGB:V, 63–64.

277. TNA: AIR 41/1, Balloon Defences, 409–410.

278. TNA: AIR 16/525, AOC-in-C Progress Report, 1 October–30 November 1942, 11.

279. TNA: AIR 16/525, AOC-in-C Progress Report, 1 October–30 November 1942, 9.

280. TNA: AIR 16/525, AOC-in-C Progress Report, 10 November 1941–31 March 1942, 11.

281. TNA: AIR 41/49; ADGB:V, 63.

282. TNA: AIR 16/525, AOC-in-C Progress Report, 1; April–15 June 1942, 8 and 1 October–30 November 1942, 9.

283. TNA: AIR 41/49; ADGB:V, 78.

284. TNA: AIR 16/525, AOC-in-C Progress Report, 10 November 1941–31 March 1942, 6.

285. Gunston, *Night Fighters*, 58.

286. TNA: AIR 16/525, AOC-in-C Progress Report, 1 July–30 September 1942, 3; and AIR 41/49; ADGB:V, 65.

287. TNA: AIR 41/4, Flying Training, 508.

288. TNA: AIR 41/71, Operational Training, 836.

289. TNA: AIR 16/874, History of Fighter OTUs, 9.

290. TNA: AIR 16/874, History of Fighter OTUs, 9.

291. TNA: AIR 16/1144, Input and Output of Pupils in 1941, 488–493.

292. TNA: AIR/1145, Input and Output of Pupils in 1942, 870–871.

293. TNA: PREM 3/29/4, Monthly Strength Returns, Fighter Command, 02.01.42 to 04.12.42.

294. TNA: CAB 106/1206, Mössel, 16 August 1942, 1.

295. TNA: AIR 41/49; ADGB:V, 66.

296. TNA: AIR 41/4, Flying Training, 355.

297. Calculated from AHB: SD (Secret Document) 96, Monthly Analysis of RAF Aircraft Accidents Metropolitan Air Force, March 1940–June 1943, 1941(7) to 1941(12).

298. TNA: AIR 41/4, Flying Training, 355–356.

299. TNA: AIR 41/49; ADGB:V, 66–67.

5. THE NIGHT RAIDS OF 1943

1. TNA: AIR 41/49; ADGB:V, 193.

2. Price, *Blitz on Britain*, 147.

3. C. Goss et al., *Luftwaffe Fighter-Bombers Over Britain* (Crécy, 2003), 177–178.

4. *Times*, 28 January 1943, 2.

5. TNA: AIR 41/49; ADGB:V, 189–190.

6. A. Price, *The Luftwaffe Data Book* (Greenhill, 1997 [1977]), 62–63.

7. Calculated from TNA: AIR 22/203, Air Ministry: Papers Accumulated by the Air Historical Branch, War Room Manual of Bomber Command Operations 1939–1945, 2; and Price, *Luftwaffe Data Book*, 32–38 and 79–80.

8. D. Edgerton, *England and the Aeroplane* (Penguin, 2013), 128.

9. J. W. R. Taylor, *Combat Aircraft of the World* (George Rainbird, 1969), 150, 185, and 187.

10. TNA: AIR 41/49; ADGB:V, 190.

11. R. Overy, "From 'Uralbomber' to 'Amerikabomber': The Luftwaffe and Strategic Bombing," *Journal of Strategic Studies* 1, no. 2 (1978): 156.

12. Galland, *First and the Last*, 71–72; and D. Irving, *The Rise and Fall of the Luftwaffe: The Life of Field Marshal Erhard Milch* (Little Brown, 1973), 174.

13. Mondey, *Axis Aircraft of World War II*, 95.

14. P. Eden, *The Encyclopedia of Aircraft of WWII* (Amber, 2004), 252. The even less complimentary 'flying coffin' was also used: Mondey, *Axis Aircraft of World War II*, 95.

15. V. Orange, "A Broad Margin—The Battle of Britain North of Watford," in *Defending Northern Skies*, ed. A. F. C. Hunter (Royal Air Force Historical Society, 1996), 73.

16. Taylor, *Combat Aircraft of the World*, 170.

17. F. K. Mason, *The British Bomber Since 1914* (Putnam, 1994), 329.

18. Mason, *The British Bomber*, 323–326, 344.

19. Overy, "From 'Uralbomber' to 'Amerikabomber,'" 162.

20. TNA: AIR 41/49; ADGB:V, 201.

21. Air Ministry, *Rise and Fall of the GAF*, 158–159.

22. Murray, *Strategy for Defeat*, 160–163.

23. Murray, *Strategy for Defeat*, 254 and 312.

24. TNA: AIR 41/49; ADGB:V, 201.

25. TNA: AIR 40/1526, Orders of Battle for 31.05.43, 31.07.43, and 15.10.43.

26. Air Ministry, *Rise and Fall of the GAF*, 198.

27. TNA: AIR 41/49; ADGB:V, 200.

28. TNA: AIR 40/1645, Tabular Record, 1943; and AIR 40/1654, Commentary, 83, 102, 120, and 131.

29. Collier, *Defence of the United Kingdom*, 314–315.

30. Price, *Blitz on Britain*, 149.

31. TNA: AIR 41/49; ADGB:V, 190. This source (from the opposing side) defends the *Luftwaffe* for following 'the only practicable policy'.

32. Goebbels, *Diaries Diaries*, 214.

33. Price, *Blitz on Britain*, 149.

34. Air Ministry, *Rise and Fall of the GAF*, 198.

35. Price, *Blitz on Britain*, 145.

36. TNA: AIR 16/584, Notes on Re-Equipment and Future Deployment of Night Fighter Squadrons, 13 February 1943, 1; and AIR 50/13/137, Air Ministry: Combat Reports, Second World War, Fighter Command, 25 Squadron, 19–20/5/1942, 390.

37. TNA: CAB 66/33/36, Paper No. WP (43) 36, Weekly Résumé (No. 177), 14–21 January 1943, 7; and AIR 41/49; ADGB:V, 193.

38. Goss et al., *Luftwaffe Fighter-Bombers*, 174.

39. Collier, *Defence of the United Kingdom*, 313.

40. TNA: AIR 41/49; ADGB:V, 193–194.

41. TNA: AIR 40/1654, Commentary, 105; HO 192/338, Air Raid Damage, Region No. 5, London, 17/18.1.43, Ref. Raid on London, 17/18.1.43, 1; and AIR 41/49; ADGB:V, 193–194.

42. Collier, *Defence of the United Kingdom*, 313.

43. O'Brien, *Civil Defence*, 437; and TNA: AIR 40/1645, Tabular Record, January 1943.

44. TNA: HO 201/21, Weekly Appreciation of Damage, 13–20 January 1943, 1–7.

45. TNA: HO 198/18, Form IB1, Incendiary Bomb Census, London Region, 17/18.1.43.

46. TNA: HO 198/183, bomb tonnage calculated from Form L, January 17–18, Region 5, 1–3.

47. TWAS: T170/8, Bulletin No. 133: 13–20 January 1943, 1.

48. TNA: AIR 25/194, No. 11 Group ORB, 17 January 1943.

49. TNA: AIR 16/889, Combats and Casualties, 17–18 January 1943.

50. Price, *Blitz on Britain*, 147.

51. Collier, *Defence of the United Kingdom*, 313.

52. TNA: AIR 25/205, No. 11 (Fighter) Group ORB: Appendices, January–May 1943, 11 Group Intelligence Bulletin No. 309, Defensive Operations by the Group; and Goss et al., *Luftwaffe Fighter-Bombers*, 176.

53. TNA: AIR 41/49; ADGB:V, 178; and Price, *Blitz on Britain*, 147.

54. TNA: AIR 16/1493, Records Research Department (RRD) Tactical Summary No. 10, January 1943, 11.

55. Price, *Blitz on Britain*, 147.

56. TNA: AIR 41/49; ADGB:V, 177.

57. Collier, *Defence of the United Kingdom*, 313; and Goss et al., *Luftwaffe Fighter-Bombers*, 177.

58. TNA: AIR 41/49; ADGB:V, 177; *Times*, 21 January 1943, 4; and Goss et al., *Luftwaffe Fighter-Bombers*, 177.

59. TNA: HO 198/18, BC2, London, 20.1.43, 1.

60. TNA: HO 201/21, Weekly Appreciation of Damage, 20–27 January 1943, 2–3.

61. Ramsey, *Blitz*, 3, 205; and TNA: HO 198/18, London, 20.1.43, 2.

62. TNA: HO 192/341, Air Raid Damage, Region No. 5, London, Lewisham 20 January 1943, RE/B15/14/2, 1.

63. Goss et al., *Luftwaffe Fighter-Bombers*, 178.

64. *Times*, 21 January 1943, 4; and Ramsey, *Blitz*, 3, 204–205.

65. TNA: AIR 41/49; ADGB:V, 176.

66. Ramsey, *Blitz*, 3, 204.

67. Ordnance Survey, Six-Inch, England and Wales, *London, Sheet P* (Ordnance Survey Office, 1946); and TNA: HO 201/21, Weekly Appreciation of Damage, 20–27 January 1943, 4.

68. Ordnance Survey, *London, Sheet P*.

69. *Times*, 28 January 1943, 2.

70. Mason, *Battle Over Britain*, 259.

71. Goss et al., *Luftwaffe Fighter-Bombers*, appendix 10.

72. TNA: AIR 25/194, No. 11 Group ORB, 20 January 1943.

73. Goss et al., *Luftwaffe Fighter-Bombers*, appendix 10.

74. TNA: AIR 40/1654, Commentary, 105; and HO 191/11, Chronological Record, 13.

75. Price, *Blitz on Britain*, 147.

76. TNA: AIR 41/49; ADGB:V, 177; and HO 199/487, Lack of warnings: evidence submitted to Fighter Command of public disquiet, Monthly Appreciation Reports from Chief Constables of Winchester, Dudley and Canterbury.

77. TNA: AIR 41/49; ADGB:V, 177–178.

78. *Times*, 28 January 1943, 2.

79. Süss, *Death From the Skies*, 409.

80. J. Rugg, "Managing 'Civilian Deaths due to War Operations': Yorkshire Experiences During World II," *Twentieth Century British History* 15, no. 2 (2004): 164; and N. Longmate, *The Workhouse* (Maurice Temple Smith, 1974), 281.

81. Rugg, "Managing 'Civilian Deaths,'" 167.

82. *Daily Express*, 6 March 1943, 3.

83. Süss, *Death From the Skies*, 116.

84. Calder, *People's War*, 226.

85. Titmuss, *Problems of Social Policy*, 282.

86. Süss, *Death From the Skies*, 191.

87. Titmuss, *Problems of Social Policy*, 282.

88. Süss, *Death From the Skies*, 194.

89. Longmate, *The Workhouse*, 276.

90. Collier, *Defence of the United Kingdom*, 314.

91. TNA: AIR 41/49; ADGB:V, 194–195.

92. TNA: AIR 40/1645, Tabular Record, May 1943.

93. TNA: AIR 40/1654, Commentary, 109.

94. TNA: HO 201/21, Weekly Appreciation of Damage, 3–10 March 1943, 2–4.

95. Price, *Blitz on Britain*, 147.

96. TNA: HO 192/347, Air Raid Damage, Region No. 5, London, 3–4 March 1943, 1–2.

97. *Guardian*, 15 February 2003, C34; and *Independent*, 19 February 2009, 15.

98. R. Fountain, *Mr Morrison's Conjuring Trick* (RTFMedia, 2012), 2 and 8.

99. Fountain, *Mr Morrison's Conjuring Trick*, 8, 86, and 110.

100. *Times*, 5 March 1943, 4.

101. *Daily Telegraph*, 5 March 1943, 1; TNA: HO 207/518, Ministry of Home Security, Civil Defence Regions, Headquarters and Regional Files; Region No. 5 (London): Bethnal Green: Tube Shelter Disaster, Newspaper Cuttings.

102. TNA: HO 192/348, Panic in Public Shelter, 1.

103. *Daily Herald*, 8 March 1943, 3.

104. *Daily Mail*, 8 March 1943, 3.

105. TNA: HO 192/348, Ministry of Home Security to All Technical Coordinating Officers, 12 March 1943, 1.

106. TNA: HO 192/348, Home Security to Technical Coordinating Officers, 3.

107. Fountain, *Mr Morrison's Conjuring Trick*, 34–38.

108. TNA: MEPO 3/1942, Report on an Inquiry into the Accident at Bethnal Green Tube Station Shelter, Ministry of Home Security (subsequently Dunne Report), 23 March 1943, 6.

109. TNA: MEPO 3/1942, Dunne Report, 11.

110. TNA: MEPO 3/1942, Dunne Report, 12.

111. TNA: CAB 66/35/37, Paper No. WP (43) 137, Tube Shelter Inquiry: Report by Mr. Dunne, 1–2.

112. *Times*, 18 July 1944, 8.

113. Fountain, *Mr Morrison's Conjuring Trick*, 95–96.

114. TNA: MEPO 3/1942, Dunne Report, 14.

115. TNA: HO 207/997, Region No. 5 (London): Bethnal Green, Tube Shelter, Metropolitan Borough of Bethnal Green to London Civil Defence Headquarters, 18 and 20 August 1941.

116. TNA: HO 207/997, London Passenger Transport Board to London Civil Defence Headquarters, 23 August 1941.

117. TNA: MEPO 3/1942, Dunne Report, 15–16; and HO 207/997, Metropolitan Borough of Bethnal Green to London Civil Defence Headquarters, 30 September 1941.

118. TNA: HO 207/519, Region No. 5 (London): Bethnal Green, Emergency Entrance to Tube Shelter After the Disaster in March 1943, Specification of Works to Be Carried Out, 12 March 1943.

119. O'Brien, *Civil Defence*, 545.

120. *Times*, 25 November 2017, 5.

121. www.bbc.co.uk/news/uk-42138437, 'Is It Right to Say People Caught in a Terror Scare "Panic"?', 28 November 2017.

122. Y. Y. Haimes, *Risk Modeling, Assessment, and Management* (Wiley-Interscience, 1998), 19.

123. Fountain, *Mr Morrison's Conjuring Trick*, 21–22 and 141.

124. TNA: PREM 3/18/1, Minister of Production to the Prime Minister, 19 January 1943.

125. TNA: HO 198/18, Anti-Personnel Bombs: Surrey, Langley Vale, Epsom.

126. TNA: AIR 25/205, 11 Group Intelligence Bulletin No. 316, Defensive Operations by the Group.

127. TNA: AIR 41/49; ADGB:V, 196.

128. Goss et al., *Luftwaffe Fighter-Bombers*, 233.

129. Price, *Blitz on Britain*, 149.

130. Collier, *Defence of the United Kingdom*, 316.

131. TNA: AIR 41/49; ADGB:V, 196.

132. Goss et al., *Luftwaffe Fighter-Bombers*, 287–289.

133. TNA: AIR 40/2444, Air War Against Great Britain, 12–13. The loss of twenty-six aircrews by KG2 during March 1943 may have influenced this policy change.

134. BA-MA: RL 7/111, *Tätigkeitsbericht der Luftflotte 3 für den Monat April 1943, (Luftflottenkommando 3*, 10.5.1943).

135. Not included on the Air Ministry list of 'chief targets' for 1943, TNA: AIR 40/1654, Commentary, 120. In a rare lapse, one source misidentifies the target as Cheltenham; Price, *Blitz on Britain*, 149.

136. Ramsey, *Blitz*, 3, 193; TNA: AIR 16/1044, Operational Research Section Reports, 1st Series, Report No. 455, Night Interception System and Operations, April 1943, App. 1; and AIR 40/1045, Tabular Record, April 1943.

137. TNA: AIR 40/1045, Tabular Record, April 1943. The standard bombload for a Ju 88 was 2,000kg, Mondey, *Axis Aircraft of World War II*, 126.

138. Collier, *Defence of the United Kingdom*, 315.

139. TNA: CAB 66/36/7, Paper No. WP (43) 157, Weekly Résumé (No. 189), 8–15 April 1943, 11; and HO 201/21, Weekly Reports, 30 December 1942–29 December 1943, Weekly Appreciation of Damage to Key Points, 14–21 April 1943, 2.

140. TNA: CAB 66/36/7, Paper No. WP (43) 157, 7; and Ramsey, *Blitz*, 3, 246.

141. TNA: AIR 41/49; ADGB:V, 196.

142. Collier, *Defence of the United Kingdom*, 316.

143. TWAS: T170/8, Bulletin No. 147: 21–28 April 1943, 1; and AIR 25/250, No. 14 (Fighter) Group ORB, January 1940–July 1943, 22 April 1943. AIR 40/1045, Tabular Record, April 1943, records a total of 121 bombs. No *Luftwaffe* aircraft could carry 5,000kg of bombs, and for such a long-range operation, extra fuel would reduce payload.

144. TNA: HO 192/1172, Surveys of Damage in Great Britain: Aberdeen, 21–22 April 1943, 1–4.

145. Ramsey, *Blitz*, 3, 250–251.

146. TNA: HO 192/1172, *Aberdeen*, 2–3.

147. TNA: AIR 25/250, No. 14 Group ORB, 22 April 1943; and AIR 41/49; ADGB:V, appendix 16.

148. Ramsey, *Blitz*, 3, 249; and TNA: CAB 106/1206, Lecture given by Major Leythaeuser, 14 February 1944, 1.

149. Collier, *Defence of the United Kingdom*, 316; TNA: AIR 40/1654, Commentary, 115.

150. Ramsey, *Blitz*, 3, 267.

151. TNA: AIR 40/1045, Tabular Record, May 1943.

152. TNA: AIR 41/49; ADGB:V, 191.

153. TNA: AIR 25/205, No. 11 (Fighter) Group ORB: Appendices, January–May 1943, 11 Group Intelligence Bulletin No. 327, Defensive Operations by the Group, 4; and HO 198/13, Forms BC2 and BC4, Region 4, Eastern, 4–5 May–22–23 June 1943, BC2, Colchester, 13/14.5.43, 1, RAF Bomb Census Squad No. 2, 13–14 May 1943, 1; and No. 9 Team RAF, Attack by Enemy Aircraft on May 13/14 1943, 3.

154. TWAS: T170/8, Bulletin No. 150: 12–19 May 1943, 1.

155. TNA: HO 201/21, Weekly Appreciation of Damage, 12–19 May 1943, 2.

156. TNA: HO 191/11, Chronological Record, 13.

157. TNA: HO 198/13, Investigation of Raid on Suffolk County on May 13–14 1943, 1.

158. TNA: AIR 16/889, Combats and Casualties, 14 May 1943.

159. Ramsey, *Blitz*, 3, 267.

160. Mason, *Battle Over Britain*, 416; and J. Vasco, *Messerschmitt Bf 110: Bombsights Over England* (Schiffer, 2002), 157.

161. TNA: AIR 40/1045, Tabular Record, May 1943; and HO 198/13, BC2s, Felixstowe and Southwold, 15/16.5.43.

162. TNA: AIR 25/194, No. 11 Group ORB, 15 May 1943; and AIR 16/889, Enemy Aircraft Casualties due to Anti-Aircraft Fire, 12–19 May 1943.

163. TNA: AIR 41/49; ADGB:V, 197.

164. TNA: AIR 40/1654, Commentary, 116; and AIR 40/1645, May 1943.

165. TNA: HO 198/3, Forms BC2 and BC4, Region 1, Northern, 13–14 January–23–24 May 1943, IB Investigation, Sunderland CB, 22 May 1943, 1. The Observer Corps reported a He 111 amongst the attackers, a type not operated over the United Kingdom since 1942, making the estimated total unreliable and indicating a lower quality of Civil Defence personnel following the 1942 manpower cuts.

166. TNA: HO 201/21, Weekly Appreciation of Damage, 12–19 May 1943, 4.

167. TWAS: T170/8, Bulletin No. 150, 2.

168. TNA: CAB 66/37/13, Paper No. WP (43) 213, Weekly Résumé (No. 194), 13–20 May 1943, 9.

169. TNA: HO 198/3, *IB Investigation*, 1; bomb tonnage calculated from BC4, Sunderland CB, 15/16-5-43, 1–16.

170. TNA: HO 198/3, BC4, Sunderland CB, 15/16-5-43, 1; and HO 191/11, Chronological Record, 13.

171. TNA: AIR 25/233, No. 13 Group ORB, 16 May 1943. Recognising a Lancaster avoided the embarrassment of shooting down a RAF aircraft, but the 'Bf 110' was clearly a misidentified Do 217.

172. J. Sweetman, *The Dambusters Raid* (Arms and Armour, 1990), xi.

173. N. Parker, *Luftwaffe Crash Archive*, Vol. 10 (Red Kite, 2017), 1215.

174. TNA: AIR 40/1654, Commentary, 116, HO 198/61, Forms BC2 and BC4, Region 8, Wales, 28–29 November 1941–23 July 1943, BC2, Cardiff CB, 17/18.5.43 and AIR 40/1645, Tabular Record, May 1943. AIR 16/1044, Report No. 471, appendix 1 confirms the aircraft number and approach.

175. TNA: AIR 41/49; ADGB:V, 198.

176. TNA: AIR 25/182, No. 10 Group ORB, 18 May 1943.

177. TNA: HO 201/21, Weekly Appreciation of Damage, 12–19 May 1943, 6.

178. TNA: HO 192/931, Air Raid Damage, Region 8, Wales, Disruption of Rail Communications, Cardiff General Station: Raid 17/18.5.1943, 1.

179. TNA: HO 198/61, 4, HE and Incendiary Attack on Cardiff, 4, HO 201/21, Weekly Appreciation of Damage, 12–19 May 1943, 9; and AIR 25/182, No. 10 Group ORB, 18 May 1943.

180. TNA: HO 191/11, Chronological Record, 13; and CAB 66/37/13, Paper No. WP (43) 213, 9.

181. TNA: AIR 25/182, No. 10 Group ORB, 18 May 1943; and AIR 16/889, Enemy Aircraft Casualties due to Anti-Aircraft Fire, 12–19 May 1943.

182. Bomb tonnage calculated from TNA: HO 198/3, BC4, Sunderland CB, 23/24-5-43, 1–14.

183. TNA: HO 201/21, Weekly Appreciation of Damage, 19–26 May 1943, 2.

184. TWAS: 209.113, Sunderland County Borough Council: Reports on Air Raids, 1940–1968, Report on Air Raid Damage—Monday 24 May 1943, 1; T170/8, Bulletin No. 151: 19–26 May 1943, 1; and TNA: HO 201/21, Weekly Appreciation of Damage, 19–26 May 1943, 2.

185. TNA: HO 198/3, BC2, Sunderland CB, 23/24-5-43, 2.

186. TNA: HO 201/21, Weekly Appreciation of Damage, 19–26 May 1943, 6; and TNA: HO 191/11, Chronological Record, 14.

187. TNA: AIR 25/233, No. 13 Group ORB, 24 May 1943.

188. O' Brien, *Civil Defence*, 438; and TWAS: 209.113, Report of Air Raids on Sunderland: 1939–1945.

189. Collier, *Defence of the United Kingdom*, 316.

190. Middlebrook and Everitt, *Bomber Command War Diaries*, 390; and IWM: MCR 18: GAF Losses, Reel 17.

191. Combined British destroyed and damaged claims match the number actually lost.

192. Collier, *Defence of the United Kingdom*, 316.

193. Ramsey, *Blitz*, 3, 249.

194. TNA: AIR 40/1645, Tabular Record, June 1943.

195. TNA: HO 201/21, Weekly Appreciation of Damage, 9–16 June 1943, 2.

196. TNA: HO 198/59, Forms BC2 and BC4, Region 7, South-Western, 8 January–12–13 June 1943, Report from Chief Constable, Plymouth, 13.6.43 and TWAS: T170/8, Bulletin No. 154: 9–16 June 1943, 1; HO 191/11, Chronological Record, 14; and HO 201/21, Weekly Appreciation of Damage, 9–16 June 1943, 2.

197. TNA: AIR 25/182, No. 10 Group ORB, 13 June 1942.

198. TNA: CAB 66/37/50, Paper No. WP (43) 250, Weekly Résumé (No. 198), 10–17 June 1943, 6 and 10.

199. TNA: AIR 40/1645, Tabular Record, June 1943; and HO 201/21, Weekly Appreciation of Damage, 3.

200. TNA: AIR 41/49; ADGB:V, 197; and Price, *Blitz on Britain*, 152.

201. O'Brien, *Civil Defence*, 438; and *Daily Mail*, 8 March 1943, 3.

202. TNA: AIR 41/49; ADGB:V, 197.

203. TNA: HO 191/11, Chronological Record, 14; and AIR 41/49; ADGB:V, 197.

204. TNA: HO 191/11, Chronological Record, 14.

205. TNA: HO 198/138, Hull: Various Reports, 23–24 June 1943–20–21 March 1945, Hull 23/24.6.43, 1 and RE/B 57/2/1.

206. TNA: AIR 16/889, Enemy Aircraft Casualties due to Anti-Aircraft Fire, 7–14 June 1943.

207. TNA: AIR 40/1645, Tabular Record, June 1943.

208. TWAS: T170/8, Bulletin No. 155: 16–23 June 1943, 1; and TNA: CAB 66/38/20, Paper No. WP (43) 270, Weekly Résumé (No. 199), 17–24 June 1943, 8.

209. TNA: AIR 40/1645, Tabular Record, June 1943.

210. TNA: AIR 40/1645, Tabular Record, June 1943; and HO 198/138, BC2, Hull 23/24.6.43, 1.

211. BA-MA: RL 7/112, *Tätigkeitsbericht der Luftflotte 3 für den Monat Juni 1943*, (*Luftflottenkommando 3*, 12.7.1943).

212. TNA: HO 192/156, Air Raid Damage, Region No. 2, North-Eastern, Hull 23/24.6.43, 1.

213. TWAS: T170/8, Bulletin No. 156: 23–30 June 1943, 1; and TNA: HO 191/11, Chronological Record, 14.

214. TNA: AIR 25/220, No. 12 Group ORB, 23 June 1943.

215. TNA: HO 198/245, Civilian War Deaths: Yearly Totals, Hull.

216. Graystone, *Blitz on Hull*, 3–4.

217. Calculated from TNA: HO 198/243, Houses Demolished in Administrative Areas as a Result of Enemy Action: Monthly Totals; and HO 198/245, Civilian War Deaths: Yearly Totals, for Gateshead, Hebburn, Hull, Jarrow, Newcastle, Seaham, South Shields, Sunderland, Tynemouth, Wallsend and Whitley Bay.

218. TNA: CAB 66/39/13, Paper No. WP (43) 313, Weekly Résumé (No. 202), 8–15 June 1943, 9 and 11.

219. BA-MA: RL 7/113, *Tätigkeitsbericht der Luftflotte 3 für den Monat Juli 1943*, (*Luftflottenkommando 3*, 13.8.1943).

220. BA-MA: RL 7/113, *Tätigkeitsbericht, Juli 1943.*

221. TNA: HO 201/21, Weekly Appreciation of Damage, 7–14 July 1943, 2–3.

222. TWAS: T170/8, Bulletin No. 158: 7–14 June 1943, 2.

223. TNA: HO 191/11, Chronological Record, 14.

224. TNA: AIR 25/220, No. 12 Group ORB, 13 July 1943.

225. TNA: HO 198/138, Hull, 13 July 1943.

226. TNA: HO 201/21, Weekly Appreciation of Damage, 7–14 July 1943, 4.

227. BA-MA: RL 7/113, *Tätigkeitsbericht, Juli 1943.*

228. TNA: CAB 66/39/13, Paper No. WP (43) 313, 11; and HO 192/158, Hull Appreciation: 13/14 July 1943, 1.

229. TNA: HO 192/158, Hull Appreciation: 13–14 July 1943, 2; and HO 191/11, Chronological Record, 14.

230. TNA: AIR 25/226, No. 12 (Fighter) Group ORB: Appendices, 1943, No. 12 Group Intelligence Bulletin No. 5, 1.

231. BA-MA: RL 7/113, *Tätigkeitsbericht, Juli 1943.*

232. TNA: AIR 40/1654, Commentary, 121.

233. TNA: AIR 41/49; ADGB:V, 207.

234. Middlebrook and Everitt, *Bomber Command War Diaries*, 410–411, Ramsey, *Blitz*, 3, 289; and H. St G. Saunders, *Royal Air Force 1939–1945*, Vol. III (HMSO, 1954), 9.

235. Saunders, *RAF*, III, 9; and Middlebrook and Everitt, *Bomber Command War Diaries*, 414. High winds caused by large fires had been noted during the raid on Exeter in May 1942.

236. TNA: HO 191/11, Statement of Civilian Casualties, 1–2.

237. Middlebrook and Everitt, *Bomber Command War Diaries*, 411.

238. Goebbels, *Diaries Diaries*, 333.

239. TNA: AIR 16/1044, Report No. 503, Night Interception System and Operations, August 1943, appendix 1; and AIR 25/182, No. 10 Group ORB, 12 August 1943.

240. TNA: HO 198/56, Forms BC2 and BC4, Region 6, Southern, 11–12 August 1943–27–28 May 1944, BC2s, Bournemouth and Poole, 11/12/8/43, 1; and HO 198/60, Forms BC2 and BC4, Region 7, South-Western, 22–23 July 1943–29–30 May 1944, BC2, Plymouth, 11/12.8.43, 1. Fighter-bombers did not carry incendiaries, implying most twin-engine aircraft attacked Plymouth.

241. TNA: HO 201/21, Weekly Appreciation of Damage, 11–18 August 1943, 2–3.

242. TNA: HO 198/60, Report on IB Raid on Plymouth, 11/12.8.43.

243. TWAS: T170/8, Bulletin No. 163: 11–18 August 1943, 2.

244. TNA: HO 191/11, Chronological Record, 14. The Bournemouth casualties were not recorded in the usual way, so they are taken from TWAS: T170/8, Bulletin No. 163, 2.

245. TNA: AIR 25/182, No. 10 Group ORB, 12 August 1943.

246. TNA: AIR 40/1654, Commentary, 122; and Price, *Blitz on Britain*, 152.

247. TNA: HO 201/21, Weekly Appreciation of Damage, 11–18 August 1943, 4; and HO 191/11, Chronological Record, 14.

248. TWAS: T170/8, Bulletin No. 163, 2.

249. TNA: AIR 16/889, Combats and Casualties, 15 August 1943, and Enemy Aircraft Casualties due to Anti-Aircraft Fire, 11–18 August 1943.

250. TNA: HO 201/21, Weekly Appreciation of Damage, 11–18 August 1943, 4; and AIR 41/49; ADGB:V, 207.

251. TNA: AIR 40/2444, Air War Against Great Britain, 14; and Collier, *Defence of the United Kingdom*, 318.

252. TNA: AIR 41/49; ADGB:V, 205.

253. Irving, *Rise and Fall of the Luftwaffe*, 241–242.

254. Collier, *Defence of the United Kingdom*, 318.

255. TNA: AIR 41/49; ADGB, V, 205.

256. Price, *Blitz on Britain*, 155.

257. TNA: AIR 16/615, AM Sir T. L. Leigh-Mallory, C-in-C Fighter Command: Correspondence with ACM Sir C. F. A. Portal, Chief of Air Staff, Report on Night Operations: 7–8 October 1943, 1–4.

258. TNA: AIR 41/49; ADGB:V, 206.

259. TNA: AIR 40/1654, Commentary, 125–126; and HO 201/21, Weekly Appreciation of Damage, 6–13 October 1943, 1–4.

260. TWAS: T170/8, Bulletin No. 171: 6–13 October 1943.

261. TNA: CAB 66/42/9, Paper No. WP (43) 459, Weekly Résumé (No. 215), 7–14 January 1943, 13.

262. TNA: HO 191/11, Chronological Record, 14.

263. TNA: AIR 16/1045, Operational Research Section Reports, 2nd Series, Report No. 1, Enemy Activity and Interception Operations in 11 and 12 Groups, Night 7 October 1943, 5–6.

264. TNA: AIR 16/890, Casualty Returns, September 1943–April 1945, Combats and Casualties, 7 October 1943; and Return of Enemy Aircraft Casualties due to Anti-Aircraft Fire, 6–13 October 1943.

265. TNA: AIR 16/1045, Report No. 1, Enemy Activity and Interception Operations, 7 October 1943, 6. German records confirm a Do 217M and Me 410 lost, with another crash landing in France. The other two aircraft lost were Ju 188s, but the two aircraft had similar pointed wings and noses, so from some angles and at high speed, they could have been confused, especially as the Ju 188 had just begun operations; IWM: MCR 18: GAF Losses, Reel 22.

266. TNA: HO 201/21, Weekly Appreciation of Damage, 13–20 October 1943, 1; and HO 191/11, Chronological Record, 14.

267. TNA: AIR 40/1654, Commentary, 127.

268. TNA: HO 191/11, Chronological Record, 14.

269. TNA: AIR 41/49; ADGB:V, 206.

270. BA-MA: RL 7/110, *Kampfeinsatz: Störangriffe, zusammengefasste Angriffe, Mineneinsatz im November 1943, (Anlage 2a zu Lfl.Kdo.3, Führ. Abt.* (1)/1c Nr.15684/43, *g.Kdos.*).

271. TNA: AIR 40/1654, Commentary, 128–129.

272. TWAS: T170/8, Bulletin No. 175: 3–10 November 1943.

273. BA-MA: RL 7/110, *Kampfeinsatz: Störangriffe, zusammengefasste Angriffe, November 1943.*

274. Sharp and Bowyer, *Mosquito*, 301.

275. BA-MA: RL 7/110, *Kampfeinsatz: Störangriffe, zusammengefasste Angriffe, November 1943*; and Sharp and Bowyer, *Mosquito*, 304–305.

276. TNA: AIR 41/49; ADGB:V, 206; and IWM: MCR 18: GAF Losses, Reel 23.

277. Collier, *Defence of the United Kingdom*, 318.

278. TNA: AIR 40/1654, Commentary, 131.

279. TNA: CAB 66/43/5, Paper No. WP (43) 505, Weekly Résumé (No. 218), 28 October–4 November 1943, 11; and CAB 66/43/25, Paper No. WP (43) 525, Weekly Résumé (No. 220), 11–18 November 1943, 11.

280. TWAS: T170/8, Bulletin No. 176: 10–17 November 1943; and TNA: AIR 40/1654, Commentary, 129.

281. TNA: AIR 40/1645, Tabular Record, January–December 1943.

282. TNA: AIR 16/525, AOC-in-C Progress Report, 1 December 1942–28 February 1943, 4.

283. TNA: AIR 16/584, Future Deployment of Night Fighter Squadrons, 13 February 1943, 1.

284. Sharp and Bowyer, *Mosquito*, 160.

285. TNA: AIR 16/525, AOC-in-C Progress Report, 1 December 1942–28 February 1943, 3–4.

286. TNA: AIR 41/49; ADGB:V, 196.

287. TNA: AIR 16/525, AOC-in-C Progress Report, 1 December 1942–28 February 1943, 5; and 1 March–31 May 1943, 6.

288. The AHB narrative identifies all remaining metric AI equipment as Mk V, which is clearly an error, as this was never fitted to Beaufighters, TNA: AIR 41/49, 202 and 210. Bingham, *Bristol Beaufighter*, 84, confirms that solely AI Mark IV was used.

289. Calculated from TNA: AIR 41/49; ADGB:V, 201, 207, and 225.

290. TNA: AIR 41/49; ADGB:V, 226.

291. TNA: AIR 16/525, AOC-in-C Progress Report, 1 December 1942–28 February 1943, 4.

292. TNA: AIR 16/525, AOC-in-C Progress Report, 1 December 1942–28 February 1943, 8–9.

293. TNA: AIR 41/49; ADGB:V, 193.

294. TNA: AIR 16/525, AOC-in-C Progress Report, 1 March–31 May 1943, 10.

295. TNA: AIR 16/526, Night Air Defence Committee, Minutes of Meetings and Reports, September 1943–July 1944, Progress Report by Air Officer Commanding-In-Chief on the Developments and Results Obtained in Night Interception for the Period 1 September 1943–22 February 1944, 6.

296. TNA: AIR 41/49; ADGB:V, 193.

297. TNA: AIR 16/525, Progress Report by General Officer Commanding-In-Chief, Anti-Aircraft Command, 8 June 1943, appendix 'B'. Most of the towns reinforced had been attacked either during the *Baedeker* period or in the spring of 1943.

298. TNA: AIR 41/17; ADGB:III, 118, and Pile, 'The Anti-Aircraft Defence of the United Kingdom', *London Gazette*, number 38149, 5984.

299. TNA: AIR 16/526, AOC-in-C Progress Report, 1 June–31 August 1943, 6–7.

300. TNA: AIR 16/526, AOC-in-C Progress Report, 1 September 1943–22 February 1944, 4.

301. TNA: AIR 16/525, AOC-in-C Progress Report, 1 December 1942–28 February 1943, 10. This report refers to such GCI stations as both 'Fixed' and 'Final'.

302. TNA: AIR 16/526, AOC-in-C Progress Report, 1 June–31 August 1943, 10.

303. TNA: AIR 16/525, AOC-in-C Progress Report, 1 March–31 May 1943, 11.

304. TNA: AIR 16/526, AOC-in-C Progress Report, 1 June–31 August 1943, 10.

305. TNA: AIR 41/12, Signals, Vol. IV: Radar in Raid Reporting (1950), 634.

306. TNA: AIR 16/874, History of Fighter OTUs, 12.

307. TNA: AIR 16/1147, Summary, 15 April–31 October 1943, 1385.

308. TNA: AIR 16/874, History of Fighter OTUs, 13–14.

309. TNA: AIR 16/1148, Summary, 1759.

310. TNA: AIR 41/49; ADGB:V, 226.

311. C. Webster, *The National Health Service: A Political History* (Oxford University Press, 1998), 3.

312. G. Rivett, *From Cradle to Grave* (King's Fund, 1997), 1.

313. R. Klein, *The Politics of the National Health Service* (Longman, 1989), 3.

314. Rivett, *From Cradle to Grave*, 7–9.

315. Klein, *Politics of the NHS*, 3–4.

316. Webster, *National Health Service*, 4.

317. Klein, *Politics of the NHS*, 6.

318. Rivett, *From Cradle to Grave*, 12.

319. Webster, *National Health Service*, 7.

320. Titmuss, *Problems of Social Policy*, 183 and 194.

321. Titmuss, *Problems of Social Policy*, 188–189, 443, 455, and 489–490.

322. Webster, *National Health Service*, 6.

323. Titmuss, *Problems of Social Policy*, 502–503.

324. Webster, *National Health Service*, 7.

325. Rivett, *From Cradle to Grave*, 2.

326. Buckley, *Air Power*, 16.

327. Todman, *Britain's War*, 656.

328. Calder, *People's War*, 405.

329. Titmuss, *Problems of Social Policy*, 194.

330. Central Statistical Office, *Statistical Digest of the War*, 37 and 40.

331. Süss, *Death From the Skies*, 223 and 230.

332. J. J. Hasegawa, "The Rise and Fall of Radical Reconstruction in 1940s Britain," *Twentieth Century British History* 10, no. 2 (1999): 146.

333. Süss, *Death From the Skies*, 235.

334. J. Glancey, "Life After Carbuncles," *The Guardian*, 17 May 2004, https://www.theguardian.com/artanddesign/2004/may/17/architecture.regeneration.

335. TNA: AIR 41/49; ADGB:V, 65 and 224; Webster and Frankland, *SAOAG*, IV, 456.

CONCLUSIONS

1. TNA: AIR 41/49; ADGB:V, iii.

2. Todman, *Britain's War*, 520.

3. TNA: AIR 40/1653, Maps for Gazetteer, 1942 and 1943, Number of Incidents by Counties.

4. TNA: AIR 41/17; ADGB:III, 121.

5. TNA: AIR 40/2444, Air War Against Great Britain, 14.

6. Calculated from TNA: AIR 40/2444, Air War Against Great Britain, appendix 2; and AIR 40/1045, Tabular Record.

7. Buckley, *Air Power*, 16.

8. *Times*, 15 June 1917, 3.

9. TNA: AIR 41/49; ADGB:V, 67.

10. Stephen Robinson, *The Blind Strategist: John Boyd and the American Way of War* (Exisle, 2021), 98.

Bibliography

I. PRIMARY SOURCES

Ia. Unpublished

Air Historical Branch (RAF) [AHB]. RAF Northolt, London, UK

Aircraft Deliveries Against Contract by Manufacturer. Vol. I: A–G.

Aircraft Record Cards (Air Ministry Form 78):

Beaufighter: Serial Range R–X.

Havoc: Serial Range AE–DG.

Ministry of Aircraft Production Statistical Review 1939–1945 (1946).

SD (Secret Document) 96, Monthly Analysis of RAF Aircraft Accidents Metropolitan Air Force, March 1940–June 1943.

Bath Record Office (BRO), Bath, UK

0146, Maps Showing Bomb Damage to Properties in Bath.

BC/2/1. Minutes of Bath City Council, 1631–1974.

War Damage List of Houses. Specifications and Plans: No. 1.

Bundesarchiv-Militärarchiv (BA-MA), Freiburg, Germany

RL 2-IV/28, *Luftkrieg gegan England: Gefechtskalender Juli–Dez 1941* (*Luftwaffe*: 8 *Abteilung*, 5 *Okt* 1944).

RL 2-IV/33, *Angriffe auf England*: *Materialsammlung*, 1940–41 (*Luftwaffe*: 8 *Abteilung*).

RL 7/110, *Kampfeinsatz: Störangriffe, zusammengefasste Angriffe, Mineneinsatz im November 1943, (Anlage 2a zu Lfl.Kdo.3, Führ. Abt.* (1)/1c Nr.15684/43, *g.Kdos.*).

RL 7/111, *Tätigkeitsbericht der Luftflotte 3 für den Monat April 1943,* (*Luftflottenkommando* 3, 10.5.1943).

RL 7/112, *Tätigkeitsbericht der Luftflotte 3 für den Monat Juni 1943,* (*Luftflottenkommando* 3, 12.7.1943).

RL 7/113, *Tätigkeitsbericht der Luftflotte 3 für den Monat Juli 1943,* (*Luftflottenkommando* 3, 13.8.1943).

RL 10/38, Vol. III: 1, *Kampfgeschwader* 4 (09.05.1941–18.06.1941), *Angriffe auf London, Birmingham und Chatham.*

Central Archive of the Ministry of the Russian Federation (TsAMO), Podolsk; f.500, *Findbuch* 12452, *Generalstab der Luftwaffe*, *Luftwaffe Führungsstab* papers (via Professor Richard Overy), File 107, *'Bemerkungen zum Einsatz der Luftwaffe'.*

Hull History Centre (HHC), Hull, UK
    C TYA: Air Raid Incident Files.
    C TYC: Summary of Air Raid Casualties.
Imperial War Museum (IWM). Duxford, UK
    German Miscellaneous MCR 18: GAF Losses.
Mass Observation Archive (M-O). University of Sussex, Brighton, UK.
    File Reports (FR):
        FR844: Hull, 23 August 1941.
        FR 1285, Reports on Two Baedeker Raids, 30 May 1942.
        FR 1423, Night Bombing and the People, 17 September 1942.
    Topic Collections (TC):
        TC23: Air Raids 1938–1945.
National Archives of the United Kingdom (TNA), London, UK
    AIR 2: Air Ministry: Registered Files (1936–1953).
    AIR 10: Air Ministry: Air Publications and Reports.
    AIR 16: Air Ministry: Fighter Command, Registered Files.
    AIR 19: Air Ministry: Private Office Papers.
    AIR 20: Air Ministry: Papers Accumulated by the Air Historical Branch.
    AIR 22: Air Ministry: Periodical Returns, Intelligence Summaries and Bulletins.
    AIR 24: Air Ministry: Operations Record Books, Commands.
    AIR 25: Air Ministry: Operations Record Books, Groups.
    AIR 27: Air Ministry: Operations Record Books, Squadrons.
    AIR 29: Air Ministry: Operations Record Books, Miscellaneous Units.
    AIR 40: Air Ministry: Directorate of Intelligence: Intelligence Reports and Papers.
    AIR 41: Air Ministry: Air Historical Branch: Narratives and Monographs.
    AIR 50: Air Ministry: Combat Reports, Second World War.
    CAB 65: War Cabinet and Cabinet, Minutes (WM and CM Series).
    CAB 66: War Cabinet and Cabinet, Memoranda (WP and CP Series).
    CAB 106: War Cabinet and Cabinet Office: Archivist and Librarian Files: (AL Series).
    HO 186: Ministry of Home Security, ARP Registered Files.
    HO 191: Ministry of Home Security, Research and Experiments Department, Unregistered Papers.
    HO 192: Ministry of Home Security, Research and Experiments Department, Registered Papers.
    HO 198: Ministry of Home Security, Research and Experiments Department, Bomb Census Papers.
    HO 199: Ministry of Home Security, Intelligence Branch, Registered Files.
    HO 201: Ministry of Home Security, Key Points Intelligence Directorate, Daily Reports.
    HO 205: Ministry of Home Security: 'O' Division, Correspondence and Papers.
    HO 207: Ministry of Home Security, Civil Defence Regions, Headquarters and Regional Files.
    INF 1: Ministry of Information: Files of Correspondence.
    MEPO 3: Metropolitan Police: Office of the Commissioner, Correspondence and Papers, Special Series.

PREM 3: Prime Minister's Office: Operational Correspondence and Papers.
Tyne and Wear Archive Services (TWAS), Discovery Museum, Newcastle upon Tyne, UK
255: Wallsend MBC.
209.113: Sunderland County Borough Council.
2239: Newcastle upon Tyne Air Raid Precautions.
PA.NC/5: Newcastle City Police, Wartime Records, Correspondence Files.
T15: Tynemouth County Borough Clerks Department, ARP Files, 1938–1974.
T170: Sunderland County Borough Council, Town Clerks Department, Civil Defence and ARP Records.
York City Archives (YCA), Explore York, York, UK
89.32: Reports on Air Raids: York: 28 October 1940.
89.38: Civil Defence.
Zuckerman Archive (SZ), University of East Anglia, Norwich, UK
OEMU/50/2, Effects of Raids 1942–1945:
OEMU/50/2/9, RE8 Assessment of the 1000 Bomber Raid on Cologne.
OEMU/50/2/16, RE8 Report on Dusseldorf Raids, August and September 1942.

Ib. Published

Contemporary Publications

Baedeker, Karl. *Great Britain: Handbook for Travellers*. Old House, 2013 [1937].
Goebbels, Joseph. *The Goebbels Diaries*. Translated and edited by Louis P. Lochner. Hamish Hamilton, 1948.
Universal Knowledge A to Z: A New Encyclopaedia of General Knowledge. Odhams, 1938.

Memoirs

Brandon, Lewis. *Night Flyer*. Goodall, 1992 [1961].
Churchill, Winston S. *The Second World War, Vol. II: Their Finest Hour*. Cassell, 1949.
Churchill, Winston S. *The Second World War, Vol. III: The Grand Alliance*. Cassell, 1950.
Douglas, Sholto. *Years of Command*. Collins, 1966.
Galland, Adolph. *The First and the Last: The German Fighter Force in World War II*. Translated by Mervyn Savill. Methuen, 1955.
Gibson, Guy. *Enemy Coast Ahead*. Goodall, 1986 [1946].
Harris, Arthur. *Bomber Offensive*. Collins, 1947.
Harrisson, Tom. *Living Through the Blitz*. Penguin, 1990 [1979].
Howard-Williams, Jeremy. *Night Intruder*. Purnell, 1972.
Kesselring, Albert. *The Memoirs of Field-Marshal Kesselring*. Greenhill, 2007 [1954].
Zuckerman, Solly. *From Apes to Warlords*. Hamish Hamilton, 1978.

Official Histories

Boog, Horst, Werner Rahn, Reinhard Stumpf, and Bernd Wegner, eds. *Germany and the Second World War. Vol. VI, The Global War*. Translated by Ewald Osers, John Brownjohn, Patricia Crampton, and Louise Willmot. Oxford University Press, 1991.

Collier, Basil. *The Defence of the United Kingdom*. HMSO, 1957.

Dunn, C. L. *The Emergency Medical Services*. Vol. II. HMSO, 1953.

Maier, Klaus A., Horst Rohde, Bernd Stegemann, and Hans Umbreit, eds. *Germany and the Second World War. Vol. II, Germany's Initial Conquests in Europe*. Translated by Daen S. McMurray and Ewald Osers. Oxford University Press, 1991.

O'Brien, T. H. *Civil Defence*. HMSO, 1955.

Parker, H. M. D. *Manpower*. HMSO, 1950.

Postan, M. M., D. Hay, and J. D. Scott. *Design and Development of Weapons*. HMSO, 1964.

Richards, Denis. *Royal Air Force 1939–1945*. Vol. I. HMSO, 1954.

Richards, Denis, and Hilary St G. Saunders. *Royal Air Force 1939–1945*. Vol. II. HMSO, 1954.

Roskill, S. W. *The War at Sea*. Vol. I. HMSO, 1954.

Roskill, S. W. *The War at Sea*. Vol. II. HMSO, 1956.

Saunders, Hilary St G. *Royal Air Force 1939–1945*. Vol. III. HMSO, 1954.

Titmuss, Richard M. *Problems of Social Policy*. HMSO, 1950.

Webster, Charles, and Noble Frankland. *The Strategic Air Offensive Against Germany, 1939–1945*. Vol. I. HMSO, 1961.

Webster, Charles, and Noble Frankland. *The Strategic Air Offensive Against Germany, 1939–1945*. Vol. IV. HMSO, 1961.

Official Publications

Air Ministry. *Bomber Command*. HMSO, 1941.

Air Ministry. *Bomber Command Continues*. HMSO, 1942.

Air Ministry. *The Rise and Fall of the German Air Force, 1933–1945*. The National Archives, 2008 [1948].

Central Statistical Office. *Statistical Digest of the War*. HMSO, 1951.

Arthur Harris. *Despatch on War Operations*. Frank Cass, 1995.

Ministry of Information. *Front Line 1940–1941: The Official Story of the Civil Defence of Britain*. HMSO, 1942.

Parliamentary Debates (Commons).

Journals

International History Review.

International Journal of Psychoanalysis.

Journal of Strategic Studies.

Labour History Review.

Twentieth Century British History.

War in History.

II. PUBLISHED SECONDARY SOURCES

Addison, Paul, and Jeremy A. Crang, eds. *The Burning Blue: A New History of the Battle of Britain*. Pimlico, 2000.

Arnold-Forster, Mark. *The World at War*. Methuen, 1983 [1974].

Baldoli, Claudia, and Andrew Knapp. *Forgotten Blitzes: France and Italy Under Allied Air Attack, 1940–1945*. Continuum, 2012.

Baldoli, Claudia, Andrew Knapp, and Richard Overy, eds. *Bombing, States and Peoples in Western Europe 1940–1944*. Continuum, 2011.

Barke, Michael, Brian Robson, and Anthony Champion. *Newcastle Upon Tyne: Mapping the City*. Birlinn, 2021.

Bekker, Cajus. *The Luftwaffe War Diaries*. Translated by Philip Ziegler. Macdonald, 1967.

Bingham, Victor. *Bristol Beaufighter*. Airlife, 1994.

Boog, Horst, ed. *The Conduct of the Air War in the Second World War: An International Comparison*. Translated By Karl B. Keenan. Berg, 1992.

Bowen, E. G. *Radar Days*. Adam Hilger, 1987.

Buckley, John. *Air Power in the Age of Total War*. UCL, 1999.

Butler, Richard, and Roslyn Russell, eds. *Giants of Tourism*. CAB International, 2010.

Calder, Angus. *The Myth of the Blitz*. Pimlico, 1992 [1991].

Calder, Angus. *The People's War: Britain 1939–1945*. Pimlico, 1992 [1969].

Cox, Sebastian, and Peter Gray, eds. *Air Power History: Turning Points from Kitty Hawk to Kosovo*. Frank Cass, 2002.

Deighton, Len. *Fighter*. Jonathan Cape, 1977.

Dildy, Douglas C., and Paul F. Crickmore. *To Defeat the Few: The Luftwaffe's Campaign to Destroy Fighter Command*. Osprey, 2020.

Dobinson, Colin. *Fields of Deception: Britain's Bombing Decoys of World War II*. Methuen, 2000.

Dupuy, R. Ernest, and Trevor N. Dupuy. *The Collins Encyclopedia of Military History: From 3500 B.C. to the Present Day*. HarperCollins, 1993.

Eden, Paul. *The Encyclopedia of Aircraft of WWII*. Amber, 2004.

Edgerton, David. *England and the Aeroplane*. Penguin, 2013.

Fountain, Rick. *Mr Morrison's Conjuring Trick*. RTFMedia, 2012.

Frankland, Noble. *History at War: The Campaigns of an Historian*. Giles de la Mare, 1998.

Gardiner, Juliet. *The Blitz: The British Under Attack*. HarperPress, 2010.

Gardiner, Juliet. *Wartime: Britain 1939–1945*. Review, 2005.

Geraghty, T. *A North-East Coast Town: Ordeal and Triumph*. Hull Academic Press, 2002 [1951].

Gilbert, Martin. *Second World War*. Weidenfeld & Nicolson, 1989.

Goss, Chris. *The Luftwaffe's Blitz: The Inside Story, November 1940–May 1941*. Crécy, 2010.

Goss, Chris, Peter Cornwell, and Bernd Rauchbach. *Luftwaffe Fighter-Bombers Over Britain*. Crécy, 2003.

Graystone, Philip. *The Blitz on Hull (1940–45)*. Lampada, 1991.

Groundwater, Ken. *Maritime Heritage: Newcastle and the River Tyne*. Silver Link, 1990.

Gunston, Bill. *Night Fighters: A Development and Combat History*. Sutton, 2003 [1976].

Haapamaki, Michelle. *The Coming of the Aerial War*. I. B. Tauris, 2014.

Haimes, Yacov Y. *Risk Modeling, Assessment, and Management*. Wiley-Interscience, 1998.

Halley, James J. *Royal Air Force Aircraft, L1000-N9999*. Air Britain, 1993.

Hastings, Max. *Bomber Command*. Michael Joseph, 1979.

Hippler, Thomas. *Bombing the People: Giulio Douhet and the Foundations of Air-Power Strategy, 1884–1939*. Cambridge University Press, 2013.

Holman, Brett. *The Next War in the Air*. Ashgate, 2014.

Holmes, Richard. *The World at War: The Landmark Oral History From Previous Unpublished Archives*. Ebury, 2007.

Irons, Roy. *The Relentless Offensive*. Pen & Sword, 2009.

Irving, David. *The Rise and Fall of the Luftwaffe: The Life of Field Marshal Erhard Milch*. Little Brown, 1973.

Jackson, Dan. *The Northumbrians: North-East England and Its People*. Hurst, 2019.

Jackson, Robert. *Air War at Night*. Howell, 2000.

Jackson, Robert. *Before the Storm: The Story of Bomber Command 1939–42*. Cassell, 2001.

Johnson, Brian. *The Secret War*. Pen & Sword, 2004 [1978].

Jones, R. V. *Most Secret War*. Hamish Hamilton, 1978.

Keegan, John. *The Second World War*. Hutchinson, 1989.

Klein, Rudolph. *The Politics of the National Health Service*. Longman, 1989 [1983].

Latham, Colin, and Anne Stobbs. *Radar: A Wartime Miracle*. Sutton, 1996.

Leapman, Michael. *Travel Guide to Britain*. Reader's Digest, 1999.

Levine, Joshua. *Forgotten Voices of the Blitz and the Battle of Britain*. Ebury, 2007.

Levine, Joshua. *The Secret History of the Blitz*. Simon & Schuster, 2015.

Liddell Hart, B. H. *History of the Second World War*. Cassell, 1970.

Longmate, Norman. *How We Lived Then: A History of Everyday Life During the Second World War*. Hutchinson, 1971.

Longmate, Norman. *The Workhouse*. Maurice Temple Smith, 1974.

Lukacs, John. *The Last European War, September 1939–December 1941*. Routledge & Kegan Paul, 1976.

Mason, Francis K. *Battle Over Britain*. McWhirter Twins, 1969.

Mason, Francis K. *The British Bomber Since 1914*. Putnam, 1994.

Mason, Francis K. *The British Fighter Since 1912*. Putnam, 1992.

Middlebrook, Martin, and Chris Everitt. *The Bomber Command War Diaries, An Operational Reference Book: 1939–1945*. Penguin, 1990 [1985].

Mondey, David. *Axis Aircraft of World War II*. Chancellor, 1996 [1984].

Murray, Williamson. *Strategy for Defeat: The Luftwaffe 1933–1945*. Apple, 1983.

Murray, Williamson, and Allan R. Millett. *A War to Be Won: Fighting in the Second World War*. Belknap Press of Harvard University Press, 2000.

Norman, Bill. *Air Raid Diary: The Luftwaffe Attacks on Tees-Side, 1940–1943*. Norman, 2010.

Orange, Vincent. *Dowding of Fighter Command*. Grub Street, 2008.

Overy, Richard. *Bomber Command 1939–1945*. HarperCollins, 1997.

Overy, Richard. *The Bombing War: Europe 1939–1945*. Allen Lane, 2013.

Overy, Richard. *Interrogations: The Nazi Elite in Allied Hands*. Allen Lane, 2001.

Overy, Richard. *Why the Allies Won*. Pimlico, 2006.

Overy, Richard J. *The Air War, 1939–1945*. Potomac, 2005.

Parker, Nigel. *Luftwaffe Crash Archive*. Vol. 10. Red Kite, 2017.

Price, Alfred. *Blitz on Britain 1939–1945*. Ian Allan, 1977.
Price, Alfred. *The Hardest Day*. Arms and Armour, 1988.
Price, Alfred. *The Luftwaffe Data Book*. Greenhill, 1997 [1977].
Purdue, Bill, and James Chapman. *The People's War? A Study Guide*. Open University, 2004.
Ramsey, Winston G., ed. *The Blitz: Then and Now*. Vol. 2. Battle of Britain Prints, 1988.
Ramsey, Winston G., ed. *The Blitz: Then and Now*. Vol. 3. Battle of Britain Prints, 1990.
Ray, John. *The Night Blitz, 1940–1941*. Arms & Armour, 1996.
Richards, Steve. *The Luftwaffe Over Brum: Birmingham's Blitz From a Military Perspective*. Richards, 2015.
Rivett, Geoffrey. *From Cradle to Grave*. King's Fund, 1997.
Roberts, Andrew. *The Storm of War: A New History of the Second World War*. Allen Lane, 2009.
Robinson, Stephen. *The Blind Strategist: John Boyd and the American Way of War*. Exisle, 2021.
Rothnie, Niall. *The Baedeker Blitz: Hitler's Attack on Britain's Historic Cities*. Ian Allan, 1992.
Rowse, A. L. *Heritage of Britain*. Putnam, 1977.
Sharp, C. Martin, and Michael J. F. Bowyer. *Mosquito*. Faber and Faber, 1971 [1967].
Snelling, Steve. *Norwich: A Shattered City*. Halsgrove, 2012.
Süss, Dietmar. *Death From the Skies: How the British and Germans Survived Bombing in World War II*. Translated by Lesley Sharpe and Jeremy Noakes. Oxford University Press, 2014.
Sweetman, John. *The Dambusters Raid*. Arms and Armour, 1990.
Taylor, John W. R. *Combat Aircraft of the World*. George Rainbird, 1969.
Terraine, John. *The Right of the Line: The Royal Air Force in the European War, 1939–1945*. Hodder and Stoughton, 1985.
Thetford, Owen. *Aircraft of the Royal Air Force*. Putnam, 1988.
Todman, Daniel. *Britain's War: Into Battle, 1937–1941*. Allen Lane, 2016.
Townsend, Peter. *Duel in the Dark*. Harrap, 1986.
Vasco, John. *Messerschmitt Bf 110: Bombsights Over England*. Schiffer, 2002.
Wainright, Martin. *The Bath Blitz*. DK, 1992 [1975].
Warner, Graham. *The Bristol Blenheim: A Complete History*. Crécy, 2002.
Webb, Edwin, and John Duncan. *Blitz Over Britain*. Spellmount, 1990.
Webster, Charles. *The National Health Service: A Political History*. Oxford University Press, 1998.
White, Graham. *Allied Aircraft Piston Engines of World War II*. Society of Automotive Engineers, 1995.
White, Ian. *The History of Air Intercept Radar and the British Nightfighter 1935–1959*. Pen & Sword, 2007.
Whiting, Charles. *Britain Under Fire: The Bombing of Britain's Cities, 1940–45*. Leo Cooper, 1999.
Whiting, Charles. *Three Star Blitz: The Baedeker Raids and the Start of Total War*. Leo Cooper, 1987.

Wood, Derek. *Attack Warning Red: The Royal Observer Corps and the Defence of Britain 1925 to 1975*. McDonald and James, 1976.

Wood, Derek, and Derek Dempster. *The Narrow Margin: The Battle of Britain and the Rise of Air Power 1930-40*, Arrow, 1969 [1961].

Zimmerman, David. *Britain's Shield: Radar and the Defeat of the Luftwaffe*. Sutton, 2001.

Index

A Mitchell Institute Book
Aviation and Air Power
Series Editor: Brian D. Laslie

In his work *Winged Defense*, Brigadier General William "Billy" Mitchell stated, "Air power may be defined as the ability to do something in the air." Since Mitchell made this statement, the definition of air power has been contested and argued about by those on the ground, those in the air, academics, industrialists, and politicians.

Each volume of the Aviation and Air Power series seeks to expand our understanding of Mitchell's broad definition by bringing together leading historians, fliers, and scholars in the fields of military history, aviation, air power history, and other disciplines in the hope of providing a fuller picture of just what air power accomplishes.

This series offers an expansive look at tactical aerial combat, operational air warfare, and strategic air theory. It explores campaigns from the First World War through modern air operations, along with the heritage, technology, culture, and human element particular to the air arm. In addition, this series considers the perspectives of leaders in the US Army, Navy, Marine Corps, and Air Force, as well as their counterparts in other nations and their approaches to the history and study of doing something in the air.